365 days with **Spurgeon**

Volume **4**

A further collection of daily
readings from sermons preached by
Charles Haddon Spurgeon
from his Metropolitan Tabernacle Pulpit

Selected and arranged by
Terence Peter Crosby

DayOne

© Day One Publications 2007
First printed 2007

ISBN 978-1-84625-090-3

Unless otherwise stated, all Scripture quotations are from
the Authorised Version Crown Copyright

British Library Cataloguing in Publication Data available

Published by Day One Publications
Ryelands Road, Leominster, HR6 8NZ
☎ 01568 613 740 FAX 01568 611 473
email—sales@dayone.co.uk
web site—www.dayone.co.uk
North American—e-mail—sales@dayonebookstore.com
North American web site—www.dayonebookstore.com

Chief Sub-Editor: David Simm
Designed by Steve Devane and printed by Gutenberg Press, Malta

Dedication

In memory of Gordon Rutherford Sayer (1916–1985), late Librarian and Secretary of the Evangelical Library, who introduced me to the riches to be found in that treasure-house of Christian literature during the five years in which I worked with him there.

Certainly many will join me in welcoming the publication of the fourth volume of *365 Days with Spurgeon*. On behalf of all who read this book, thanks go to Terence Crosby for dedicating many hours to gathering a fine collection of Spurgeon gems. Through his evident editorial skill and diligent research, along with ready and able assistance from Day One Publications, he has laid in our hands a beneficial source of spiritual nourishment to add to the previous three gladly received.

Charles Haddon Spurgeon
photographed in the New Forest on his
39th birthday, 19 June 1873.
He said 'I like this photograph better than
any portrait ever taken of me.'

A careful observer of these volumes of *365 Days with Spurgeon* will note they follow the preaching of Spurgeon chronologically, each covering approximately six years of his ministry, with the daily readings drawn from sermons preached as near as possible to the actual dates. The present volume covers Spurgeon's preaching ministry from 1873 to 1879.

Those were fruitful and happy years for C. H. Spurgeon. Behind him lie the varied taunts he received during the early days of his London ministry. His continued and maturing presence in the pulpit of the Metropolitan Tabernacle long silenced those who had prophesied the quick extinguishing of his brilliant star. Some years ahead of him waited the awful Downgrade Controversy. And approaching, just off the horizon, was the warring disease that would come with such fury it often struck Spurgeon from his gospel steed and finally silenced him at the age of fifty-seven.

Biographer Arnold Dallimore said of this middle season of Spurgeon's life, 'Between 1875 and 1885 Spurgeon's ministry reached heights it had never attained before. Although the seeds sown in London had already brought a great harvest, during these years the fruit proved still more abundant, and it came with the richness and a steadiness that was new even to a work so blessed of God as his had been.'[1]

Space doesn't allow a full listing of the many efforts that prospered under Spurgeon's care. A few of the more influential ministries were the Pastor's College, the Stockwell Orphanage, and the Metropolitan Tabernacle Colporteurs Association. Other well-known ministries found first form during these years of Spurgeon's life—the Pastor's Aid Society and the Book Fund ministry to name two.

Many today know Spurgeon solely through his sermons published in many forms, including helpful books like *365 Days with Spurgeon*. Nothing in English church literature can compare to the usefulness found from his preaching—it is a lasting legacy. But a fruitful bounty remains to this very day from his enthusiastic support of church planting. As early as 1859, he declared,

God sparing my life, if I have my people at my back I will not rest until the dark county of Surrey be covered with places of worship ... I announce my own schemes: visionary they may appear, but carried out they will be. It is only within the last six months that we have started two churches—one in Wandsworth and the other in Greenwich, and the Lord has prospered them. The pool of baptism has been stirred with converts. And what we have done in two places I am about to do in a third, and we will do it not for the third or the fourth, but for the hundredth time, God being our helper ... We must go from strength to strength, and be a missionary church, and never rest until not only this neighbourhood, but our country, of which it is said that some parts are as dark as India, shall have been enlightened with the gospel.[2]

These excerpts from documents electronically preserved at www.british-history.ac.uk provide a snapshot of the fruitful blessing God poured upon Spurgeon's church-planting labours:

'Enfield Baptist church was founded with help from C. H. Spurgeon in 1867, when services were held in a room over the Rising Sun, Church Street.' 'Totteridge Road church was opened with help from Spurgeon in 1868.' 'Hornchurch Baptist church: In 1877 the members of the mission formed a church ... they sought the help of Spurgeon, who sent students from his Baptist college at the Metropolitan Tabernacle.' 'Westminster Baptist Church: Spurgeon preached at the stone-laying and gave £100 to the building fund.' And another church had this record: 'Closed 1865, but reopened same year by C.H. Spurgeon.'

Estimates of upwards of two hundred churches were started by Spurgeon, the people of the Metropolitan Tabernacle and the men of the Pastor's college. In London alone, Spurgeon claimed that over forty churches were started. Of particular interest to Terence Crosby and me is the influence C.H. Spurgeon had on Trinity Road Chapel, Upper

Tooting, London—the church I presently serve as pastor and where Terence holds membership.

Here's the story:

William Winsford, a member of the Metropolitan Tabernacle, moved to then rural Upper Tooting and came across a few others with a desire to see an evangelical church established. Three Sundays after services began, C.H. Spurgeon invited Winsford to his nearby home on Nightingale Lane, relayed his approval of the work, and generously offered to help. His involvement in those early days set the trajectory of the church—an influence that lasts to this day.

When it was clear the growing church needed larger accommodations, Spurgeon came and preached, and issued an appeal to other churches to provide financial help for the church's building project. His interest in the success of the church is clear when he wrote, 'Our friends have made a good beginning, and if my purse holds out I will double all they can raise in the next year up to £250. I wish the friends every success.'[3]

The money was soon raised, Spurgeon kept his promise, donated the £250, and offered to preach at the stone-laying. The preacher Winsford purchased the property, but soon fell ill and couldn't conduct the services. Spurgeon heard of the church's need, surveyed the property, and encouraged the church to get on with building the chapel. On June 6, 1877, Spurgeon laid the memorial stone and gave what was described as 'a wise and happy address'. That evening, his sons joined him—Charles led in prayer and Thomas delivered an address.

On Thursday, 27 September 1877, the new building opened with Spurgeon preaching from Ecclesiastes 8:4 'Where the word of the king is.' The sermon is found in volume 28 of *The Metropolitan Tabernacle Pulpit* (sermon 1,697). He closed with this charge, 'Preach the King's word, for it will give you power in private prayer, power in the Sunday School, power in the prayer meeting, power in everything that you do; because you will live upon the King's own word, and his word is meat to the soul.'

Spurgeon stamped an indelible mark on Trinity Road Chapel that has continued long after his death. One pastor was a student at the Pastor's College and another, Henry Oakley, supported Spurgeon through the Downgrade Controversy and maintained Spurgeon's model for biblical, Christ-centered preaching.

In the 1940s, Ernest Kevan kept the church closely in line with its past by writing an article on the church's faith and practice as set out in its trust deeds. Explaining that document, Kevan wrote, 'The accurate interpretation of these requirements with regard to the life of the Church and the character of its ministry seems to be summed up by saying that as a Baptist Church, it is required that the minister who is called shall be a convinced Baptist, and that his views shall be Calvinistic, or, rendered in more modern terms, along the lines of teaching such as we have come to associate with the name of Charles Haddon Spurgeon.'

A quote of Spurgeon found in the church's magazine, *The Witness*, summarizes what that means, 'As the hammer comes down on the anvil ever with the same ring, so we will preach Christ, Christ, Christ and nothing else but Christ.'

May God empower us to do that! And through reading *365 Days with Spurgeon*, may you be inspired and equipped to hold high the gospel torch among our generation, just like C.H. Spurgeon did so wonderfully in his.

Doug McMasters
Pastor, Trinity Road Chapel
Upper Tooting, London

Notes

1 **Arnold Dallimore,** *Spurgeon* (Chicago: Moody Press, 1984), p. 381.

2 **C.H. Spurgeon,** *New Park Street Pulpit*, vol. 5 (Pilgrim Publications, 1981 reprint), p. 354.

3 **Henry Oakley,** *All the Way* (The Book Society, 1930), p. 8.

This fourth volume of *365 Days with Spurgeon* takes the reader well into the second half of Spurgeon's 37–year London ministry, covering a further six-year period from 11 May 1873 to 27 April 1879.

Those who have used any of the earlier volumes may notice some significant developments, perhaps the most obvious being the exceptional number of undated sermons, there being no less than a hundred of these. A further twelve undated sermons (nos. 1117, 1174, 1212–3, 1239, 1259, 1265, 1336, 1393, 1506, 1520 & 1697) can be fairly accurately dated by internal details or external sources. The last of these is of particular interest to the compiler as it was preached at Trinity Road Chapel, the church which he has attended for over thirty years. At the time when it was preached Spurgeon was still living in Nightingale Lane, Wandsworth Common, less than a mile away. Further information about these sermons can be found in the index section, which has been extended to include a chronological list of Spurgeon's dateable New Park Street and Metropolitan Tabernacle Pulpit sermons from 1853 to 1891. I am grateful to Doug McMasters, pastor of Trinity Road Chapel, not only for providing the Foreword, but also for the loan of the volumes of the Metropolitan Tabernacle Pulpit published after Spurgeon's death; this has greatly facilitated the dating of some of the numerous undated sermons.

As in previous volumes the presence of undated sermons has allowed for the inclusion of several short topical series, particularly in February, for which there are only four dated sermons during the period covered by this volume. This was due to Spurgeon's frequent illnesses which had now become an almost annual interruption to his ministry. The longest of these interruptions, apart from a single sermon in the middle, lasted from November 1878 to April 1879, a period of over five months. As noted in the previous volume several mainly undated sermons are accompanied by sick notes or letters (see nos. 1153, 1156, 1158, 1213, 1215–7, 1220–1, 1396–7, 1453, 1455–8, 1460–1, 1463, 1465–6). A number of undated sermons at the beginning of 1879 are also prefaced by a series of short written sermons, namely 1451–2 (from Spurgeon's sick room), 1454 (written when away) and 1457, 1459, 1461, 1463–4 & 1467 (all written at Mentone). These have been omitted for the purposes of the present volume, but details can be found in the index. The physical weakness under which Spurgeon often laboured is illustrated by an incident during no. 1396 (13 January 1878) when he had to stop and ask for a hymn to be sung mid-sermon while he recovered his strength. This occasion was also followed by two months of recuperation in Mentone, South France.

Another change which can only in part be attributed to Spurgeon's winter absences is the almost complete disappearance of topical Christmas sermons, there being only two genuine articles in the period covered by this volume. In some years he now chose not to preach on a Christmas text on occasions when it had previously been his annual practice. But this seems to have been a period during which he deliberately avoided drawing attention to Christian festivals in general. This volume includes readings from five sermons preached on Easter Sunday morning, but in none of these is attention drawn to the resurrection of our Lord Jesus Christ. Prior to 1874 Spurgeon had often chosen to preach on an Easter text on Easter Sunday and from 1880 onwards this was to be his practice nearly every year. Likewise there is a complete absence of sermons about the Holy Spirit on Whit Sunday, though it has to be admitted that he rarely celebrated Whit Sunday in his preaching anyway except during the years 1882 to 1886.

As in previous volumes of *365 Days with Spurgeon* the majority of readings have been allocated to coincide with the actual dates on which the sermons were preached. Each reading indicates Spurgeon's sermon-title and text; particularly long texts have been abbreviated, but listed in their fulness in the Scripture index. The reader's attention has been drawn to contemporary topics of personal, national and international interest to which Spurgeon occasionally referred. There has been a minimum of sympathetic updating of the original material to remove antiquated language and terminology and where necessary Spurgeon's Scripture quotations (probably made from memory) have been corrected to remove any inaccuracies.

The footnotes for meditation have been added by the compiler, but this volume sees a difference due to a major innovation in the format of most of the sermons from no. 1116 onwards. This was the regular inclusion of the numbers of the two, three (usually) or four hymns sung from *Our Own Hymnbook*, which had been published seven years earlier in September 1866. These, in addition to the listing of Spurgeon's Scripture reading, give us more of an insight into the occasion on which each sermon was preached. A verse or two from one of the hymns sung has been extracted to serve as a meditation on those occasions when the thoughts conveyed are particularly appropriate to the chosen sermon-extract. However, one drawback has emerged; the first 150 numbers in *Our Own Hymnbook* relate to the 150 Psalms, but there are multiple paraphrases or sections of certain Psalms and it was not always indicated in Spurgeon's sermons which particular one of these was actually sung on the occasion! Part or the whole of Spurgeon's own Scripture readings have been selected for the further suggested reading on 46 days on which they also were particularly appropriate to the chosen sermon-extract. Otherwise the further suggested readings have been selected by the compiler.

Another practice which seems to have commenced during this period involved a form of evangelistic outreach perhaps influenced by the recent evangelistic campaigns of Moody and Sankey, for whom Spurgeon voiced support, as seen in the titles of nos. 1238–9; in no. 1247 he also called for prayerful follow-up to their campaigns and (as indicated especially in the posthumously-published Sunday evening sermons for 1875–6) he often at this time chose to have a hymn sung from Sankey's *Sacred Songs and Solos*. On certain Sunday evenings (see nos. 1315, 1322, 1355, 1389, 1414 & 1466) the regular congregation of the Metropolitan Tabernacle deliberately vacated their seats and stayed away so that the usually packed building could be thrown open to 'strangers' and afford an opportunity for the gospel to be preached to crowds of unconverted men and women. What a contrast to the days in which we live! The spiritual decline suffered by 'the land of the Book' is highlighted by the almost scandalous absence of so many of the Lord's people from the Lord's house on the evening of the Lord's Day—one wonders whether the Lord's Day ought to be renamed 'The Lord's Morning' in many a Christian household. There would be plenty of room for the unconverted to come in vast numbers every Sunday without any of us deliberately vacating our seats to make room for them! But alas, the vast majority of needy sinners are content to continue on their way to a lost eternity anyway without any thought of their Maker or concern for their souls. What a desperate spiritual state we are in. May the Lord use this volume to do some good for both saint and sinner alike.

My thanks once again to all at Day One, and especially to David Simm and Digby James, for their encouragement and assistance in the production of this further volume, also to The Evangelical Library for the long-term loan of the relevant years of The Metropolitan

Tabernacle Pulpit and for help with other enquiries. As you use this volume, please remember to pray for these organisations and the valuable work they do in continuing to promote the eternal gospel of our Lord Jesus Christ.

Terence Peter Crosby
Wandsworth, London

Sihon and Og, or Mercies in detail

'To him which smote great kings: for his mercy endureth for ever: and slew famous kings: for his mercy endureth for ever: Sihon king of the Amorites: for his mercy endureth for ever: and Og the king of Bashan: for his mercy endureth for ever.' Psalm 136:17–20
SUGGESTED FURTHER READING: Nehemiah 9:16–31

These mercies come quickly one after the other, and so they show the continuance of the mercy, while the unbroken succession of wave upon wave in ceaseless regularity gives sanction to the chorus, 'his mercy endureth for ever.' Were we in the habit of dwelling distinctly upon God's distinct mercies, do you not think we should have in our souls a firmer faith as to the endurance, continuity and everlastingness of the mercy of God? When we think of what the Lord did for us when we were babes in grace, we say, 'his mercy endureth for ever.' Then consider what he did for us when we were young men in Christ Jesus—'his mercy endureth for ever.' Think of what he has done for us after we have grown to be fathers—'his mercy endureth for ever.' And, you grey heads, tell of what the Lord has done for you, for when you put all four ages together, you can say with special emphasis, 'his mercy endureth for ever.' I wish I had a memory strong enough to recollect all the mercies of God to me in the past year. They have been very many, very great, and, taken one by one, very sweet. As I look at them one after the other, the evidence seems to accumulate until the argument becomes conclusive that 'his mercy endureth for ever.' It has endured all through the year, it was connected with all the years that went before, it is gathering fresh force in the year that is current. So I may trust for the years that are yet to come that he who was yesterday so full of mercy, and is today so full of grace, will be for ever the same. Do you not see that the striking of these bells one by one, the bringing out of each mercy in its distinctiveness one after the other, goes to illustrate the precious and ever-blessed truth that 'his mercy endureth for ever'?

FOR MEDITATION: (*Our Own Hymn Book* no.136 song 1 v.7—John Milton, 1645)
'Let us then, with gladsome mind, praise the Lord, for He is kind:
For His mercies shall endure, ever faithful, ever sure.'

SERMON NO. 1285

Pride catechized and condemned

'For who maketh thee to differ from another? and what hast thou that thou didst not receive? now if thou didst receive it, why dost thou glory, as if thou hadst not received it?' 1 Corinthians 4:7
SUGGESTED FURTHER READING: Obadiah 3–12

Pride grows apace like other ill weeds. It will live on any soil. In the natural heart it flourishes, springing up without sowing and growing without watering; even in the renewed heart it all too readily takes root when Satan casts abroad a handful of its seed. Of all creatures in the world the Christian is the last who ought to be proud; and yet, alas, we have had mournful evidence both in past history and in our own observation, and worst of all in our own personal experience, that Christians may become lifted up to their own shame. Paul set himself very earnestly to deal with this disease when he saw it raging among the Corinthians. He felt it needful to do so, for it was leading to other mischiefs of the most disgraceful kind. Pride and self-conceit had led the members of the church in Corinth to choose for themselves distinct leaders and to arrange themselves under separate banners, the followers of this man thinking themselves better than the followers of that. Thus the body of Christ was divided, and all sorts of ill-feeling, jealousy, emulation and envy sprang up in the church of God where all ought to have been mutual helpfulness and loving unity. Paul, therefore, earnestly and with great wisdom assailed the spirit of pride. He was well aware that pride is shallow and superficial. It cannot endure honest questioning and so he tried it by the Socratic method and put it through a catechism. He puts three questions to it in this verse, which all called upon his friends to go a little lower in their contemplation of themselves than their pride had before allowed them to go. Pride said, 'I have such and such gifts', but Paul replied, 'What hast thou that thou didst not receive?' Thus he digged deeper and undermined pride.

FOR MEDITATION: (*Our Own Hymn Book* no.235 v.1—Horatius Bonar, 1856)
>'All that I was, my sin, my guilt, my death, was all mine own;
>All that I am, I owe to Thee, my gracious God, alone.'

SERMON NO. 1271

Solemn pleadings for revival

'*Keep silence before me, O islands; and let the people renew their strength: let them come near; then let them speak: let us come near together to judgment.*' *Isaiah 41:1*
SUGGESTED FURTHER READING: Psalm 85:1–13

The text is a challenge to the heathen to enter into a debate with the living God. The Lord bids them argue at their best, and let the controversy be calmly carried out to its issues, so as to be decided once for all. He bids them be quiet, reflect and consider, in order that with renewed strength they may come into the discussion and defend their gods if they can. He urges them not to bring flippant arguments, but such as have cost them thought and have weight in them, if such arguments can be. He bids them be quiet till they are prepared to speak, and then, when they can produce their strong reasons and set their cause in the best possible light, he challenges them to enter the lists and see if they can maintain for a moment that their gods are gods or anything better than deceit and falsehood. We also who worship the Lord God Most High have a controversy with him. We have not seen his church and his cause prospering in the world as we could desire; as yet heathenism is not put to the rout by Christianity, neither does the truth everywhere trample down error; nations are not born in a day; the kingdoms of the world have not become the kingdom of our Lord and of his Christ. We desire to reason with God about this, and he himself instructs us how to prepare for this sacred debate. He bids us be silent, consider and then draw near to him with holy boldness, plead with him, produce our cause and bring forth our strong reasons. It seems to me that at the beginning of the year I cannot suggest to Christian people a more urgent topic than this, that we should plead with God that he would display among us greater works of grace than as yet our eyes have seen.

FOR MEDITATION: 'A time to keep silence' comes before 'a time to speak' (Ecclesiastes 3:7). God's holiness should cause us all to fall silent before him (Habakkuk 2:20; Zechariah 2:13). Unbelievers need to shut up before God (Romans 3:19) before they speak up to God (Romans 10:13). Sometimes the converted also need to exercise quietness before God (Psalm 4:4; 46:10). Do you talk too much?

SERMON NO. 1215

Life more abundant

'I am come that they might have life, and that they might have it more abundantly.' John 10:10

SUGGESTED FURTHER READING: Psalm 16:1–11

Abundance of life is often seen in the overflow of enjoyment. On a spring morning, when you walk in the field and see the lambs frisking so merrily, you have said, 'There is life for you.' You see a company of little children, all in excellent health—how they amuse themselves and what pranks they play! You say, 'What life there is in those little children!' Catch one of the little urchins and see if he does not wriggle out of your arms, and you say, 'Why, he is all life.' Just so and hence his mirth. In youth there is much life and overflow of spirits. When Israel came out of Egypt, she was young Israel and how merrily did she smite her timbrels and dance before Jehovah. When churches are revived, what life there is in them and then what singing! Never comes a revival of religion without a revival of singing. As soon as Luther's Reformation comes, the Psalms are translated and sung in all languages; and when Whitefield and John Wesley are preaching, then Charles Wesley and Toplady must be making hymns for the people to sing, for they must show their joy, a joy born of life. When the Lord gives you, dear friend, more life, you also will have more joy. You will no more go moping about the house, or be thought melancholy and dull when the Lord gives you life more abundantly. I should not wonder if you get into the habit of singing at your work and humming tunes in your walks. I should not wonder if people ask, 'What makes So-and-so so happy? What makes his eyes twinkle as with some strange delight? He is poor and sick, but how blissful he appears to be!' This will be seen when you not only 'have life', but when you 'have it more abundantly.'

FOR MEDITATION: Life does not consist of an abundance of physical possessions (Luke 12:15), but spiritual life in Christ brings with it an abundance of spiritual possessions. For a sample of these read Psalm 36:7–10.

SERMON NO. 1150

A catechism for the proud

'For who maketh thee to differ from another? and what hast thou that thou didst not receive? now if thou didst receive it, why dost thou glory, as if thou hadst not received it?' 1 Corinthians 4:7
SUGGESTED FURTHER READING: Luke 18:35–19:10

The text is an encouragement for seekers. You have begun another year and are you yet unsaved? But still you do desire to become children of God. Now, do you know an eminent Christian? Perhaps it is your revered grandmother or it may be some earnest Christian minister. You greatly admire those people, do you not? Now remember that there is nothing good in them but what they have received from God. The Lord can give the like grace to you and you can receive even as they have received. Do you believe that? It is true whether you believe it or not. The Lord in his abundant mercy can give to you what he has given to the best of his saints, whoever you may be. 'Then what have I to do?' says one. What you have to do is, according to the text, to be a receiver. Reception is a faculty which belongs to us however low we may sink. When a person is covered with rags, filth and disease, he can still become a receiver; and even if he cannot stretch out his hand, he can find ways and means for receiving. Receiving implies neither strength, nor merit, nor wisdom. It requires no power, no faculty, no virtue, no anything; the power to be a receiver dwells with the weakest of the weak and the worst of the worst. The emptier you are, the more room there is for reception; the blacker you are, the more room to receive washing; the fouler you are, the more reason to receive cleansing; the more sick and near to death, the more room to receive healing. Will you have the blessing which God in Christ Jesus is ready to give? If you will be saved, hearken to the voice of God and live! If you are willing to accept his Son Jesus Christ as your Saviour, and put your whole trust in him, you shall be saved.

FOR MEDITATION: We can receive only what God has given us from above (John 3:27), but this includes the Saviour; wonderful promises are made to all who receive him (John 1:12,16; 7:39). However, those who fail to do so (John 1:11) will face serious consequences (John 12:48). The gospel command is not 'take him or leave him', but 'Believe on the Lord Jesus Christ, and thou shalt be saved' (Acts 16:31).

SERMON NO. 1392

The peace of God

'And the peace of God, which passeth all understanding, shall keep your hearts and minds through Christ Jesus.' Philippians 4:7
SUGGESTED FURTHER READING: 1 Thessalonians 5:16–24

'The peace of God ... shall keep your hearts and minds.' Three rules are added by the apostle, which you will be sure to recollect. He tells us to be careful for nothing, to be prayerful for everything and to be thankful for anything. Anyone who can keep these three rules will be quite sure to have a peaceful mind. *'Be careful for nothing';* leave your care with God. Having done your best to 'provide things honest in the sight of all men', take no distressing, disturbing, anxious thought about anything, but cast your burden on the Lord. Then *pray about everything,* little as well as great, joyous as well as sad; 'in everything by prayer and supplication ... let your requests be made known unto God.' That which you pray over will have the sting taken out of it if it be evil, and the sweetness of it will be sanctified if it be good. The tribulation which you pray over will become bearable, even if it be not changed into a subject for rejoicing. A trouble prayed over is a dead lion with honey in the carcase. And then we are bidden to *be thankful for anything,* for the apostle says, 'in every thing ... with thanksgiving let your requests be made known unto God.' Thankfulness is the great promoter of peace; it is the mother and nurse of restfulness. Doubtless our peace is often broken because we receive mercies from God without acknowledging them: neglected praises sour into unquiet forebodings. If we render to the Lord the fragrant incense of holy gratitude we shall find our soul perfumed with the sweet peace of God.

FOR MEDITATION: Be careful for nothing (1 Peter 5:7), be prayerful for everything (Ephesians 6:18) and be thankful for anything (Ephesians 5:20). Consider the turmoil and conflict that accompany anxiety (Luke 10:40–41), prayerlessness (James 4:1–2) and thanklessness (Romans 1:21).

SERMON NO. 1397

Our urgent need of the Holy Spirit

'Through the power of the Holy Ghost ... by the power of the Spirit of God.' Romans 15:13,19
SUGGESTED FURTHER READING: Psalm 67:1–7

If you lived in Egypt, you would notice, once in the year, the Nile rising; and you would watch its increase with anxiety, because the extent of the overflow of the Nile is very much the measure of the fertility of Egypt. Now the rising of the Nile must depend upon those far-off lakes in the centre of Africa, whether they shall be well filled with the melting of the snows or not. If there be a scanty supply in the higher reservoirs, there cannot be much overflow in the Nile in its after-course through Egypt. Let us translate the figure and say that, if the upper lakes of fellowship with God in the Christian church are not well filled, if the soul's spiritual strength be not sustained by private prayer and communion with God, the Nile of practical Christian service will never rise to the flood. The one thing I want to say is this: you cannot get out of the church what is not in it. The reservoir itself must be filled before it can pour forth a stream. We must ourselves drink of the living water till we are full, and then out of the midst of us shall flow rivers of living water, but not till then. Out of an empty basket you cannot distribute loaves and fishes, however hungry the crowd may be. Out of an empty heart you cannot speak full things, nor from a lean soul bring forth fat things full of marrow, which shall feed the people of God. Out of the fulness of the heart the mouth speaks, when it speaks to edification at all. So the first thing is to look well to home affairs and pray that God would 'bless *us;* and cause his face to shine upon *us;*' that his 'way may be known upon earth,' and his 'saving health among all nations.'

FOR MEDITATION: We are commanded to go on being filled with the Spirit (Ephesians 5:18). Such filling can never take place while we are fighting him, either by resisting him (Acts 7:51) or restricting him (Isaiah 63:10; Ephesians 4:30; 1 Thessalonians 5:19), but only as we are following him (Galatians 5:16–18,22–25).

SERMON NO. 1332

Manoah's wife and her excellent argument

'And Manoah said unto his wife, We shall surely die, because we have seen God. But his wife said unto him, If the LORD *were pleased to kill us, he would not have received a burnt offering and a meat offering at our hands, neither would he have shewed us all these things.' Judges 13:22–23*
SUGGESTED FURTHER READING: Proverbs 31:10–31

Women's perceptions are generally far clearer than men's reasonings: they look at once into a truth, while we hunt for our spectacles. Their instincts are generally as safe as our reasonings, and when they also have a clear logical mind they make the wisest of counsellors. Manoah's wife not only had clear perceptions, but she had capital reasoning faculties. She argued that it was not possible that God should kill them after what they had seen and heard. Oh that every man had such a prudent, gracious wife as Manoah had! Oh that whenever a man is cast down, a Christian brother or sister stood ready to cheer him with some reminder of the Lord's past goodness, or with some gracious promise from the divine word. It may be the husband who cheers the wife, and in such a case it is equally beautiful. We have known a Christian sister to be very nervous, depressed and troubled: what a mercy to her to have a Christian husband whose strength of faith can encourage her to smile away her griefs, by resting in the everlasting faithfulness and goodness of the Lord. How careful ought young people to be in the choosing of their partners in life! When two horses pull together how smoothly the chariot runs, but if one draws one way and the other pulls in the opposite direction, what trouble there is sure to be. Suppose Manoah had happened to have an unbelieving wife. How his spirit would have gone down into despair, till he would have fulfilled his own sad prophecy. If he had been troubled with a wife like Mistress Job and she had uttered some bitter saying just when he was in anguish, how much more severe would his griefs have become. But Mistress Manoah was a believing woman; she argued out the question most discreetly, and her husband found peace again.

FOR MEDITATION: A marriage made in heaven is a great blessing (Proverbs 18:22; 19:14), if it remains heavenly-minded (Ephesians 5:22–25). But consider the harm that a wife (Proverbs 12:4; 19:13) or a husband (Colossians 3:19) can inflict.

SERMON NO. 1340

A God ready to pardon

'Thou art a God ready to pardon.' Nehemiah 9:17
SUGGESTED FURTHER READING: Genesis 3:8–21

The Lord at all times is 'a God ready to pardon.' It is true of him by nature, for mercy is an essential attribute of God. We must never think that our Lord Jesus died to make God merciful; on the contrary, the death of the Lord Jesus is the result of the mercy of God. When man sinned, God was willing enough to pardon him, for the death of a sinner is no pleasure to him. Judgment is his strange work. The way in which the Lord came to Adam at the first showed his mercy. He came, if you remember, 'in the cool of the day', not at the instant the crime was committed. God is not in a hurry to accuse man or to execute vengeance upon him; he therefore waited until the cool of the day. He did not address rebellious man in the language of indignation, but he kindly called to Adam, 'Where art thou?' And when he had questioned the guilty pair and convicted them and the sentence was passed, it was certainly terrible, but how mildly tempered; the curse was as much as possible made to fall obliquely: 'cursed is the ground for thy sake'. Though the woman was made to feel great sorrows, yet those were connected with a happy event which causes the travail to be forgotten. There was tenderness in the dread utterances of an offended God, and mainly so because almost as soon as he declared that man must labour and die, he promised that the seed of the woman should bruise the serpent's head. Assuredly the Lord our God is by nature very pitiful and full of compassion. This truth is evident when we remember that God was abundantly ready to pardon, for he himself removed the impediment which lay in the way of forgiveness.

FOR MEDITATION: 'Who is a God like unto thee, that pardoneth iniquity' (Micah 7:18)? If we seek him, call upon him, forsake our wicked ways and return to him, 'he will abundantly pardon' (Isaiah 55:7). David said to God, 'For thy name's sake, O LORD, pardon mine iniquity; for it is great' (Psalm 25:11). Have you ever approached God like this?

Free pardon

'I, even I, am he that blotteth out thy transgressions for mine own sake, and will not remember thy sins.' Isaiah 43:25
SUGGESTED FURTHER READING: 1 Peter 3:18–4:6

In the ordinance of baptism the believer sets forth the doctrine of salvation by death and burial. That was Noah's salvation. He went into the ark as one dead to the world; he was buried in the ark, and then he floated out from the dead world into the new. Peter says, 'The like figure whereunto even baptism doth also now save us (not the putting away of the filth of the flesh, but the answer of a good conscience toward God,) by the resurrection of Jesus Christ.' That is to say, baptism is a like figure of salvation, for it sets forth in a figure, and only in a figure, our death with Christ, our burial with Christ and our resurrection with Christ. Therefore where there is true faith and the soul has communion with Christ, we are buried with him in baptism unto death, 'that like as Christ was raised up from the dead by the glory of the Father, even so we also should walk in newness of life.' Death has passed upon us, for the apostle says, 'because we thus judge, that if one died for all, then *all died:*'—for such is the literal Greek—'and that he died for all, that they which live should not henceforth live unto themselves, but unto him which died for them, and rose again.' Well then, beloved, if we are dead, I do not wonder that God says he does not remember our sins, for we are new creatures; 'we have passed from death unto life'. We have come into a new life; God looks upon us from a new point of view and regards us under a new aspect as members not of the first Adam condemned and dead, but of the second Adam, the Lord from heaven, the living and the quickening Spirit. Well may he say to men who are new creatures, 'I will not remember your sins.'

FOR MEDITATION: Meditate on the aspects of salvation which have been associated with and illustrated by baptism (1 Peter 3:21)—repentance (Mark 1:4; Acts 19:4), cleansing (Acts 22:16), death, burial and resurrection to new life (Romans 6:3–4). Have you experienced this transformation and have you portrayed it in believer's baptism?

A revival promise

'One shall say, I am the LORD*'s; and another shall call himself by the name of Jacob; and another shall subscribe with his hand unto the* LORD*, and surname himself by the name of Israel.' Isaiah 44:5*
SUGGESTED FURTHER READING: Acts 2:37–47

One memorable thing about conversions wrought by the Holy Spirit is this, that these converted people shall be led to confess their faith. They shall not, like Nicodemus, come to Jesus by night; they shall not hope to go to heaven creeping all the way behind the hedge, but they shall avow their allegiance. 'One shall say, I am the LORD's; and another shall call himself by the name of Jacob; and another shall subscribe with his hand unto the LORD, and surname himself by the name of Israel.' The God of Israel shall be their God, and the people of Israel shall be their people. I love to see both these things in young converts. Some appear to dedicate themselves to God, but they feel themselves such superior beings that they do not join with any church, but hold themselves in the isolation which practically means, 'Stand by; I am holier than thou.' They do not think any church good enough for them, but my private opinion is that they are not good enough for any church. On the other hand, some will join a church, but do not seem to have had enough respect to the inward, vital part of religion in giving themselves up to the Lord, and therefore no church will find them to be any great gain. There must be the two together, a surrender to God and then a union with the people of God. Consider the first of these points—'One shall say, I am the LORD's'. He shall confess that from head to foot, body, soul and spirit, he is not his own but Christ's. He will feel, 'I have been washed in his blood; I have been pardoned all my sins and been renewed in heart; and now I am the Lord's and desire to live to his praise. Tell me what I can do and how I can serve the Lord, for I am his and mean to be his for ever.' This is delightful.

FOR MEDITATION: (*Our Own Hymn Book* no.95 song 2 v.4—Isaac Watts, 1719)
    'Today attend His voice, nor dare provoke His rod;
    Come, like the people of His choice, and own your gracious God.'

SERMON NO. 1151

Opening the mouth

'Open thy mouth wide, and I will fill it.' Psalm 81:10
SUGGESTED FURTHER READING: Ezekiel 34:1–10

Open your mouths wide, dear friends, and ask great things for the church. The church of God, I hope, is in a better condition than she was some years ago, but we have not yet learned what it is to believe in great works being done for God. There are still churches which, if they were to have half-a-dozen added to them in a year, would be intensely satisfied, if not overjoyed, instead of calling for prayer, fasting and humiliation because so few are brought to Christ. There are church members around us who do not believe in many people being converted at once. If the gospel were preached so that a dozen were brought in at one time, they would impute it to undue excitement, and doubt its being the work of the Spirit of God, though we have the New Testament, and the Acts of the Apostles especially, to lead us to expect such things. There are churches which, if God were to send them a hundred converts at once, would not receive them, but would put them through a rigid quarantine; and you may be sure our heavenly Father will not send his new-born babes to places where they will not be cheerfully admitted. There are certain churches whose modes of testing and trying are such that the young lambs would be torn to bits before they would get into the green pastures, and there would hardly be two legs and a piece of an ear left after they had passed the examination: the Good Shepherd will not send his lambs where such a tribe of wolves stand gaping for prey. Pray for the church that she may have greater faith in her God, greater belief in the gospel which she preaches, greater closeness of walk with Jesus and greater care to obey her Master's precepts; and then you may open your mouth wide and expect to see the kingdom of Christ more fully come.

FOR MEDITATION: (*Our Own Hymn Book* no.980 v.2—John Newton, 1779)
> 'Thou art coming to a King,
> Large petitions with thee bring;
> For His grace and power are such,
> None can ever ask too much.'

The day of salvation

'Behold, now is the day of salvation.' 2 *Corinthians* 6:2
SUGGESTED FURTHER READING (Spurgeon): Isaiah 49:8–13

Beloved, are you in deep trouble just now? Is your spirit overwhelmed within you? Be of good cheer, for this is the day of salvation. It is not a time for saints to die in; it is not a day in which the enemy shall triumph over believers; it is for us the day of salvation. Be glad, then, you who are assailed by the enemy. Though your foe may put his foot upon your neck, yet he cannot crush your life out, but you may boldly cry, 'Rejoice not against me, O mine enemy: when I fall, I shall arise.' It is the day in which believers must be saved. Did not Christian, in *Pilgrim's Progress,* find it so from the very day in which he left the City of Destruction to the time when he passed through the river and Hopeful said to him, 'I feel the bottom, and it is good'? He had days of conflict, days of weariness and days of deep distress of mind, but all along he was saved, saved from the lions, saved from Giant Despair, saved from the flatterer's net and saved from the last river with its chill floods. We also live in the day of salvation. 'Ah', said a Popish bishop once to one of our martyrs, 'You are a heretic and you will be damned.' 'My lord,' said the heroic man, 'there I am at a pass with you; I may be burned, but I never shall be damned.' 'Why so?' said his adversary. The man replied by quoting that passage in the old translation, 'There is therefore now no damnation to them that are in Christ Jesus, who walk not after the flesh but after the Spirit.' Who shall condemn those for whom Christ has died? It is the day of salvation, not of accusation. It is the day of victory, not of defeat, not of captivity, much less a day of destruction to the true people of God.

FOR MEDITATION: (*Our Own Hymn Book* no.406 v.6—John Kent, 1803)
  'Saints dejected, cease to mourn,
  Faith shall soon to vision turn;
  Ye the kingdom shall obtain,
  And with Christ exalted reign.'

SERMON NO. 1394

'Rest in the Lord'

'Rest in the LORD.' Psalm 37:7
SUGGESTED FURTHER READING: 2 Chronicles 14:1–15

Rest in each one of the attributes of God. Are you conscious of sin? Come and rest in the mercy which blots it out. Poor sinner, I would invite you with the burden of your guilt upon you to remember that God delights in mercy and that it is his joy to pass by transgression. You will never escape from the bondage of your sin, except by coming to the mercy of God in Jesus Christ his Son. Rest in boundless mercy. Beloved child of God, are you troubled about inward sin? Then rest in his power to break the neck of corruption. Perhaps your affliction concerns your worldly affairs; then rest in the power of God to help you: he is great at a dead lift, and when none can help us but God, then is God most ready to come to the rescue. Rest, beloved brother, in God's wisdom. You cannot see your way, but he can see it; leave it to him, for there is no possibility of error in his counsels. Rest also in his immutability, that sure anchorage amid the troubled sea of life. You have changes every day; he never changes. Come back to him whose constancy of love is a mountain of strength. He has set his mind upon saving you, and he is of one mind, so who shall turn him? This is his mind, that 'He that believeth and is baptized shall be saved', and he will perform that salvation: neither death, nor hell shall thwart the sacred purpose of an unchanging God. He will carry out his gracious work and glorify himself therein. Rest also in his faithfulness. What he has promised he will perform. 'God is not a man, that he should lie; neither the son of man, that he should repent: hath he said, and shall he not do it?' Take his promise and believe it to be as good as the fulfilment, for so it is.

FOR MEDITATION: (*Our Own Hymn Book* no.708 v.6—Ann Letitia Waring, 1850)
   'My heart is resting on His truth,
   Who hath made all things mine;
   Who draws my captive will to Him,
   And makes it one with Thine.'

SERMON NO. 1333

Reasons for turning to the Lord

'Come and let us return unto the LORD: *for he hath torn, and he will heal us; he hath smitten, and he will bind us up.'* Hosea 6:1
SUGGESTED FURTHER READING (Spurgeon): Psalm 32:1–11

The writer of these words discerns the presence of the Lord, for he is convinced that his trials come from God. Ungodly men set down their troubles to chance, and sometimes even trace them to the devil, as if they expected their father to have dealings with them. Frequently they lay their ills at the door of their fellow men, and grow quarrelsome, malicious and revengeful. It is a happy day for a man when he knows in whose hand is the rod, and learns to trace his troubles to God. Alas, even some children of God greatly err in this matter when under affliction; they spend their time in bewailing second causes and do not look at the first cause. This is brutish. If you strike a dog with a stick he will bite at it; had he a little intelligence he would bite at you and know that the blow came, not from the stick, but from the hand that used it. So unbelievers in trouble usually look at the secondary agent and spend their anger or thoughts entirely there. If in the day of adversity they would consider, they would perceive that affliction does not spring out of the ground, neither do distresses come by chance, but that the hand of the Lord is in all these things. 'Shall there be evil in a city, and the LORD hath not done it?' Whichever way the trial came, it came from him. If the trouble was caused by a triumphant enemy or by a deceitful friend, if it came as a loss in business or as a sickness of body, or if it wounded us through the arrows of death piercing the heart of our beloved, it was the Lord. Learn that lesson. *He* has smitten you; *he* has torn you: *he* has done it all. He has ordained our trials for judgment and established them for correction; let us not despise them by refusing to see his hand or by angrily rebelling against him.

FOR MEDITATION: Misinterpretation can arise from ignorance of the unseen spiritual battle. Resist blaming the devil (2 Peter 2:10–12; Jude 8–10). Religious men attributed even our Saviour's work to him (Matthew 9:34; 12:24; John 8:48–52).

N.B. A hymn was sung in the middle of this sermon while Spurgeon, who was very unwell, regained his strength. He did not preach again until 17 March.

SERMON NO. 1396

The oil of gladness

'*Thou lovest righteousness, and hatest wickedness: therefore God, thy God, hath anointed thee with the oil of gladness above thy fellows.*'
Psalm 45:7
SUGGESTED FURTHER READING (Spurgeon): Isaiah 61:1–3

We know that the anointing received by our Lord Jesus Christ was the resting of the Spirit of God upon him without measure. We are not left to any guesswork about this, for in Isaiah 61:1 we are told, 'The Spirit of the Lord GOD is upon me; because the LORD hath anointed me'. Our Lord appropriated these very words to himself when he went into the synagogue at Nazareth, opened the book at the place wherein these words are written, and said, 'This day is this scripture fulfilled in your ears.' The apostle Peter also, in Acts 10:38, speaks of 'how God anointed Jesus of Nazareth with the Holy Ghost and with power', so that we know on both Old and New Testament authority that the anointing which rested upon the Lord Jesus Christ was the unction of the Holy Spirit. Therefore, by 'the oil of gladness', which we have before us in the text, is intended the Holy Spirit himself, or one of the gracious results of his sacred presence. The divine Spirit has many attributes, and his benign influences operate in divers ways, bestowing upon us benefits of various kinds, too numerous for us to attempt to catalogue. Amongst these is his comforting and cheering influence—'the fruit of the Spirit is ... joy'. In Acts 13:52 we read, 'the disciples were filled with joy, and with the Holy Ghost.' Wherever he comes as an anointing, whether upon the Lord or upon those whom he anoints, in every case the ultimate result is joy and peace. On the head of our great High Priest he is joy, and this 'oil of gladness' flows 'down to the skirts of his garments'. To the Comforter, therefore, we ascribe 'the oil of gladness'.

FOR MEDITATION: Read more about the anointing of the believer and the resulting blessings in Psalm 23:5–6, 2 Corinthians 1:21–22 and 1 John 2:20–21,26–27.

A cheery word in troublous times

'Wherefore, sirs, be of good cheer: for I believe God, that it shall be even as it was told me.' Acts 27:25
SUGGESTED FURTHER READING: Psalm 34:1–22

I learned a lesson the other day which, I think, I never can forget. I was asked after preaching a sermon to go and see a lady who suffered from rheumatism. Now, I know by bitter experience what rheumatism is, but when I saw one whose fingers and hands had all lost their form through pain, so that she was incapable of any motion beyond the mere lifting up of her hand and letting it fall again, and when I saw the pain marked on her countenance, and knew that for twenty-two years she had suffered an agony, then I said, 'You have preached me a sermon upon patience and I hope I shall profit by it. How dare I be impatient if you have to suffer so!' Now, if you go and see sick folk (and I suppose you do), say to them, 'be of good cheer, for it shall be even as God has told me;' and what has he told me? Why, that he will support his people in the severest afflictions. 'He shall deliver thee in six troubles: yea, in seven there shall no evil touch thee.' Tell them that the Lord will bless his people's troubles, for 'all things work together for good to them that love God'. Tell them that God will bring his people out of the trouble some way or other, for he has said, 'Many are the afflictions of the righteous: but the LORD delivereth him out of them all.' And if you will tell them these precious things, believing them yourself and having experienced the truth of them yourself, your testimony will comfort them. You will meet with some that have been bereaved, who have lost the light of their house, and have seen the desire of their eyes taken away with a stroke. Cheer them and tell them of the sweet things that God has said concerning the bereaved. He is 'A father of the fatherless, and a judge of the widows'. Make a point of declaring your belief that he is so.

FOR MEDITATION: God expects his people to visit the sick (Matthew 25:36,39–40). Failure to do so can be held against us (Ezekiel 34:4; Matthew 25:43–45). But a cold clinical attitude is not acceptable; genuine concern and warmth is required. Consider the attitudes of Job (Job 29:15–16), David (Psalm 35:13–14) and the apostle Paul (Philippians 2:25–30) towards the sick.

SERMON NO. 1335

Am I my brother's keeper?

'Am I my brother's keeper?' Genesis 4:9
SUGGESTED FURTHER READING (Spurgeon): 1 John 3:10–18

The whole example of Jesus Christ, whom we call Master and Lord, lies in the direction of our being the keeper of our brother; for what was Jesus' life but entire unselfishness. What was said of him at his death but that 'He saved others; himself he cannot save'? The very fact that there is a Christ at all means that there was one who cared for others, and the fact that our Lord became a man means that he loved his enemies and came here to rescue those who rebelled against his authority. If we are selfish, if we make our own going to heaven to be the one end of life, we are not Christians. We may call whom we please Master, but we are not following Jesus Christ. Tears do you shed? But do you weep over Jerusalem? Tears for yourself are poor things if there are never any for others. You pray and agonize: but is your grief ever caused by bearing the burden of other men's souls? Otherwise, are you like him with whose name Gethsemane must ever be connected in our memories? Oh, though we gave our bodies to be burned, yet if we had not love for mankind, it would profit us nothing. We may go a long way, and apparently all the way, in the externals of the Christian faith, but we are still aliens to the commonwealth of which Jesus is the great head. I am sure it is so. I speak not my own mind, but the mind of Christ. If he were here, what would he say to anyone who called himself his disciple and yet never lifted his hand or moved his tongue to snatch the firebrand from the flame or save the sinner from the error of his ways? It must be so, then: we must be our brothers' keepers.

FOR MEDITATION: A failure to have a genuine concern for the welfare of others amounts to looking after our own interests instead of those of Jesus Christ (Philippians 2:20–21). His example teaches us to please others for their good rather than pleasing ourselves (Romans 15:1–3).

Concern for other men's souls

'I say the truth in Christ, I lie not, my conscience also bearing me witness in the Holy Ghost, that I have great heaviness and continual sorrow in my heart. For I could wish that myself were accursed from Christ for my brethren, my kinsmen according to the flesh.' Romans 9:1–3
SUGGESTED FURTHER READING: Philippians 3:17–4:3

Love mankind with all your soul, and you will feel no difficulty in exercising patience, forbearance and forgiveness. This spirit will also keep you from very many other griefs. Some people are always fretting for want of something to fret about. No people are more uneasy than those who have nothing to do and nothing to think about; such persons keep a little growlery in the house, and use it as a trouble factory, where they invent grievances. There are people that I know of who ought to be as merry as the birds of the morning, and yet they are always worrying and stewing about nothing at all. Now, the best way to kill one grief is to introduce another. John Foster wrote of the expulsive power of a new affection and I want you to experience it. Get love for the souls of men: then you will not be whining about a dead dog, or a sick cat, or about the crochets of a family and the little disturbances that John and Mary may make by their idle talk. You will be delivered from petty worries, if you are concerned about the souls of men. When certain persons come to me with their sentimental sorrows, I wish the Lord would fill them with the love of souls, and make their hearts break with anxiety for their conversion: then would their griefs be of a nobler kind. You would no longer weep over a molehill if you began to move mountains. Get your soul full of a great grief, and your little griefs will be driven out. These thoughts of Paul about his brethren cause us to feel that we too may make our lives sublime, if in our hearts there shall burn the selfsame ardent affection towards our fellow-men.

FOR MEDITATION: Our service for God is bound to be hindered even by things which are right and proper in themselves (1 Corinthians 7:32–34), but it is a tragedy when faithful gospel-workers get distracted by petty in-fighting (Philippians 4:2–3). Even the apostle Paul discovered that gospel-workers who are more concerned for others than themselves tend to be few and far between (Philippians 2:20–22).

SERMON NO. 1425

The soul-winner

'The fruit of the righteous is a tree of life; and he that winneth souls is wise.' Proverbs 11:30
SUGGESTED FURTHER READING (Spurgeon): Romans 10:1–17

You will be wise, if for you the one absorbing desire is that you may turn the ungodly from the error of their ways. For you there will be a crown glittering with many stars, which you shall cast at Jesus' feet in the day of his appearing. Further, it is not only wise to make this your aim, but you will have to be very wise if you succeed in it, because the souls to be won are so different in their constitutions, feelings and conditions, and you will have to adapt yourself to them all. The trappers of North America have to find out the habits of the animals they wish to catch, and so you will have to learn how to deal with each class of cases. Some are very depressed; you will have to comfort them. Perhaps you will comfort them too much and make them unbelieving, and, therefore, possibly instead of comforting them you will need sometimes to administer a sharp word to cure the sulkiness into which they have fallen. Another person may be frivolous, and if you put on a serious face you will frighten your bird away; you will have to be cheerful and drop a word of admonition as if by accident. Some people, again, will not let you speak to them, but will talk to you; you must know the art of putting a word in edgeways. You will have to be very wise and become 'all things to all men', and your success will prove your wisdom. Theories of dealing with souls may look very wise, but they often prove to be useless when actually tried: he who by God's grace accomplishes the work is a wise man, though perhaps he knows no theory whatever. This work will need all your wit, and far more, and you will have to cry to the great winner of souls above to give you of his Holy Spirit.

FOR MEDITATION: Dealing with the souls of others requires wisdom and discernment far above our own. Consider how the Christian is taught to approach the believer who has sinned (Galatians 6:1; 1 John 5:16), the wanderer who was once 'not far from the kingdom of God' (Mark 12:34: James 5:19–20) and a variety of unbelievers who simply need to be saved (Jude 22–23).

SERMON NO. 1292

Love's medicines and miracles

'Behold, for peace I had great bitterness: but thou hast in love to my soul delivered it from the pit of corruption: for thou hast cast all my sins behind thy back.' Isaiah 38:17
SUGGESTED FURTHER READING: Micah 7:18–20

The Lord becomes oblivious of his people's sins. Somebody said the other day concerning a certain piece of business, 'I shall never think of it again; it has gone as though it had never been.' The Lord means all that concerning his people's sins: 'I shall never think of them again; they are quite gone as far as I am concerned; I have thrown them where I shall never see them any more; their sins and iniquities will I remember no more.' What a gracious mode of pardoning sin! God himself passes an act of oblivion and declares, 'I will not remember their sins.' He looks upon his people who have been so provoking and are still so prone to sin, and yet 'He hath not beheld iniquity in Jacob, neither hath he seen perverseness in Israel'. He sees his people washed in the blood of the Lamb, robed in the righteousness which is in God by faith, and he beholds in them neither 'spot, or wrinkle, or any such thing', for he has cast their sins so far away that they are out of sight of omniscience and out of mind of omnipresence. Again, I would remind you of the words 'behind thy back'. Where is that? All things are before God's face: he looks on all the works of his hands, and he sees all things that exist. Behind his back! It must mean annihilation, non-existence and non-entity. O my soul, your God has flung your sin into non-entity and effectually made an end of it: he treats you as though it never had been, and as far as his justice is concerned through the vicarious sacrifice of Christ, it is to the Lord as though we had never transgressed at all: 'thou hast cast all my sins behind thy back.'

FOR MEDITATION: God's grace in casting all our sins behind his back is magnified when we realise that we by our sins had in effect cast God (1 Kings 14:9; Ezekiel 23:35) and his law (Nehemiah 9:26) behind our backs.

SERMON NO. 1337

A remonstrance and a rejoinder

'For in Jesus Christ neither circumcision availeth anything, nor uncircumcision; but faith which worketh by love.' Galatians 5:6
SUGGESTED FURTHER READING: Romans 6:15–23

You who profess to have found Christ, do not make any sham of it. Do let it be salvation from sin that you have got. Salvation from hell—is that what you want? That is not the salvation you ought to try after. It is salvation from sin. That will bring salvation from hell. You know that every thief would like to get salvation from going to prison, and that would not be of any particular use to him. The salvation that is worth having is the salvation from thieving any more. Mr. Thief, if you get that, you will get salvation from prison too. Salvation from hell is not the matter, but salvation from sinning. Now let us see how you live, you converts. You go home, sir, and growl at your wife; you go home, madam, to be snappish with your servant; you go home, housemaid, to be slovenly over your duty; you go hence, working man, resolved to give half a day's work for a whole day's wage; you go home, master, to act the tyrant over your men. Well, you have been converted, have you? I pray God to undo such a conversion and begin again with you. There are lots of people who need to be unconverted before they are converted, to have the rubbish they have built up themselves pulled down before Christ can begin. Suppose you have some freehold ground and it has an old remarkable building on it. With a new edifice in view, you need to clear away every vestige of the former house. There are plenty of people who have a good-for-nothing conversion that needs sweeping away before God can do anything with them. Do pray to the Lord in this way—'Lord, I beseech thee, save me from my sin.' Let me have a perfect faith which works, not a faith that sends me to sleep.

FOR MEDITATION: A profession of salvation which is only an insurance for the afterlife and which makes no difference to the present life, is no more than a variation on the worthless theme of faith without works. Such faith is dead and cannot save anyone (James 2:14–26).

One greater than the temple

'But I say unto you, that in this place is one greater than the temple.'
Matthew 12:6
SUGGESTED FURTHER READING: Hebrews 9:1–14

He is 'greater than the temple', because he is a more sure place of consolation. Brethren, when a guilty conscience wished for relief, the man in the olden times went up to the temple and presented his sin offering; but you and I find a more effectual sin offering in our crucified Lord whenever our soul is burdened, for by it we are in very deed cleansed from sin. The Jew was not really cleansed, but only typically; ours is an actual and abiding deliverance from sin, its guilt and its defilement. We have no more consciousness of it when the blood of Jesus Christ is applied to our souls. Come evermore, burdened ones, to Christ's body as to a temple, see your sin put away by his finished atonement and then go your way comforted. The Israelites were accustomed to go to the temple in time of trouble to make supplication: it is very pleasant to think of broken-hearted Hannah standing in the tabernacle before the Lord and pouring out her silent complaint. Come, beloved, you too may speak in your heart unto the Lord whenever you will, and you will be heard. No Eli is near to judge you harshly and rebuke you sharply, but a better priest is at hand to sympathise with you, for he himself is 'touched with the feeling of our infirmities'. Fear not, you shall obtain an answer of peace, and the blessing given shall bear the sweet name of Samuel, because you asked it of the Lord. To Jesus you may come as to the temple, when like Hezekiah you are made to smart by a blasphemous letter or any other oppression: here you may spread the matter before the Lord with a certainty that the Lord, who is 'greater than the temple', will give you an answer of peace in reference to the trial which you leave in his hands.

FOR MEDITATION: The Lord Jesus Christ is superior to the temple both on earth and in heaven. On earth the temple was to be destroyed (Luke 21:5–6), but 'the temple of his body' was to be raised soon after destruction (John 2:19–22). In heaven there will be no temple, but 'the Lord God Almighty and the Lamb are the temple of it' (Revelation 21:22). The temple was temporary, but he is eternal.

SERMON NO. 1275

The heart full and the mouth closed

'And I will establish my covenant with thee; and thou shalt know that I am the LORD: *That thou mayest remember, and be confounded, and never open thy mouth any more because of thy shame, when I am pacified toward thee for all that thou hast done, saith the Lord* GOD.' *Ezekiel 16:62–63*
SUGGESTED FURTHER READING: 1 Timothy 1:8–17

It ought to encourage every one who has not found peace with God to hear us tell of what we feel of our own sinfulness, because, sinner, where one sinner gets through, there is room for another. If a prison door is broken down and a man gets out, another man who is in the same prison may safely say, 'Why should I not escape too?' Supposing we were all beasts in Noah's ark and we could not get down from the ark to the ground except by going down that slanting ramp which most of the painters have sketched when they have tried to depict the scene. We must go down that ramp. Are you, sheep and hares, afraid that the ramp will not bear you up? Listen, then. I am an elephant and I have come down out of the ark over that bridge; therefore it is clear that all of you who are smaller than I am can come over too. There is strength enough to bear up the hare, the coney, the ox and the sheep, for it carried the elephant. The way down has been trodden by that heavy, lumbering creature, so it will do for you, whoever you may be. Ever since the Lord Jesus Christ saved me, I made up my mind that I should never meet another person who was harder to save than I. Somebody said to me once when I was a child, when it was very dark and I was afraid to go out, 'What are you afraid of? You won't meet anything uglier than yourself.' Surely as to my spiritual condition that is true; I never did meet anything uglier than myself and I never shall. And if there is a great big, ugly sinner here, you are not uglier than I was by nature, and yet the Lord Jesus Christ loved me. Why should he not love you too?

FOR MEDITATION: (*Our Own Hymn Book* no.546 v.5—Charlotte Elliott, 1836)
'Just as I am—Thou wilt receive, Wilt welcome, pardon, cleanse, relieve;
Because Thy promise, I believe, O Lamb of God, I come.'

The new fashion

'And immediately he arose, took up his bed, and went forth before them all; insomuch that they were all amazed, and glorified God, saying, We never saw it on this fashion.' Mark 2:12
SUGGESTED FURTHER READING: 2 Chronicles 33:1–16

That regeneration which produces no effect is nothing — less than nothing. It would be like saying, 'That man is saved from the paralysis.' 'Well, but he lies on the bed.' 'Yes, he lies on the bed the same as he did before, but he is delivered from the paralysis.' 'But how do you know?' 'Well, of course, it may not be an actual cure, but it is a virtual cure, because he has undergone a ceremony and therefore it must be so; you are to believe it.' This is fine talk; but when the man rose, rolled up his bed and carried it on his back, that was a deal more convincing. Now, when God's providence brings in a man who has been a drunkard, and he hears the gospel of Jesus Christ, believes in Jesus, turns his cups upside down and becomes a sober man, there is something in that. If there comes a man who is proud, haughty, a hater of the gospel, a man who can swear and who has no regard for the Sabbath day, and he believes in Jesus, becomes at home as gentle as a lamb, so that his wife hardly knows that he is the same man, and delights to go to the house of God on the Sabbath, there is something real and tangible to be seen in that, is there not? Here is a man that would cheat you in his business, as soon as look at you, but the grace of God comes to him, and he becomes scrupulously honest. Here is a man that used to associate with the lowest of the low, but the gospel of Jesus Christ is received by him, and he seeks godly companions and loves only those whose talk is sweet, clean and holy. Why, you can see it. And this is the kind of salvation we want in these days, a salvation that can be seen, which makes the paralysed sinner roll up his bed and carry it away.

FOR MEDITATION: The new birth produces new life (1 Peter 1:23–2:2; 1 John 2:29; 4:7; 5:1,4). Being spiritually stillborn does not qualify as being born again (John 8:39–42).

Eternal faithfulness unaffected by human unbelief

'If we believe not, yet he abideth faithful: he cannot deny himself.'
2 *Timothy* 2:13
SUGGESTED FURTHER READING: Acts 20:17–32

One of the most shocking trials to young Christians is the fall of an eminent teacher. I have known some that have been almost ready to give up their faith when some one who appeared to be very earnest and faithful has suddenly apostatized. Such things have happened in our memory, to our intense grief. I want, therefore, to put it very plainly. If it should come to pass that any one whom you revere as having been a blessing to your soul—whom you love because you have received from him the word of life—if such a one upon whom you may, perhaps, have leaned too much, should in the future turn out not to be true and faithful, and should not believe, do not follow his unbelief, for 'if we believe not, yet *he* abideth faithful: he cannot deny himself'. Peter denies his Master: do not follow Peter when he is doing that, for he will have to come back weeping, and you will hear him preaching his Master again. Worse still, Judas sells his Master: do not follow Judas, for Judas will die a wretched death, and his destruction shall be a warning to others to cling more closely to the faith. You may see the man who stood like a cedar in Lebanon fall by one stroke of the devil's axe, but do not, therefore, think that the trees of the Lord, which are full of sap, will fall too. He will keep his own, for he knows 'them that are his'. Pin not your faith to any man's sleeve. Let not your confidence rest on any arm of flesh, neither say, 'I believe because of the testimony of such a one and I hold to the form of sound words because my minister has held it', for all such props may be smitten away and on a sudden may fail you.

FOR MEDITATION: Backsliding, apostasy or error on the part of others ought not to take us completely by surprise. Such disappointments must never be used as an excuse for doing likewise, but should always be seen as a warning and an encouragement to go on with the Lord regardless (Acts 20:28–32; Philippians 3:16–19; 2 Timothy 3:12–14; 2 Peter 3:17–18; 1 John 2:19,24; 2 John 7–8; Jude 19–21).

Offended with Christ

'And blessed is he, whosoever shall not be offended in me.' Matthew 11:6
SUGGESTED FURTHER READING (Spurgeon): Matthew 10:24–39

There are not a few who professed to become Christians and who thought that they were always going to be happy. The evidence that they gave of being Christians was that they felt so happy. I do not know that mere happiness is any evidence of being a Christian at all, for many are living far from God and yet account themselves very happy, while some of those who live near to God are groaning because they cannot get nearer still. Yet a joyful feeling is by many regarded as conclusive evidence of salvation; they add to this the notion that as soon as ever they believed in Jesus Christ the conflict was all over, and there remained nothing more to be done in the way of resisting sin and denying the lusts of the flesh. They dreamed that they had only to start on pilgrimage and get to the Celestial City in a trice, only to draw the sword from the scabbard and all Canaan would be conquered in an hour. Very soon they find that it is not so. Their old corruptions are alive; the flesh begins to pull a different way from that which they profess to have chosen, the devil tempts them and they are so disappointed by their new discovery that they become offended with Christ altogether. A sudden victory would suit them, but to carry a cross before winning a crown is not to their mind. Others of them have met an opposition they did not expect from their adversaries, while from their friends they have not met with all the respect that they think they ought to have. Their friends and acquaintances have laughed at them; they did not reckon on this, they never counted the cost, and so they are offended with Christ.

FOR MEDITATION: (*Our Own Hymn Book* no.671 vv.2&3—Isaac Watts, 1721)
'Must I be carried to the skies on flowery beds of ease
While others fought to win the prize, and sailed through bloody seas?
Are there no foes for me to face? Must I not stem the flood?
Is this vile world a friend to grace, to help me on to God?'

Seekers directed and encouraged

'And ye shall seek me, and find me, when ye shall search for me with all your heart.' Jeremiah 29:13
SUGGESTED FURTHER READING: 1 Kings 15:1–14

Some seek God *with a false heart*. They flame with zeal and would have their friends know it, for they say as Jehu did to Jehonadab, 'Come with me, and see my zeal for the LORD'; but their heart is not true towards God. Their piety is an affectation of feeling and not deep soul-work; it is sentimentality, not the graving of God's Spirit upon the heart. Beware of a false religious excitement, of being borne up with religious gas as some are, inflated like balloons by a revival, only to burst by-and-by when most they need something to support them. God grant us to be saved from a lie in the heart, for it is a deadly canker, fatal to all hope of finding the Lord. Some seek him, too, *with a double heart,* as the Hebrew puts it. They have a heart towards God and they have a heart towards sin: they have a heart towards the pardon, but they have also a heart towards the transgression. They would serve God and Mammon: they would build an altar for Jehovah and still keep Dagon in his place. If your heart is divided you will be found wanting. Those prayers will never get to heaven which fly upward with only one wing. If one oar pulls towards earth and the other towards heaven, the boat of the soul will revolve in a circle of folly, but never reach the happy shore. Beware of a double heart. And some seek God *with half a heart*. They have a little concern and are not altogether indifferent; they do think when they pray, read and sing, but the thought is not very intense. Superficial in all things, the seed is sown in stony ground and soon it is withered away, because there is no depth of earth. The Lord save us from this.

FOR MEDITATION: General ungodliness can be expected when the heart is false (Isaiah 59:12–13) or double (Psalm 12:1–2). David urged Solomon to cultivate 'a perfect heart' (1 Chronicles 28:9) and prayed the same for him (1 Chronicles 29:19), but Solomon was not careful to maintain one (1 Kings 11:4), even though he himself had urged his people to do so (1 Kings 8:61). Each one of us needs to heed the instruction, 'Keep thy heart with all diligence' (Proverbs 4:23).

SERMON NO. 1457(B)

Why men cannot believe in Christ

'How can ye believe, which receive honour one of another, and seek not the honour that cometh from God only?' John 5:44
SUGGESTED FURTHER READING: Hebrews 11:23–28

Some cannot believe in Jesus Christ because they are very fond of what they call pleasure. Every man desires happiness and is not to be condemned for this. The human mind was constituted to enjoy pleasure, but it was never created to be content with the vanities which are falsely called pleasures. It makes one blush to think of the trifles in which our neighbours take delight. Sinful pleasures are a great bar to faith and must be renounced. That evil companion who has charmed you with questionable jests must be given up. Do you say that you cannot quit him? Then I see why you cannot believe in Jesus. Unbelievers know that if they believe in Christ they must forsake that house of unclean amusement which leads to vice, and they cannot believe because they love the place of temptation. They hesitate, deliberate and say that they cannot believe in Jesus; but if they would speak the truth, they mean they cannot give up sweet sin. Sin is such a dainty, that they must roll it again under the tongue and relish it once more. They prefer pleasure to the Saviour. There are some who are unable to believe in Jesus Christ for reasons which I hardly care to utter publicly, and yet I must. I have sometimes had sorrowful proof of the reason why some men have lived in unbelief of Christ. After a death I have heard what would have been a shame to whisper in the ear of an unsuspecting wife. The man was a respectable merchant in the city and went into the 'best society', but he was keeping a mistress and living in fornication all the while. He said he could not believe in Christ! Do you wonder? How could he? I speak plainly, because these things are common among respectable merchants and they need to be told plainly of their sins. Do not come whining to me about 'can't believe in Jesus Christ'. Of course you cannot while you live in filthy lusts.

FOR MEDITATION: (*Our Own Hymn Book* no.572 v.1—Charles Wesley, 1749)
'Oh! that I could repent, with all my idols part,
And to Thy gracious eyes present a humble, contrite heart.'

SERMON NO. 1245

Unconditional surrender

'Submit yourselves therefore to God.' James 4:7
SUGGESTED FURTHER READING: Romans 7:7–17

'In what respect am I to submit myself?' First submit yourself by confessing your sin. Cry, 'I have sinned.' Do not brazen it out and say, 'I have not sinned.' You will never be pardoned while that is the case. He that confesses his sin shall find mercy. Sinner, choose between one of two things; judge yourself, or be judged by God. If you will judge yourself and put in a plea of guilty, then will the Great Judge grant you forgiveness, but not otherwise. Condemn yourself and you shall not be condemned. Confess the indictment to be true, for true it is; to deny it is to seal your doom. Next, honour the law which condemns you. Do not persevere in picking holes in it and saying that it is too severe and requires too much of a poor fallible creature; 'the law is holy, and the commandment holy, and just, and good'. Kiss it, though it condemns you, and say, 'Though it charges me with guilt and convicts me of deadly sin, yet it is a good law and ought not to be altered, even to save me.' Next, own the justice of the penalty. Your sins condemn you to hell; do not say, 'God is too severe; this is a punishment disproportionate to the offence.' You will never be pardoned if you think so, but God will be justified in your condemnation: the pride of your heart will be a swift witness against you. Confess with your heart, 'If my soul were sent to hell, it is no more than I deserve.' When you have confessed your guilt, honoured the law and acknowledged the justice of the penalty, then you are nearing the position in which God can be merciful to you. Submit yourself, sinner—do it now—submit yourself to God as your king.

FOR MEDITATION: Read Isaiah 1:18–20. God is ready and willing to reason with sinners and to forgive and bless all who submit to him and trust in the Lord Jesus Christ to be their saviour. But those who are obstinate and who continue to resist him will just as surely be punished by him. In which category are you?

SERMON NO. 1276

Dagon's ups and downs

'*And when they arose early on the tomorrow morning, behold, Dagon was fallen upon his face to the ground before the ark of the* LORD; *and the head of Dagon and both the palms of his hands were cut off upon the threshold; only the stump of Dagon was left to him.*' 1 Samuel 5:4
SUGGESTED FURTHER READING (Spurgeon): Romans 7:18–25

'The stump of Dagon was left to him.' I wish it were not. I have heard some say that they have no sin remaining in them. Well, the Lord convert them! Every child of God who knows anything about himself and the experience of a real believer, knows that there is indwelling sin in him, and that to a most fearful extent, so as to make his very soul cry out in agony, 'O wretched man that I am! who shall deliver me from the body of this death?' I could not go the length of singing, with Ralph Erskine, as a description of myself, what he wrote in his *Believer's Sonnets*—'To good and evil equal bent, and both a devil and a saint.' But yet, taken with a large lump of salt, there is a good deal of truth even in that unguarded expression. There is the old corruption within us, and there is no use denying it, because denying it will put us off our guard, make many of the puzzles of life to be quite unanswerable, and often bring upon us great confusion of soul. 'Another law' is within us as well as the law of grace. Can you draw near to God and not see that he can justly charge you with folly? Can you stand in his presence, as Job did, behold his glory and not say, 'I abhor myself, and repent in dust and ashes'? Can you have dealings with perfection and not perceive your faultiness? Can you come near unto the innermost court of the temple, stand in that excessive light of fellowship which is the portion of the Lord's chosen, and not see within yourself thousands of spots and wrinkles, so as to make you cover your face for shame and adore the amazing grace which loves you still?

FOR MEDITATION: (*Our Own Hymn Book* no.631 v.2—John Fawcett, 1782)
'What though Satan's strong temptations vex and tease thee day by day?
And thy sinful inclinations often fill thee with dismay?
Thou shalt conquer, through the Lamb's redeeming blood.'

The yoke removed and the Lord revealed

'They … shall know that I am the LORD, *when I have broken the bands of their yoke.' Ezekiel 34:27*
SUGGESTED FURTHER READING: Galatians 5:13–17

The moment we become Christians an inward battle begins. The old self will not tolerate the intruder, the new creature in Christ Jesus, and a conflict ensues. The converted man will be clean rid of some sins and scarcely ever feel a temptation to them. Notably some men, who have been given to certain evil habits, have never been tempted that way again, but the flesh has taken a turn and rebelled in another direction. I have known a man, after conversion, tempted to commit a totally new sin for him and the suggestion has been a galling yoke to him. A passion which before he did not know to be in his soul has been aroused, and he has seen the meshes of a net gradually encompassing him. Then he has cried out because of the oppression put upon his sin-hating heart. If a believer has gone very deep in sin before conversion, he will often have a hard battle of it arising from the recollection of old transgressions, old habits and old lusts. You may get the serpent out, but the slime of the reptile still remains; it needs the sanctifying power of the Spirit of God to purge its former lurking place. If a lion has long had his lair in a thicket, the hunters may chase him out, but his den is there and likely enough cubs will come forth when least expected; so it is with evil in the heart of man. An old cask smells of the wine it held; it will need a great deal of scalding to sweeten it; and even then, if you put pure water into it, there will still be a taste of the old liquor about it. In certain of our petty wars we never seem to come to an end; the natives are not at peace nor will they keep quiet; they watch an opportunity and break out again. It is so with the war in the Christian's soul.

FOR MEDITATION: The Christian must recognize and resist the specific temptations which once led regularly into sin (Ephesians 4:25–28; 1 Peter 4:3), but remain on guard for the unexpected which can also lead astray (2 Samuel 11:2–4; Matthew 16:21–23; Galatians 6:1). Whether the temptation is habitual or a novelty, God always gives the Christian a way to endure and resist it (1 Corinthians 10:13).

SERMON NO. 1462

The dual nature and the duel within

'But I see another law in my members, warring against the law of my mind, and bringing me into captivity to the law of sin which is in my members.' Romans 7:23
SUGGESTED FURTHER READING: Exodus 13:17–22

I am not sure that the conflict between the new nature and the old is felt by all young Christians at the first. Frequently Christian life may be divided into three stages: the first period is that of *comfort,* in which the young Christian rejoices in the Lord; his principal business is to sing and tell what God has done for him. The more of this the better. After that, very often comes the stage of *conflict:* instead of being children at home we have grown into men and therefore we must go to war. Under the old law when a man was married or had built a house, he was excused from fighting for a season, but when that was over, he must take his place in the ranks: and so it is with the child of God; he may rest awhile, but he is destined for the war. The period of conflict is often succeeded, especially in old age, by a third stage which we may call *contemplation,* in which the believer sits down to reflect upon the goodness of the Lord towards him, and upon all the good things which are in store for him. This is the land Beulah, which John Bunyan describes as lying on the edge of the river and so near to the Celestial City that you can hear the heavenly music across the stream, and, when the wind blows that way, you can smell the sweet perfumes from the gardens of the blessed. That is a stage which we must not expect to reach just now. My young friend, inasmuch as you are at the first weak and tender, the Lord may be pleased to screen you from a great many temptations and from uprisings of your flesh, but the probabilities are that before long you will put down your harp and take up your sword, and your joy of spirit will give place to the agony of conflict.

FOR MEDITATION: Read again how carefully God avoided allowing the children of Israel to face too much temptation at the start of their long journey (Exodus 13:17–18). He still does not allow his people to be tempted beyond their ability to resist (1 Corinthians 10:13), but that gives us no excuse for pushing young converts too quickly into circumstances where they will face unnecessarily premature temptations (1 Timothy 3:6).

SERMON NO. 1459(B)

'Lead us not into temptation'

'Lead us not into temptation.' Matthew 6:13
SUGGESTED FURTHER READING: Galatians 5:26–6:5

Two men were condemned to die as martyrs in the burning days of Queen Mary. One of them boasted very loudly to his companion of his confidence that he should play the man at the stake. He did not mind the suffering; he was so grounded in the gospel that he knew he should never deny it. He said that he longed for the fatal morning even as a bride for her wedding. His companion in prison in the same chamber was a poor trembling soul, who could not and would not deny his Master, but he told his companion that he was very much afraid of the fire. He said he had always been very sensitive of suffering, and he was in great dread that, when he began to burn, the pain might cause him to deny the truth. He besought his friend to pray for him, and he spent his time very much in weeping over his weakness and crying to God for strength. The other continually rebuked him and chided him for being so unbelieving and weak. When they both came to the stake, he who had been so bold recanted at the sight of the fire and went back ignominiously to an apostate's life, while the poor trembling man whose prayer had been, 'lead me not into temptation,' stood firm as a rock, praising and magnifying God as he was burnt to a cinder. Weakness is our strength and our strength is weakness. Cry unto God that he try you not beyond your strength, and in the shrinking tenderness of your conscious weakness breathe out the prayer, 'lead us not into temptation'. Then if he does lead you into the conflict, his Holy Spirit will strengthen you and you will be brave as a lion before the adversary. Though trembling and shrinking within yourself before the throne of God, you would confront the very devil and all the hosts of hell without one touch of fear. It may seem strange, but so the case is.

FOR MEDITATION: (*Our Own Hymn Book* no.1001 v.4—James Montgomery, 1825)
'From dark temptation's power,
From Satan's wiles defend;
Deliver in the evil hour,
And guide us to the end.'

SERMON NO. 1402

Daniel facing the lions' den

'Now when Daniel knew that the writing was signed, he went into his house; and his windows being open in the chamber toward Jerusalem, he kneeled upon his knees three times a day, and prayed, and gave thanks before his God, as he did aforetime.' Daniel 6:10
SUGGESTED FURTHER READING: Nehemiah 6:1–16

Believe me, to be decided for the right is not only the right thing but the easiest thing. It is wise policy as well as true probity. If you will not yield an inch, then somebody else must move out of the way. If you cannot comply with their proposals, then other people will have to rescind their resolutions. So you will find that, if you suffer and perhaps suffer severely at first, for decision of character, you will get speedy recompense for all you endure and a grand immunity in the future. There will be an end to the indignities that are offered you. If it be not obstinacy, but real conscience that prompts you, you will rise to a position which otherwise you could not have attained. The opposition, so strong against you at first, will very likely lead to your enemies endorsing your views, and the dishonour you have meekly to bear will be followed by a deference flattering to your vanity, if not perilous to your future consistency. Only put your foot down now; be firm and unfaltering now. If you yield today, you will have to yield more tomorrow. Give the world an inch, and it will take a mile. Be resolved, therefore, that no inch will you give, that to the lions' den you would sooner go than that there should be equivocation, prevarication, or anything approaching to falsehood. However great the difficulty may be at the outset, yet do it and you will be unhurt: you will be an immediate gainer by it and, to the rest of your days, God will give you a better and happier life than ever you have had before. 'When a man's ways please the LORD, he maketh even his enemies to be at peace with him.'

FOR MEDITATION: If you are unsure where you stand on certain issues, how can you expect anybody else to know where you stand? Note how God honours those who refuse to compromise (Daniel 1:8–9; 3:16–18,28; 6:21–22) even if it still involves persecution and suffering (Acts 5:27–29,40–42).

The best burden for young shoulders

'It is good for a man that he bear the yoke in his youth.' Lamentations 3:27
SUGGESTED FURTHER READING: Romans 5:1–5

If it were possible to take every young Christian and put him into a pious family and not let him go into the world at all, but always keep him in his mother's lap, if it were possible to take every working man and guarantee that he should only work in a shop where they sing psalms from morning to night, where nobody ever swears, where nobody ever utters a word of chaff against him, I do not know that it would be wise. To keep people out of temptation is exceedingly proper, and none of us have any right to put a temptation in another's way; but it is good for us to be tempted sometimes, otherwise we should not know the real condition of our hearts and might be rotting with inward pride while blooming with outward morality. Temptation lets us know how weak we are and drives us to our knees. It tests our faith, tries our love, and lets us see whether our graces are genuine or not. When religion puts on her silver slippers, everybody is quite content to go with her, but the honest, hearty Christian will follow Jesus Christ's truth when she goes barefoot through the mire and slough, and when her garments are bespattered by unholy hands. Herein is the trial of the true and the unmasking of the deceitful. It would not be good for us to be kept from persecution, slander and trial. 'It is good for a man that he bear the yoke in his youth.' A Christian is a hardy plant. Many years ago a larch was brought to England. The gentleman who brought it put it in his hothouse, but it did not develop in a healthy manner. It was a spindly thing, and therefore the gardener, feeling that he could not make anything of it, threw it upon the dunghill. There it grew into a splendid tree, for it had found a temperature suitable to its nature. The tree was meant to grow near the snow; it loves cold winds and rough weather, and they had been sweating it to death in a hothouse. So it is with true Christianity.

FOR MEDITATION: Consider Joseph. As a teenager he suffered hatred, jealousy and plotting (Genesis 37:2–5,8,11,18–20). Sold into slavery (Genesis 37:28; Psalm 105:17–18), he endured slander and imprisonment (Genesis 39:14–20). Contrast his understandable complaints then (Genesis 40:14–15) with his later testimony to God's goodness (Genesis 41:50–52) and sovereignty (Genesis 45:4–8; 50:20).

SERMON NO. 1291

Trial by the word

'Until the time that his word came: the word of the LORD *tried him.'*
Psalm 105:19
SUGGESTED FURTHER READING: James 1:1–12

While Joseph was tried in prison, God's great object was to prepare him for the government which awaited him. It was designed first to give him power to bear power, a rare acquirement. Solomon says, 'As the fining pot for silver, and the furnace for gold; so is a man to his praise.' Many a man can bear affliction, but few men can endure prosperity; the most perilous thing in the world is to step suddenly from obscurity into power. Have we not seen men, illiterate and unknown, suddenly introduced to the Christian pulpit and made much of, and has it not frequently turned out that their names have been by-and-by prudently forgotten, for they were overthrown by the dizzy heights to which they were lifted? It is far better that a man should fight his way up to his position, that he should be assailed by enemies, distrusted by friends and pass through a probationary career. Even then he can only stand as the Lord holds him, but without it he is in great peril. Hence the apostle says, 'Not a novice, lest being lifted up with pride he fall into the condemnation of the devil.' If I knew that some young man would be greatly owned of God in the future and become a prince in our Israel, and if by lifting up this finger I could screen him from fierce criticism, misrepresentation and abuse, I would not do it, because, severe as the ordeal might be to him, I am persuaded it is needful that he should pass through it in order to make him able to bear the giddy heights of the position for which God intends him.

FOR MEDITATION: (*Our Own Hymn Book* no.750 v.2—William Cowper, 1779)
'God in Israel sows the seeds
Of affliction, pain, and toil;
These spring up and choke the weeds
Which would else o'erspread the soil:
Trials make the promise sweet;
Trials give new life to prayer;
Trials bring me to His feet,
Lay me low and keep me there.'

SERMON NO. 1277

The poor man's prayer

'Remember me, O LORD, *with the favour that thou bearest unto thy people: O visit me with thy salvation; that I may see the good of thy chosen, that I may rejoice in the gladness of thy nation, that I may glory with thine inheritance.' Psalm 106:4–5*
SUGGESTED FURTHER READING: Job 8:11–22

Just think for a moment. Supposing you are living now without seeing the good of God's chosen, without being saved, what a wretched life it is to live! I cannot understand what men do without God: I cannot comprehend how they live. Do you have no cares? 'We have anxieties in shoals' you say. Well, where do you take them? I have troubles enough, but I have a God to take them to. What do you do with many troubles and no God? Do your children never distress your mind? How can you live with bad children and no God? Do you never lose money in business? Do you never feel distracted? Do you never say, 'What shall I do? Which way shall I turn?' I suppose you do. Then what do you do without a helper or guide? Poor, weak thing as I am, I run under the shelter of my Father's wing and feel safe enough. But where do you go? Where do you fly? What is your comfort? I suppose you are something like the poor creatures condemned to death in olden times to whom they gave a stupefying cup, so that they might die without feeling the horror of death: surely you must be under a strong delusion that you can believe a lie, for if you were in your senses, you could not do without God, even with your beautiful gardens, fine parks, wealth and riches, or, many of you, with your poverty and hard labour. Poor man without God, how do you keep up your spirits? What comfort is there in your life? No prayer in the morning or at night: what days, what nights! I could as soon think of living without eating or breathing, as living without prayer. Wretched naked spirits your souls must be with no God to cover them!

FOR MEDITATION: (*Our Own Hymn Book* no.556 v.1—Charles Wesley, 1739)
> 'Jesus, the sinner's Friend, to Thee,
> Lost and undone, for aid I flee;
> Weary of earth, myself, and sin,
> Open Thine arms and take me in.'

SERMON NO. 1454(B)

The sad plight and sure relief

'For when we were yet without strength, in due time Christ died for the ungodly.' Romans 5:6
SUGGESTED FURTHER READING: Mark 2:1–17

The description of those for whom Christ died has not one letter of goodness in it. It describes them as hopelessly bad. Yet for such Christ died. I am not going to tell you that Christ died for saints. He died for sinners, not for the godly, but 'for the ungodly', not for the strong in grace, morals and the like, but for those who were 'without strength'. Truly I know he died for the saints, but who made them saints? When he died for them they were sinners. I know he died for those whom he has made 'strong in the Lord, and in the power of his might', but who made them strong? When he died for them they were as weak as others. All the difference between Peter in heaven and Judas in hell is a difference made by free rich sovereign grace. There was the same raw material to begin with in one as in another; and Jesus Christ looked upon men not at their best, when he laid down his life for their redemption, but at their worst. This is clear; it is self-evident: had they been whole, they would not have needed a physician; if they had not been lost, they would not have needed a Saviour; if the disease had not been very bad, they would not have needed so matchless a medicine as the blood of Christ; if they had not been helplessly lost, there could have been no necessity for omnipotence to step in to effect their rescue, and had not the ruin been terrible to the last degree, it would not have been demanded that God himself should come in human flesh and make expiation for guilt by his own death upon the cross. The glory of the remedy proves the desperateness of the disease. The grandeur of the Saviour is a sure evidence of the terribleness of our lost condition.

FOR MEDITATION: The description of those for whom Christ died is hardly calculated to flatter our pride. Our spiritual sickness (Mark 2:17) includes being blind (John 9:39; 2 Corinthians 4:4), deaf (Matthew 13:15) and even dead (Ephesians 2:1). Read what Jesus had to say to those who dared to disagree with his diagnosis (John 9:40–41).

SERMON NO. 1184

The weaned child

'My soul is even as a weaned child.' Psalm 131:2
SUGGESTED FURTHER READING: Jeremiah 17:1–10

Big as men may account themselves to be on account of their ancestors, we all trace our line up to a gardener, who lost his place through stealing his Master's fruit, and that is the farthest we can possibly go. Adam covers us all with disgrace, and under that disgrace we should all sit humbly down. Look into your own heart, and, if you dare to be proud, you have never seen your heart at all. It is a mass of pollution: it is a den of filthiness. Apart from divine grace, your heart is a seething mass of putrefaction, and, if God's eternal Spirit were not to hold it in check, but to let your nature have its way, envyings, lustings, murders and every foul thing would come flying forth in your daily life. A sinner and yet proud! It is monstrous. As for children of God, how can they be proud? I fear we are all too much so; but what have we to be proud of? What have we that we have not received? How then can we boast? Are we dressed in the robe of Christ's righteousness? We did not put a thread into it; it was all given us by the charity of Jesus. Are our garments white? We have washed them in the blood of the Lamb. Are we new creatures? We have been created anew by omnipotent power, or we should still be as we were. Are we holding on our way? It is God that enables us to persevere, or we should long ago have gone back. Have we been kept from the great transgression? Who has kept us? We certainly have not kept ourselves. There is nothing that we have of which we can say, 'I did this and it is all my own,' except our faults and our sins, and over these we ought to blush.

FOR MEDITATION: A proud person, whether sinner or saint, is an abomination to God (Proverbs 6:16–17; 16:5). Pride can only bring trouble upon us (Proverbs 11:2; 16:18; 29:23). We all need to recognise pride for what it is in God's sight—'sin' (Proverbs 21:4).

SERMON NO. 1210

The hospital of waiters visited with the gospel

'Jesus saith unto him, Rise, take up thy bed, and walk.' John 5:8
SUGGESTED FURTHER READING (Spurgeon): John 4:46–54

A crowd of waiters are waiting for dreams and visions. Perhaps you think these are very few, but they are not so few as you may imagine. They have a notion that perhaps one of these nights they will have such a vivid dream of judgment that they will wake up alarmed, or such a bright vision of heaven that they will wake up fascinated by it. They have been reading in somebody's biography that he saw something in the air, or heard a voice, or had a text of Scripture 'laid home to him', as it is called; they are waiting until the like signs and wonders shall happen to them. I bear them witness that they are very anxious for this thing to happen, but their mistake is that they want it at all or expect it to happen, and they lie there by the Pool of Bethesda waiting and waiting and waiting, as though they could not believe God, but they could believe in a dream. They could not confide in the teaching of Holy Scripture, but they could believe in a voice which they imagined to be sounding in their ears, though it might be the chirp of a bird or nothing at all. They could trust their imagination, but they cannot trust the word of God as it is written in the inspired volume. They want something over and above the sure word of testimony; the witness of God is not enough for them. They demand the witness of fancy, or the witness of feeling, and they are waiting in the porch by the pool until that comes. What is this but an insulting unbelief? Is not the Lord to be believed until a sign or a wonder shall corroborate his testimony? Such waiting provokes the Most High.

FOR MEDITATION: (*Our Own Hymn Book* no.546 v.2—Charlotte Elliott, 1836)
'Just as I am—and waiting not
To rid my soul of one dark blot,
To Thee, whose blood can cleanse each spot,
O Lamb of God, I come.'

Idols abolished

'Ephraim shall say, What have I to do any more with idols?' Hosea 14:8
SUGGESTED FURTHER READING (Spurgeon): Hosea 13:1–6

The essence of idolatry is this—to love anything better than God, to trust anything more than God, to wish to have a God other than we have, or to have some signs and wonders by which we may see him, some outward symbol or manifestation that can be seen with the eye or heard with the ear, rather than to rest in an invisible God and believe the faithful promise of Him whom 'eye hath not seen, nor ear heard'. In some form or other this great sin is the main mischief in the heart of man; even in saved men this is one of the developments of remaining corruption. We may very easily make an idol of anything, and in different ways. No doubt many mothers and fathers make idols of their children; so many husbands and wives idolize each other, and we may even make idols of ministers, even as there were idol shepherds of old. Equally is it certain that many a thoughtful man makes an idol of his intellect, and many another makes an idol of his gold, or even of that little home wherein he enjoys so much content. The ignorant papist holds up his crucifix and worships that, and that is his idol; but men who are better instructed often take the Bible and read that, but, failing to get through the letter into the spirit, they trust in the mere act of Scripture reading and make even the word itself to become an idol to them through their resting in a mere creed, or in bare Bible reading, and not pressing through it to hearty spiritual worship of God himself. Anything, however holy, which comes between us and the personal dealing of our soul with God, as he is revealed in Christ Jesus, by faith, love and hope, becomes an idol to us.

FOR MEDITATION: Whether before our eyes (Ezekiel 6:9; 18:12; 20:24; 33:25) or in our hearts (Ezekiel 14:3–4,7), idols are a cause of defilement (Ezekiel 20:7,18; 22:3–4; 23:7) and pollution (Ezekiel 20:31; 23:30). The only proper course of action is to turn from them in repentance and to call upon God himself to lay hold of our hearts (Ezekiel 14:5–6).

SERMON NO. 1339

Let him alone

'Ephraim is joined to idols: let him alone.' Hosea 4:17
SUGGESTED FURTHER READING (Spurgeon): Proverbs 1:20–33

Any vice deliberately harboured, any one sin persistently indulged, may bring about this fearful result. God will speak of you, then, not as an erring creature whom it is possible to reclaim, but as a wretched outcast whom it is necessary to abandon. A man may be overtaken with a fault. If he has been guilty of drunkenness his conscience rebukes him. Falling into that sin once or twice, he has felt, as well he may, that he has been degraded by it. Let that man continue—and I might especially say, 'Let that woman continue' (for the common use or the constant abuse of intoxicating drinks exerts its baneful spell over both sexes)—let any one continue to violate the laws of sobriety, and before long that sin will become a rooted habit. Then conscience will cease to accuse and God will practically say, 'Ephraim is given to his cups: let him alone!' Or let a man begin some practice of fraud in his business. At first it will trouble him: he will feel uneasy. By-and-by his systematic dishonesty will not prick his conscience. He will become so familiar with crime that he will call it custom and wonder how ever he could have been so chicken-hearted as to feel any trouble about it at all. God will let him alone and leave him to eat the fruit of his own ways. He is given to his sin, and his sin will bind him with iron chains and hold him a captive. I cannot, of course, pick out the special sin of everyone, but whatever your sin is, you are warned against it. Your conscience tells you it is wrong. If you persevere in it, it may come to be your eternal ruin. God will say, 'The man is joined to idols: let him alone.' Continuance in sin provokes that sentence, especially when that continuance in sin is perpetrated in the teeth of many admonitions.

FOR MEDITATION: Deliberate continuance in sin, far from providing fresh opportunities for God's grace to be displayed (Romans 6:1–2), instead provokes God's wrath (Romans 2:4–5). Contemplate the terrible finality of the repetitive phrases 'God gave them up' and 'God gave them over' which toll like a funeral bell in Romans 1:24–28.

SERMON NO. 1140

Reasons for parting with sin

'*Come now, and let us reason together, saith the* LORD: *though your sins be as scarlet, they shall be as white as snow; though they be red like crimson, they shall be as wool.*' *Isaiah 1:18*
SUGGESTED FURTHER READING: Isaiah 59:1–13

It is most certain that the real reason why men who have an earnest desire to be saved and sincere religiousness of a certain sort, do not find peace is this—they are in love with sin. Either some one sin is secretly indulged, or many sins are unrepented of and unforsaken. They provoke the Lord with their trespasses and then hope to pacify him with their prayers. Hence it is altogether vain for them to tread God's courts: in vain they pray, and in vain they attend upon religious ceremonies with the view of finding peace, for they have hidden the accursed thing in the midst of the camp; they are harbouring a traitor, and until this accursed thing is destroyed and the traitor is driven out, they cannot be acceptable to God. To all such God asks, 'What have you to do with peace while your offences are so many?' O, ungodly man, your heart can never rest in God while it goes forth after its idols. As long as you and your sins are at peace, God and your soul must be at war. Until you are ready to be divorced from sin, you can never be married to Christ. God will give salvation and the pardon of sin, and give them freely to the very chief of sinners, but the sinner must confess and forsake his sin. The Lord graciously says, 'Let the wicked forsake his way, and the unrighteous man his thoughts: and let him return unto the LORD, and he will have mercy upon him; and to our God, for he will abundantly pardon.' But 'There is no peace, saith my God, to the wicked.' His word solemnly declares that 'God shall wound the head of his enemies, and the hairy scalp of such a one as goeth on still in his trespasses.'

FOR MEDITATION: The comforting teaching that God automatically hears all our prayers is simply not true. The Bible teaches us that God, although not deaf, does not hear the prayers of those who are separated from him by their sin (Isaiah 59:1–2); he will, however, answer the sinner's sincere prayer for the forgiveness of sin (Luke 18:13–14). God will not even listen to the prayers of his saved people when they harbour sin in their hearts (Psalm 66:18).

SERMON NO. 1278

Glorying in the Lord

'He that glorieth, let him glory in the Lord.' 1 Corinthians 1:31
SUGGESTED FURTHER READING: Jeremiah 9:23–10:7

Glory in the Lord practically, by having a contempt for those things which others value so much. Do not be greedy after the world. Love God too much to care for earthly treasures. If God gives you wealth, thank him for it and use it. If he does not, do not worry about it. Feel that you are rich enough without heaps of yellow metal. You have your God and that is the best wealth; you have a heaven to go to and a little heaven below. Rejoice in that which you find in your God. Live above the world. 'For our conversation is in heaven.' May God's Spirit help you. Thus glorify God and when men look at you, compel them to feel that there is something in you and about you which they cannot understand, for you have been with Jesus and you have learned of him. In all these ways, 'He that glorieth, let him glory in the Lord.' I am sorry to feel compelled to say that I am afraid many do not understand this. Perhaps you have gloried in your priests and thought they were great. Very possibly some of you glory in your minister; you think he is very eminent. Some of you, it may be, glory in your purses and your possessions. Some of you glory in your broad acres and large houses. Some of you glory in the skill you have in your trade or your quickness in business. It may be many of you glory in the fact that you are not as other men are. All these gloryings are evil. God help you to put them down. Even to glory in your church, your sect and your creed is wrong. To glory in the Lord is the work of his Spirit, and to live to make him glorious in the esteem of men is the only thing worthy of an immortal mind. You will never glory in God until first of all God has killed your glorying in yourself.

FOR MEDITATION: (*Our Own Hymn Book* no.242 v.3—Philip Doddridge, 1755)
'Perish each thought of human pride,
Let God alone be magnified;
His glory let the heavens resound,
Shouted from earth's remotest bound.'

SERMON NO. 1178

The overflowing cup

'My cup runneth over.' Psalm 23:5
SUGGESTED FURTHER READING: Jeremiah 2:4–13

If your cup is running over, let it stay where it is. Understand my meaning: the cup stands under the spring; the spring keeps running into it, and so the cup runs over, but it will not run over long if you take it from where the spring pours into it. The grateful heart runs over because the fountain of grace runs over. Keep your cup where it is. It is our folly that we forsake 'the fountain of living waters' and apply to the world's 'broken cisterns'. We say in the old proverb, 'Let well alone', but we forget this practical maxim with regard to the highest good. If your cup runs over, hear Christ say, 'Abide in me.' David had a mind to keep his cup where it was and he said, 'I will dwell in the house of the LORD for ever.' When I preach abroad I always like to go to the same house in the town, and I say to my host, 'I shall always come to you, as long as you invite me, for I do not think there is a better house.' If a man has a good friend, it is a pity to change him; the older the friend the better. The bird which has a good nest had better keep to it. Gad not abroad, I charge you, but let the Lord be your dwelling-place for ever. Many have been fascinated by new notions and new doctrines, and every now and then somebody tells us he has found a wonderful diamond of new truth, but it generally turns out to be a piece of an old bottle: as for me, I want nothing new, for the old is better, and my heart cries, 'Return unto thy rest, O my soul; for the LORD hath dealt bountifully with thee.' Until they find me a better fountain than the Lord has opened in Christ Jesus his Son, my soul will abide in her old place and plunge her pitcher into the living waters.

FOR MEDITATION: (*Our Own Hymn Book* no.708 v.1—Anna Letitia Waring, 1850)
    'My heart is resting, O my God;
    I will give thanks and sing;
    My heart is at the secret source
    Of every precious thing.'

SERMON NO. 1222

Jesus near but unrecognised

'But their eyes were holden that they should not know him.' Luke 24:16
SUGGESTED FURTHER READING: Lamentations 3:16–33

I remember years ago visiting a woman, whom I never could comfort until she died, and then she died triumphantly. I said to her, 'What do you come to the chapel for? What is the good of it if there is nothing there for you?' 'No,' she said, 'still I like to be there. If I perish, I will perish listening to the precious word.' 'But why is it you remain a member of the church, as you say you are not a saved soul?' 'Well,' she said, 'I know I am not worthy, but unless you turn me out I will never go out, for I like to be with God's people. I desire to be numbered with them, too, though I know I am not worthy, for I have no hope.' I said, 'Well now, I will give you five pounds if you will give up your hope altogether;' and I drew out my purse. 'Five pounds!' she said, and looked at me with utter horror; 'Five pounds!' She would not give Christ up for five thousand worlds. 'But you have not got him, you said.' 'No, sir, I am afraid I have not got him, but I will never give him up.' There came out the real truth. So it was with these two disciples; they talked as if they could not give him up; though they were afraid that he had not risen from the dead, yet they remained his disciples and spoke of 'certain women also of our company'. They were half-unconsciously clinging to the forlorn cause in its very worst estate. And so will we. We will say with Job, 'Though he slay me, yet will I trust in him.'

> 'Yea, when thine eye of faith is dim,
> Rest thou on Jesus, sink or swim;
> And at His footstool bow the knee,
> And Israel's God thy peace shall be.'

FOR MEDITATION: Peter felt that his sinfulness demanded a parting of the ways (Luke 5:8), but underneath was in no mood to give up his Lord (Matthew 26:33; John 6:67–69; 13:37). When he actually did the unthinkable, he had no peace (Luke 22:55–62). Do you experience these contradictory feelings? Be encouraged by the fact that the Lord was in no way going to give Peter up (Luke 22:31–32). 'He will never, never leave us; Nor will let us quite leave Him' (Joseph Hart).

SERMON NO. 1180

A voice from heaven

'And I heard a voice from heaven saying unto me, Write, Blessed are the dead which die in the Lord from henceforth: Yea, saith the Spirit, that they may rest from their labours; and their works do follow them.'
Revelation 14:13
SUGGESTED FURTHER READING: Colossians 1:1–10

Books written for the Master and his truth, though buried in obscurity, are sure of a resurrection. Fifty years ago our old Puritan authors, yellow with age and arrayed in dingy bindings, 'wandered about in sheepskins and goatskins; being destitute, afflicted, tormented', But they have been brought forth in new editions and every library is enriched with them; the most powerful religious thought is affected by their utterances and will be till the end of time. You cannot kill a good man's work, nor a good woman's work either, though it be only the teaching of a few children in the Sunday-school. You do not know to whom you may be teaching Christ, but assuredly you are sowing seed which will blossom and flower in the far-off ages. When Mrs Wesley taught her sons, little did she think what they would become. You do not know who may be in your class. You may have there a young Whitefield, and if the Lord enables you to lead him to Jesus, he will bring thousands to decision. Good woman, you may be nursing one whom God will make a burning and a shining light; and if you train that little one for Jesus your work will never be lost. No holy tear is forgotten; it is in God's bottle. No desire for another's good is wasted; God has heard it. A word spoken for Jesus, a mite cast into Christ's treasury, a gracious line written to a friend—all these are things which shall last when the sun has blackened into a coal and the moon has curdled into a clot of blood. Deeds done in the power of the Spirit are eternal. 'Therefore, my beloved brethren, be ye stedfast, unmoveable, always abounding in the work of the Lord, forasmuch as ye know that your labour is not in vain in the Lord.'

FOR MEDITATION: Sowing the seed of the gospel can seem an uncertain business, but that should not deter us (Ecclesiastes 11:4–6), because God's word will fulfil its purpose (Isaiah 55:10–11) and some of the seed will eventually be fruitful (Psalm 126:5–6), perhaps way beyond our wildest expectations (Matthew 13:8,23).

SERMON NO. 1219

Morning and evening songs

'To shew forth thy lovingkindness in the morning, and thy faithfulness every night.' Psalm 92:2

SUGGESTED FURTHER READING: Psalm 36:1–12

It was said of Mr Whitefield that he could have moved an audience to tears by saying the word 'Mesopotamia'; I think he could have done it better with the word 'lovingkindness'. Put it under your tongue; let it lie there—lovingkindness. Kindness—does that mean kinnedness? Some say that it is the root-sense of the word—kinned-ness, such feeling as we have to our own kin, for blood is ever thicker than water, and we act towards those who are our kindred as we cannot readily do towards strangers. Now, God has made us of his kin. In his own dear Son he has taken us into his family. We are children of God, 'heirs of God, and joint-heirs with Christ;' there is a kinned-ness from God to us through our great kinsman Jesus Christ. But then the word is only half understood when you get to that, for it is loving-kindness. For a surgeon to set a man's limb when it is out of joint or broken is kindness, although he may do it somewhat roughly and in an off-hand manner, but if he does it very tenderly, covering the lion's heart with the lady's hand, then he shows loving-kindness. A man is picked up on the battle-field, put into an ambulance and carried to the hospital; that is kindness; but if that poor soldier's mother could come into the hospital and see her boy suffering, she would show him loving-kindness, which is something far more. A child run over in the street and taken to hospital would be cared for, I have no doubt, with the greatest kindness; but, send for its mother, for she will give it loving-kindness. And so the Lord deals with us. He gives us what we want, in a fatherly manner. He does to us what we need, in the tenderest fashion. It is kindness; it is kinned-ness; but it is loving-kindness. The very heart of God seems written out in this word.

FOR MEDITATION: God's loving-kindnesses are marvellous (Psalm 17:7), excellent (Psalm 36:7), better than life (Psalm 63:3) and multitudinous (Isaiah 63:7). Try to count your blessings and praise God for them.

SERMON NO. 1138

Compassion on the ignorant

'Who can have compassion on the ignorant, and on them that are out of the way; for that he himself also is compassed with infirmity.' Hebrews 5:2
SUGGESTED FURTHER READING: Mark 8:1–10

If you want to draw people around you, you must have sympathy with them: compassion magnetizes a man and makes him attract as the loadstone fascinates the needle. A big heart is one of the main essentials to great usefulness. Try and cultivate it. Do not let another man's sorrow fall upon a deaf ear as far as you are concerned, but sorrow with the sorrowful and 'have compassion on the ignorant, and on them that are out of the way': they will soon perceive it and do to you as they did to your Master, of whom we read, 'Then drew near unto him all the publicans and sinners.' Men will cluster around you like bees around their queen; they will not be able to help it; they will not wish to help it. Love is the queen bee and where she is you will find the centre of the hive. By this same means you will hold those whom you gather, for men will not remain with an unloving leader: even little children in our classes will not listen long to an unsympathetic teacher. Great armies of soldiers must be led by a great soldier and children must be held in hand by childlike instructors. When human beings surround an uncompassionate person, they soon find it out and fly off at a tangent as if by instinct. You may collect people for a time by some extraneous means, but unless they perceive that you love them and that your heart goes out with desires for their good, they will soon weary of you. The multitude still clung to the skirts of Jesus even to the last, whenever he preached, because they saw that he really desired their good. You must have compassion if you are to keep up the attention of those whom you address. The earth is held together by the force of attraction, and to the men upon it that same power is exercised by love and compassion.

FOR MEDITATION: Consider Rehoboam's leadership (2 Chronicles 10). When people came to him with grievances (vv.3–4), wise elders advised him to react kindly, knowing that he would win their allegiance (vv.6–7). His foolish preference for the advice of his contemporaries (vv.8–11) led him to answer roughly (vv.12–14). This drove the people away and into rebellion (vv.16–19). Rehoboam had only himself to blame.

SERMON NO. 1407

Forgiveness made easy

'Forgiving one another, even as God for Christ's sake hath forgiven you.'
Ephesians 4:32
SUGGESTED FURTHER READING: Matthew 7:1–5

There is something wrong about me that needs to be forgiven by my brother, but there is also something wrong about my brother which needs to be forgiven by me, and this is what the apostle means—that we are all of us mutually to be exercising the sacred art and mystery of forgiving one another. If we always did this, we should not endure those who have a special faculty for spying out faults. There are some who, whatever church they are in, always bring an ill report of it. I have heard this sort of thing from many—'There is no love among Christians at all.' I will tell you the character of the gentleman who makes that observation; he is both unloving and unlovely, and so he is out of the track of the pilgrims of love. Another cries, 'There is no sincerity in the world now.' That man is a hypocrite: be quite sure of that. Judge a bird by its song and a man by his utterance. The censorious measure our corn, but they use their own bushels. You may know very well what a man is by what he says of others. It is a gauge of character which very seldom will deceive you, to judge other men by their own judgment of their fellows. Their speech betrays their heart. Show me your tongue, sir! Now I know whether you are sick or well. He that speaks with an ill tongue of his neighbour has an ill heart; rest assured of that. Let us begin our Christian career with the full assurance that we shall have a great deal to forgive in other people, but that there will be a great deal more to be forgiven in ourselves, and let us set our account upon having to exercise gentleness and needing its exercise from others, 'forgiving one another, even as God for Christ's sake hath forgiven you'.

FOR MEDITATION: Correctly understood and accepted, the forgiveness of our sins will bear fruit not only in forgiving others, but also in fearing God (Psalm 130:4), patient longsuffering (Matthew 18:21) and heartfelt love (Luke 7:47).

The God of Bethel

'I am the God of Beth-el.' Genesis 31:13
SUGGESTED FURTHER READING (Spurgeon): Genesis 28:10–22

Jacob promised that he would give a tenth unto the Lord. I do not know whether any of you have made any vow of that kind. I suppose there are few Christians who have not, at some time or other, made a vow. Well, brethren and sisters, perform your vows unto the Lord. God forbid that we should ever say anything in the heat of emotion or make any pledge without due premeditation, for God is not to be mocked. When we have once devoted anything unto the Lord, let us not draw back our hand. I have known Christian men who have said, 'If the Lord should prosper me till I am worth such and such an amount, all that I gain beyond it shall be given as a free-will offering to him.' I know one or two of the largest givers in Christendom who are thus fulfilling the vows they made. Yet I have also known some people entangled by their vows. They have had in perplexity to ask, 'What am I to do? I am in such a position that a larger capital than I ever contemplated is really necessary for the carrying on of my business: yet I have pledged myself to save and call my own no more than a definite sum which I have already in possession.' You must take heed how you vow, for you may entangle yourself. Very often it is best not to vow at all; but if in the hour of sorrow you have opened your mouth unto the Lord, take heed that you do not withdraw from the thing your heart has purposed and your lips have uttered. Sometimes the Lord directs his people to make some solemn pledge, which otherwise they might not have done, on purpose that they may do more for the glory and honour of his name than they have ever done before.

FOR MEDITATION: Read Ecclesiastes 5:4–6. Though paying what has been vowed can be a joyful experience (Jonah 2:9), making a vow can be a dangerous thing (Judges 11:30–40); breaking one can be even more serious (Malachi 1:14). If it is better not to vow than to vow and not pay (Ecclesiastes 5:5), Christians especially should think very seriously before taking marriage vows which one day they may not be prepared to keep.

SERMON NO. 1267

Counting the cost

'For which of you, intending to build a tower, sitteth not down first, and counteth the cost, whether he have sufficient to finish it?' Luke 14:28
SUGGESTED FURTHER READING: 2 Peter 1:1–11

The word here used for 'tower' has often been employed to signify a turreted house, a villa, or a country mansion. 'Which of you,' says Jesus to the people, 'intending to build for himself a mansion in which to reside at his ease would not first of all count the cost?' The building is to be a costly one. That it would cost a considerable sum is clear from the Saviour's saying that the wise man sits down and counts the cost. He does not merely stand up, pass his hand over his brow and say, 'This tower will cost me so many pounds,' but it is to be an elaborate construction, an almost palatial edifice, and therefore he sits down, like a merchant at his desk, and thoughtfully considers the undertaking; he consults the architect and the mason, and calculates what will be the expense of the outer walls, the roof, the interior fittings, and the like; he does not make a rough guess, but counts the cost as men count their gold. It is evidently a matter of consequence with them, and so is true religion—it is no trifle, but an all-important business. He who thinks that a careless, hit-or-miss, headlong venture will suffice for his eternal interests is the reverse of wise. True godliness is the building up of a character which will endure the day of judgment. It begins in laying deep the foundations in faith, love and a renewed heart; it is carried on by putting patiently, carefully and often painfully, stone upon stone the materials of the fair edifice, diligently adding 'to your faith virtue; and to virtue knowledge; and to knowledge temperance; and to temperance patience; and to patience godliness; and to godliness brotherly kindness; and to brotherly kindness charity.' Your life-work consists in 'building up yourselves on your most holy faith'. Do you see that it is a glorious palace to which the Christian character is likened?

FOR MEDITATION: While the Lord Jesus Christ is preparing many mansions for his people in heaven (John 14:2–3), it is the individual responsibility of those who trust in him to be busy building a godly character on earth (Jude 20).

SERMON NO. 1159

The rider on the white horse and the armies with him

'And I saw heaven opened, and behold a white horse; and he that sat upon him was called Faithful and True, and in righteousness he doth judge and make war. His eyes were as a flame of fire, and on his head were many crowns; and he had a name written, that no man knew, but he himself. And he was clothed with a vesture dipped in blood: and his name is called The Word of God. ... And out of his mouth goeth a sharp sword, that with it he should smite the nations: and he shall rule them with a rod of iron: and he treadeth the winepress of the fierceness and wrath of Almighty God. And he hath on his vesture and on his thigh a name written, KING OF KINGS, AND LORD OF LORDS.' Revelation 19:11–13, 15–16*

SUGGESTED FURTHER READING: Daniel 7:9–14

It was natural that John should carry his glance from the eyes to the brow; and as he looked at our champion on the white horse he saw that 'on his head were many crowns'. The last he had seen there was a crown of thorns; but that was gone, and in the place of the one crown of the briars of the earth, he saw many crowns of the jewels of heaven. There rests the crown of creation, for this Word made heaven and earth, the crown of providence, for this man now rules the nations with a rod of iron, the crown of grace, for it is from his royal hand that blessings are bestowed, and the crown of the church, for be it known to all men that there is no head of the church but Christ, and woe unto those who steal the title. He is 'head over all things to the church', and king in the midst of her. Yes, on his head are many crowns placed there by individual souls that he has saved. We have each one tried to crown him in our poor way, and we will do so as long as we live. All power is given unto him in heaven and in earth, and well may multitudes of diadems encircle that august brow which once was crowned with thorns. Glory be unto thee, O Son of God! Our hearts adore thee as we contemplate thee on thy white horse.

FOR MEDITATION: (*Our Own Hymn Book* no.351 v.1—Edward Denny, 1837)

'Bright with all His crowns of glory, see the royal Victor's brow;
Once for sinners marred and gory, see the Lamb exalted now:
While before Him all his ransomed brethren bow.'

SERMON NO. 1452(B)

The Master

'She called Mary her sister secretly, saying, The Master is come, and calleth for thee.' John 11:28
SUGGESTED FURTHER READING: 1 Corinthians 1:1–17

I hear a great deal said of sundry 'Bodies of Divinity', but my own impression is that there has been and will be only one body of divinity, and that is Jesus Christ, 'For in him dwelleth all the fulness of the Godhead bodily.' To the true church her body of divinity is Christ. Some churches refer to other standards, but we know no standard of theology except our Master. 'I, if I be lifted up from the earth, will draw all men unto me.' We feel no drawings towards any other master. He is the standard—'unto him shall the gathering of the people be.' We are not of those who will go no further than Martin Luther. Blessed be God for Martin Luther! God forbid that we should say a word in depreciation of him. But were we baptized unto Martin Luther? I think not. Some can never budge an inch beyond John Calvin, whom I reverence first of all merely mortal men; but still John Calvin is not our master, but only a more advanced pupil in the school of Christ. He teaches and, as far as he teaches what Christ taught, he is authoritative, but where Calvin goes apart from Jesus, he is no more to be followed than Voltaire himself. There are brethren whose one reference for everything is to the utterances of John Wesley. 'What would Mr Wesley have said?' is a weighty question with them. We think it a small matter what he would have said, or what he did say for the guidance of Christians, now so many years after his departure; far better is it to enquire what Jesus says in his word. One of the grandest of men that ever lived was Wesley, but he is no master of ours. We were not baptized in the name of John Wesley, or John Calvin, or Martin Luther; 'one is your Master, even Christ.'

FOR MEDITATION: (*Our Own Hymn Book* no.769 v.3—Augustus M.Toplady, 1759)
'Nothing, save Jesus, would I know;
My friend and my companion Thou!
Lord, seize my heart, assert Thy right,
And put all other loves to flight.'

The way to honour

'Whoso keepeth the fig tree shall eat the fruit thereof: so he that waiteth on his master shall be honoured.' Proverbs 27:18
SUGGESTED FURTHER READING: Ephesians 6:5–9

A Christian man is thoughtful; he studies, reads and investigates: still, for all that, philosophy does not rule him, nor the news of the day, nor the science of the times. Christ is our Master, master of our thoughts and meditations, the great leader and teacher of our understandings. We are his disciples, and disciples of none besides. We are affected by the love of family, the love of friendship and the love of country, but there is a love that is higher than all these, a master-love, and this is love to Jesus our Well-beloved, the Bridegroom of our souls. The text, 'No man can serve two masters', is frequently misread. The stress is not to be laid on the word 'two'. For that matter a man might serve three, half-a-dozen or twenty; but the stress is to be laid upon the word 'masters'—'No man can serve two *masters*'. Only one thing can be the master-passion; only one power can completely master us, so as to be supremely dominant and exercise imperial lordship over us. No man can have two imperial master-faculties, master-motives and master-ambitions; 'one is your Master, even Christ.' We are compelled, while we are in this body, to yield to this impulse and to that, we are urged forward by this motive and by that, we pursue this end and that; subordinately none of these things may be sinful, but the master-impulse must be the love of Christ, the master-aim must be Christ's glory, and the master-power that possesses us, as the Spirit took possession of the prophets of old and carried them right away, must be loyalty to Jesus Christ our Lord. He is our Master and we stand before him as servants who desire to obey his bidding.

FOR MEDITATION: (*Our Own Hymn Book* no.664 v.3—Isaac Watts, 1709)
'All that I am, and all I have,
Shall be for ever Thine;
Whate'er my duty bids me give,
My cheerful hands resign.'

SERMON NO. 1118

The best beloved

'Yea, he is altogether lovely.' Song of Solomon 5:16
SUGGESTED FURTHER READING: Philippians 3:7–11

The best thing about Christ is Christ himself. We prize his, but we worship him. His gifts are valued, but he himself is adored. With mingled feelings of awe, admiration and thankfulness we contemplate his atonement, his resurrection, his glory in heaven and his second coming, but it is Christ himself, stupendous in his dignity as the Son of God and superbly beautiful as the Son of man, who sheds an incomparable charm on all those wonderful achievements, wherein his might, merit, goodness and grace appear so conspicuous. For him let our choicest spices be reserved and to him let our sweetest anthems be raised. Our choicest ointment must be poured upon his head, and for his own self alone our most costly alabaster boxes must be broken; 'yea, he is altogether lovely.' Not only is his teaching attractive, his doctrine persuasive, his life irreproachable, his character enchanting, and his work a self-denying labour for the common good of all his people, but he himself is altogether lovely. I suppose at first we shall always begin to 'love him, because he first loved us'. Even to the last his love to us will always be the strongest motive of our affection towards him; still there ought to be added to this another reason less connected with ourselves and more entirely arising out of his own superlative excellence; we ought to love him because he is lovely and deserves to be loved. The time should come when we can heartily say, 'we love him because we cannot help it, for his all-conquering loveliness has quite ravished our hearts.' Surely it is but an unripe fruit to love him merely for the benefits which we have received at his hand.

FOR MEDITATION: (*Our Own Hymn Book* no.793 v.2—John Berridge, 1785)
'None among the sons of men,
None among the heavenly train,
Can with Jesus then compare,
None so sweet, and none so fair!'

SERMON NO. 1446

'Lovest thou me?'

'Simon, son of Jonas, lovest thou me?' John 21:16
SUGGESTED FURTHER READING: 1 Peter 1:1–9

If we have no love for Jesus Christ's person, our piety lacks the *adhesive element;* it fails in that which will help us stick to the good old way to the end and hold out to the end. Men often leave what they like, but never what they love; men can deny what they merely believe as a matter of mental conviction, but they will never deny that which they feel to be true and accept with heartfelt affection. If you are to persevere to the end, it must be in the power of love. Love is the great *inspiriting force.* Many a deed in the Christian life is impossible to everything but love. If in serving Christ you come across a difficulty far too great for judgment and far too hard for prudence, unbelief sits down, weighs and calculates, but love, mighty love, laughs at the impossibility and accomplishes it for Jesus Christ. Love breaks through troops, leaps over walls and hand-in-hand with faith she is all but omnipotent; through the power of God which is upon her, she can do all things for Jesus Christ her Lord. If you lack love your energy is gone; the force which nerves the man and subdues his foes is lacking. Without love, too, you are without the *transforming force.* Love to Christ is that which makes us like him. The eyes of love, like windows, let in the Saviour's image, and the heart of love receives it as upon a sensitive plate, until the whole nature bears its impress. You are like that which you love or you are growing like it. If Christ is loved, you are growingly becoming like him; but without love you will never bear the image of the heavenly. O Spirit of God, with wings of love brood over us, until Christ is formed in us.

FOR MEDITATION: (*Our Own Hymn Book* no.640 v.5—Samuel Stennett, 1787)
  'A very wretch, Lord! I should prove,
  Had I no love for Thee:
  Rather than not my Saviour love,
  Oh may I cease to be!'

Romans, but not Romanists

'*I commend unto you Phebe our sister, which is a servant of the church which is at Cenchrea: that ye receive her in the Lord, as becometh saints, and that ye assist her in whatsoever business she hath need of you: for she hath been a succourer of many, and of myself also.*' Romans 16:1–2
SUGGESTED FURTHER READING: Romans 12:6–13

According to this passage (Romans 16:1–16) the early Christians were accustomed to show their love to one another by practical help; in the second verse Paul says of Phebe, 'receive her in the Lord, as becometh saints, and ... assist her in whatsoever business she hath need of you: for she hath been a succourer of many, and of myself also.' I do not think that the apostle alluded to any church business, but to her own business, whatever that may have been; she may have had moneys to gather in or some complaint to make at headquarters about an exacting tax-gatherer. I do not know what it was, and it is quite as well that Paul did not tell us. It is no part of an apostle's commission to tell us other people's business; but whatever business it was, if any Christian in Rome could help her, he was to do so. And so if we can help our Christian brethren in any way or shape, as much as is in us, we are to endeavour to do it. Our love must not lie in words alone or it will be as unsubstantial as the air. Mark you, you are not called upon to become sureties for your brethren, or to put your name on the back of bills for them; do that for nobody, for you have an express word in Scripture against it—'He that is surety for a stranger shall smart for it: and he that hateth suretiship is sure,' says Solomon. I could wish that some brethren had been wise enough to have recollected the teaching of Scripture upon that point, for it might have saved them a sea of troubles. But for your fellow Christians do anything that is lawful for you to do; do it for one another out of love to your common Lord. 'Bear ye one another's burdens, and so fulfil the law of Christ.'

FOR MEDITATION: God is able to be surety for his people (Psalm 119:122; Hebrews 7:22), but loving others does not mean that we must accept such responsibility for their obligations. Scripture discourages this (Proverbs 11:15; 17:18; 22:26) and advises a hasty retreat from it (Proverbs 6:1–5). Paul's approach to Onesimus' obligations (Philemon 18–19) is an exception which proves the rule.

SERMON NO. 1113

The entreaty of the Holy Ghost

'Wherefore, as the Holy Ghost saith, To day if ye will hear his voice, harden not your hearts.' Hebrews 3:7–8
SUGGESTED FURTHER READING (Spurgeon): Psalm 95:1–11

Today attend the voice of God. Today, that is, especially while the Holy Spirit is leading others to hear and to find mercy; today, while the showers are falling; today, receive the drops of grace; today, while there are prayers offered up for you; today, while the hearts of the godly are earnest about you; today, while the footstool of heaven's throne is wet with the tears of those who love you; today, lest lethargy should seize the church again; today, lest the preaching of the word of God should come to be a matter of routine, and the preacher himself, discouraged, should lose all zeal for your soul; today, while everything is peculiarly propitious, hear the voice of God. While the wind blows, hoist the sail; while God is abroad on errands of love, go forth to meet him. Today, while yet you are not utterly hardened, while still there is a conscience left within you; today, while yet you are conscious of your danger in some degree, while yet there is a lingering look towards your father's house, hear and live, lest, slighting your present tenderness, it should never come again, but you should be abandoned to the shocking indifference which is the prelude of eternal death. Today, young people, while yet you are undefiled with the grosser vices; today, young men who are new to this polluting city, before you have steeped yourselves in its streams of lust; today, while everything is helpful to you, hear the loving, tender, wooing voice of Jesus, and 'harden not your hearts'. To me the text seems wonderfully gospel-like when it says 'today', for what is it but another way of putting the doctrine of the blessed hymn, *'Just as I am, without one plea'*? Today—that is, in the circumstances, sins and miseries in which you now are, hear the gospel and obey it.

FOR MEDITATION: (*Our Own Hymn Book* no.497 v.3—Albert Midlane, 1865)
> 'Soon that voice will cease its calling, now it speaks, and speaks to thee;
> Sinner, heed the gracious message, to the blood for refuge flee;
> Take salvation, take it now, and happy be.'

SERMON NO. 1160

A clear conscience

'Then shall I not be ashamed, when I have respect unto all thy commandments.' Psalm 119:6

SUGGESTED FURTHER READING: 2 Thessalonians 3:6–16

We must not forget or be negligent concerning morals, which some have accounted to be minor obligations, pretending to abound in prayer, but positively 'slothful in business', content to wait but not to work. They said that they were serving at the altar, but we saw that they were indolent enough in the shop. Christian men who stand up for the truth should take care not to be lax in their conduct when they are so wonderfully strict in their creed. Do not trifle with truth in speaking to your fellow man while you insist on respecting the truth of God. Can anything be more despicable than the pietists who prate much about the faithfulness of God's promises, but are not very particular about keeping their own promises? They say that they will let you have an article home on Friday night, but you do not get it until the following Wednesday; that is telling a falsehood. If you saw yourselves as others see you, though you might account yourselves spiritually true, you would know for a certainty that you were morally false. Little duties are almost too insignificant for such high-flying spiritual professors. They are brethren that can pray at a prayer-meeting; therefore, they need not do an honest day's work for an honest day's wage. On the other hand, they can oppress the labourer in his wages because they mean to give a donation to the hospital. It will not do. In vain you pretend to be spiritual and attend to spiritual duties, while you leave the commonplace morals in abeyance. Depend upon it, if you are not moral, you are not a disciple of Christ. It is all nonsense about your experience. If you occasionally get drunk, or if you now and then let fall an oath, or if in your business you would make twice two into five or three, according as your profit happens to run, why, do not talk about being a Christian.

FOR MEDITATION: (*Our Own Hymn Book* no.119 song 2 v.4—Isaac Watts, 1719)

'Order my footsteps by Thy word,
And make my heart sincere;
Let sin have no dominion, Lord,
But keep my conscience clear.'

SERMON NO. 1443

Enlivening and invigorating

'Quicken thou me according to thy word.' Psalm 119:25
SUGGESTED FURTHER READING: Romans 8:1–13

How are we to understand this quickening? It means making alive, keeping alive, and giving more life—in a word, enlivening. The Psalmist was alive, a spiritual man, or else he would not have asked for life; dead men never pray, 'Quicken me.' It is a sign that there is life already when a man can say, 'Give me life, O Lord!' This is not the prayer of the unconverted; it is the prayer of a man who is already regenerate and has the love of God in his soul: 'Quicken thou me according to thy word.' Quickening, of course, comes to us at first by regeneration. It is then that we receive spiritual life; and as there is no natural life in the world except that of which God is the author, so assuredly in the new world there is no spiritual life except that which God has created. The first quickening is that which comes upon us when we begin to feel our need of a Saviour, when we begin to perceive the preciousness of that Saviour, and when with a feeble finger we touch the hem of the Saviour's garment: then are we quickened into newness of life. But that spiritual life needs every day to be kept alive. It is like the life of a fire, which must be fed with fuel and supported with air. It is like our natural life, which needs food to sustain it, and needs to breathe the atmosphere in order to continue. We are as much creatures of God's power in continuing to live as in commencing to live, and, spiritually, we owe as much to divine grace that we remain believers as that we became believers. As soon as we get spiritual life, this prayer is most proper as a sacred instinct; 'Lord, continue this life in my soul; continue to quicken me; for, if thou dost not, I have no life in myself apart from thee, and I should die were I severed from thee, as doth a branch when severed from the vine. Continue therefore, good Lord, to quicken me.'

FOR MEDITATION: At what stage of quickening are you? Have you been made alive together with Christ (Ephesians 2:5; Colossians 2:13)? If not, you are still dead in your trespasses and sins (Ephesians 2:1). Spiritual life comes from God alone, from Father and Son (John 5:21) and Holy Spirit (John 6:63). Do not resist any desires you get to seek him.

SERMON NO. 1350

The student's prayer

'Make me to understand the way of thy precepts: so shall I talk of thy wondrous works.' Psalm 119:27
SUGGESTED FURTHER READING: 2 Timothy 3:10–17

O Lord, what foolish creatures we are! When thou dost exhort us one way, we run to such an extreme therein that we forget that thou hast given us any other counsel than that which is just now ringing in our ears. We have known some commanded to be humble, who have bowed down till they have become timorous and desponding. We have known others exhorted to be confident, who have gone far beyond a modest courage and grown so presumptuous that they have presently fallen into gross transgressions. Is fidelity to the truth your cardinal virtue? Take heed of being uncharitable. Is love to God and man your highest aspiration? Beware lest you become the dupe of false apostles and foul hypocrites. Have you clad yourself with zeal as with a garment? Have a care now, lest by one act of indiscretion your garment should be rolled in blood. How easy it is to exaggerate a virtue until it becomes a vice. A man may look to himself, examine himself and scrutinize all his actions and motives till he becomes deplorably selfish; on the other hand a man may look to others, counselling and cautioning them, preaching to them and praying for them, till he grows oblivious of his own estate, degenerates into hypocrisy and discovers to his surprise that his own heart is not right with God. There is a 'way' about the precepts: there is a chime about them in which every bell gives out its note and makes up a tune. There is a mixture, as of old, of the anointing oil, so much of this, that and the other; if any ingredient were left out, the oil would have lost its perfect aroma. So is there an anointing of the holy life in which there is precept upon precept skilfully mingled, delicately infused, gratefully blended and grace given to keep each of these precepts.

FOR MEDITATION: Scriptural obedience and doctrinal understanding must not be taken to unscriptural extremes: without care Christian liberty may develop into licence (Galatians 5:13; 1 Peter 2:16), church discipline into hostility (2 Corinthians 2:6–8; 2 Thessalonians 3:14–15), and opportunities for sharing the gospel into quarrels or rudeness (2 Timothy 2:24–25; 1 Peter 3:15).

SERMON NO. 1344

Conversions desired

'And the hand of the Lord was with them: and a great number believed, and turned unto the Lord.' Acts 11:21

SUGGESTED FURTHER READING: 1 Corinthians 9:19–23

God speed every effort to promote sobriety, chastity, thrift, honesty and morality, but you and I are sent for something more than this; our work goes deeper and is more difficult; we do not so much pray that the lion may be tamed as that he may be turned into a lamb. It may be well to lop the branches of the tree of sin, but our business is to lay the axe at the root of the trees by leading men to turn to God. This is a change, not of the outward conduct merely, but of the heart; if we do not see this result and if men do not believe and turn to God, we have laboured in vain, and spent our strength for nothing. If there are no believings and turnings to the Lord, we may get to our secret chambers and bewail ourselves before God because none have believed our report, and the arm of the Lord has not been revealed. There is the object; aim at it, saying, 'this one thing I do'. Praying in the Holy Spirit and depending upon his power, push on with this one sole object. Drive at it, you teachers in the Sunday-school; do not be satisfied with instructing the children, but labour to have them converted. Drive at it, you preachers; do not believe that you have done your work when you have taught the people; you must never rest till they believe in Jesus Christ. Pursue this end in every sermon or Sunday-school address; throw your whole soul into this one object. Yours must not be a cold inculcation of an external morality, but a warm enthusiasm for an inward regeneration. You are not to bring men to believe in themselves and so become self-made men, but to lead them to believe in Jesus and to become new creatures in him.

FOR MEDITATION: (*Our Own Hymn Book* no.331 v.4—Charles Wesley, 1749)

> 'His only righteousness I show,
> His saving truth proclaim;
> 'Tis all my business here below
> To cry, "Behold the Lamb!"'

SERMON NO. 1282

Wake up! Wake up!

'That, knowing the time, that now it is high time to awake out of sleep: for now is our salvation nearer than when we believed.' Romans 13:11
SUGGESTED FURTHER READING: Jonah 1:1–6

Into what a deep slumber some professing Christians have fallen! How utterly insensible they are to the sins and sorrows of those around them. They believe God has a people, and are very glad he has, as far as they are capable of being glad of anything that does not concern themselves. But, 'the world lieth in wickedness' and multitudes are perishing. They are sorry it is so, that is to say, they go as far as saying they are sorry. It does not cause them any sleepless nights, it does not disturb their digestion, and it in no way interferes with their comfort, for they do not seem to think that it has anything to do with them. I know some in such a sleep who drug themselves with almost as much regularity as they feed themselves. They take that great and precious truth of the divine sovereignty, and turn it to a most detestable use, for they say, 'What is to be will be, and the Lord's purpose will be fulfilled. There will be some saved and others lost.' All this is said as coolly as if they were talking of a wasp's nest. As for those that are lost, they dare not injure their logic by indulging a little mournful emotion. Were their minister to weep over the lost, as Jesus wept over Jerusalem, they would say he was unsound, a duty-faith man and, probably, an Arminian. They would straightway leave him and think that he could not have really received the mind of the Spirit of God. Yet, in the judgment of all who think right, one of the finest traits in a Christian's character is the deep sorrow which he feels over souls that are being lost and the great longing of his own soul that men would turn unto God and find peace through Jesus Christ. I fear there are many professors in a deep sleep as to whether others are going to heaven or to hell!

FOR MEDITATION: The Lord Jesus Christ told his apostles to lift up their eyes to see fields already white for harvest (John 4:35). If you feel too sleepy to care for souls, be warned that 'he that sleepeth in harvest is a son that causeth shame' (Proverbs 10:5) and remember that the enemy of souls is busy vandalising the harvest-field even while you sleep (Matthew 13:24–25).

SERMON NO. 1445

'Without money and without price'

'Without money and without price.' Isaiah 55:1
SUGGESTED FURTHER READING: Acts 8:14–25

Would you have the King of kings sell forgiveness to the sons of men at so much per head? Would you have him sell his Holy Spirit and come like Simon Magus offering money for him? Would you have him give to you, as the reward of merit, adoption into his family, that you might become his sons and brag even in the halls of heaven that you climbed to this dignity by your own good works? Talk not so exceeding proudly. The great King has made a great supper. Would you have him demand a price for entrance, sit as a receiver at the gates of mercy, and stop each one who comes to see if he has brought a price to pay for entrance there? No, it is not like our God. He does not deal thus. When the prodigal came back, imagine the father keeping his son in quarantine to see if he had a clean bill of health! Imagine him saying, 'My son, have you brought me a gift with which to reconcile me?' The parable would be spoiled by the hint of such a thing. Its glory lies in the freeness of the father's love, which asked no questions, but accepted the repenting child just as he was. God, the great Father, must not be so dishonoured in your thoughts as to be conceived of as requiring a price of you. You displease him when you think that you are to do something, feel something and bring something in your hand as a recommendation to him. Could you picture Jesus going about selling his cures, saying to the blind beggar, 'How much have you left of the alms of the charitable to give to me for your eyesight?' or saying to Martha and Mary, 'Bring me all you have, and I will raise your brother Lazarus.' Oh, I loathe to speak of it; it makes me sick to imagine such a thing.

FOR MEDITATION: (*Our Own Hymn Book* no. 552 v.3—Augustus M.Toplady, 1776)
'Nothing in my hand I bring,
Simply to Thy cross I cling;
Naked, come to Thee for dress;
Helpless, look to Thee for grace;
Foul, I to the fountain fly;
Wash me, Saviour, or I die.'

SERMON NO. 1161

Redemption and its claims

'Ye are bought with a price.' 1 Corinthians 6:20 & 7:23
SUGGESTED FURTHER READING: 1 Peter 1:14–21

'Ye are bought', not merely made and preserved, but 'bought with a price'. You who are children of God, you were bought as the devils never were, for Jesus never died to save them; 'he took not on him the nature of angels; but he took on him the seed of Abraham.' You are bought as the ungodly were not, for they remain the slaves of Satan and are not redeemed from their 'vain conversation received by tradition from' their fathers. They have rejected the purchase price: they remain unredeemed from their slavery to sin; but you have been redeemed 'with the precious blood of Christ, as of a lamb without blemish and without spot'; and therefore Christ lays his pierced hand upon you and says, 'You are mine.' Your King sets the broad arrow on you and marks you as royal property. There was one possession which Jacob greatly valued, and which he gave to his darling son Joseph, because, he said, 'I took it out of the hand of the Amorite with my sword and with my bow.' You also are the possession which Christ values beyond everything, because he has delivered you out of the hand of sin and Satan by his own sufferings and death; because of this he has the highest conceivable right of property in you. He is not merely your Creator and Preserver, but he is your Redeemer, and, therefore, if all the world should refuse him homage, and all men should revolt from him, and even if the angels should desert his standard, yet you must not, for you 'are bought with a price'. Other claims are forcible, but this claim is overwhelming. Other bands are strong, but these cords of love are invincible. 'For the love of Christ constraineth us.'

FOR MEDITATION: (*Our Own Hymn Book* no.663 v.1—James George Deck, 1837)
'Jesus, spotless Lamb of God,
Thou hast bought me with Thy blood,
I would value nought beside
Jesus—Jesus crucified.'

SERMON NO. 1163

The blind befriended

'I will bring the blind by a way that they knew not: I will lead them in paths that they have not known: I will make darkness light before them, and crooked things straight. These things will I do unto them, and not forsake them.' Isaiah 42:16
SUGGESTED FURTHER READING: Hebrews 11:8–16

When a blind man knows the way, he can almost go without the guide. Many of our friends afflicted with the loss of sight find their way day by day along the accustomed road; there have been some that have been so expert, though blind, that they could go over fifty miles of country, or thread their way in town up and down the streets of a milkman's walk, serving at each customer's house without ever making a mistake. They have often acted as guides to others; but, then, it has always been along a way that they have known. There is many a blind sinner who could guide others in the ways that he knows. He could guide others in the way of the drunkard, the licentious, or the swearer. He knows that way very well. He could guide young people into the way of infidelity, putting a thousand horrible thoughts into their minds. But when the Lord takes such a man as that in hand, he does not lead him that way, but in a way that he never went before. I remember being led by the divine hand down the dark lane of repentance with many a sigh and many a groan. I remember being led into the more pleasant way of faith by the same divine hand, and brought to the Saviour's feet; since then I have not known the way and have not expected to know it; for the way of grace that lies before us may be described as the Lord described the way of Israel in the wilderness: 'ye have not passed this way heretofore.' It is a new way, and when God undertakes to be our guide it is all new. Is it not written, 'Behold, I make all things new'? I hope that many of us know what it is to be led in a way we have not known.

FOR MEDITATION: (*Our Own Hymn Book* no.23 version 3 v.3—Isaac Watts, 1719)
'If e'er I go astray,
He doth my soul reclaim;
And guides me in His own right way,
For His most holy name.'

SERMON NO. 1310

The chariots of Ammi-nadib

'Or ever I was awake, my soul made me like the chariots of Ammi-nadib.' Song of Solomon 6:12
SUGGESTED FURTHER READING: John 16:16–28

The rule of the Christian life is, 'if any would not work, neither should he eat.' If you will not serve God as Christians, you shall not feed upon the sweet things of the kingdom to your own soul's comfort. A little more service and your souls would become 'like the chariots of Ammi-nadib'. I say this to bring up your grateful memories that you may thank God for what he has done, for whatever he has done in the past he will do again in the future. When the Lord has come once to his people he says, 'I will see you again, and your heart shall rejoice.' Of everything he has ever given you, he has got as much in store, and he is quite as able to give it to you now as he was before. You have never gone so high in joy that you cannot go higher yet; you have never drunk such draughts from the well of Bethlehem as left the well empty; you shall drink again of it. Do not say, 'I had those sweet times when I was young; I shall never have them again.' You shall have precious times again. Get back to your first love; get forward to a higher love than ever you had, for God will help you. Do you look back and say this?

> 'What peaceful hours I once enjoyed!
> How sweet their memory still!
> But now I find an aching void
> The world can never fill.'

Thank God for that ache. Bless God for the aching void. If your soul aches for God, he will come to your relief before long. Whenever a soul puts up a flag of distress at the mast-head, he may be sure that Christ is on the look-out for just such a soul.

FOR MEDITATION: Whereas salvation is limited to those who admit they can do nothing to deserve it (Romans 4:4–5; Ephesians 2:8–9), spiritual blessing in the Christian life is promised only to those who serve and obey God (Malachi 3:10; John 14:21–23).

SERMON NO. 1155

Jesus, the substitute for his people

'*Who is he that condemneth? It is Christ that died, yea rather, that is risen again, who is even at the right hand of God, who also maketh intercession for us.*' Romans 8:34
SUGGESTED FURTHER READING: Colossians 3:1–4

'Who is even at the right hand of God.' Bear in mind that what Jesus is, his people are, for they are one with him. His condition and position are typical of their own. 'Who is even at the right hand of God'—that means love, for the right hand is for the beloved. That means acceptance: who shall sit at the right hand of God but one who is dear to God? That means honour: to which of the angels has he given to sit at his right hand? Power also is implied! No cherub or seraph can be said to be at the right hand of God. See the force, then, of the interrogation, 'Who is he that condemneth?' It may be made apparent in a twofold manner. Who can condemn me while I have such a friend at court? While my representative sits near to God, how can I be condemned? But next, I am where he is, for it is written that he 'hath raised us up together, and made us sit together in heavenly places in Christ Jesus'. Can you suppose it possible to condemn one who is already at the right hand of God? The right hand of God is a place so near and so eminent that one cannot suppose an adversary bringing a charge against us there. Yet there the believer is in his representative, and who dare accuse him? It was laid at Haman's door as his worst crime that he sought to compass the death of queen Esther herself, so dear to the king's heart; and shall any foe condemn or destroy those who are dearer to God than ever Esther was to Ahasuerus, for they sit at his right hand, vitally and indissolubly united to Jesus.

FOR MEDITATION: (*Our Own Hymn Book* no.329 v.3—Isaac Watts, 1709)
'He lives, He lives, and sits above,
For ever interceding there;
Who shall divide us from His love?
Or what should tempt us to despair?'

SERMON NO. 1223

Conversions encouraged

'(For the LORD *thy God is a merciful God;) he will not forsake thee, neither destroy thee, nor forget the covenant of thy fathers which he sware unto them.' Deuteronomy 4:31*
SUGGESTED FURTHER READING: Matthew 18:10–14

Any animal which belongs to us causes us concern if we lose it, or it is in trouble. I noticed the other night how even the little kitten could not be missing without causing anxiety to the household. What calling and searching! Rougher natures would say, 'If the kitten will keep out of doors at night, let it do so.' But the owner thought not so, for the night was cold and wet. I have seen great trouble when a bird has been lost through the opening of a cage door, and many a vain struggle to catch it again. What a stir there is in the house about a little short-lived animal. We do not like to lose a bird or a kitten, and do you think the good God will willingly lose those whom he has made in his own image, and who are to exist for ever? I have used a very simple and homely illustration, but it commends itself to the heart. You know what you would do to regain a lost bird, and what will not God do to save a soul! An immortal spirit is better than ten thousand birds. Does God care for souls? That he does, and in proof thereof Jesus has come to seek and to save the lost. The Shepherd cannot rest while one of his flock is in danger. 'It is only one sheep! You have ninety-nine more, good man; why do you fret and bother yourself about one?' He cannot be pacified. He is considering where that sheep may be. He imagines all sorts of perils and distresses. Perhaps it is lying on its back and cannot turn over, or it has fallen into a pit, or is entangled among briars, or the wolf is ready to seize it. It is not merely its intrinsic value to him, but he is concerned for it because it is his sheep and the object of his care. God has such a care for man.

FOR MEDITATION: God cares for animals and so should we. But he cares even more for people (Luke 12:6–7,24) and the Lord Jesus Christ posed searching questions to those who treated animals better than other people (Matthew 12:11–12; Luke 13:15–16; 14:5). Even the prophet Jonah was concerned for a single plant without a soul, rather than about thousands of people who could lose their souls (Jonah 4:9–11).

SERMON NO. 1283

Hold fast your shield

'Cast not away therefore your confidence, which hath great recompense of reward.' Hebrews 10:35
SUGGESTED FURTHER READING: Philippians 1:3–20

Do not cast away your confidence, for it has 'great recompense of reward'. There is a reward in it now, for it makes us *happy*. When we are sweetly confident in God and do not molest ourselves with doubts and fears, how happy we are! Who has not read Cowper's beautiful description of the cottager with her pillow-lace and bobbins, who knew no more than 'her Bible true, a truth the learned Frenchmen never knew', who was just as happy as the days were long. We are never so happy as when, in childlike simplicity, we trust our God without a doubt. Do not cast away your confidence, since it yields you such pure delight. But it makes you so *strong,* too, strong both to bear and labour. When you are like a child in confidence before God, you can endure pain and reproach bravely. You can bear, like Atlas, a world upon your shoulders when you have God within you. If he be near, you laugh at difficulties and, as for impossibilities, there are no such things. Brethren, hold fast your confidence, because it ministers to your strength. And, moreover, it makes you *victorious*. Many a man has been won to Christ by the confidence of simple Christians. Our doubts and fears are mischievous; they are thistle seed and sow unbelief in others; but our childlike reliance upon God, our humble joy in our dear Father's care, and our unmoved resolution through thick and thin to stick to our Master is likely to convert others, by God's good Spirit, to the right way. 'Cast not away therefore your confidence.'

FOR MEDITATION: (*Our Own Hymn Book* no.675 v.1—Philip Doddridge, 1755)
'Now let the feeble all be strong,
And make Jehovah's arm their song,
His shield is spread o'er every saint,
And thus supported, who shall faint?'

SERMON NO. 1263

Retreat impossible

'*I have opened my mouth unto the* LORD, *and I cannot go back.*' Judges
11:35
SUGGESTED FURTHER READING: Hebrews 10:26–39

We cannot go back! To go back is death, shame and eternal ruin. And to
go back would be so unreasonable. Why should I leave my Lord? Why
should I let my Saviour go? In my heart of hearts I cannot think of a
reason why I should forsake my Master. Do I seek pleasure? What
pleasure is equal to that which he can give me? Do I seek gain? What gain
could there be if I lost him? Do I seek ease? To leave him would be to
forfeit eternal rest. To whom should we go? That was a forcible question
of the disciples when the Master enquired, 'Will ye also go away? Then
Simon Peter answered him, Lord, to whom shall we go?' To whom can
we go? If you give up the religion of Jesus Christ, what other religion
would you have? 'We could go into the world,' says one. Could you? If
you are a child of God, you are spoiled for the world. Before you became
a Christian you could have done very well in the world, but now you
know too much to be happy there. While the sow is a sow, the mud is
good enough for her. Turn that sow into an angel, and if the angel has
no place in heaven, where shall it go? It cannot go back to the sty. What
could it do there? The wash of the trough was good enough for the sow,
but the angel has eaten heavenly food. It cannot roll in the mire, nor
consort with swine; it must have heaven or nothing. If you can go back
to the world, you will go back to the world; but if you are a child of God
you cannot go back, because grace has so changed your nature that you
would not be in an element in which you could exist.

FOR MEDITATION: (*Our Own Hymn Book* no.661 v.1—John Newton,
1779)
'From pole to pole let others roam,
And search in vain for bliss;
My soul is satisfied at home,
The Lord my portion is.'

Saving faith

'Thy faith hath saved thee.' Luke 7:50 & 18:42
SUGGESTED FURTHER READING: Romans 3:21–30

I do not remember that this expression is found anywhere else in the word of God. It is found in these two places in the Gospel by Luke, but not in any other Gospel. Luke also gives us in two other places a kindred and almost identical expression, 'thy faith hath made thee whole.' This you will find in reference to the woman whose issue of blood had been staunched (Luke 8:48), and in connection with that one of the ten lepers who returned to praise the Saviour for the cure he had received (Luke 17:19). You will find the expression, 'thy faith hath made thee whole' once in Matthew and twice in Mark, but you find it twice in Luke together with the twice-repeated words of our text, 'thy faith hath saved thee.' Are we wrong in supposing that the long intercourse of Luke with the apostle Paul led him not only to receive the great doctrine of justification by faith which Paul so plainly taught, and to attach to faith that high importance which Paul always did, but also to have a peculiar memory for those expressions which were used by the Saviour, in which faith was manifestly honoured to a very high degree? Albeit Luke would not have written anything which was not true for the sake of maintaining the grand doctrine so clearly taught by the apostle, yet I think his full conviction of it would help to recall to his memory more vividly those words of the Lord Jesus from which it could be more clearly learned or illustrated. Be that as it may, we know that Luke was inspired, and that he has written neither more nor less than what the Saviour actually said, and hence we may be quite sure that the expression, 'thy faith hath saved thee', fell from the Redeemer's lips, and we are bound to accept it as pure unquestionable truth and may repeat it ourselves without fear of misleading others.

FOR MEDITATION: When it comes to the matter of salvation, the Lord Jesus Christ is the agent (Hebrews 2:10; 5:9), and his shed blood the instrument (Acts 20:28; Romans 5:9; Ephesians 1:7; 1 Peter 1:18–19; Revelation 1:5), but faith in him and in his shed blood is also essential as the channel (Romans 3:25; Ephesians 2:8).

SERMON NO. 1162

Two sorts of hearers

'But be ye doers of the word, and not hearers only, deceiving your own selves.' James 1:22
SUGGESTED FURTHER READING: Romans 1:28–2:5

Certain ministers are not content with sowing the old seed, which, from the hand of apostles, confessors, fathers, reformers and martyrs, produced a harvest unto God; they spend time speculating whether the seed of the tares grown under certain circumstances may not bring forth wheat, and whether good wheat would not be the better for the admixture of just a little sprinkling of tare seed. We want somebody to take these bits of preaching, put them into a cauldron, boil them down, and see what is the essential practical product of them. A short time ago an article in the newspapers fastened itself upon my mind, with regard to the moral state of Germany. The writer, a German, says that the scepticism of the professed preachers of the word, the continual doubts which have been suggested by scientific men and more especially by professedly religious men as to revelation, have now produced upon the German nation the most frightful consequences. The picture which he gives makes us fear that our Germanic friends are treading upon a volcano which may explode beneath their feet. The authority of the government has been so severely exercised that men begin to be weary of it, and the authority of God has been put so much out of the question that the basis of society is undermined. I need not, however, ground my remarks upon that article, for the French revolution at the end of the eighteenth century remains in history as an enduring warning of the dread effects of philosophy when it has cast suspicion upon all religion and created a nation of infidels. I pray God that the like may not happen here; but the party of 'modern thought' seem resolved upon repeating the experiment. So greatly is the just severity of God ignored, and so trifling an evil is sin made out to be, that if men were to be doers of what they hear and to carry out what is taught from certain professedly Christian pulpits, anarchy would result. Free-thinking always leads that way.

FOR MEDITATION: Empty religiosity, devoid of power and love towards God, can lead to appalling ungodliness (2 Timothy 3:1–5). Paul says what our attitude should be towards those who practise and teach it—'from such turn away' (2 Timothy 3:5).

SERMON NO. 1467(B)

God's advocates breaking silence

'Suffer me a little, and I will shew thee that I have yet to speak on God's behalf.' Job 36:2
SUGGESTED FURTHER READING: Romans 3:1–9

He who preaches the gospel only from its manward side is apt to forget its major part. He regards man with a pity and sympathy most fitting and proper, but fails in sympathy with God, and in distinct recognition of the claims and rights of the great Sovereign. How seldom is divine sovereignty spoken of! Man is looked upon as though he were a deserving creature and had a right to salvation. One would think, to hear some preachers, that God was under obligation to man, or that he had no will of his own, but had left man's will to be supreme. The truth is that if all had been condemned, God would have been infinitely just, and if he spares one and not another, none can say to him, 'What doest thou?' His declaration is 'I will have mercy upon whom I will have mercy, and I will have compassion on whom I will have compassion.' I sympathise with man, but I have in my soul an infinitely deeper sympathy with God. I am bound to love my neighbour as myself, but the still higher law calls on me to love the Lord my God with all my heart, soul, mind and strength. Speaking on behalf of man may be carried so far that you come to look upon sin as his misfortune rather than his fault, and to view the fact that sin is punished at all as a matter to be deplored. In some professed Christians their pity for the criminal has overcome their horror at the crime. Eternal punishment is denied, not because the Scriptures are not plain enough on that point, but because man has become the god of man, and everything must be toned down to suit the tender feelings of an age which excuses sin but denounces its penalties, which has no condemnation for the offence, but spends its denunciations upon the Judge and his righteous sentence. By all means have sympathies manward, but at the same time show some tenderness towards the dishonoured law and the insulted Lord.

FOR MEDITATION: Putting the just God and Saviour (Isaiah 45:21) on trial is futile and dangerous; those who try this will have to defend their actions without having a leg to stand on (Isaiah 45:9–11; Romans 9:14,19–20). Abraham didn't have all the answers but still trusted the Judge of all the earth to do right (Genesis 18:25).

SERMON NO. 1403

The jewel of peace

'Now the Lord of peace himself give you peace always by all means. The Lord be with you all.' 2 Thessalonians 3:16
SUGGESTED FURTHER READING: Isaiah 26:1–12

Without peace you cannot grow. A shepherd may find good pasture for his flock, but if his sheep are hunted about by wild dogs, so that they cannot rest, they will become mere skin and bone. The Lord's lambs cannot grow if they are worried and harried; they must enjoy 'the rest wherewith' the Lord makes 'the weary to rest'. If your soul is always sighing, moaning, and questioning its interest in Christ, if you are always in suspense as to what doctrine is true and what is false, if there is nothing established and settled about you, you will never come to the fulness of the stature of a man in Christ Jesus. Neither without peace can you bear much fruit, if any. If a tree is frequently transplanted you cannot reasonably look for many golden apples upon its boughs. The man who has no root-hold, who neither believes, nor grasps, nor enjoys the gospel, can ever know what it is to be 'stedfast, unmoveable, always abounding in the work of the Lord'. We know, too, some who, because they have no conscious peace with God, lack all stability and are the prey of error. That doctrine can soon be driven out of a man's head which affords no light and comfort to his heart. If you derive no sweetness from what you believe, I should not marvel if you soon begin to doubt it. The power of the gospel is its best evidence to the soul; a man always believes in that which he enjoys. Only make a truth to be a man's spiritual food, let it be marrow and fatness to him, and I warrant you he will believe it. When truth becomes to a proud carnal mind what the manna became to murmuring Israel, namely, 'light bread' that his 'soul loatheth', then the puffed-up intellect cries after something more pleasing to the flesh; but to the mind which hungers and thirsts after righteousness, the gospel is so soul-satisfying that it never wearies of it.

FOR MEDITATION: Meditate on verses which teach us about some of the blessings which accompany peace—growth (Psalm 85:8–12; Isaiah 9:6–7), fruit (James 3:17–18) and stability (Psalm 119:165; Philippians 4:7; 1 Thessalonians 5:23).

SERMON NO. 1343

Now—a sermon for young men and young women

*'Son of man, behold, they of the house of Israel say, The vision that he
seeth is for many days to come, and he prophesieth of the times that are
far off.' Ezekiel 12:27*
SUGGESTED FURTHER READING: Acts 24:10–27

The evil argument mentioned in the text has been used from Ezekiel's
day right down to the present, and has served Satan's turn in ten
thousand cases. By its means men have delayed themselves into hell.
When they hear of the great atonement made upon the cross by the Lord
Jesus and are bidden to lay hold upon eternal life in him, men still say
concerning the gospel, 'The vision that he seeth is for many days to
come, and he prophesieth of the times that are far off.' That is to say,
they pretend that the matters whereof we speak are not of immediate
importance and may safely be postponed. They imagine that religion is
for the weakness of the dying and the infirmity of the aged, but not for
healthy men and women. They meet our pressing invitation, 'All things
are now ready, come to the supper,' with the reply, 'Religion is meant to
prepare us for eternity, but we are far off from it as yet, and are still in
the heyday of our being; there is plenty of time for those dreary
preparations for death. Your religion smells of the vault and the worm.
Let us be merry while we may. There will be room for more serious
considerations when we have enjoyed life a little, or have become
established in business, or can retire to live upon our savings. Religion is
for the sere and yellow leaf of the year's fall, when life is fading, but not
for the opening hours of spring, when the birds are pairing and the
primroses smiling under the returning sun. You prophesy of things that
are for many days to come, and of times that are far off.' Very few young
people may have said as much as this, but that is the secret thought of
many: and with this they resist the admonition of the Holy Spirit, who
says, 'To day if ye will hear his voice, harden not your hearts.'

FOR MEDITATION: (*Our Own Hymn Book* no.497 v.4—Albert Midlane,
1865)
  'Life is found alone in Jesus, only there 'tis offered thee—
  Offered without price or money, 'tis the gift of God sent free;
  Take salvation, take it now, and happy be.'

SERMON NO. 1164

The sealing of the Spirit

'In whom ye also trusted, after that ye heard the word of truth, the gospel of your salvation: in whom also after that ye believed, ye were sealed with that Holy Spirit of promise.' Ephesians 1:13
SUGGESTED FURTHER READING: Romans 8:12–17

There can be no doubt about the seal of the text. You have been taught of God what no one but the Spirit of God could have taught you; you have a life in you which no one but the Spirit could have given you: of that knowledge and that life you are perfectly conscious; you do not want to ask anybody else about them. A man may ask me whether I know so and so, but I am the best witness whether I do or not. If I am asked, 'How do you know you are alive?', well, I walk about; that is all, but I am quite sure about it, and I do not want any further evidence. The best seal to a man's heart must be that of which he is conscious, and about which he need not appeal to others. Give me a seal that is as sure as my own existence: I fail to see how God himself can give me anything more sure than the gift of his Spirit working knowledge and life in me. 'But if only I could hear a voice,' says one. Suppose you did. Then the argument of fear would be that there are countless voices, and one may be mistaken for another. You were in the street when you heard it; perhaps it was a parrot or a starling in the upper window. Who knows? It is so easy for the ear to be deceived. Many a time you have said, 'I know I heard so and so,' when you did not hear it, but something very like it. I would not believe my own ears, if their evidence had to do with my soul, one half so readily as I would believe my own consciousness. Since knowledge, life and other things I have just mentioned, are all matters of consciousness, they are much better seals than anything which appealed like an angelic vision to the eye, or like a mysterious voice to the ear. Here you have something sure and steadfast.

FOR MEDITATION: (*Our Own Hymn Book* no.468 v.3—Isaac Watts, 1709)
'Assure my conscience of her part
In the Redeemer's blood,
And bear Thy witness with my heart,
That I am born of God.'

The three whats

'That ye may know what is the hope of his calling, and what the riches of the glory of his inheritance in the saints, and what is the exceeding greatness of his power to us-ward who believe.' Ephesians 1:18–19
SUGGESTED FURTHER READING: Hebrews 6:9–20

We want you to know *'the hope of his calling,'* that you may not neglect it, nor set anything in competition with it. What a hope the calling of God gives the Christian. Do not let it go. If any ask you, 'What said the man?' I would like you to be compelled to say, 'He said that there is a future before us of such glory that he charged us not to lose it. There are possibilities of such intense delight for ever and ever that he besought us to ensure that delight by accepting Christ and his way of salvation.' Next we want you to believe *'the riches of the glory of his inheritance in the saints'*, that you may see where your hope lies. Your hope lies in not being your own any more, but in being the Lord's, and so realizing 'the riches of the glory of his inheritance in the saints'. The saints belong to their Lord: your salvation will be found in experimentally knowing that you are not your own, because you are bought with a price, and in admitting that your honour and happiness is found in being the Lord's. If you are your own, you will spend yourself and be ruined, but if you are Christ's, he will take care of you. If I thought that I had a hair of this head that belonged to myself alone, I would tear it out; but to be owned by Jesus altogether, spirit, soul and body, to be Christ's man in the entireness of my being, this is glory, immortality and eternal life. Be your own and you will be lost: be Christ's and you are saved. We want you to know *'the exceeding greatness of his power'*, that you may not doubt, despond or despair, but come, cast yourselves upon the incarnate God, and let him save you. Yield yourselves to him, that the great glory of his power may be manifest in you.

FOR MEDITATION: (*Our Own Hymn Book* no.757 v.1—Isaac Watts, 1721)
'How vast the treasure we possess!
How rich Thy bounty, King of grace!
This world is ours, and worlds to come:
Earth is our lodge, and heaven our home.'

SERMON NO. 1466

The Christian's motto

'I do always those things that please him.' John 8:29
SUGGESTED FURTHER READING: 1 Thessalonians 4:1–12

If you want to know what things please God, let me refer you to one or two passages of Scripture. David says in Psalm 69:30–31, 'I will praise the name of God with a song, and will magnify him with thanksgiving. This also shall please the LORD better than an ox or bullock that hath horns and hoofs.' The apostle says in Hebrews 13:16, 'But to do good and to communicate forget not: for with such sacrifices God is well pleased.' Let us, then, constantly praise God. Let us have hymns in store for moments when we can sing, and thoughts in store for moments when the tongue must be silent, but when the heart may yet sing aloud unto the Most High. Bless the Lord, for 'Whoso offereth praise glorifieth' him. A thankful spirit is always pleasing to God; therefore cultivate it and shake off, as you would shake off a viper from your hand, the spirit of murmuring against the Most High. A thankful humble poor woman may please God better than the most talented minister who is evermore complaining of the dispensations of God. John tells us in 1 John 3:22–23 that we are to 'do those things that are pleasing in his sight', and adds, 'this is his commandment, That we should believe on the name of his Son Jesus Christ, and love one another'. Faith, therefore, is one of the pleasing graces. We read of Enoch that 'before his translation he had this testimony, that he pleased God. But without faith it is impossible to please him'. Love to the brethren is also another of the graces which please God. He would have us love his people, care for the poor, relieve those that are sick and cheer those who are cast down. Brethren, if you would please the Lord, put aside all petty jealousies and labour to prevent disunion, for brotherly love is one of the most pleasing sights which the Father of mercies sees.

FOR MEDITATION: If our aim is to please God, we will also seek to avoid those things which obviously displease him, such as complaining (Numbers 11:1), scandalous behaviour (2 Samuel 11:27), rejoicing at another's misfortune (Proverbs 24:17–18), injustice (Isaiah 59:15), opposing the gospel (1 Thessalonians 2:15–16) or simply neglecting to believe God (Hebrews 11:6).

SERMON NO. 1165

Godly fear and its goodly consequence

'In the fear of the LORD *is strong confidence: and his children shall have a place of refuge.' Proverbs 14:26*
SUGGESTED FURTHER READING (Spurgeon): Psalm 37:27–33

'In the fear of the LORD there is strong confidence.' It was bravely done by old Hugh Latimer when he preached before Henry VIII. It was the custom of the Court preacher to present the king with something on his birthday; Latimer presented Henry VIII with a pocket-handkerchief with this text in the corner, 'whoremongers and adulterers God will judge', a very suitable text for bluff Henry. Then he preached a sermon before his most gracious majesty against sins of lust, and delivered himself with tremendous force, not forgetting or abridging the personal application. The king said that next time Latimer preached—the next Sunday—he should apologise, and he would make him so mould his sermon as to eat his own words. Latimer thanked the king for letting him off so easily. When the next Sunday came, he stood up in the pulpit and said, 'Hugh Latimer, thou art this day to preach before the high and mighty prince Henry, King of Great Britain and France. If thou sayest one single word that displeases his Majesty he will take thy head off; therefore, mind what thou art at.' But then said he, 'Hugh Latimer, thou art this day to preach before the Lord God Almighty, who is able to cast both body and soul into hell, and so tell the king the truth outright.' And so he did. His performance was equal to his resolution. However, the king did not take off his head, but respected him all the more. The 'fear of the LORD' gave him strong confidence, as it will to any who cleave close to their colours. *'Fear him, ye saints, and ye will then have nothing else to fear.'* Drive straight ahead in the fear of the everlasting God, and whoever comes in your way had better mind what he is at. It is yours to do what is right, and bear everything they devise that is wrong. God will bless you therein, and you shall praise him therefore.

FOR MEDITATION: Even if it seems to get us off the hook, cowardly compromise will never do us any spiritual good. Contrast Peter's bitter weeping after denying his Lord (Luke 22:54–62) with the boldness and joy felt by him and the other apostles when they refused to repeat the cowardly deed (Acts 4:18–31; 5:27–29,40–42).

Over against the sepulchre

'Sitting over against the sepulchre.' Matthew 27:61
SUGGESTED FURTHER READING (Spurgeon): Luke 23:50–56

'Sitting over against the sepulchre' while Christ lies in it, my first thought about it is, I will rest, for he rests. What a wonderful stillness there was about our Lord in that rocky grave. He had been daily thronged by thousands: even when he ate bread they disturbed him. He scarce could have a moment's stillness in life; but now how quiet is his bed! Not a sound is heard. The great stone shuts out all noise and the body is at peace. Well, if he rests, I may. If for a while the Lord seems to suspend his energies, his servants may cry unto him, but they may not fret. He knows best when to sleep and when to wake. As I see the Christ resting in the grave, my next thought is, he has the power to come forth again. When the disciples were alarmed because Jesus was asleep, they were in error, for his sleep was the token of their security. When I see a captain on board ship pacing anxiously up and down the deck, I may fear that danger is suspected; but when the captain turns into his cabin, then I may be sure that all is right, and there is no reason why I should not turn in too. So if our blessed Lord should ever suffer his cause to droop, and if he should give no marvellous manifestations of his power, we need not doubt his power; let us keep our Sabbath, pray to him and work for him, for these are duties of the holy day of rest; but do not let us fret and worry, for his time to work will come. The rest of the Christian lies in believing Christ under all circumstances. Go in for this, beloved.

FOR MEDITATION: Those who come to Christ and are united to him are promised rest by him in this life (Matthew 11:28–29), after death (Revelation 14:13) and after his second coming (2 Thessalonians 1:7). Be sure not to miss out on this (Hebrews 4:1,10–11), because throughout eternity there will never be any rest for those who are still outside of Christ (Revelation 14:11).

SERMON NO. 1404

Guile forsaken when guilt is forgiven

'Blessed is the man unto whom the LORD *imputeth not iniquity, and in whose spirit there is no guile.'* Psalm 32:2
SUGGESTED FURTHER READING: 1 Peter 3:8–17

Be honest. Sinner, may God make you honest. Do not deceive yourself. Make a clean breast of it before God. Have an honest religion, or have none at all. Have a religion of the heart, or else have none. Put aside the mere vestment and garment of piety, and let your soul be right within. Be honest. And you that are Christians, recollect that your blessedness will never be enjoyed by yourselves unless you continue to be without guile. Some Christians live rather by policy than by honesty; I hope they are Christians, but I am not sure, for their life is full of scheming. They never go straight; they would not care to go straight; they rather like going a little round about just to show that they can dodge in and out. There are men of this sort in business, and you need not go out of your road to meet them. Even their thinking seems to revolve on a wheel—all round about and round about. Now, friends, you will never be happy while you act craftily. The only life in which a man can enjoy the blessedness of pardoned sin is a downright straightforward life. Be like clear glass, so that all who choose to do so may see right through you. There is a way of living guardedly, in which you never speak your mind, but are diplomatic and reserved; you take your words out of your mouth, look at them, judge what other people will think of them, and then you put the best of them back again. There is a system of living, as it were, in armour, buckled up, with your visor down; you never dare show your real self, but maintain great prudence and reserve. What is this but to live in fetters? I would sooner die at once. To speak his heart and to act honestly is to a true believer the path of peace and happiness.

FOR MEDITATION: Christianity has no place for guile. The Lord Jesus Christ lacked it (1 Peter 2:22), the apostle Paul denied it (1 Thessalonians 2:3) and we are to avoid it (Psalm 34:13; 1 Peter 2:1; 3:10). Its absence from our lips and lives is commendable (John 1:47; Revelation 14:5); 'let your yea be yea; and your nay, nay' (James 5:12).

SERMON NO. 1346

A weighty charge

'Keep yourselves in the love of God.' Jude 21
SUGGESTED FURTHER READING: Luke 10:38–42

If you want to be kept in the love of God, follow earnestly the means of grace. Do not neglect the hearing of the word, nor the reading of it in private, nor secret prayer, nor the assembling of yourselves together. Come often to the Lord's table; you will find it a very blessed means of quickening the pulse of your soul. There are God's appointed ordinances for stirring up your love; do not be so proud as to think you can do without them. I fear there are some Christians who are so busy in doing good that they do not allow themselves opportunities of getting good. Incessantly do I urge Christian people to be engaged in some work for Christ; I would urge it again and again, but some of you young people ought not to absent yourselves from public worship, in order to go and teach in ragged schools or elsewhere; you have not yet enough knowledge, nor enough strength to be able to bear the frequent loss of the instructive ordinances; and even those of you who can bear to go upon half rations will be wise not to do so, for a man who works so long every day, that he does not sleep enough, or eat enough, will in the long run be less capable of labour than if he had attempted less and had taken more time for the feeding and resting of his body. Remember that Martha, though she was very busy, was not so much commended as Mary who 'sat at Jesus' feet'. Be busy as Martha, but be devout as Mary: so will you keep your heart in the love of God. You will do this very much, too, by communing with the Lord. Never spend a day without hearing your Master's voice. Do not come down from your chamber to see the face of man till you have seen the face of God.

FOR MEDITATION: (*Our Own Hymn Book* no.811 v.4—Isaac Watts, 1709)
'Till Thou hast brought me to Thy home,
Where fears and doubts can never come,
Thy countenance let me often see,
And often Thou shalt hear from me.'

For whom is the gospel meant?

'I came not to call the righteous, but sinners to repentance.' Mark 2:17
'Christ died for the ungodly.' Romans 5:6
'While we were yet sinners, Christ died for us.' Romans 5:8
'Christ Jesus came into the world to save sinners.' 1 Timothy 1:15
SUGGESTED FURTHER READING (Spurgeon): Galatians 3:5–14

Concerning the gospel, there are many who might cry out, 'Manna?' for they know not what it is. Frequently they make a mistake as to its bearings and objects, dreaming that it is a kind of improved law, or an easier system of salvation by works; hence they err in their idea of the persons for whom it is designed. They imagine that surely the blessings of salvation must be meant for deserving persons, and Christ must be the Redeemer of the meritorious. On the principle of 'good for the good' they infer that grace is for the excellent and Christ for the virtuous. Hence it is a most useful thing for us continually to be reminding men what the gospel is and for whom it is sent into the world; though most of you know full well and do not need to be told, yet there are multitudes around us who persist in grave mistakes and need to be instructed over and over again in the very simplest of the doctrines of grace. There is less need for laborious explanations of profound mysteries than for simple explanations of plain truths. Many need only a simple latchkey to lift the latch and open the door of faith, and such a key I hope God's infinite mercy may put into their hands. Our business is to show that the gospel is intended for sinners and has an eye to guilty persons, that it is not sent into the world as a reward for the good and excellent, or for those who think they have any measure of fitness or preparation for the divine favour, but that it is intended for law breakers, for the undeserving, for the ungodly, for those who have gone astray like lost sheep, or left their father's house like the prodigal. Christ died to save sinners, and justifies the ungodly.

FOR MEDITATION: (*Our Own Hymn Book* no.545 v.1—Russell Sturgis Cook, 1850)
'Just as thou art, without one trace
Of love, or joy, or inward grace,
Or meetness for the heavenly place,
O guilty sinner, come!'

The secret of health

'I shall yet praise him, who is the health of my countenance and my God.' Psalm 42:11
SUGGESTED FURTHER READING (Spurgeon): Jeremiah 30:12–17

What a difference grace makes to the spiritual *forehead* when it works with power. By nature our forehead is as brass, hard, bold and presumptuous, but see what grace makes it. 'Thy temples are like a piece of pomegranate within thy locks.' The pomegranate, when you open it, is red and white, and the Christian's brow is full of the blushes of a sacred shamefacedness; 'within thy locks', says the Song of Solomon, as though concealed with holy fear, but what you did see of her brow was red and white, blushing with bashfulness and holy love in the presence of her Lord. I pray that all of you who are converted may know what holy shamefacedness means. Confidence in Christ is admirable, but not effrontery and self-confidence. I am afraid of those who are so very sure and confident all on a sudden, and yet have never felt the burden of sin. Be ashamed and confounded while you lay hold on Christ, for the more he does for you, the less you must think of yourself. You may very accurately measure the reality of your grace by the reality of your self-loathing. The bridegroom also describes the *lips* of his beloved. 'Thy lips are like a thread of scarlet, and thy speech is comely.' Before her health returned her lips were livid, before she had received comfort they were white with fear, but now they wear a healthy redness and are lovely to her Lord. How about your lips, beloved friends? Are they praying, singing, confessing lips? Do you speak well of the Redeemer and rejoice whenever you tell what his love has done for you? Well is it with us when to our Lord our *cheeks* 'are comely with rows of jewels', our 'neck with chains of gold', while our whole countenance shines with holiness.

FOR MEDITATION: Contrast the beauty of holiness with the spiritual ugliness of a stiff neck (2 Chronicles 36:13; Jeremiah 17:23), a filthy mouth (Romans 3:13–14), adulterous and lustful eyes (2 Peter 2:14; 1 John 2:16) and itching ears (2 Timothy 4:3–4). Holiness involves taking steps to hear no evil (Isaiah 33:15), see no evil (Isaiah 33:15; Matthew 5:27–29) and speak no evil (Psalm 34:13; Ephesians 4:29; Titus 3:2; James 4:11). Pray for God's help (Psalm 119:37; 141:3).

Marrow and fatness

'Thou hast spoken also of thy servant's house for a great while to come.'
2 Samuel 7:19
SUGGESTED FURTHER READING: 2 Corinthians 4:13–5:5

Your God has spoken of you 'for a great while to come'. He has said, 'I will never leave thee, nor forsake thee.' Is not that 'for a great while to come'? He has bidden you say, 'Surely goodness and mercy shall follow me all the days of my life: and I will dwell in the house of the LORD for ever.' Is not that 'for a great while to come'? He has promised to give you all you ever shall require. 'No good thing will he withhold from them that walk uprightly.' Note well that text ever to be remembered, 'because I live, ye shall live also', and that petition of our Lord, 'Father, I will that they also, whom thou hast given me, be with me where I am; that they may behold my glory.' These and a hundred other gracious words all concern 'a great while to come'. You have not obtained transient blessings, boons which will be gone tomorrow, gifts which will decay as the year grows old and the autumn leaves flutter to the ground. You have not obtained a mercy which will leave you when you tremble in decrepitude; rather your God will not forsake you when you are old and grey-headed; you 'shall still bring forth fruit in old age … to shew that the LORD is upright'. 'When thou passest through the waters, I will be with thee; and through the rivers, they shall not overflow thee:' therefore may you boldly say, 'Yea, though I walk through the valley of the shadow of death, I will fear no evil: for thou art with me.' When you die you shall rise again. In your flesh you shall see God and shall rejoice before him. For ever shall you be satisfied when you wake up in his likeness; you shall go into everlasting joy, and so shall be for ever with the Lord. He has spoken to you 'for a great while to come'. Sit down and wonder: wonder and adore for evermore.

FOR MEDITATION: (*Our Own Hymn Book* no.775 v.6—John Mason, 1683)
'My God, I'll praise Thee while I live,
And praise Thee when I die,
And praise Thee when I rise again,
And to eternity.'

SERMON NO. 1166

My God

'My God.' Psalm 91:2
SUGGESTED FURTHER READING: Romans 11:33–36

The wise man was asked 'What is God?' and he requested that he might have a day to consider his answer. When the sun had set he said that he must have three days, for in thinking of it the subject grew. They gave him three days, and when these were over he demanded six days more, for the subject was greater than ever. When they called upon him at the six days' end, he claimed twelve days more, for the subject was still beyond him. They bade him take the twelve days, and they would hear the result of his thoughts. The next time he said that he must have a month, and at the month's end, he gave them no information, but assured them he must have a year. When the year was over, he confessed that he should need a lifetime: he should never be able to tell them what God was so long as he lived. There is no defining the Incomprehensible One. Yet, you and I can call him 'My God'. Let us reflect upon his being ours as to his nature, his person, his essence. There is Father, Son and Holy Spirit, three in one: then the Father is my God: he has loved me, he has chosen me, he has begotten me and provided for me; he is my Father, my all. Then too the adorable Son is mine; Jesus, the Redeemer, the Prophet, Priest and King, the Intercessor, the Judge; he is mine. Then the Holy Spirit is mine; the Instructor, the Quickener, the Sanctifier, the Comforter. Dew, fire, wind, dove, whatever the metaphor under which he veils himself, he is mine. The Father, the Son and the Holy Spirit, to these beloved and glorious persons of the one undivided Godhead faith says, 'My God'.

FOR MEDITATION: (*Our Own Hymn Book* no.774 v.1—Isaac Watts, 1709)
    'My God, my life, my love,
    To Thee, to Thee I call:
    I cannot live, if Thou remove,
    For Thou art all in all.'

SERMON NO. 1297

Remember!

'Thou shalt remember that thou wast a bondman in the land of Egypt, and the LORD *thy God redeemed thee.' Deuteronomy 15:15*
SUGGESTED FURTHER READING: Isaiah 58:6–14

'The seventh day is the sabbath of the LORD thy God: in it thou shalt not do any work, thou, nor thy son, nor thy daughter, nor thy manservant, nor thy maidservant, nor thine ox, nor thine ass, nor any of thy cattle, nor thy stranger that is within thy gates; that thy manservant and thy maidservant may rest as well as thou. And remember that thou wast a servant in the land of Egypt, and that the LORD thy God brought thee out thence through a mighty hand and by a stretched out arm: therefore the LORD thy God commanded thee to keep the sabbath day.' You were a bondman. What would you have given for rest then? Now that the Lord has given you this hallowed day of rest, guard it sacredly. When you were a bondman you knew the heart of a servant and you sighed because your toil was heavy; now that you are set free, if you have servants, think of them, and so order your household that they may as much as possible enjoy their Sabbath. Certain household duties must be performed, but plot and plan to make these as light as possible 'that thy manservant and thy maidservant may rest as well as thou'. If you meet with any that are in bondage of soul and cannot rest, obey the text in its spiritual teaching. Rest in the Lord Jesus yourself, but endeavour to bring all your family into the same peace, 'that thy manservant and thy maidservant may rest as well as thou.' Surely if you have been set free from the iron bondage, you ought not to want urging to keep with all sacredness this holy day, which the mercy of God has hedged about, nor should you need exhorting to rest in the Lord, and to endeavour to lead others into his rest.

FOR MEDITATION: 'The sabbath was made for man' (Mark 2:27). Consider some of the words associated with it: rest (Exodus 16:23), holy (Exodus 20:8), blessed (Exodus 20:11), delight (Isaiah 58:13). These are a far cry from the world's view of the Lord's Day as a killjoy! What was prohibited on the Sabbath was labour and work (Exodus 20:9–10) including burden-carrying (Jeremiah 17:21–22), the very kind of thing that can so easily kill joy!

SERMON NO. 1406

How is salvation received?

'Therefore it is of faith, that it might be by grace; to the end the promise might be sure to all the seed; not to that only which is of the law, but to that also which is of the faith of Abraham; who is the father of us all.'
Romans 4:16
SUGGESTED FURTHER READING: Hebrews 11:1–6

'It is of faith.' What does the 'it' refer to? If you read the context, I think you will consider that it refers to the promise, although some have said that the antecedent word or thought is 'the inheritance'. This matters very little, if at all: it may mean the inheritance, the covenant, or the promise, for these are one. To give a wide word which will take in all, the blessedness which comes to a man in Christ, the blessedness promised by the covenant of grace 'is of faith': in one word, salvation 'is of faith'. And what is faith? It is believing the promise of God, taking God at his word, and acting upon that belief by trusting in him. Some of the Puritans used to divide faith, improperly but still instructively, into three parts. The first was self-renunciation, which is, perhaps, a preparation for faith rather than faith itself, in which a man confesses that he cannot trust in himself, and so goes out of self and all confidence in his own good works. The second part of faith, they said, was reliance, in which a man, believing the promise of God, trusts him, depends upon him, and leaves his soul in the Saviour's hands: and then the third part of faith, they said, was appropriation, by which a man takes to himself that which God presents in the promise to the believer, appropriates it as his own, feeds upon it, and enjoys it. Certainly there is no true faith without self-renunciation, reliance, and at least a measure of appropriation; where these three are found, there is faith in the soul. The blessing was of faith in Abraham's case, and it is precisely the same with all those who by faith are the children of believing Abraham.

FOR MEDITATION: Trace these definitions of faith as illustrated by Abraham's experience in Romans 4—self-renunciation (vv.5–6), reliance on the promise of God (vv.3,17) and appropriation of the promised blessings (vv.18–21). Are you following Abraham's example of faith in the living God (vv.16,23–25)?

Strengthening words from the Saviour's lips

'And he said unto me, my grace is sufficient for thee: for my strength is made perfect in weakness. Most gladly therefore will I rather glory in my infirmities, that the power of Christ may rest upon me.' 2 Corinthians 12:9

SUGGESTED FURTHER READING: Ephesians 6:10–17

Dr Adam Clarke furnishes us on the last part of the text with a useful observation—'Most gladly therefore will I rather glory in my infirmities, that the power of Christ may rest upon me.' The Greek word interpreted 'rest' is the same word employed by John when he says, 'the Word was made flesh, and', as the Greek runs, '*tabernacled* among us, (and we beheld his glory, the glory as of the only begotten of the Father,) full of grace and truth.' The passage before us means: 'I rather glory in my infirmities, that the power of Christ may *tabernacle in* me.' Just as the Shekinah light dwelt in the tent of the wilderness beneath the rough badger skins, so I glory to be a poor frail tent and tabernacle, that the Shekinah of Jesus Christ may dwell in my soul. Do you catch the thought? Is it not full of beauty? First, Paul puts the power of Christ in opposition to his own power, because if he is not weak, then he has strength of his own; if what he does is done by his own strength, there is no room for Christ's strength; but if his own power be gone, there is space for the power of Christ. If my life is sustained by my own strength, and my good works are done in my own strength, there is no room for Christ's strength; but the apostle found that it was not so, and therefore he said, 'I glory in my strengthlessness, that the power of Christ may tabernacle in me.' But what is the power of Christ? Let the text I quoted tell you: 'the glory as of the only begotten of the Father, full of grace and truth.' What power was this which Paul expected to tabernacle in him but the power of grace and truth? It must be so, because God had said, 'my grace is sufficient for thee'.

FOR MEDITATION: (*Our Own Hymn Book* no.681 v.2—Isaac Watts, 1709)
'I glory in infirmity,
That Christ's own power may rest on me:
When I am weak, then am I strong,
Grace is my shield, and Christ my song.'

SERMON NO. 1287

A sermon upon one nothing by another nothing

'Though I be nothing.' 2 *Corinthians* 12:11
SUGGESTED FURTHER READING: 1 Corinthians 12:28–13:8

I remember well a talkative Christian, who supposed herself to possess very remarkable attainments. This superior person was talking of the marvellous things which she had felt, known and done. She was, if not quite perfect, in remarkable danger of becoming so. She turned to an aged Christian in the company and said, 'But you, dear brother, do not say a word.' Now, you know there are individuals who say little but think all the more; our old friend was one of them and still remained silent. 'Come,' said she, 'have you no religious experience?' The old man said very quietly, 'I never had any to boast about.' That remark I heartily endorsed. If we attain to the highest experience, rise very near to God, and conquer open sin, we shall still have to look within and say, 'I am nothing.' Boasting is a sure sign of failure wherever it is found; even a giant like Goliath had hardly done boasting before he fell beneath the sling and stone of a ruddy youth. Restrain every feeling of pride; chase it from your soul, for it is foolish and will lead to further folly; it is a noxious insect which will corrupt whatever it lights upon, gaudy though its wings may be. King Herod was soon eaten of worms when he began to be fly-blown with pride. Where there is the most precious grace, there is always a jewel-case of humility to keep it in. Gilded wood may float, but an ingot of gold will sink. Diotrephes was a nobody and loved the pre-eminence; Paul 'was not a whit behind the very chiefest apostles', yet he said, 'though I be nothing.' If we reach the apostle's point of conscious nothingness we had better stop there, for there is no place safer and happier, and none more consistent with the facts of the case. Those who are lowly are excellent, but pride is pestilent.

FOR MEDITATION: Those who know themselves to be 'nothing' are well aware that they have in themselves nothing in which to glory (1 Corinthians 9:16). Those who go in for boasting reveal by so doing that they in fact know nothing (1 Corinthians 8:1–2; Galatians 6:3; 1 Timothy 6:4).

SERMON NO. 1458

Spiritual appetite

'The full soul loatheth an honeycomb; but to the hungry soul every bitter thing is sweet.' Proverbs 27:7
SUGGESTED FURTHER READING: John 12:12–26

Have an appetite for Christ and the little prayer meeting, though there be only a few poor people at it, will be sweet to you. That poor broken-down preaching, which is the best that the minister is able to give, will become sweet to you because there is a savour of Christ in it. If you can only get a leaf torn out of the Bible, or half a leaf, it will be precious to you. Even to hear a child sing a hymn about Christ will be pleasant. Dr Guthrie, when dying, asked his friend to sing him 'a bairn's hymn'. He wanted a child's hymn then; a little simple ditty about Christ was what the grand old man desired in his departing moments; and when your soul hungers after Jesus Christ you will love simple things if they speak of him. You will not be so dainty as some of you are. You must have a comfortable cushion to sit upon; when you are hungry you are glad to stand in the aisles. Full souls must have a very superior preacher; they say of the most successful evangelist, there is nothing in him, he only tells a lot of anecdotes: but when you are hungry, you will rejoice that the man preaches Christ, and the faults will vanish. I remember my father telling me when I was a boy and did not like my breakfast, that he thought it would do me good to be sent to the workhouse for a month and see if I did not get an appetite. Many Christians need to be sent under the law a little while, and Moses would cure them of squeamishness, so that when they came back to Jesus and his love, they would have a zest for the gospel. The lesson from all this is, pray for a good appetite for Christ, and, when you have it, keep it. Do not spoil it with the unsatisfying dainties of the world, or by sucking down modern notions and sceptical philosophies.

FOR MEDITATION: (*Our Own Hymn Book* no.436 v.4—John Fawcett, 1782)
    'Millions of happy spirits live
    On Thy exhaustless store;
    From Thee they all their bliss receive,
    And still Thou givest more.'

SERMON NO. 1227

Additions to the church

'And the Lord added to the church daily such as should be saved.' Acts 2:47
SUGGESTED FURTHER READING: Acts 8:1–13

We are just coming to the most beautiful season of the year, the spring, when everything around us is shaking off the chill grave-clothes of winter and putting on the beautiful array of a new life. The church of God was in that condition at Pentecost; her winter was past and the flowers appeared on the earth. She enjoyed the spring breezes, for the breath of the Holy Spirit refreshed her garden: there was spring music—the time of the singing of birds was come, for her preachers testified faithfully of Jesus, and so many and varied were the sweet notes which welcomed the new season, that many nations of men heard in their own tongue 'the wonderful works of God'. There was, also, the spring blossoming, the fig tree put forth her green figs, and the vines with the tender grapes gave a good smell, for all around multitudes inquired, 'Men and brethren, what shall we do?' and many avowed their faith in Jesus. There were the spring showers of repentance, the spring sun-gleams of joy in the Holy Spirit and the spring flowers of newly-given hope and faith. May we behold just such another spring-time in all the churches of Jesus Christ throughout the world, and meanwhile let us arouse ourselves suitably to so gladsome a season. Let us rise up and meet the Well-Beloved, and in concert with him let us sow in hope and look for a speedy upspringing. The Sun of Righteousness is coming forth as a bridegroom out of his chamber, and the weary night is melting into welcome day; let us hear the Beloved's voice as he cries to us, 'Rise up, my love, my fair one, and come away.'

FOR MEDITATION: (*Our Own Hymn Book* no.972 v.4—James Montgomery, 1825)
'O Spirit of the Lord, prepare
All the round earth her God to meet;
Breathe Thou abroad like morning air,
Till hearts of stone begin to beat.'

N.B. A footnote to this sermon indicates that 107 believers were to be received into membership at the evening service.

SERMON NO. 1167

Rubbish

'There is much rubbish; so that we are not able to build the wall.'
Nehemiah 4:10
SUGGESTED FURTHER READING: 1 Peter 2:1–11

There is a building going on in us. It is the Spirit's work to edify us, that is to say, to build us up in grace, and that building is carried on by the grace of love. 'Knowledge puffeth up, but charity edifieth.' We are each one of us called to be builders, builders in God's strength, and let that not be forgotten; but, beloved, I am afraid most of us have to say, 'there is much rubbish; so that we are not able to build the wall.' Do you not often feel that you cannot be built up in heavenly graces, because of the rubbish of your own corrupt nature? What a fall the fall was! What a total ruin did it make of our moral nature! Brethren, do you not discover—I do, almost every day—some fresh heap of rubbish which you hardly knew was there? Points in which we thought ourselves strong turn out to be our weaknesses. There was an infirmity from which we half indulged the thought that we were clear, and therefore we were rather severe upon others for having such an infirmity and sin; but at last it broke out in ourselves; it always had been in us, but it had not had the occasion and opportunity; at length the provocation came and the hidden evil was revealed. Much more of such rubbish remains in us. Oh, the rubbish of pride, of unbelief, of evil lustings, of anger, of despondency, of self-exaltation! Brethren, it is not worth while to stir it; it is such a foul heap! I have no desire to turn cinder-sifter to it, for there is never a jewel in it that will pay for the sifting; but there it is, and the building of grace does not advance as we could wish, because of the corruption which still abides in us, notwithstanding all that some may say.

FOR MEDITATION: The apostle Paul regarded everything which could come between him and the Lord Jesus Christ as rubbish (Philippians 3:8), which he was determined to dispose of as he aimed to be built up in his Christian faith (Philippians 3:12–14). He calls us to share the same attitude (Philippians 3:15).

The reason why many cannot find peace

'Be afflicted, and mourn, and weep: let your laughter be turned to mourning, and your joy to heaviness.' James 4:9
SUGGESTED FURTHER READING: Ecclesiastes 7:1–6

'Be afflicted, and mourn, and weep: let your laughter be turned to mourning, and your joy to heaviness.' I grieve to say that I have met with people who say, 'I cannot find peace, I cannot get salvation,' and who talk very prettily in that way; but outside the door they are giggling one with another, as if it were a matter of amusement. The Sabbath day is spent in vain, idle, frivolous conversation; seriousness they do not seem even to have felt. The whole matter appears to be a mere sport. Some seem to jump into religion as people do into a bath, and jump out again about as fast; they never weigh the matter, they have no thought, no sorrow for sin, no humiliation before God. For decency's sake, stop that laughter if you are an unsaved soul. To laugh whilst in danger of being lost sounds to me as ghastly and grim as if the fiends of hell were to set up a theatre and act a comedy in the pit. What right have you with laughter while sin is unforgiven and while God is angry with you? Go to him in fitter form and fashion, or he will refuse your prayers. Be serious, begin to think of death, judgment and the wrath to come. These are not trifles, nor things to make sport about, neither is true religion a thing to be attended to as easily as when one snaps his finger and says, 'Heigh presto! Quick. It's done!' By no means. If you are saved, your mind is solemnly impressed by eternal realities and you are serious about matters of life and death; the very thought of sin pains you, and since you meet with it in your daily life you have cause for daily humbling, and are afflicted because of it. Many fail to get peace because it is not a solemn matter at all.

FOR MEDITATION: There is 'a time to weep, and a time to laugh' (Ecclesiastes 3:4), but 'sorrow is better than laughter' because it leads to true heartfelt joy (Ecclesiastes 7:3). Jesus pronounced a blessing upon those 'that weep now' for they 'shall laugh' (Luke 6:21), but woe upon those 'that laugh now' for they 'shall mourn and weep' (Luke 6:25). The superficial fun generated in some churches is no substitute for the joy of the Lord, acquired by soul-dealings with him.

SERMON NO. 1408

The great house and the vessels in it

'But in a great house there are not only vessels of gold and of silver, but also of wood and of earth; and some to honour, and some to dishonour. If a man therefore purge himself from these, he shall be a vessel unto honour, sanctified, and meet for the master's use, and prepared unto every good work.' 2 Timothy 2:20–21
SUGGESTED FURTHER READING: 1 Samuel 16:1–13

There are some Christians whom the Lord cannot much use because they are not cleansed from selfishness; they have an eye to their own honour or aggrandisement. The Lord will not be in complicity with selfish aims. Some are self-confident: there is too much of the 'I' about them, and the Master will not use them. He will have our weakness, but not our strength; if we are great somebodies he will pass us by, take some little nobody and make use of him. The Lord cannot use some men because they are too apt to be proud; if he were to give them a little success it would be dangerous to their Christian existence; their poor brain would begin to swim and they would think the Lord could hardly do without them; when they meet with a little encouragement they swell into such wonderful people that they expect everybody to fall down and worship them. God will not use them, neither will he set upon his table vessels which are in any way defiled. There must be purity; a man may work his heart out in the ministry or Sunday-school, but if he is practising some secret sin he cannot prosper; it is not possible that God should honour him. There may be a measure of apparent success for a time, and divine sovereignty may use the truth itself despite the man, but the man himself will not be useful to the Master. Littleness of grace and contentedness with that spiritual poverty also puts many a man aside. We must be full if God is to pour out of us to the thirsty, and full of his light if we are to illuminate the darkness of others: we cannot reveal to the world what the Lord has not revealed to us. O for a holy character and holy communion with God; then we shall be golden vessels fit for the Master's use.

FOR MEDITATION: David dispensed with physical aids which would have hindered his service for God (1 Samuel 17:38–39). To be useful to God we often need to exercise a similar spiritual bodily repentance (Mark 9:43–47; 1 Corinthians 9:25–27; Hebrews 12:1).

SERMON NO. 1348

Truly eating the flesh of Jesus

'Then Jesus said unto them, Verily, verily, I say unto you, Except ye eat the flesh of the Son of man, and drink his blood, ye have no life in you. Whoso eateth my flesh, and drinketh my blood, hath eternal life.' John 6:53–54
SUGGESTED FURTHER READING: Mark 10:46–52

What a man eats and drinks he appropriates to himself, and that not by laying it on one side in a treasury or casket, but by receiving it into himself. You appropriate money and put it in your pocket—you may lose it; you secure a piece of land and put your hedge about it, but that hedge may be broken down; but when you receive by eating and drinking, you have placed the good things where you will never be robbed of them; you have received them in the truest and surest sense, for you have real possession and enjoyment in your own person. To say, 'Christ is mine' is a blessed thing; but really to take Christ into you by the act of faith, is at once the vitality and the pleasure of faith. In eating and drinking a man is not a producer, but a consumer; he is not a doer or a giver forth; he simply takes in. If a queen should eat, if an *empress* should eat, she would become as completely a receiver as the pauper in the workhouse. Eating is an act of reception in every case. So it is with faith: you do not have to do, to be, or to feel, but only to receive; the saving point is not a something which comes from you, but the reception of something imparted to you. Faith is an act which the poorest, vilest, weakest, most condemned sinner may perform, because it is not an act requiring power on his part, nor the going forth of anything from him, but simply the receiving into himself. An empty vessel can receive and so much the better because it is empty. Are you willing to receive Jesus Christ as the free gift of divine mercy? Do you this day say, 'I have received him'? Well then, you have eaten his flesh and drunk his blood.

FOR MEDITATION: We initially receive the Lord Jesus Christ at conversion (John 1:12), but that initial reception needs to be followed up by a growing knowledge of him (Colossians 2:6–7). Sometimes, especially after a period of barrenness or backsliding, it may almost feel like starting all over again (Revelation 3:20).

N.B. Queen Victoria was soon to be proclaimed Empress of India on 1 May 1876.

SERMON NO. 1288

The leading of the Spirit, the secret token of the sons of God

'As many as are led by the Spirit of God, they are the sons of God.'
Romans 8:14
SUGGESTED FURTHER READING: Galatians 5:16–26

The Spirit of God leads the sons of God into holiness. I shall not attempt to define what holiness is. That is best seen in the lives of holy men. Can it be seen in your life? If you are of a fierce, unforgiving spirit, the Holy Spirit never led you there; if you are proud and hectoring, the Holy Spirit never led you there; if you are covetous and lustful after worldly gain, the Holy Spirit never led you there; if you are false in your statements and unjust in your actions, the Holy Spirit never led you there. If I hear of a professor of religion in the ball-room or the theatre, I know that the Holy Spirit never led him there; if I find a child of God mixing with the ungodly, using their speech and doing their actions, I am persuaded the Holy Spirit never led him there. But if I see a man living as Christ would have lived, loving, tender, fearless, brave, honest, in all things minding to keep a good conscience before God and men, I hope that the Spirit of God has led him; if I see that man devout before his God and full of integrity before his fellow men, then I hope and believe that the Spirit of God is his leader and influences his character; 'the fruit of the Spirit is love, joy, peace, longsuffering, gentleness, goodness, faith, meekness, temperance: against such there is no law. And they that are Christ's have crucified the flesh with the affections and lusts.' I do not wish to speak sharply, but I feel that I must speak plainly, and I feel bound to say that there is far too much hypocrisy among professing Christian people. Many wear the name of Christian, but have nothing else that is Christian about them. It is sorrowful that it should be so, but so it is: false professors have lowered the standard of Christian character, and made the church so like the world that it is hard to say where one begins and the other ends.

FOR MEDITATION: The perfect holiness of the Lord Jesus Christ is linked in Scripture to the work of the Holy Spirit (Luke 1:35; Acts 10:38). Unholiness on the part of a Christian contradicts the work of the Holy Spirit (1 Corinthians 6:18–19; 1 Thessalonians 4:7–8) and positively grieves him (Ephesians 4:28–31).

Salvation by faith and the work of the Spirit

'*For we through the Spirit wait for the hope of righteousness by faith.*'
Galatians 5:5
SUGGESTED FURTHER READING: 1 John 3:19–4:6

Whoever has this 'hope of righteousness by faith', has the Spirit of God. If your hope is based upon your being righteous through faith in Jesus Christ, you have been born again and renewed in heart by the Holy Spirit. Many are puzzled and say, 'I wish I knew I had the Spirit.' They fancy that the Spirit of God would cause some singular excitement in them, very different from quiet penitence and humble trust: I have known them suppose that this would cause some very astounding swoonings, palpitations and I do not know what besides. The best evidence of your having the Spirit of God is your depending upon Christ as a little child depends upon its mother. Others may bring other evidence to prove that they are born from above: let them bring the evidence and be thankful that they can bring it, but if you have no other evidence but this, 'Jesus Christ is my sole reliance, and on him do I depend,' that is enough: all the rest will follow in due course. 'He that believeth on the Son of God hath the witness in himself.' 'He that believeth on him is not condemned.' Draw a second inference. Wherever there is any other hope, or a hope based upon anything else but this, the Spirit of God is not present. Much talk about him there may be, but the Spirit himself is not there, for 'other foundation can no man lay than that is laid, which is Jesus Christ'. The Spirit will not bear witness to man's home-born presumptuous hopes. He bears witness to the finished work of Jesus Christ, and if you are relying upon that, you have the Spirit. If you are building upon sacraments, works, orthodoxies, feelings, or anything but Jesus Christ, you have not the Spirit of God, for the Spirit of God never taught a man to place his house upon such sandy foundations.

FOR MEDITATION: (*Our Own Hymn Book* no.533 v.1—Joseph Hart, 1759)
   'The moment a sinner believes, and trusts in his crucified God,
   His pardon at once he receives, redemption in full through His blood;
   Though thousands and thousands of foes against him in malice unite,
   Their rage he through Christ can oppose led forth by the Spirit to fight.'

SERMON NO. 1228

The crown of thorns

'And when they had platted a crown of thorns, they put it upon his head.' Matthew 27:29
SUGGESTED FURTHER READING: Hebrews 2:5—18

The coronation of Christ with thorns was symbolical and had great meaning in it, for, first, it was to him *a triumphal crown.* Christ had fought with sin from the day when he first stood foot to foot with it in the wilderness up to the time when he entered Pilate's hall, and he had conquered it. As a witness that he had gained the victory, behold sin's crown seized as a trophy! What was the crown of sin? Thorns. These sprang from the curse; 'thorns also and thistles shall it bring forth to thee' was the coronation of sin, and now Christ has taken away its crown and put it on his own head. He has spoiled sin of its richest regalia and he wears it himself. Glorious champion, all hail! What if I say that the thorns constituted *a mural crown?* Paradise was set round with a hedge of thorns so sharp that none could enter it, but our champion leaped first upon the bristling rampart and bore the blood-red banner of his cross into the heart of that better new Eden, which thus he won for us never to be lost again. Jesus wears the mural chaplet which denotes that he has opened Paradise. It was *a wrestler's crown* he wore, for he wrestled 'not against flesh and blood, but against principalities, against powers', and he overthrew his foe. It was *a racer's crown* he wore, for he had run with the mighty and outstripped them in the race. He had well-nigh finished his course, and had but a step or two more to take to reach the goal. Here is a marvellous field for enlargement. It was a crown rich with glory, despite the shame which was intended by it. We see in Jesus the monarch of the realms of misery, the chief among ten thousand sufferers. Never say, 'I am a great sufferer.' What are our griefs compared with his?

FOR MEDITATION: (*Our Own Hymn Book* no.336 v.1—Thomas Kelly, 1820)
'The head that once was crowned with thorns,
Is crowned with glory now;
A royal diadem adorns
The mighty Victor's brow.'

SERMON NO. 1168

The philosophy and propriety of abundant praise

'They shall abundantly utter the memory of thy great goodness, and shall sing of thy righteousness.' Psalm 145:7
SUGGESTED FURTHER READING: Jeremiah 31:10–14

We are to acquaint ourselves thoroughly with God as he has made himself known, and we are to consider continually his great goodness, that we may retain the memory of it. If we are willing to see, we shall not lack for opportunities of beholding his goodness every day, for it is to be seen in so many acts that I will not commence the catalogue, since I should never complete it. His goodness is seen in creation; it shines in every sunbeam, glitters in every dewdrop, smiles in every flower and whispers in every breeze. Earth, sea and air, teeming with innumerable forms of life, are all full of the goodness of the Lord. Sun, moon and stars affirm that the Lord is good, and all terrestrial things echo the proclamation. His goodness is also to be seen in the providence which rules over all. Let rebellious spirits murmur as they may, goodness is enthroned in Jehovah's kingdom, and evil and suffering are intruders there. God is good towards all his creatures, and especially towards the objects of his eternal love, for whom 'all things work together for good'. It is, however, in the domain of grace that the noblest form of divine goodness is seen. Begin with the goodness which shines in our election, and follow the silver thread through redemption, the mission of the Holy Spirit, the calling, adoption, preservation and perfecting of the chosen, and you will see riches of goodness which will astound you. Dwell where you may within the kingdoms of redemption, and you will see rivers and oceans of goodness. I leave your own minds to remember these things, and your own lips abundantly to utter the memory of the Lord's great goodness in the wonders of his salvation, for it is not my design to speak for you, but to stir you up to speak for yourselves.

FOR MEDITATION: Take time to 'praise the LORD for his goodness' (Psalm 107:8,15,21,31) as seen in creation (Genesis 1:4,10,12,18,21,25,31), in provision (Psalm 21:3; 65:11: 68:10) and especially in the life of the Lord Jesus Christ (Mark 7:37: Acts 10:38).

The shortest of the seven cries

'After this, Jesus knowing that all things were now accomplished, that the scripture might be fulfilled, saith, I thirst.' John 19:28
SUGGESTED FURTHER READING: Psalm 22:14–31

It seems to me very wonderful that this 'I thirst' should be, as it were, the clearance of it all. Jesus had no sooner said 'I thirst' and sipped the vinegar, than he shouted, 'It is finished' and all was over: the battle was fought and the victory won for ever, and our great Deliverer's thirst was the sign of his having smitten the last foe. The flood of his grief had passed the high-water mark and began to be assuaged. The 'I thirst' was the bearing of the last pang; what if I say it was the expression of the fact that his pangs had at last begun to cease, and their fury had spent itself and left him able to note his lesser pains? The excitement of a great struggle makes men forget thirst and faintness; it is only when all is over that they come back to themselves and note the spending of their strength. The great agony of being forsaken by God was over, and he felt faint when the strain was withdrawn. I like to think of our Lord's saying, 'It is finished' directly after he had exclaimed, 'I thirst', for these two voices come so naturally together. Our glorious Samson had been fighting our foes; 'heaps upon heaps' he had slain his thousands, and now like Samson 'he was sore athirst'. He sipped of the vinegar and he was refreshed, and no sooner had he thrown off the thirst than he shouted like a conqueror, 'It is finished', and quitted the field, covered with renown. Let us exult as we see our Substitute going through with his work even to the bitter end, and then with an 'It is finished' returning to his Father, God. O souls, burdened with sin, rest here and, resting, live.

FOR MEDITATION: Meditate on the 'things' that 'were now accomplished' at this momentous point in history. The ending of the three hours of darkness indicated that the separation of the Lord Jesus Christ from his Father in heaven was now finished (Mark 15:33–34); the tearing of the temple curtain showed that the separation between sinful man and his Maker was now finished (Matthew 27:50–51; Luke 23:44–46); the bodily resurrection of many of the saints proved that the power of death was now finished (Matthew 27:52–53).

SERMON NO. 1409

Faith purifying the heart

'Purifying their hearts by faith.' Acts 15:9
SUGGESTED FURTHER READING: 2 Thessalonians 2:13–17

'As ye have therefore received Christ Jesus the Lord, so walk ye in him.' As you believe in him unto justification, believe in him to sanctification. If anybody tells you that you are to get justification in one way and sanctification in another way, do not believe him. Jesus Christ is 'of God made unto us … sanctification, and redemption'. Pharisees virtually teach us that we are to be sanctified by the law, though justified by faith; but we know better. These are twin covenant blessings and are not to be had apart. Believe in Christ to conquer sin as well as to pardon sin. Believe that the only power which can subdue a base passion in you is the power which washed you from your iniquity of old. Trust Christ with the power of sin as well as the guilt of sin. You need not go through a round of performances in order to be purified in heart; you need not look for a higher life than Jesus gave you when you looked and lived: there is no higher life, for he gave you his own. What more do you want than the Holy Spirit who quickens you? What is higher than that? What more can you have than faith has brought you and will bring you? Jesus has given you himself. Did you believe in half a Christ at the beginning? Did you receive from him a lower and inferior life? Shame on you to think so. You trusted your soul wholly with him, did you not, and did he not give his whole self to you? Do you mean to say that you trusted him to save you from hell, and not from sin? Did you trust him to blot out the past, and were you fool enough to trust to yourself for keeping in the future? If so, you did not believe in him at all; your faith was faulty at the very core, for Christ must be everything or nothing.

FOR MEDITATION: Saving faith also functions both as a shield (Ephesians 6:16) and a breastplate (1 Thessalonians 5:8). Old Testament heroes won physical battles through faith (Hebrews 11:32–34) and ongoing faith is essential to the Christian in winning the battles of spiritual warfare (1 Timothy 1:18–19; 6:11–12; 1 Peter 5:8–9; 1 John 5:4–5).

Clearing the road to heaven

'Gather out the stones.' Isaiah 62:10
SUGGESTED FURTHER READING: Matthew 27:27–50

It was needful before you could be saved that in the person of man the Son of God should die. I can conceive him living on earth, but who shall conceive him dying? God was in Christ as he died upon the accursed tree. He who spread the heavens, made the earth and piled the mountains, he was here in the form of man; and the soldiers came and seized him in the garden as though he had been a thief; they took him away to Pilate's hall and there they scourged him; there they spit in his face; there they crowned him with a crown of thorns and then condemned him to bear his cross. Him, the Eternal God in human flesh, they hounded along Jerusalem's streets, then flung him down upon his back on the transverse wood, and drove the cruel nails through his blessed and tender hands and feet; then they lifted up the cross and dashed it into its socket in the earth till all his bones were dislocated, and he cried, 'I am poured out like water, and all my bones are out of joint'. It was he who but a little while before had heard the songs of angels, and at whose feet the seraphim and cherubim adored. He on that tree was fastened and lifted up, and there he died in infinite agonies; it were not possible to describe them, for none knew their terror. God forsook him: his Father turned away his face, and in the bitterness of his anguish he said, 'My God, my God, why hast thou forsaken me?' Thus on the tree he died, and in that death he took the punishment due on account of the sin of all who shall believe on him. He suffered in their stead an equivalent for all that they would have had to suffer had they been cast into the pit of hell. This being done, salvation is not only possible, but achieved. Believe in it, sinner! What stone remains now that Jesus has died?

FOR MEDITATION: By his death on the cross the Lord Jesus Christ has removed all kinds of obstacles and threats which used to stand in the way of those who now trust in him as their Saviour—the wrath of God (Romans 5:9), the controlling power of sin (Romans 6:6), the unfulfilled demands of the law (Colossians 2:13–14) and the rule of evil spirits (Colossians 2:15). All you have to do to ensure that these things remain in your way is to continue in your unbelief.

SERMON NO. 1131

Peace: a fact and a feeling

'Therefore being justified by faith, we have peace with God through our Lord Jesus Christ.' Romans 5:1
SUGGESTED FURTHER READING: Hebrews 10:1–14

Faith comes into contact with pardon when faith believes that the Son of God came and stood in the sinner's stead, accepts this substitution as a glorious boon of grace, rests in it, and says, 'Now I see how God is just and smites Christ in my stead. Seeing he condemned me before I had personally sinned, because of Adam's sin, I see how he can absolve me, though I have no righteousness, because of Christ's righteousness. In another I fell and in another I rise. By one Adam I was destroyed: by another Adam I am restored. I leap for joy and accept it as from the Lord.' This is not quite all, for now here stands the guilty one, who has owned the sentence, and he has seen the sentence executed upon another. What then? He takes his place as no longer liable to that sentence. The penalty cannot be exacted twice. It is neither in accord with human or divine righteousness that two should be punished for the same offence unless both are guilty. When God devised the plan of substitution, the full penalty demanded of the guilty surety was clearly intended to bring exemption to the guilty sinners. That Jesus should suffer vicariously, and yet those for whom he paid the quittance in drops of blood should obtain no acquittal, could not be. When God laid sin upon Christ it must have been in the intent of his heart that he would never lay it on those for whom Christ died. So there stands the man who was once guilty, but he is no more condemned, because another has taken upon him the condemnation to which he was exposed. Still more, inasmuch as the Lord Jesus Christ came voluntarily under the law, obeyed, fulfilled and made the law honourable, according to the infinite purpose and will of God the righteousness of Christ is imputed to the believer. While Christ stands in the sinner's place, the believing sinner stands in Christ's place.

FOR MEDITATION: (*Our Own Hymn Book* no.397 v.3—Count Zinzendorf, 1739; tr. by John Wesley, 1740)
   'Bold shall I stand in that great day,
   For who aught to my charge shall lay?
   While through Thy blood absolved I am
   From sin's tremendous curse and shame.'

Decision—illustrated by the case of Joshua

'As for me and my house, we will serve the LORD.*' Joshua 24:15*
SUGGESTED FURTHER READING (Spurgeon): Psalm 101:1–8

Some have avowed themselves on the Lord's side and yet do not serve the Lord; their names are down in the church book and they attend to the outward ordinances, but as for serving the Lord, you will have to search for it, and search in vain. Joshua went in for serving God in truth. He was a soldier and if anyone had asked him, 'whose soldier are you, Joshua?' he would have answered, 'I am God's soldier.' 'Whose battles do you fight?' 'I fight the battles of Jehovah.' 'And what is your object in fighting?' 'To glorify Jehovah.' He was committed to the Lord's cause from head to foot. Many professors do not understand what this means; they view religion as a kind of off-hand farm; they have another estate, which is their home and main care, and the kingdom of God is an off-hand farm, to be managed mainly by the minister as a bailiff. Their religion gets their spare time and odd thoughts; Jesus comes in for the cold meat that is left over, and the world has the hot joints. Religion is by no means the great channel along which the strength of their life runs, but it is a sort of backwater: they let the waste water run there, when they have more than enough to turn the mill-wheel of business. They are seen at prayer meetings when there are no accounts to settle and no new books to read; they do something for the church of God when they have nothing on hand, no friend coming to spend the evening with them, and no amusement available. They treat the Lord Jesus Christ very cavalierly. They hope they will be saved by him—I hope they will! They say they will be wonders of grace if they are, and I think they will! Such conduct to the bleeding Lamb is base and I hate it. 'As for me' I will be bold enough to say with Joshua, 'I will serve the LORD.'

FOR MEDITATION: (*Our Own Hymn Book* no.671 v.1—Isaac Watts, 1721)
  'Am I a soldier of the cross,
  A follower of the Lamb?
  And shall I fear to own His cause,
  Or blush to speak His name?'

The fulness of Christ the treasury of the saints

'For it pleased the Father that in him should all fulness dwell.' Colossians
1:19
'And of his fulness have all we received, and grace for grace.' John 1:16
SUGGESTED FURTHER READING: Colossians 2:8–15

Behold the plan which infinite wisdom has devised! The Eternal Son of God becomes man, the divine nature comes in all its fulness and dwells in the Mediator Christ Jesus. Coming into him he was made to feel the mighty burnings of justice, which caused him agony but could not consume him, for in him was no sin. Justice burned and blazed within him, and brought him to the cross and death, because he stood in the sinner's place; but this golden vessel, though heated, was not melted; it could contain the divine fire and yet not be destroyed; and now in Christ Jesus dwells 'all the fulness of the Godhead bodily', and, moreover, the divine nature is in him in such a way as to be capable of communication to the sons of men; of course the essence of Deity is not communicated, for that would be to make men into gods, but we are made 'partakers of the divine nature' in the sense of receiving the same character and becoming the children of God. That which God could not bring to us directly by reason of our inability to receive it, he has now brought to us through a Mediator, by placing it in the man Christ Jesus, that we, coming to him, might freely receive of it. The next step in the plan of salvation is this—after the fulness of God has come to man in the person of his Son, every one that comes to him by faith receives of his grace. Salvation is not by what you bring to Christ, but by what you take from him. You are to be receivers first, and then by-and-by, through the power of grace you shall give forth from yourselves rivers of living water to others. In your first coming you come empty, having nothing but your sin and misery; as empty, undeserving sinners you receive of his fulness, and all your life long continue to do the same.

FOR MEDITATION: (*Our Own Hymn Book* no.415 v.2—John Cennick, 1742)
'Fulness of riches is in Thee!
From Thee all mercies spring:
And grace and love, divine and free,
And power enlivening.'

SERMON NO. 1169

Prayer perfumed with praise

'In everything by prayer and supplication with thanksgiving let your requests be made known unto God.' Philippians 4:6
SUGGESTED FURTHER READING: Philemon 1–7

We must mingle our thanksgivings with our prayers, or else we may fear that our mind is not in harmony with the divine will. Recollect that prayer does not alter the mind of God: it never was the intent of prayer that it should attempt anything of the kind. Prayer is the shadow of the decrees of the Eternal. God has willed such a thing, and he makes his saints to will it and express their will in prayer. Prayer is the rustling of the wings of the angels who are bringing the blessing to us. It is written, 'Delight thyself also in the LORD; and he shall give thee the desires of thine heart.' It is not said that he will give the desire of his heart to every Jack and Tom, but you must first delight in the Lord, and when your mind finds all her joy in God, then it is clear that God and you, as far as it can be, are standing on the same plane and moving in the same direction, and now you shall have the desire of your heart, because the desire of your heart is the desire of God's heart. Character, as much as faith, lies at the basis of prevalence in prayer. I do not mean in the case of the prayer of the sinner when he is seeking mercy, but I mean in the habitual prayers of the godly. There are some who cannot pray so as to prevail, for sin has made them weak, and God walks contrary to them, because they walk contrary to him. He who has lost the light of God's countenance has also lost much of the prevalence of his prayers. You do not suppose that every Israelite could have gone to the top of Carmel and opened the windows of heaven as Elijah did. No, he must first be Elijah, for it is the 'effectual fervent prayer' not of every man, but 'of a righteous man' that 'availeth much'.

FOR MEDITATION: God delights to hear and answer the prayers of 'the upright' and 'the righteous' (Proverbs 15:8,29), but even the prayers of such godly people need to be 'effectual' and 'fervent' (James 5:16). For our prayers to prevail we need to continue 'instant in prayer' (Romans 12:12), to 'strive' in prayer (Romans 15:30), to 'give' ourselves to prayer (1 Corinthians 7:5), to labour 'fervently' in prayer (Colossians 4:12) and to pray in faith (James 5:15).

SERMON NO. 1469

Believers free from the dominion of sin

'For sin shall not have dominion over you: for ye are not under the law, but under grace.' Romans 6:14
SUGGESTED FURTHER READING: Galatians 4:21–5:4

'Not under the law,' being interpreted, means that we are not trying to be saved by obedience to law; we do not pretend to earn eternal life by merit, nor hope to claim anything of the Lord as due to us for good works. The principle which rules our life is not mercenary; we do not expect to earn a reward, neither are we flogged to duty by dread of punishment. We are 'under grace', that is to say, we are treated on the principle of mercy and love, not on that of justice and desert. Freely of his own undeserved favour God has forgiven us for Christ's sake. He has regarded us with favour, not because we deserved it, but simply because he willed to do so, according to that ancient declaration, 'I will have mercy on whom I will have mercy, and I will have compassion on whom I will have compassion.' The Lord did not choose us because of any goodness in us, but he has saved us and called us according to the purpose of his own will. Moreover, our continuance in a state of salvation depends upon the same grace which first placed us there. We do not stand or fall according to our personal merit, but because Jesus lives we live, because Jesus is accepted we are accepted, and because Jesus is beloved we are beloved: in a word, our standing is not based upon merit, but upon mercy, not upon our changeable character, but upon the immutable mercy of God. Grace is the tenure upon which we hold our position before the Lord. 'For by grace are ye saved through faith; and that not of yourselves: it is the gift of God.' 'But that no man is justified by the law in the sight of God, it is evident: for, The just shall live by faith. And the law is not of faith: but, The man that doeth them shall live in them.'

FOR MEDITATION: (*Our Own Hymn Book* no.647 v.6—William Cowper, 1779)
'To see the law by Christ fulfilled,
And hear His pardoning voice,
Changes a slave into a child,
And duty into choice.'

The divine call for missionaries

'Also I heard the voice of the Lord, saying, Whom shall I send, and who will go for us? Then said I, Here am I; send me.' Isaiah 6:8
SUGGESTED FURTHER READING: Acts 22:6–21

This is the voice of the one God, and it is also the question of the sacred Trinity: 'Whom shall I send, and who will go for us?' The Father, Son and Spirit thus question us; shall not the threefold voice be regarded? Notice the particular kind of man for whom this voice is seeking. It is a man who must be sent, a man under impulse, a man under authority— 'Whom shall I send?' But it is a man who is quite willing to go, a volunteer, one who in his inmost heart rejoices to obey—'who will go for us?' What a strange mingling this is! 'Woe is unto me, if I preach not the gospel', and yet 'taking the oversight thereof, not by constraint, but willingly'. Irresistible impulse and cheerful choice, omnipotent compulsion and joyful eagerness most mysteriously combine! We must have a mingling of these two. I do not know that I could put into so many words that wonderful feeling of freeness and overpowering impulse, of necessity and freedom, but our experience understands what our language cannot express. We are willing, and yet a power is over us; we are 'willing in the day of' God's power, coming forth as freely as the dew-drops 'from the womb of the morning', and yet as truly the product of divine power as they are. Such must God's servant be. 'Whom shall I send?' It is Jehovah's voice; 'and who will go for us?' It is the voice of the bleeding Lamb, the loving Father, and the ever-blessed Spirit. Does no one leap up at this moment and freely offer himself? Must I speak in vain? That would be a light thing—must the voice from heaven be in vain? Did the child Samuel reply, 'Here am I; for thou didst call me', and will no full-grown man answer to the voice of the Eternal?

FOR MEDITATION: The calling and sending of the apostle Paul can be attributed to all three persons of the Trinity, to the Father (Acts 22:14–15), to the Son (Acts 20:24; 26:14–18) and to the Holy Spirit (Acts 13:2). The Great Commission to all Christians also involves all three persons of the Trinity (Matthew 28:19–20). Does your response resemble that of the apostle Paul (Acts 26:19–20) or is it more like that of either of the two sons in the story Jesus told (Matthew 21:28–31)?

SERMON NO. 1351

Nevertheless, hereafter

'Jesus saith unto him, Thou hast said, nevertheless, I say unto you, Hereafter shall ye see the Son of man sitting on the right hand of power.'
Matthew 26:64
SUGGESTED FURTHER READING: Matthew 27:50–28:15

There came to the members of the Sanhedrim a messenger, who told them that 'the veil of the temple was rent in twain'. At that moment, when the Saviour died, that splendid piece of tapestry seemed to tear itself asunder from end to end as if in horror at the death of its Lord. The members of that council, when they met each other in the street and spoke of the news, must have been dumb in sheer astonishment; but while they looked upon each other, the earth they stood upon reeled, and they could scarcely keep their feet. This was not the first wonder which had startled them that day, for the sun had been beclouded in unnatural darkness. At midday it had ceased to shine, and now the earth ceased to be stable. Also, in the darkness of the evening, certain members of this council saw the sheeted dead, newly arisen from their tombs, walking through the streets; for 'the earth did quake, and the rocks rent; and the graves were opened; and many bodies of the saints ... appeared unto many.' Thus early they began to know that the man of Nazareth was at 'the right hand of power'. Early on the third morning, when they met together, there came a messenger in hot haste, who said, 'That stone is rolled away from the door of the sepulchre. Remember that you placed a watch and set your seal upon the stone. But early this morning the soldiers say that he came forth. He rose, that dreaded One whom we put to death, and at the first sight of him the keepers did shake, and became as dead men.' Now these members of the Sanhedrim believed that fact, and we have clear evidence that they did, for they bribed the soldiers, and said, 'Say ye, His disciples came by night, and stole him away while we slept.' Then did the word also continue to be fulfilled, and they plainly saw that Jesus whom they had condemned was at 'the right hand of power'.

FOR MEDITATION: (*Our Own Hymn Book* no.414 v.2—Isaac Watts, 1709)
'Worthy is He that once was slain, the Prince of Peace that groaned and died
Worthy to rise, and live, and reign at His Almighty Father's side.'

SERMON NO. 1364

The Son glorified by the Father and the Father by the Son

'These words spake Jesus, and lifted up his eyes to heaven, and said, Father, the hour is come; glorify thy Son, that thy Son also may glorify thee.' John 17:1
SUGGESTED FURTHER READING: Acts 3:11–21

The rending of the veil at the moment of his death was the glorifying of Christ, for now there is for us a way to the throne of God, which before had been closed. Then the opening of his pierced side was another glorifying of him, for the fount is to believers the effectual cleansing of both the guilt and power of sin; and thus the Saviour's pierced heart glorified him in its power to bless. Then that poor body lay in the grave, wrapped in the linen and spices. But the Father glorified even that dead body which men thought to be corruptible, for it saw no corruption. During the three days and nights no worm could come near it, nor trace of decay. That crystal vase in which the rich ointment of the Saviour's soul had dwelt must not be injured. 'A bone of him shall not be broken.' Beautified by those scars, that body must be safely guarded by watching angels till the morning came. It barely dawned. As yet the sun was rising, and lo the Sun of righteousness himself arose! As a man rising from his couch puts on his garments, so did our Lord put on the vesture of the body which he had laid aside, and came again into the world, alive as to his body and soul, a perfect man. It was a grand glorifying of Christ when the Father raised him from the dead, and he was seen by his disciples once again. Death had no bands wherewith to hold him. The sepulchre's ward could not confine the unequalled prisoner. Declared to be glorious by the resurrection from the dead, his prayer was heard. And after only a few weeks there came another glory; from the brow of Olivet he gently ascended, floating in the air from the company of his disciples, rising up in the midst of angels till a cloud received him out of human sight. His Father glorified him.

FOR MEDITATION: Jesus was raised on a tree (John 12:32), from the tomb and to the throne. Though 'humbled for a season' he is highly exalted to the glory of God the Father (Philippians 2:8–11). Unless we honour him fully, we dishonour the Father who loves him (John 5:20,23). Jesus must always be lifted up, never lowered down.

SERMON NO. 1464(B)

The sure triumph of the crucified one

'Behold, my servant shall deal prudently, he shall be exalted and extolled, and be very high.' Isaiah 52:13
SUGGESTED FURTHER READING: Luke 12:35–48

A portion of the church not only expects the Lord's second advent, but gets into a state of feverishness about the matter. 'Surely,' say they, 'his delays have been very great. "Why is his chariot so long in coming?"' Brethren, the Master knows best. It may please him to finish up the present dispensation today; if so, he will doubtless 'deal prudently' in so doing: but it may be that myriads of years are yet to elapse before his appearing, and if so there will be wisdom in the delay. Let us leave the matter alone, for while the general fact that he will come is clearly revealed in order to quicken our diligence, the details are veiled in mystery, since they would only gratify our curiosity. If I knew that our Lord would come this evening, I should preach just as I mean to preach; if I knew he would come during this sermon, I would go on preaching until he did. Christian people ought not to be standing with their mouths open, gazing up into heaven and wondering what is going to happen, but they should abide with 'loins ... girded about' and 'lights burning', ready for his appearing, whenever it may be. Go straight ahead upon the business your Lord has appointed you, and you need be under no apprehension of being taken by surprise. On one occasion I called to see one of our friends and I found her whitening the front steps. When she saw me she jumped up and blushingly said, 'Oh dear, sir, I am sorry you caught me like this; I wish I had known you were coming.' 'My dear sister,' I said, 'I hope that is how the Lord will find me at his coming—doing my duty.' I should like to be found whitening the steps when the Lord comes, if that were my duty. Steady perseverance in appointed service is far better than prophetical speculation.

FOR MEDITATION: Being ready for the Lord's second coming involves living soberly and expectantly (1 Thessalonians 5:6,8; Titus 2:12–13; 1 Peter 1:13). Unbelievers should beware of a sense of false security (1 Thessalonians 5:3) or scoffing (2 Peter 3:3–4) because of his apparent delay, but Christians should also beware of being deceived as a result of their own impatience (2 Thessalonians 2:1–3).

SERMON NO. 1231

'By all means save some'

'That I might by all means save some.' 1 Corinthians 9:22
SUGGESTED FURTHER READING: Matthew 13:10–17

There was never a man more stern for principle than Paul; in things where it was necessary to take his stand he was firm as a rock, but in merely personal and external matters he was the servant of all. Adaptation was his forte. Beloved, if you have to talk to children, be children, and do not expect them to be men. Think their thoughts, feel their feelings, and put truth into their words. You will never get at their hearts till your heart is in sympathy with their childhood. If you have to comfort the aged, enter also into their infirmities, and do not speak to them as if they were still in the full vigour of life. Study persons of all ages and be as they are, that they may be led to be believers, as you are. Are you called to labour among the educated? Then choose out excellent words, and present them as apples of gold in baskets of silver. Do you work among the illiterate? Let your words be as goads; speak their mother tongue and use great plainness of speech, so that you may be understood, for what avails to speak to them in an unknown tongue? Are you cast among people with strange prejudices? Do not unnecessarily jar with them, but take them as you find them. Are you seeking the conversion of a person of slender understanding? Do not inflict upon him the deeper mysteries, but show him the plain man's pathway to heaven in words which he who runs may read. Are you talking with a friend who is of a sorrowful spirit? Tell him of your own depressions, enter into his griefs, and so raise him as you were raised. Like the good Samaritan, go where the wounded man lies, and do not expect him to come to you. A real passion for winning souls reveals the many sides of our manhood and uses each one as a reflector of the divine light of truth.

FOR MEDITATION: Even within the church the apostles chose carefully what to say to people according to their spiritual maturity (1 Corinthians 3:1–3; Hebrews 5:11–14), social status (Ephesians 5:22–6:9; Colossians 3:18–4:1) and age (1 John 2:12–14). Timothy and Titus were instructed to do likewise (1 Timothy 5:1–3; Titus 2:1–10). How much more care is needed to speak appropriately to the unconverted.

Concealing the words of God

'I have not concealed the words of the Holy One.' Job 6:10
SUGGESTED FURTHER READING (Spurgeon): Luke 11:44–54

What will it be to meditate upon a dying bed on having known the truth, but having never in any way assisted to spread it? What will it be to lie with eternity just before you and to reflect, 'I have been a member of a church many years, but have never brought in a single convert. I sat in my pew and knew the divine secret, but never told even a child of it. Neither by pen nor tongue did I make Jesus known. I left that to the minister. I knew there were good people about who cared for men's souls, but I had no such feeling: I kept myself to myself and felt no anxiety about my neighbours. I had very little care as to whether souls were saved or not. I was glad when I heard of an increase to the church, but not very particularly so; I was sorry when things were down, but not so sorry that I lost my appetite or lay awake. I did not trouble myself more than I could help, for I was foolish enough to dream that the best thing I could do was to consult my own interests; I fancied that my chief end was to enjoy myself for ever.' I can imagine such a man beset with horrors when he comes to die, and struggling to get anything like a glimpse of hope. His life has been one of selfishness; how can he be a Christian? Conscience will ask, 'Is this Christlike, this keeping back of the divine bread from the perishing, this concealing of the light of God? Surely you are no follower of the Crucified?' How will such conduct look at the last great day?

FOR MEDITATION: (*Our Own Hymn Book* no.900 vv.1&4—John Joseph Winkler, 1714; tr. John Wesley, 1739)
'Shall I, for fear of feeble man,
Thy Spirit's course in me restrain?
Or undismayed in deed and word,
Be a true witness for my Lord?

The love of Christ doth me constrain
To seek the wandering souls of men;
With cries, entreaties, tears, to save,
To snatch them from the fiery wave.'

SERMON NO. 1471

Under constraint

'For the love of Christ constraineth us; because we thus judge, that if one died for all, then were all dead.' 2 Corinthians 5:14
SUGGESTED FURTHER READING: 2 John 1–11

He who does not hate the false does not love the true; he to whom it is all the same whether it be God's word or man's, is himself unrenewed at heart. If some of you were like your fathers, you would not have tolerated in this age the wagon loads of trash under which the gospel has been of late buried by ministers of your own choosing. You would have hurled out of your pulpits the men who are enemies to the fundamental doctrines of your churches, and yet are crafty enough to become your pastors and undermine the faith of a fickle and superficial generation. These men steal the pulpits of once orthodox churches, because otherwise they would have none at all. Their powerless theology cannot of itself arouse sufficient enthusiasm to enable them to build a mousetrap at the expense of their admirers, and therefore they profane the houses which were built for the preaching of the gospel, and turn aside the organisations of once orthodox communities to help their infidelity: I call it by that name in plain English, for 'modern thought' is not one whit better, and of the two evils I give infidelity the palm, for it is less deceptive. I beg the Lord to give back to the churches such a love for his truth that they may discern the spirits and cast out those which are not of God. I feel sometimes like John, of whom it is said that, though the most loving of all spirits, yet he was the most decided of all men for the truth; when he went to the bath and found that the heretic Cerinthus was there, he hurried out of the building and would not stay in the same place with him. There are some with whom we should have no fellowship, not even so much as to eat bread; for though this conduct looks stern and hard, it is after the mind of Christ.

FOR MEDITATION: The early Christians were warned about the dangers posed by false apostles (2 Corinthians 11:13), false brethren (2 Corinthians 11:26; Galatians 2:4), false Christs (Mark 13:22–23), false prophets (Matthew 7:15; 24:11; 1 John 4:1) and false teachers (2 Peter 2:1). The modern church should stop pretending that it has grown sufficiently mature not to have to worry about such things.

SERMON NO. 1411

Strong consolation for the Lord's refugees

'That by two immutable things, in which it was impossible for God to lie, we might have a strong consolation, who have fled for refuge to lay hold upon the hope set before us.' Hebrews 6:18
SUGGESTED FURTHER READING (Spurgeon): Hebrews 3:12–19

In the forcible language of the Greek 'lay hold' would imply firm retention of that which we have seized. I remember well when first I 'lay hold upon the hope' that God had set before me. I was terribly afraid to grasp it for I thought it was too good to be true: but I saw that there was no other chance for me, and therefore I was driven right out of myself to be bold and venture all. I knew that I must flee somewhere and it seemed to be that or nothing; I was forced to believe in the wondrous plan of salvation by another and in another, even in salvation by Jesus Christ. I made a dash at it and believed it, and joy and peace filled my spirit. That is twenty-seven years ago now and I am laying hold upon it still. Brethren and sisters, I have not gone an inch beyond the old hope. Jesus Christ was all in all to me then, and he is the same now, only I am more resolved than ever to lean my soul on him and upon him alone. I profess to you this day that I dare not place a shadow of reliance upon any sermons I have preached, or any alms I have given, or any prayers I have offered, or any communions with Christ I have enjoyed, or on anything that I have done, said or thought: but I rely wholly on what Jesus did and is doing as my covenant Head and Surety. I know he bore my sin 'in his own body on the tree', I know he buried my sin where it never shall have a resurrection, I know he sits as my representative at the eternal throne, and I also know that I shall soon be where he is, because I am one with him, since I have believed in him.

FOR MEDITATION: For our sakes the Lord Jesus Christ made no attempt to hold on to all that had always been his by right (Philippians 2:6–7), but we need to lay hold of and to keep hold of eternal life (1 Timothy 6:12,19), by holding on to our faith (1 Timothy 1:19; Hebrews 10:23), confidence (Hebrews 3:6,14) and hope (Hebrews 6:18).

The great emancipator

'And thou shalt say unto Pharaoh, thus saith the LORD, *Israel is my son, even my firstborn: and I say unto thee, Let my son go, that he may serve me.' 'Then the* LORD *said unto Moses, Now shalt thou see what I will do to Pharaoh.' Exodus 4:22–23; 6:1*
SUGGESTED FURTHER READING: Luke 6:17–23

It sometimes happens that the ungodly themselves become very glad to get rid of God's chosen people, whom they are prone to persecute. 'Their melancholy ill comports with our liveliness,' so they say. They did all they could to invite them to their parties and get them into their frivolities again; they laid traps for them to keep them away from hearing the gospel; but now the Lord has begun to deal with them, their old companions say, 'Now we must give them up.' 'I have tried all I could to get our old comrade back to our old convivialities,' says one, 'but, really, he said such things that he quite poisoned all our pleasures. We could not enjoy ourselves. Let us get rid of him. Do not let him be in our company any more.' Yes, it is a grand thing when the preaching of the gospel makes the ungodly want to keep the converts away from their cliques, when they say, 'Oh, go off to your Tabernacle: we do not want you here; you have pestered us enough with your religion, your prayers, your crying, your tears, your talk about being lost, and your wanting to find a Saviour. You are bad company and you had better be gone.' A lady who joined this church some years ago, moving in the higher circles of society, said to me, 'I was quite willing to continue my acquaintance with my friends, but I found they gave me the cold shoulder and did not want me.' Just so. It is a great mercy when the Egyptians say, 'Get gone,' and when they are ready to give you jewels of silver and gold to get rid of you. The Lord wants his people to come right out and to be separate.

FOR MEDITATION: The godly can take great comfort when they are cast out and snubbed by the ungodly (Luke 6:22–23), but the ungodly who cast out God's people are the ones who should start getting worried about what God is going to do to them (Isaiah 66:5; John 9:34–41; 1 Peter 4:3–5).

Family reformation; or, Jacob's second visit to Bethel

'And God said unto Jacob, Arise, go up to Bethel, and dwell there.'
Genesis 35:1
SUGGESTED FURTHER READING: Titus 2:1–15

Every now and then, dear brothers and sisters, we shall find it necessary to say to ourselves and to our family, 'We must come out from among worldlings; we must be separate. We are forming connections which are injurious to us, and we must snap the deceitful bonds. We are being led into habits and customs in the management of the household which are not such as God would approve. We are doing this to secure favour of one, and doing that to escape frowns from another, and we are not walking straight with the Lord; therefore, to bring us back to our moorings, we must come right out and go to Bethel, to the place where God met with us at the first. We must go to our first meeting-place and meet with our Lord again, cost whatever the journey may: though some may feel it to be a cross, yet we must begin again and work upon the old lines. Back to our old Puritanism and precision we must go and renew our vows. Let us go right away from worldliness, get to the Bethel of separation, and draw near to God again.' Have you never found, beloved, when you have been very deep in business and very much in the world, that you begin to feel heart-sick and begin to cry, 'It won't do; I must get out of this; I must retreat into a holy solitude and enjoy a little quiet communion with God'? Have you not sometimes felt concerning your family, 'We are not serving the Lord aright, nor becoming more holy or devoted; everything appears to be going downhill. We must steer the other way. We must alter our present declining state in the name of God, or else we cannot expect to have his blessing'? I know that you have come to such a pass and have resolved to take a decided step. May the Lord help all of us when we see clearly that something is to be done.

FOR MEDITATION: Consider Joshua' determination to distance his family from ungodly ways, regardless of what others chose to do (Joshua 24:14–15). Contrast this with the behaviour of Achan, whose worldliness implicated the rest of his family and brought disaster upon them (Joshua 7:1,19–25).

Solomon's plea

'For thou didst separate them from among all the people of the earth, to be thine inheritance.' 1 Kings 8:53
SUGGESTED FURTHER READING: 2 Corinthians 6:14–7:1

Many of us are not separated enough from the world. God intends the difference to be very marked; he would have the line between the church and the world drawn very clearly. I could wish to obliterate for ever the unhappy and artificial distinction which is constantly made between sacred and secular, for a world of mischief has come out of it. The truth is that a real Christian may be known by this, that to him everything secular is sacred, and the commonest matters are holiness unto the Lord. I do not believe in the religion which only lifts its head above water on Sunday, and confines itself to praying, preaching and carrying hymn books about: we must have a religion which gives a true yard when it is measuring its cloth, a religion which weighs a true pound when it is dealing out shop goods, a religion which scorns to puff, lie and take advantage of a gullible public, a religion which is true, upright, chaste, kind and unselfish. Give me a man who would not lie if the whole earth or heaven itself were to be won thereby. We need among professed Christians a high morality; far more, we need unsullied holiness. O Holy Spirit, work it in us all! Holiness means wholeness of character in contradistinction to the cultivation of some few virtues and the neglect of others. O that we were like the Lord in this, that we loved only that which is right, and abhorred that which is evil; that we kept along the straight and narrow path, and could not be decoyed from it, fearing not the frown of man nor courting his smile, but resolved as God lives in us that we will live in our daily actions according to his will. This would make Christians to be indeed a separated people, and this is precisely what their God would have them to be.

FOR MEDITATION: God commanded Israel to be different from all other nations (Leviticus 20:23), but this they failed to do in both the secular (1 Samuel 8:4–7,19–20) and the sacred (2 Kings 17:33). Christians ought to be aware of the threats posed by worldliness (Colossians 2:8,20; 2 Peter 2:20; 1 John 2:15–17) instead of trying to see how far they can go and still get away with being worldly.

SERMON NO. 1232

The ear bored with an awl

'And if the servant shall plainly say, I love my master, my wife, and my children; I will not go out free: Then his master shall bring him unto the judges; he shall also bring him to the door, or unto the door post; and his master shall bore his ear through with an aul; and he shall serve him for ever.' Exodus 21:5–6

SUGGESTED FURTHER READING (Spurgeon): John 6:60–71

This is a very memorable night to me. It was exactly twenty-four years ago that I put on the Lord Jesus Christ publicly in baptism, avowing myself to be his servant; I have served him since, and I think he says to me, 'You may go free if you will; I will not hold you in unwilling servitude.' He says the same to every one of you. There are plenty of places you can go; there are the world, the flesh and the devil. For a master you may choose any of these three. Jesus will not hold you against your will. Do you desire to go free from the yoke of Jesus? 'Blessed be his name,' I never wish to be free from his dear yoke. Rather would I say:—

'Oh, to grace how great a debtor, daily I'm constrained to be!
Let that grace, Lord, like a fetter, bind my wandering heart to thee.'

I wish to serve him not another four and twenty years, but four and twenty million years, and for ever and ever, for his yoke is easy and his burden is light. It is said, 'if they had been mindful of that country from whence they came out, they might have had opportunity to have returned.' And so have we, but will we return to the land of destruction? Will we go back into perdition? Will we renounce our Lord? No, by God's grace it cannot be! We are bound for the land of Canaan, and to Canaan we will go. Wandering hearts we have, but grace still holds them fast.

FOR MEDITATION: (*Our Own Hymn Book* no.663 v.2—James George Deck, 1837)
'I am Thine, and Thine alone, this I gladly, fully own;
And, in all my works and ways, only now would seek Thy praise.'

N.B. Spurgeon's testimony dates this undated sermon to the evening of 3 May 1874, exactly 24 years since his baptism at Isleham on 3 May 1850.

SERMON NO. 1174

The Lord chiding his people

'He will not always chide: neither will he keep his anger for ever.' Psalm
103:9
SUGGESTED FURTHER READING: Revelation 2:18–29

I believe our heavenly Father at times chides his people through church
discipline. I do not mean the discipline carried on by us through minister,
deacons and the church itself, but I refer to that solemn church discipline
which goes on in the churches and is often unobserved. Paul said of the
disorders in the Corinthian church, 'For this cause many are weak and
sickly among you, and many sleep. For if we would judge ourselves, we
should not be judged. But when we are judged, we are chastened of the
Lord, that we should not be condemned with the world.' Now, there is no
reason to believe that these visitations of the Lord upon the churches have
ceased; indeed I am persuaded they have not. I have seen those who have
walked inconsistently die one after another; when their inconsistencies
have not been such as I could touch, but such as have grieved the children
of God, the Lord has himself executed discipline. Many cases which I
shall never relate are written down in the tablets of my memory with this
verdict, 'Removed by the discipline of God.' I have seen others blighted in
fortune, chastened in body, and especially depressed in spirit as the result
of grieving the Spirit of God in the church. Church sins, such as injure
peace and unity, check zeal and enterprise, hinder prayer, or grieve holy
men, are surely visited with stripes. There is no need for us to root up the
tares, for the Spirit of God does it by his own processes. That same spirit
that was in Peter and smote Ananias and Sapphira is still in the church,
not destroying souls, but taking away life or health as a solemn discipline
upon grave offences beyond the reach of human jurisdiction.

FOR MEDITATION: Corinth was not the only New Testament church
facing such church discipline (1 Corinthians 5:3–5; 11:29–30). Most of
the seven churches in Revelation were warned that they would
experience the same (Revelation 2:16,22–23; 3:3,16,19); one even faced
the ultimate removal of its lampstand ('candlestick' KJV) altogether
(Revelation 2:5). When God judges his household (1 Peter 4:17), the
church needs to undergo serious self-examination. It's all too convenient
to blame the devil for all the problems encountered in church life.

Where true prayer is found

'Therefore hath thy servant found in his heart to pray this prayer unto thee.' 2 Samuel 7:27
SUGGESTED FURTHER READING: James 5:13–18

The spirit of prayer, though it is always present in every regenerated heart, is not always alike active. It is not perhaps today nor tomorrow that every Christian will be able to say, 'I find in my heart to pray this one particular prayer unto God'; it may for the present be beyond our standard of grace, and we may therefore be unable to grasp the blessing. In some respects we are not masters of our supplications. You cannot always pray the prayer of faith in reference to any one thing; that prayer is often the distinct gift of God for an occasion. Others may ask your prayers and sometimes you may plead very prevalently for them, but at another time that power is absent. You feel no liberty to offer a certain petition, but on the contrary feel held back in the matter. Well, be guided by this inward direction, and follow rather than press forward in such a case. There are times with us when we find it in our heart to pray a prayer, and then we do so with eagerness and assurance; but we cannot command such seasons at pleasure. How freely then does prayer come from us, as freely as the leaping water from the fountain; there is no need to say, 'I long to pray'; we do pray, we cannot help praying, we have become a mass of prayer. We are walking the streets and cannot pray aloud, but our heart pleads as fast as it beats; we enter our house and attend to family business, and still the heart keeps pleading as constantly as the lungs are heaving; we go to bed and our last thought is supplication; if we wake in the night still is our soul making intercession before God, and so it continues while the visitation remains. O that it were always so. Now it is a very happy thing when the Christian finds it in his heart to pray with marked and special fervour unto God.

FOR MEDITATION: It would be sinful to waste the opportunity when prayer seems to come easily to us (1 Samuel 2:1; Acts 1:14; Romans 10:1), but the fact that this is not always the case gives us no excuse to refrain from prayer when the going is tough (1 Samuel 1:10; Nehemiah 1:4; Luke 18:1; 22:40–46; Romans 8:26). As an old Minister used to say, 'See what hard hearted prayer will do.'

SERMON NO. 1412

Ecce Rex (or, Behold the King)

'He saith unto the Jews, Behold your King.' John 19:14
SUGGESTED FURTHER READING: Matthew 21:1–11

When you look at him you are struck at once with the thought that if he be a king he is like no other monarch, for other kings are covered with rich apparel and surrounded with pomp, but he has none of these. Their glories usually consist in wars by which they have made others suffer, but his glory is his own suffering; no blood but his own has flowed to make him illustrious. He is a king, but he cannot be put in the list of sovereigns such as the nations of the earth are compelled to serve. When Antoninus Pius set up the statue of Jesus in the Pantheon as one of a circle of gods and heroes, it must have seemed strangely out of place to those who gazed upon its visage if the sculptor was at all true to life. It must have stood apart as one that could not be numbered with the rest. Neither can you set him among the masters of the human race who have crushed mankind beneath their iron heel. He was no Caesar; you cannot make him appear like one: call him not autocrat, emperor or czar—he has an authority greater than all these, yet not after their kind. His purple is different from theirs, and his crown also, but his face differs more, and his heart most of all. 'My kingdom is not of this world', he said. For troops he has a host of sorrows, for pomp a surrounding of scorn, for lofty bearing humility, for adulation mockery, for homage spitting, for glory shame, and for a throne a cross. Yet was there never truer king; indeed all kings are but a name, save this King, who is a real ruler in himself and of himself, and not by extraneous force. Right royal indeed is the Nazarene, but he cannot be likened unto the princes of earth, nor can his kingdom be reckoned with theirs.

FOR MEDITATION: (*Our Own Hymn Book* no.282 v.3—Isaac Watts, 1709)
    'See from His head, His hands, His feet,
    Sorrow and love flow mingled down!
    Did e'er such love and sorrow meet,
    Or thorns compose so rich a crown!'

SERMON NO. 1353

Underneath

Underneath are the everlasting arms.' Deuteronomy 33:27
SUGGESTED FURTHER READING: Isaiah 40:9–11

God surrounds his children on all sides: they dwell in him. The passage before us (Deuteronomy 33:26–27) shows that the Lord is *above*, for we read, 'There is none like unto the God of Jeshurun, who rideth upon the heavens in thy help, and in his excellency on the sky.' Assuredly he is *around* them, for 'The eternal God is thy refuge'; and he is *before* them, for 'he shall thrust out the enemy from before thee; and shall say, Destroy them.' Here according to the text the Lord is also *under* his saints, for 'underneath are the everlasting arms'. 'LORD, thou hast been our dwelling-place in all generations', and by thee we are everywhere surrounded as the earth by the atmosphere. The verse which contains our text should be interpreted somewhat after this fashion: 'The eternal God is thy dwelling-place, or thy rest, and underneath are the everlasting arms.' The parallel passage is Song of Solomon 2:6 where the bride exclaims, 'His left hand is under my head, and his right hand doth embrace me.' The soul has come to its resting-place in God and feels itself to be supported by the divine strength. The heart has learned to abide in Christ Jesus to go no more out for ever, but to lean on him both day and night. It is somewhat in the condition of Noah's dove which, when weary, was about to drop into the all-destroying waters, but Noah put out his hand and plucked her in unto him into the ark; when she was all safe in the hollow of his hands, held by her preserver with a firm but tender grasp, she found in that place a refuge which surrounded her and upheld her from below. The hands covered her on all sides and came beneath her too. Even thus the hand of God sustains all those who dwell 'in the secret place of the most High' and 'abide under the shadow of the Almighty'.

FOR MEDITATION: (*Our Own Hymn Book* no.732 v.1—George Keith, 1787)
    'How firm a foundation, ye saints of the Lord,
    Is laid for your faith in His excellent word!
    What more can He say than to you He hath said,
    You who unto Jesus for refuge have fled?'

SERMON NO. 1413

All the people at work for Jesus

'Let not all the people go up.' Joshua 7:3
'Take all the people of war with thee.' Joshua 8:1
SUGGESTED FURTHER READING: Matthew 20:1–8

In the days of chivalry a certain band of knights had never known defeat. In all battles their name was terrible to the foe. On their banners was emblazoned a long list of victories; but in an evil hour the leader of the knights summoned them in chapter and said, 'My brethren, we cause ourselves too much toil. We have a band of skilled warriors versed in all the arts of battle; these are quite sufficient for ordinary conflicts, and it will be wise for the many if they tarry in the camp and rest, or furbish their weapons for extraordinary occasions. Let the champions go alone. Yonder knight with his sword can cleave a man in twain at a single stroke, and his comrade can break a bar of iron with his axe; others among us are equally powerful, each one being a host in himself. With the terror of our name behind them, the chosen champions can carry on the war while the rest divide the spoil.' The saying pleased the warriors well, but from that hour the knell of their fame was rung and defeat defiled their standard. When they came together they complained about the champions because they had not sustained the honour of the order, and they bade them exert themselves more heroically. They did so, but with small success. Louder and louder were the notes of discontent and the demands for new champions. Then one of the oldest of the knights said, 'Brethren, why do you blame us? The mistake lies here. In the old time, when the enemy assailed us, a thousand men were up in arms, and we who led the van knew that a gallant army followed at our heels. But now you have made us solitary champions, and the adversary takes heart to defy us, finding us unsustained. Come you all with us to the fray as aforetime, and none shall stand against us.' Brethren, you do not need anyone to interpret this to you.

FOR MEDITATION: Not only on the mission-field but also in many churches today the words of the Lord Jesus Christ still ring uncomfortably true—'The harvest truly is great, but the labourers are few' (Luke 10:2). Are you praying about it (Luke 10:2) and doing something about it (Luke 10:3) or simply ignoring it?

SERMON NO. 1358

Healing leaves

'The leaves of the tree were for the healing of the nations.' Revelation
22:2
SUGGESTED FURTHER READING: Deuteronomy 11:13–21

It is wonderful how little a thing may save a soul, if Christ be in it. 'A
verse may strike him whom a sermon flies,' and a picture on a wall may
awaken a train of thought in a man who would not listen to that same
thought if spoken in words. Remember Colonel Gardiner and his
remarkable conversion by looking at a picture of Christ upon the cross.
While waiting to fulfil an assignation of the most infamous kind, he saw
a picture of our dying Lord, and under it written, 'I did all this for thee;
what hast thou ever done for me?' The assignation was never kept, and
the colonel became a brave soldier for Jesus Christ. We may not think
well of representations of the crucifixion, which is a theme beyond the
painter's art, but there can be no question that it is our duty to set forth
Christ among the people by our speech, so that he may be seen by their
mind's eye, evidently crucified among them. Make the passing throng see
the gospel in every corner of the streets if you can. Paste up texts of
Scripture among business announcements; hang them up in your
kitchens, parlours and drawing-rooms. I hate to see Christians hang up
abominable Popish things because they happen to be works of art. Burn
every one of such artful prints or paintings, and pictures of saints, virgins
and the like, which tempt men to idolatry. Degrade not your houses by
anything which insults your God, but let your adornments be such as
may lead men's thoughts aright; never let a man say in hell, 'I was misled
by a work of art on your wall which was also a work of the devil and
suggested evil thoughts.' Everywhere bring Christ to the front and scatter
his words, like leaves from the tree.

FOR MEDITATION: Making and worshipping graven images was forbidden
by the Ten Commandments (Exodus 20:4–5) and soon provoked God's
wrath (Exodus 32:7–10); it still does (Romans 1:18–25). However, God's
plans for the Tabernacle included a visual role for models and pictures of
cherubim (Exodus 25:18–22; 26:1,31; Hebrews 9:5); extra features
appeared in Solomon's Temple (1 Kings 6:23–32; 7:29,36; 2 Chronicles
3:7–14). In Mark 12:13–17 we see Jesus using a picture as a visual aid.

SERMON NO. 1233

The Saviour you need

'And being made perfect, he became the author of eternal salvation unto all them that obey him.' Hebrews 5:9
SUGGESTED FURTHER READING (Spurgeon): Hebrews 7:23–28

Let me compare salvation to a book of which Jesus is the sole author. No one else has contributed a line or a thought to it. He has never asked any human mind to write a *preface* to his work; the first word is from his pen. Some of you are trying to preface Christ's work, but your toil is fruitless; he will never bind up your wretched introduction with his golden lines of love. Come to him without a preface, just as you are, steeped up to the throat in the foulness of sin. Come to him without previous preparation, and lay your heart's tablets before him that he may write thereon. He is an author so skilful that none have ever discovered the smallest *errata* in his work, for there are no mistakes, and no amendments are ever needed. When he saves he saves completely. He does not ask us to revise and perfect his writing; it is perfected by his own hand. He is an author to whose writing there are no *addenda;* 'It is finished', and he is accursed who shall add a line. We have to take the finished salvation and rejoice in it, but add to it we never may. Christ is an author who needs no man's *imprimatur;* he himself has dignity and authority enough to make his work illustrious without the patronage of man. Christ is the author of salvation. What you have to do, sinner, is to take it, not preface it, improve it, or add to it, but to take it just as it is. There it is for you; it is to be had for the taking; hold out your trembling hand and receive it: bring your empty cup, hold it under the divine fountain and let it be filled. Faith to accept it is all that is required. Why is it that you delay? You want to make yourself better before you believe in Jesus, that is to say, you want to be the author of salvation, and so to elbow Christ out of his place.

FOR MEDITATION: Scripture warns us against tampering with God's written word (Deuteronomy 4:2; Proverbs 30:5–6; Revelation 22:18–19). An even worse prospect awaits those who reject, oppose or tamper with the works of God's living Word (Hebrews 10:28–31; Revelation 19:11–16). God is perfectly able to start and finish the work of salvation without our interference (Philippians 1:6; Hebrews 12:2).

SERMON NO. 1172

Motives for stedfastness

'Therefore, my beloved brethren, be ye stedfast, unmoveable, always abounding in the work of the Lord, forasmuch as ye know that your labour is not in vain in the Lord.' 1 Corinthians 15:58
SUGGESTED FURTHER READING: Colossians 2:1–8

If ever there was a period in the Christian church when professors needed to be exhorted to be 'stedfast, unmoveable', it is just now, for the foundations are removed and all things are out of course. Men remove the old landmarks and break down the pillars of the house. All things reel to and fro and stagger like a drunken man, and only he who keeps the feet of the saints can preserve our uprightness. I see the tacklings loosed and the mast unstrengthened, and the brave vessel of the church is in an evil case. Many have left their moorings and are drifting hither and thither, their helmsmen all amazed. No longer does the squadron of the Lord sail in order of battle, but the lines are broken and the vessels yield to the tossings of winds and waves. Alas that it should be so. O where is he that trod the sea, the pilot of the Galilean lake? I see him walking the waters, and he cries to us who still stand true to the one Lord, the one faith and the one baptism, 'be ye stedfast, unmoveable'. Whatever other denominations of Christians do, be true to your Lord in all things, for those who forsake him shall be written in the dust. Never stir away from the truth! Some are changeable by constitution like Reuben—'unstable as water, thou shalt not excel'. A mind on wheels knows no rest; it is as a rolling thing before a tempest. Struggle against the desire for novelty, or it will lead you astray as the will-o'-the-wisp deceives the traveller. If you desire to be useful, if you long to honour God, if you wish to be happy, be established in the truth, and be not 'carried about with every wind of doctrine' in these evil days; 'be ye stedfast, unmoveable'.

FOR MEDITATION: Novelty is God's prerogative (Isaiah 42:9; 43:19; 48:6; 62:2; 65:17; 66:22; Jeremiah 31:31; Ezekiel 11:19; 36:26; John 13:34; 2 Corinthians 5:17–18; Hebrews 8:8; 9:15; 10:20; Revelation 21:5). Even the new song we sing has been placed in our mouths by God (Psalm 40:3). Our responsibility is to seek out and walk in the good old paths, even if it goes against our own wills (Jeremiah 6:16).

No difference

'He maketh his sun to rise on the evil and on the good, and sendeth rain on the just and on the unjust.' Matthew 5:45
SUGGESTED FURTHER READING: Isaiah 1:1–20

I heard the other day an instance of a dog's returning good for evil. A man had taken a large Newfoundland dog with the intention of drowning him. He went into a boat with a big stone, intending to throw the dog out of the boat into the stream with the stone about his neck. Somehow or other before he had securely tied the stone, the dog had become free and in some little scuffle between them the boat was upset and dog and man were both in the water. The man sank and was nearly drowned, but the dog, noble creature, swam up, seized hold of the man and drew him safely to shore. Now suppose he had drowned the dog after that! Did I hear some indignant person say, 'Let him be drowned himself'? He would not deserve to live, surely. I would take such a dog as that home and say, 'While I have a crust, there shall be a bit for you, good dog, who saved my life when I was destroying yours.' Now, if even a dog, when it renders good for evil, gets a claim upon us, what shall I say of the great God who with generous liberality continues to feed and keep in life and health the undeserving sons of men, and who, more than this, has given his own Son to die, and sent a message of amazing love to mankind, in which he says, 'Come to me: I am ready to forgive you. Come and accept my love and mercy. Let us be friends, for I delight to forgive sin'? Is it not clear that to abuse such love is black-hearted baseness? I beseech you, be not guilty of it.

FOR MEDITATION: God can take evil things and work them together for the good of those who love him (Genesis 50:20; Romans 8:28), but evil on our part can never be excused whether it is in response to God's goodness (Romans 2:4–9) or even if it eventually results in God's glory (Romans 3:5–8; 6:1–2).

Our Lord's question to the blind men

'And when Jesus departed thence, two blind men followed him, crying, and saying, Thou Son of David, have mercy on us. And when he was come into the house, the blind men came to him: and Jesus saith unto them, Believe ye that I am able to do this? They said unto him, Yea, Lord. Then touched he their eyes, saying, According to your faith be it unto you. And their eyes were opened.' Matthew 9:27–30
SUGGESTED FURTHER READING: Matthew 15:21–28

When a soul says to Jesus, 'I know thou canst save me, my Lord: therefore in thee do I trust,' he cannot shake him off and cannot wish to do so, for he has said, 'him that cometh to me I will in no wise cast out.' I sometimes tell a story to illustrate this; it is a simple tale, but it shows how faith wins everywhere. Many years ago my garden happened to be surrounded by a hedge, which looked green, but was a poor protection. A neighbour's dog was very fond of visiting my garden, and, as he never improved my flowers, I never gave him a cordial welcome. Walking along quietly one evening, I saw him doing mischief. I threw a stick at him and advised him to go home; but how did the good creature reply to me? He turned round, wagged his tail, and in the merriest manner picked up my stick, brought it to me and laid it at my feet. Did I strike him? No, I am not a monster. I should have been ashamed of myself if I had not patted him on the back and told him to come there whenever he liked. He and I were friends directly, because he trusted me and conquered me. Now, simple as the story is, that is just the philosophy of a sinner's faith in Christ. As the dog mastered the man by confiding in him, so a poor guilty sinner does, in effect, master the Lord himself by trusting him, when he says, 'Lord, I am a poor dog of a sinner, and thou mightest drive me away, but I believe thee to be too good for that. I believe thou canst save me and I trust myself with thee.' You will never be lost if you thus trust.

FOR MEDITATION: Read the amazing account of a people whose faith in God led him to deliver them from the judgment he was about to inflict upon them (Jonah 3:4–10). More than once Jesus allowed himself to be mastered by the faith of needy people (Matthew 8:10; 15:28). However unworthy you feel, you will not need to go as far as Job when he said, 'Though he slay me, yet will I trust in him' (Job 13:15).

SERMON NO. 1355

The unknown ways of love

'Jesus answered and said unto him, What I do thou knowest not now; but thou shalt know hereafter.' John 13:7
SUGGESTED FURTHER READING: John 11:1–16

I hope, dear brethren, our faith in Christ does not rest upon our capacity to understand what he does: if so, I fear it is not faith at all, but a mere exercise of self-conceited carnal reason. Some things which the Lord has done bear upon their very forefront the impress of his infinite love, but I hope you know enough of him now to be able to believe that where there are no traces of love apparent to you, his love is surely there. I rejoice in that part of my text which says, 'What I do'. This washing of the feet was not being done by Bartholomew or Nathanael: it was the personal act of the Lord himself. Now, when the Master and Lord is the actor, who wants to raise a question or to suggest enquiry? It must be right if he does it: to question his conduct would be an insult to his majestic love. Do you know Christ? Then you know the character of his deeds. Do you know your Lord? Then you are sure that he will never act unkindly, unbecomingly, or unwisely. He can never send a needless sorrow or wantonly cause a tear to flow, can he? Here, then, is the question, not why is it done, but who is doing it? If the Lord is doing it, we can have no doubt about the excellence of his design. We believe that he is right when we cannot see that he is so. If we do not trust him far beyond what we know, it will show that our confidence in him is very limited. When a person only obeys another because he chooses to obey and sees it a proper thing to do, he has not the spirit of implicit obedience at all; and when a person only confides in another as far as he can see that he is safe, he is a stranger to implicit confidence. Confidence has its sphere beyond the boundaries of knowledge: where judgment ceases, faith begins. 'What I do thou knowest not now.'

FOR MEDITATION: (*Our Own Hymn Book* no.689 v.2—Thomas Kelly, 1815)
'Though enwrapt in gloomy night,
We perceive no ray of light;
Since the Lord Himself is here,
'Tis not meet that we should fear.'

SERMON NO. 1293

How a man's conduct comes home to him

'The backslider in heart shall be filled with his own ways: and a good man shall be satisfied from himself.' Proverbs 14:14
SUGGESTED FURTHER READING (Spurgeon): John 15:1–11

Look at the backslider eating the fruit of his ways. He neglected prayer and when he tries to pray he cannot; his powers of desire, emotion, faith and entreaty have failed; he kneels, but cannot pray; the Spirit of supplications is grieved and no longer helps his infirmities. He reaches down his Bible and commences to read a chapter, but he has disregarded the word of God so long that he finds it more like a dead letter than a living voice, though it used to be a sweet book before he became a backslider. The minister, too, is altered; he used to hear him with delight; but now the poor preacher has lost all his early power, so the backslider thinks. Others do not think so, the place is just as crowded, there are as many saints edified and sinners saved as before, but the wanderer in heart began criticising, and now he is entangled in the habit and criticises everything, but never feeds upon the truth. Like a madman at table he puts his fork into the morsel, holds it up, looks at it, finds fault with it and throws it on the floor. Nor does he act better towards the saints in whose company he once delighted; they are dull society and he shuns them. Of all the things which bear upon his spiritual life he is weary; he has trifled with them and now cannot enjoy them. Hear him sing, or rather sigh—

'Thy saints are comforted, I know, and love Thy house of prayer;
I sometimes go where others go, but find no comfort there.'

How can it be otherwise? He is drinking water out of his own cistern and eating bread of which he sowed the corn some years ago. His ways have come home to him.

FOR MEDITATION: (*Our Own Hymn Book* no.809 v.5—John S.B.Monsell, 1863)
'My sun is, Lord, where'er Thou art,
My cloud, where self I see,
My drought in an ungrateful heart,
My freshest springs in Thee!'

SERMON NO. 1235

Messrs Moody and Sankey defended; or, a vindication of the doctrine of justification by faith

'They that are Christ's have crucified the flesh with the affections and lusts.' Galatians 5:24
SUGGESTED FURTHER READING: Revelation 1:4–18

'He was wounded for our transgressions, he was bruised for our iniquities: the chastisement of our peace was upon him; and with his stripes we are healed.' Yet he loved us still. Many waters could not quench his love, neither could the floods drown it. When they nailed him to the tree, he loved us still. When he cried in sad soliloquy, 'I am poured out like water, and all my bones are out of joint', he loved us still. When dogs compassed him and 'bulls of Bashan' beset him round, he loved us still. When dread faintness came upon him till he was brought into the dust of death, and his heart melted like wax in the midst of his bowels, he loved us still. When God forsook him, the sun was blotted out, midnight darkness covered the midday, and a denser darkness like that of Egypt, which might be felt, veiled his spirit, he loved us still. Till he had drunk the last dregs of the unutterably bitter cup, he loved us still. When he could say, 'It is finished', the light shone on a face that loved us still. Every man who believes in Jesus and knows his love, says, 'How can I offend him? How can I grieve him? There are actions in this life in which I might otherwise indulge, but I dare not now, for I fear to vex my Lord.' And if you say, 'Dare not? Are you afraid of him?' the answer will be, 'I am not slavishly afraid, for into hell I can never go. What am I afraid of, then? I am afraid of that dear face, on which I see the gutterings of tears which he once shed for me. I am afraid of that dear brow which wore the thorn-crown for me; I cannot rebel against such kindness; his bleeding love enchains me. How can I do so great a wickedness as to put my dying Lord to shame?' Do you not feel this?

FOR MEDITATION: (*Our Own Hymn Book* no.278 v.5—Frederick William Faber, 1849)
   'A broken heart, a fount of tears ask, and they will not be denied;
   Lord Jesus, may we love and weep, since Thou for us art crucified.'

N.B. This sermon gave support to Moody and Sankey's London campaign. See 6 June.

SERMON NO. 1239

'I thought'

'I thought.' 2 Kings 5:11
SUGGESTED FURTHER READING: Isaiah 55:6–11

There are a great many things which men can discover, and the inventiveness of the human mind about earthly things appears to have scarcely any limit; but, with regard to heavenly things the natural man has not the faculty of discerning, never made a discovery yet and never will. Whatever is known of God is made known by God. Upon the face of nature the existence of God is written, but we look in vain for any indication of a plan of salvation. Jesus alone is the Saviour; how can you imagine that his way of saving can be known to men except as he has revealed it? I will ask you a question. Suppose you were sick of a mysterious and fatal disorder and a skilful physician was recommended to you, would you expect to foresee that physician's mode of action? Would you go to him and then hesitate to accept his advice because it was contrary to what you had supposed it would be? If so, I can only say that you must be very foolish to go to a physician at all. Why not heal yourself? Your case is complicated, and here is a surgeon who, by long experience and wonderful skill, has acquired power to deal with your disorder. Do you insist upon it that he shall only operate as you approve? Is he to use knife, lancet, band and splint at your dictation? If so, you had better dispense with him and call in a nurse who has never studied the art, but is quite able to do your bidding, for you are surgeon to yourself. Unconverted friend, your case is one in which you cannot help yourself, and none but Jesus can save you. How can you expect to invent for yourself a plan of salvation? You are bidden to become Christ's disciple—do you expect to know more than your Master? Are you to teach him, or is he to teach you?

FOR MEDITATION: Access to God and to salvation depends not upon what we think, but upon what God has said and done. Our sincerest thoughts, if they are out of line with God's word, are sincerely wrong. Consider some of the situations where incorrect thoughts can continue to separate us from God (Matthew 6:7; John 5:39–40; Acts 8:20).

SERMON NO. 1173

Soul-satisfying bread

'And Jesus said unto them, I am the bread of life: he that cometh to me shall never hunger; and he that believeth on me shall never thirst.' John 6:35
SUGGESTED FURTHER READING: 1 Corinthians 1:23–2:2

All believers bear witness that Jesus Christ is satisfying bread to them. When do you get most satisfied on a Sunday? I do not know whom you may happen to hear, but what Sabbath days are the best to you? When your minister rides the high horse and gives you a splendid oration, and you say, 'Dear me, it is wonderful,' have you ever felt satisfied to think it over on the Monday? Have you ever felt satisfied with sermons composed of politics and morality, or very nice essays which would suit the *Saturday Review* if they were a little more caustic? Do you enjoy such meat? I will tell you when I enjoy a Sunday most—when I preach Christ most, or when I can sit and hear a humble village preacher exalt the Lord Jesus. It does not matter if the grammar is spoilt as long as Jesus is there. What some call platitudes are dainties to me if they glorify my Lord Jesus Christ. Anything about him is satisfying to a renewed spirit—cannot you bear witness to that? Sometimes when I have preached up Jesus Christ— and I think I generally do so, for the fact is I do not know anything but him, and I am 'determined not to know any thing among you, save Jesus Christ, and him crucified'—I know you go away and say, 'That is what we want—Christ crucified, Christ the sinner's substitutionary sacrifice, no sham Christ, no mere talk about Christ as an example, but his flesh and blood, a dying, bleeding, suffering Christ: that is what we want.' Now I have the witness of every Christian here to that! You are never satisfied with anything but that, are you? No matter how cleverly the doctrine might be analysed, or however orthodox it might be, you cannot be content with it; you must have the person of Christ, the flesh and the blood of Christ, or else you are not content.

FOR MEDITATION: Preaching Christ may annoy others (Acts 4:1–2; 1 Corinthians 1:23), but this could not deter the apostles (Acts 5:40–42). When Christ is preached out of a sense of privilege (Ephesians 3:8) and love (Philippians 1:15–16), it is bound to prove a blessing to God's people (Romans 16:25; 1 Corinthians 1:23–24). What effect does hearing Christ preached have upon you?

SERMON NO. 1112

Great difference

'Where is the God of judgment?' Malachi 2:17
'Then shall ye return, and discern between the righteous and the wicked, between him that serveth God and him that serveth him not.' Malachi 3:18
SUGGESTED FURTHER READING: Isaiah 65:11–19

When Christ the Sun of righteousness shall arise upon the earth and gild it with his own light, there shall be a new heaven and a new earth; the righteous shall go forth and leap for joy, like cattle which had been penned in the stall. No works of the ungodly shall be left. They shall be utterly gone. There shall be no tavern songs or ale-house ribaldry, no village profligate around whom shall gather the youth to be led away by his libidinous and blasphemous words, no shameless reviler who shall provide a hall where blasphemers may congregate to see who can utter the blackest profanities against the Lord of hosts, no shrine of virgin or saint, no idol, image or crucifix. Superstition shall be swept away. There shall be no congregations where pretended preachers of the gospel shall deal out new philosophies and suggest newly-invented scepticisms, which they hoped men would accept as new, though they were the old errors of the past picked off the dunghill upon which they had been thrown by disgusted ages. Sin shall all be gone and not a trace of it shall be left, but here shall dwell righteousness and peace; the meek shall inherit the earth, and the saints shall stand each one in his lot, for the Lord himself shall reign amongst them gloriously. From every hill and vale shall come up the one song of glory unto the Most High and every heart shall magnify his name, who at last has answered the question, 'Where is the God of judgment?' Then, cast into hell, in the place appointed for the devil and his angels, the ungodly shall never ask again, 'Where is the God of judgment?' Saints triumphant in their Lord, with whom they shall reign for ever in eternity, shall perceive that he discerns 'between the righteous and the wicked, between him that serveth God and him that serveth him not.' Beloved hearer, where will you be on that day?

FOR MEDITATION: We can rejoice in the exclusion of sin from heaven (Luke 12:33; Revelation 21:27; 22:3) as long as we are not still among those who will be excluded along with it (1 Corinthians 6:9–10; Ephesians 5:5; Revelation 21:8).

SERMON NO. 1415

The Father's will

'And this is the Father's will which hath sent me, that of all which he hath given me I should lose nothing, but should raise it up again at the last day. And this is the will of him that sent me, that every one which seeth the Son, and believeth on him, may have everlasting life; and I will raise him up at the last day.' John 6:39–40
SUGGESTED FURTHER READING: Jonah 3:1–10

Never fear that there is anything in the secret purposes of God which can contradict the open promises of God. Never dream, if you are a believer, that there can be any dark decree that shuts you out from the benefits of grace. Decrees or no decrees, 'this is the will of him that sent me, that every one which seeth the Son, and believeth on him, may have everlasting life'. Therefore, lay hold on Christ with all your heart, poor sinner; ask not to know whether your name is in the Book of Life; come just as you are, by God's own invitation. The woman in the crowd could not tell whether it was written in the book of the decrees that she should be healed, but she came behind the Saviour, touched the hem of his garment and was made whole. The dying thief did not stop to enquire, 'Was I chosen by God before time began?' but said, 'Lord, remember me when thou comest into thy kingdom.' In like manner act upon your present need and fit your prayer to the present opportunity. The doctrine of decrees never operates upon a man's ordinary life. What hungry man would hesitate or say, 'I cannot tell whether it is the purpose of God that I should eat'? When the provision is spread out before him he eats. Would the weary man vex his soul with misgivings and say, 'I want to know whether it is the purpose of God that I should sleep'? He acts like a sensible creature and goes to his bed at the time of rest, grateful for the interval of deep repose that can renew his strength and freshen up his vital powers. Go and do likewise. Do not rebel at the purposes or deny them, but act upon the precepts and rejoice in them; they are the guide for you. Rely upon the promises.

FOR MEDITATION: Meditate on Deuteronomy 29:29. Although we cannot understand God's secret purposes, we have no right to deny their existence or to use them as an excuse for disobeying his commandments or for disbelieving his promises.

SERMON NO. 1117

The anchor

'God, willing more abundantly to shew unto the heirs of promise the immutability of his counsel, confirmed it by an oath: that by two immutable things, in which it was impossible for God to lie, we might have a strong consolation, who have fled for refuge to lay hold upon the hope set before us: which hope we have as an anchor of the soul, both sure and stedfast.' Hebrews 6:17–19

SUGGESTED FURTHER READING: Luke 1:67–75

Anchor-making is very important work. The anchor-smith has a very responsible business, for if he makes the anchor badly or of weak material, woe to the shipmaster when the storm comes on. Anchors are not made of cast iron, nor of every kind of metal that comes to hand, but of wrought iron, strongly welded, and of tough, compact material, which will bear all the strain that is likely to come upon it at the worst of times. If anything should be strong, it should be an anchor, for upon it safety and life often depend. What is our anchor? It has two great blades or flukes to it, each of which acts as a holdfast. It is made of two divine things. One is God's *promise*, a sure and stable thing indeed. We are very ready to take a good man's promise, but perhaps he may forget to fulfil it, or is unable to do so: neither of these things can occur with the Lord; he cannot forget or fail to do as he has said. Jehovah's promise, what a certain thing it must be! If you had nothing but the Lord's bare word to trust, surely your faith should never stagger. To this sure word is added another divine thing, namely God's *oath*. I scarcely dare speak upon this sacred topic. God's oath, his solemn assertion, his swearing by himself! Conceive the majesty, awe and certainty of this! Here are two divine assurances, which like the flukes of the anchor hold us fast. Who dares to doubt the promise of God? Who can have the audacity to distrust his oath?

FOR MEDITATION: (*Our Own Hymn Book* no.632 vv.2 & 3—William Williams, 1772; Charles H. Spurgeon, 1866)

'Let Satan and the world, now rage or now allure;
The promises in Christ are made immutable and sure.'
The oath infallible is now my spirit's trust;
I know that He who spake the word, is faithful, true, and just.'

All things are ready. Come.

'Come, for all things are now ready.' Luke 14:17
SUGGESTED FURTHER READING: Matthew 22:1–10

Notice the word 'now'—'all things are now ready', just now, at this moment. At feasts the good housewife is often troubled if the guests come late. She would be sorry if they came half-an-hour too soon, but half-an-hour too late spoils everything; in what a state of fret and worry she is if, when 'all things are now ready', her friends still delay. Leave food at the fire awhile, and it does not seem to be 'now ready', but something more than ready and even spoiled. So does the great householder lay stress upon this—'all things are now ready', therefore come at once. He does not say that, if you wait another seven years, all things will then be ready: God grant that long before that space of time you may have got beyond the needs of persuasion by having become a taster of the feast, but he does say that they are all ready now. Just now that your heart is so heavy, your mind so careless and your spirit so wandering, all things are ready now. Just now, though you have never thought of these things before, yet 'all things are now ready'. Though your sins are as the stars of heaven, and your soul trembles under an awful foreboding of coming judgment, yet 'all things are now ready'. After all your rejections of Christ, after the many invitations that have been thrown away upon you, come to the supper. And if they are ready now, the argument is come now, while all things are still ready. While the Spirit lingers and strives with men, while mercy's gates still stand wide open, that 'whosoever will may come', while life, health and reason are still spared to you and the ministering voice that bids you come can still be heard, come now, come at once—all things are ready—come!

FOR MEDITATION: (*Our Own Hymn Book* no.504 v.5—Albert Midlane, 1862)

"'All things are ready," Come,
To-morrow may not be;
O sinner, come, the Saviour waits,
This hour to welcome thee!'

SERMON NO. 1354

The best house-visitation

'They entered into the house of Simon and Andrew, with James and John. But Simon's wife's mother lay sick of a fever, and anon they tell him of her. And he came and took her by the hand, and lifted her up; and immediately the fever left her, and she ministered unto them.' Mark 1:29–31

SUGGESTED FURTHER READING: John 1:35–42

If you are yourself saved, you should inquire, 'To what house may I become a messenger of salvation?' Perhaps you have no family of your own; I do not know whether Andrew had: he seems at the time of this narrative to have lived in a part of the same house as Peter: possibly they each had a house at Bethsaida, which was their own city, and lived together when they went on business to Capernaum. Perhaps Andrew had no wife and no children. If so, I feel sure that he said to himself, 'I must seek the good of my brother and his family.' I believe, if we are really lively and thoughtful Christians, our conversion is an omen for good to all our kinsfolk. We shall not idly say, 'I should have looked after my own children and household, if I had owned any, but having none I am excused'; rather we shall consider ourselves to be debtors to those who are kindred householders. Uncles and aunts should feel an interest in the spiritual condition of nephews and nieces; cousins should be concerned for cousins, and all ties of blood should be consecrated by being used for purposes of grace. Moses, when he led the people out of Egypt, would not let a 'hoof be left behind', nor ought we to be content to leave one kinsman a slave to sin. Abraham in his old age took up sword and buckler for his nephew Lot, and aged believers should seek the good of the most distant members of their families; if it were always so, the power of the gospel would be felt far and wide. The household of which Peter was master might never have known the gospel if a relative had not been converted.

FOR MEDITATION: It was no coincidence that there were two pairs of brothers amongst the twelve apostles (Matthew 10:2) and another group in the early church (Acts 1:14; 1 Corinthians 9:5; Jude 1). Contrast Paul's spiritual concern for his own people (Romans 9:3–4; 10:1) with the elder brother's selfish indifference to his prodigal brother (Luke 15:28–30). How concerned are you for your relatives?

SERMON NO. 1236

Stephen's death

'And they stoned Stephen, calling upon God, and saying, Lord Jesus, receive my spirit. And he kneeled down, and cried with a loud voice, Lord, lay not this sin to their charge. And when he had said this, he fell asleep.' Acts 7:59–60
SUGGESTED FURTHER READING: Acts 21:7–14

Some, if they were going off by train and knew a month beforehand, would be all in a fever an hour before they started; though they know the time the train starts, they cannot arrive a few minutes before, but rush in just as the bell rings and leap into the carriage just in time to catch the train. Some die in that fashion, as if they had so much to do and were in such a hurry, and had so little grace that they could only be saved 'so as by fire'. When worldly Christians die, there is a deal to be done to pack up and get ready for departing, but a true Christian stands with his loins girded; he knows he has to travel; he does not know exactly when, but he stands with his staff in his hand. He knows the Bridegroom is soon coming, and therefore keeps his lamp well trimmed. That is the way to live and the way to die. May the Holy Spirit put us in such a condition, that the angel of death may not summon us unawares or catch us by surprise; then going home will be nothing out of the common, but a simple matter. Bengel, the famous commentator, did not wish to die in spiritual parade with a sensational scene, but to pass away like a person called to the street door from the midst of business. His prayer was granted. He was revising the proof sheets of his works almost to the moment when he felt the death stroke. Equally desirable was the end of the Venerable Bede, who died as he completed his translation of the gospel of John. 'Write quickly,' said he, 'for it is time for me to return to him who made me.' 'Dear master,' said the pupil, 'one sentence is still wanting.' 'Write quickly,' said the venerable man. The young man soon added, 'It is finished'; Bede replied, 'Thou hast well said; all is now finished,' and fell asleep. So would we desire to depart.

FOR MEDITATION: (*Our Own Hymn Book* no.853 v.1—Isaac Watts, 1709)
    'Father, I long, I faint to see
    The place of Thine abode;
    I'd leave Thy earthly courts, and flee
    Up to Thy seat, my God!'

SERMON NO. 1175

Onward!

'Brethren, I count not myself to have apprehended: but this one thing I do, forgetting those things which are behind, and reaching forth unto those things which are before, I press toward the mark for the prize of the high calling of God in Christ Jesus.' Philippians 3:13–14

SUGGESTED FURTHER READING: Hosea 14:1–9

The condition in which a believer should always be found is that of progress: his motto must be, 'Onward and upward!' Nearly every figure by which Christians are described in the Bible implies this. We are plants of the Lord's field, but we are sown that we may grow—'first the blade, then the ear, after that the full corn in the ear.' We are born into the family of God, but there are babes, little children, young men and fathers in Christ Jesus; and there are a few who are perfect or fully developed men in Christ Jesus. It is a growth evermore. Is a Christian described as a pilgrim? He is no pilgrim who sits down as if rooted to the place. 'They go from strength to strength'. The Christian is compared to a warrior, a wrestler, a competitor in the games: these figures are the very opposite of a condition in which nothing more is to be done. They imply energy, the gathering up of strength and the concentration of forces, in order to overthrow adversaries. The Christian is also likened to a runner in a race, and that is the figure now before us in the text. It is clear that a man cannot be a runner who merely holds his ground, contented with his position: he only runs aright who each moment nears the mark. Progress is the healthy condition of every Christian; and he only realises his best estate while he is growing in grace, adding 'to faith virtue', following 'on to know the Lord', and daily receiving grace for grace out of the fulness which is treasured up in Christ Jesus. Now to this progress the apostle exhorts us.

FOR MEDITATION: Two important lessons are to be learned from the apostle Paul's attitude towards progress in the Christian lives of those to whom he wrote. He did not neglect to express gratitude to God for their progress thus far, but would add to this a desire for his readers not to rest content, but to advance further still (Philippians 1:3–11; Colossians 1:3–10; 1 Thessalonians 3:6–4:1,9–10).

SERMON NO. 1114

Choice comfort for a young believer

'The LORD *will perfect that which concerneth me: thy mercy, O* LORD, *endureth for ever: forsake not the works of thine own hands.' Psalm 138:8*
SUGGESTED FURTHER READING (Spurgeon): Romans 8:28–39

I want you young friends especially, who are just beginning life, to feel, 'Now, I am going to put myself and all my temporal circumstances, all my fears, all my engagements, my living, my dying, into the hand of God, and there I am going to leave it. I will trust him with my all. In the beginning I will trust him, and I will do so even to the end, and go my way with this calm confidence, "The LORD will perfect that which concerneth me: thy mercy, O LORD, endureth for ever".' I remember hearing one of our evangelists once say that some Christian people, when they first profess to be Christians, are like a man who is going a long distance by rail, but only takes a ticket for a short distance; he then has to get out and make a rush for new tickets as he goes along. 'Now,' said he, 'there are other believers who know better and take a ticket all the way through at the first, which is by far the wiser way.' Some trust the Lord to keep them for a quarter of a year and others for a month, but when I believed in Christ Jesus, I thank his name, I trusted him to save me to the end. I sought for and obtained a finished salvation, which is my joy and hope at this moment. I took a ticket all the way through and I have not had to get a fresh ticket yet. I have sometimes thought I should, but when I have run to the ticket office, they have handed me back my old ticket, the one I lost, the same one as before, and I knew it to be the same, for it bore this stamp upon it—'He that believeth and is baptized shall be saved'. The believer is saved at first by believing, and he shall be so to the last.

FOR MEDITATION: (*Our Own Hymn Book* no.243 v.1—William Hammond, 1745)
'O my distrustful heart,
How small thy faith appears!
But greater, Lord, Thou art
Than all my doubts and fears:
Did Jesus once upon me shine?
Then Jesus is for ever mine.'

SERMON NO. 1506

The heavenly wind

'The wind bloweth where it listeth, and thou hearest the sound thereof, but canst not tell whence it cometh, and whither it goeth: so is every one that is born of the Spirit.' John 3:8
SUGGESTED FURTHER READING: Romans 9:14–24

The Holy Spirit is God himself, absolutely free, and works according to his own will and pleasure amongst the sons of men. One nation has been visited by the Holy Spirit and not another—who shall tell me why? Why do heathen lands lie in dense darkness while on Britain the light is concentrated? Why has the Reformation taken root in England and among the northern nations of Europe, while in Spain and Italy it has left scarce a trace? Why blows the Holy Spirit here and not there? Is it not that he does as he wills? 'I will have mercy on whom I will have mercy, and I will have compassion on whom I will have compassion' is the declaration of the divine sovereignty, and the Spirit of God in his movements confirms it. Among the nations where the Spirit of God is at work how is it that he blesses one and not another? How is it that of two men hearing the same sermon and subject to the same influences at home, one is taken and the other left? Two children, nursed and trained by the same parents, grow up to different ends. He who perishes in sin has no one to blame but himself, but he who is saved ascribes it all to grace—why came that grace to him? We never dare to lay upon God the fault of man's not repenting and believing—that rests with the evil will which refused to obey the gospel; but we dare not ascribe to any natural goodness the saving difference in the case of the one who believes, but we attribute it all to the grace of God, and believe that the Holy Spirit works in such 'to will and to do of his good pleasure'. But why works he in any of the chosen? 'The wind bloweth where it listeth'.

FOR MEDITATION: (*Our Own Hymn Book* no.448 vv.2&3—Isaac Watts, 1709)
'The sovereign will of God alone creates us heirs of grace;
Born in the image of His Son, a new peculiar race.
The Spirit, like some heavenly wind, blows on the sons of flesh;
Creates a new—a heavenly mind, and forms the man afresh.'

SERMON NO. 1356

Gone. Gone for ever

'And as thy servant was busy here and there, he was gone.' 1 Kings 20:40
SUGGESTED FURTHER READING (Spurgeon): Luke 19:12–26

Is it not a sad thing to have neglected that which is evidently the main business of life? If I am God's creature, I must have been meant to serve God, and if I have not served him, even as a creature, I have not done what I was meant for; but if I profess to be a Christian, then the thing assumes a more solemn form. Have I professed to be bought with Jesus' blood, and have I lived as if I were my own? I profess to be filled with the Spirit of God by being regenerated—have I lived like one who has been born again? If I have been baptized upon a profession of my faith, I gave myself up to be buried in the water professing that I was dead to the world—have I been dead to the world? I said that I was going to live in newness of life as one risen from the dead—have I so lived? Professing Christians, have you been true to your professions, or have those professions been only lies? Conscience, answer me, I charge you! O Spirit of God, quicken conscience in every one here present, so that none may 'be hardened through the deceitfulness of sin'. To serve God is the only thing worth living for; when we lie upon the sick bed and begin to look into the future, we judge it to be so. It makes a good man greedy to serve God when he thinks that his life will soon be over. He condemns himself for every wasted hour and laments that his every faculty has not been spurred to the uttermost in the service of him who bought him with his blood. I never yet heard regrets from dying men that they had done too much for Christ, or lived too earnestly for him, or won too many souls, or given too much of their substance to the cause of God: but the regrets all lie the other way. God save us from them for his mercy's sake.

FOR MEDITATION: (*Our Own Hymn Book* no.769 v.1—Augustus M.Toplady, 1759)
> 'Emptied of earth I fain would be,
> Of sin, myself, and all but Thee;
> Only reserved for Christ that died,
> Surrendered to the Crucified.'

SERMON NO. 1296

The faithful saying

'This is a faithful saying, and worthy of all acceptation, that Christ Jesus came into the world to save sinners; of whom I am chief.' 1 Timothy 1:15
SUGGESTED FURTHER READING: Luke 18:9–14

Salvation must be for sinners, for to them only can mercy ever come. If I am brought before a court of justice and plead 'Not guilty,' and the magistrate replies that he will have mercy upon me, I repel his observation with indignation; I want no mercy of him; I am innocent. Let him give me justice; that is all I ask. It is an insult to the innocent to offer him mercy; therefore, unless man is guilty, God cannot show him mercy. Mercy has no room to bestow her blessings of amnesty and pardon till first of all guilt is admitted. To the sinner forgiveness can come, but to none else. Moreover, the characters whom Jesus came to save are always so described that they must be sinners. Sometimes we read of them as being 'dead in trespasses and sins', and it is written, 'And you hath he quickened'. Sometimes they are represented as enemies: 'when we were enemies, we were reconciled to God by the death of his Son'. They are aliens, strangers, wandering sheep, prodigal sons, and so forth; all these imply distance from God by sin. Sometimes they are represented as debtors; when they have nothing to pay, he freely forgives them all their debt. All the descriptions of persons for whom the mercy of God is intended bear upon their forefront the notion of their being sinners; our Lord himself said, 'I came not to call the righteous, but sinners to repentance.' The coming of Christ has no bearing towards the ninety-and-nine that went not astray, except that they are left where they were. The Good Shepherd comes after the lost sheep and only the lost sheep, and if you can prove that you are not a lost sheep, then you have proved that Christ never came to save you. The whole of his errand looks this way; he came to save sinners and only sinners.

FOR MEDITATION: (*Our Own Hymn Book* no.241 v.4—Isaac Watts, 1709)
  ''Twas mercy filled the throne,
  And wrath stood silent by,
  When Christ was sent with pardons down
  To rebels doomed to die.'

How they conquered the dragon

'They overcame him by the blood of the Lamb, and by the word of their testimony; and they loved not their lives unto the death.' Revelation 12:11

SUGGESTED FURTHER READING: Hebrews 13:10–21

If you and I are ever to be amongst these victors, the blood must be our own, appropriated by faith. How is it with you? Has the blood cleansed you? Does the blood dwell in you as your life? Has the blood of the Lamb given you fellowship with God and brought you near? If so, you are on the way to overcoming 'by the blood'. The blood of the Lamb, according to the verse which precedes the text, had given them all they needed, for it gave them *salvation.* They were saved, completely saved. Jesus Christ, when they laid hold upon him and felt the power of his blood, redeemed them from all iniquity and translated them from the kingdom of Satan. Then they received *strength:* note that word. They had been dead, but they obtained life; they had been weak, but they were made strong in the Lord, for he who knows the power of the blood of Jesus is made strong to do great exploits. Then they obtained the *kingdom,* for the kingdom comes to us by the way of the conquering blood of Jesus, and he 'hast made us unto our God kings and priests' because he was slain. We are also told that they had *power,* or authority. Our Lord, who has risen from the dead, clothed all his disciples with authority when he said, 'All power is given unto me in heaven and in earth. Go ye therefore, and teach all nations, baptizing them.' If we have participated in the blood of Jesus Christ, I hope we feel it to be all these four things to us—salvation from sin, strength out of weakness, a kingdom in fellowship with Christ, and authority to speak in his name. It is the blood of the covenant, and it secures all the covenant gifts of God to us.

FOR MEDITATION: Are you enjoying these four blessings secured by the blood of the Lord Jesus Christ for all who trust in him—salvation from sin (Romans 3:25: 5:8–9; Ephesians 1:7; 1 John 1:7; Revelation 1:5); strength out of weakness (Hebrews 9:14; 13:20–21); a kingdom in fellowship with Christ (Revelation 1:5–6; 5:9–10); authority to speak in his name (Hebrews 10:19–23; 13:12–15)?

The eternal day

*'Thy sun shall no more go down; neither shall thy moon withdraw itself:
for the* LORD *shall be thine everlasting light, and the days of thy
mourning shall be ended.' Isaiah 60:20*
SUGGESTED FURTHER READING: Revelation 21:22–22:5

Some have thought the joy of heaven would lie in knowledge; they shall
have it. Others have rejoiced in the prospect of continued service; they
shall have it and 'serve him day and night in his temple'. I know not if I
be idle, but the sweetest thought of heaven to me is rest, and I shall have
it, for 'There remaineth therefore a rest to the people of God'. Peace! O
quiet soul, do you not long for it? You shall have it. Security and a sense
of calm! O, tempest-tossed one, you shall have them. Strength, power—
some have wished for that. You shall be raised in power. Fulness, the
filling up of every vacuum! You shall have it and 'be filled with all the
fulness of God'. I am a long way out of my depth now, but I am not
afraid of sinking here; I shall never exaggerate; the joys of heaven are
ecstatic, so that if we knew anything of them at this moment, we should
be like Paul, who said, 'whether in the body, I cannot tell; or whether out
of the body, I cannot tell: God knoweth.' Ecstatic—that is standing right
out of yourself; that will be your condition; you will get away from
yourself altogether and be 'Plunged in the Godhead's deepest sea, and
lost in his immensity'. It will be a rapture, as it were, a snatching away of
yourself; like the chariots of Amminadib shall be the joys into which you
shall be uplifted and borne away. We shall know all about it before long,
some of us, so there is not much need to attempt a premature
description. When the Lord is the light, who knows how bright the light
must be? And when the Lord is the Lamb, and the Lamb is the Lord, and
the Lord and the Lamb are at once the light, who knows how sweet, how
lovely that eternal light must be?

FOR MEDITATION: (*Our Own Hymn Book* no.874 v.4—Samuel Stennett,
1787)
　'All o'er those wide extended plains,
　Shines one eternal day;
　There God the Sun for ever reigns,
　And scatters night away.'

SERMON NO. 1176

The good shepherdess

'Tell me, O thou whom my soul loveth, where thou feedest, where thou makest thy flock to rest at noon; for why should I be as one that turneth aside by the flocks of thy companions? If thou know not, O thou fairest among women, go thy way forth by the footsteps of the flock, and feed thy kids beside the shepherds' tents.' Song of Solomon 1:7–8
SUGGESTED FURTHER READING: Ephesians 5:1–15

You want to get to Jesus and to bring those under your charge to him. Very well, then, do not seek out a new road, but simply go the way which all other saints have gone. If you want to walk with Jesus, walk where other saints have walked; if you want to lead others into communion with him, lead them by your example where others have gone. What is that? If you want to be with Jesus, go where Abraham went in the path of *separation*. See how he lived as a pilgrim and a sojourner with his God. If you would see Jesus, 'Come out from among them, and be ye separate … and touch not the unclean thing'. You shall find Jesus when you have left the world. If you would walk with Jesus, follow the path of *obedience*. Saints have never had fellowship with Jesus when they have disobeyed him. Keep his statutes and observe his testimonies; be jealous over your conduct and character, for the path of obedience is the path of communion. Be sure that you follow the ancient ways with regard to the Christian ordinances: do not alter them, but keep to the good old paths. Stand and enquire what apostles did, and do the same. Jesus will not bless you in using fanciful ceremonies of human invention. Keep to those which he commands, which his Spirit sanctions, and which his apostles practised. Above all, if you would walk with Jesus, continue in the way of *holiness;* persevere in the way of grace. Make the Lord Jesus your model and example; and by treading where the footprints of the flock are to be seen, 'thou shalt both save thyself, and them that hear thee'. You shall find Jesus, and they shall find Jesus too.

FOR MEDITATION: The Christian's walk should be characterised by separation (Ephesians 5:7–8), obedience (Ephesians 2:10; 2 John 6) and holiness (Romans 13:13: Ephesians 4:17). Never develop a rebellious attitude towards this, for great blessings surround this pathway alone (Psalm 1:1–3).

SERMON NO. 1115

'Thy salvation'

'Then took he up in his arms, and blessed God, and said, Lord, now lettest thou thy servant depart in peace, according to thy word: for mine eyes have seen thy salvation.' Luke 2:28–30
SUGGESTED FURTHER READING: Ecclesiastes 12:1–7

It is a great blessing to the aged man to have Jesus in his arms. Though he shall be compelled by the infirmities of age to ask with Barzillai, 'Can thy servant taste what I eat or what I drink?' yet he shall find great sweetness in the bread of heaven, and the name of Jesus shall be as 'wines on the lees well refined'. If, through age and infirmity, he cannot 'hear any more the voice of singing men and singing women', he that has Christ has music in his heart for ever. In old age Solomon tells us that 'the grasshopper shall be a burden,' but this child is none. Then the sun, the light, the moon and the stars are darkened, but this child gives light to all who see him. Then 'the keepers of the house shall tremble,' but they are strengthened as they hold the Lord: though 'those that look out of the windows be darkened,' they are bright when they gaze upon the Saviour; 'the doors shall be shut in the streets,' but no door shuts out the Lord Jesus; 'the voice of the bird' awakens the light sleeper, but no sound shall break the repose of those who rest in Jesus. With the aged desire fails, but not with the aged saint, for he sees in Christ Jesus all his desires fulfilled; and though 'man goeth to his long home,' he that has the holy child Jesus to go with him may even long for the journey, saying, 'Lord, now lettest thou thy servant depart in peace.' Though 'mourners go about the streets' of earth, he who has seen in Christ the salvation of God ascends to other streets, where 'sorrow and sighing shall flee away'. Thrice blessed old age which thus renews its youth with Christ Jesus.

FOR MEDITATION: (*Our Own Hymn Book* no.435 v.6—Horatius Bonar, 1863)
    'My life with Him is hid,
    My death has passed away,
    My clouds have melted into light,
    My midnight into day.'

A business-like account

'But what things were gain to me, those I counted loss for Christ. Yea doubtless, and I count all things but loss for the excellency of the knowledge of Christ Jesus my Lord: for whom I have suffered the loss of all things, and do count them but dung, that I may win Christ.'
Philippians 3:7–8
SUGGESTED FURTHER READING: Luke 14:25–33

Many are brought to Christ in earnest assemblies, where they are addressed in fervent language; yet a man may sit down in his study with his pen in his hand, and in the coolest manner may calculate, and, if under the Holy Spirit's guidance he is led to calculate truthfully, he will come to the conclusion that the cause of the Lord Jesus is worthiest and best. Do not imagine that religion consists of a wild fanaticism which never considers, calculates, judges, estimates or ponders, for such an imagination will be the reverse of truth. Ardour, fervour and enthusiasm are desirable, and we cannot have too much of them, but at the same time we can justify our attachment to Christ by the calmest logic and the most patient consideration. We may make a lengthy and deliberate estimate, taking both temporal and eternal things into review, and yet may challenge all gainsayers while we declare that it is the wisest and best thing in the world to be a disciple of Jesus Christ. In our text the apostle gives us the word 'count' three times. He was skilled in spiritual arithmetic and very careful in his reckoning. He cast up his accounts with caution and observed with a diligent eye his losses and gains. In his reckoning he does not ignore any losses that may be supposed to be sustained, or really may be sustained; on the other hand, he does not forget that blessed gain for which he counts it worthwhile to suffer surprising loss. Paul here seems to be in a mercantile frame of mind, adding, subtracting, counting and balancing with much quiet and decision of mind. I commend the text to business men.

FOR MEDITATION: (*Our Own Hymn Book* no.554 v.2—Isaac Watts, 1709)
    'Now for the love I bear His name,
    What was my gain I count my loss;
    My former pride I call my shame,
    And nail my glory to His cross.'

SERMON NO. 1357

Gathering to the centre

'They came to him from every quarter.' Mark 1:45
SUGGESTED FURTHER READING: John 1:43–51

There is only one Christ, but many are the quarters from which men come to him. It would be impossible to describe all the ways by which men come to Christ, and all the quarters from which they come. To our first believings we are all led by the Spirit of God, but very singular are the experiences of God's people, and perhaps each man has a road peculiar to himself. We do not know all the ways by which souls arrive at Christ, but there is this mercy—he knows the ways by which his redeemed are coming to him, and he knows where they are. I recollect being at Wotton-under-Edge in Mr Hills' garden, and being informed that on the Sabbath morning the quaint old gentleman would go into his garden and watch the people coming to the meeting-house. He would sit in his garden with his telescope in the centre of an amphitheatre of hills, observe the country people coming down, notice any peculiar action, and mention it in his sermon very much to the astonishment of the people concerned. Our Lord Jesus, sitting in the centre to which his redeemed are coming, sees them all, even when they are 'yet a great way off'. If we can conceive a soul millions of miles off from him, as far off as a comet has gone from the sun when it wanders to its utmost tether, yet our Lord Jesus Christ knows from where the wanderer comes, and notes the time when the turning begins and the hour when the face is set towards himself. He can spy out grace in a man's heart long before the man himself is conscious of it and long before the most hopeful minister in the world could see a trace of divine life in the soul. What a mercy this is! They come 'to him from every quarter', and he knows from where they come and how far they are on the road.

FOR MEDITATION: Men and women can come to the Lord Jesus Christ from all directions geographically (Luke 13:29), sinfully (1 Corinthians 6:9–11), socially (Galatians 3:28) and nationally (Revelation 7:9–10), but there is only one direction from which we can come to him spiritually (Ephesians 2:1–3; 5:14).

The blessings of following on

'Then shall we know, if we follow on to know the LORD: his going forth is prepared as the morning; and he shall come unto us as the rain, as the latter and former rain unto the earth.' Hosea 6:3
SUGGESTED FURTHER READING: John 5:39–47

We may read the Bible—I trust we shall; but there is such a thing as resting in Bible reading, and if we do so we shall fall short. Our Lord denounced that in his day when he said, 'Search the scriptures; for in them ye think ye have eternal life: and they are they which testify of me. And ye will not come to me, that ye might have life.' As much as if he had said, 'Your searching the scriptures is well enough, but coming to me is the main business.' It is not the letter-God, but the living God that we want. It is not the book of God so much as the God of the book that we must know. We must seek Christ Jesus, the personal Christ, really existent to ourselves; falling at his feet, confessing our sin, looking up to his wounds, trusting and confiding in him, we shall be indeed blessed. You cannot know the Lord in any other way than by his coming to you in the reality of his incarnation as the very Christ of God. I wish I knew how to put the matter so that every one would recognise to the full my meaning. You know the moment people begin to think about religion they say, 'Well, yes, we must keep the Sabbath, we must attend a place of worship and we must have family prayer.' Thus they dwell upon the many things that they 'must do', all of which things are right enough, but they are only the shell. What the sinner has to say is not, 'I will arise and go to church.' No! 'I will arise and go to my closet and pray.' No, that is not it, first. 'I will arise and go and read a chapter of the Bible.' No, that is not it, good as that is: but 'I will arise and go to my father.' That is where you have to go—to a real God.

FOR MEDITATION: Coming to God requires faith alone (Hebrews 11:6) in the Lord Jesus Christ alone (John 14:6; Hebrews 7:25). The Lord Jesus Christ said 'Come unto me' (Matthew 11:28) and his apostles repeated the same invitation and command (1 Peter 2:4). Have you heeded his call and obeyed him?

SERMON NO. 1246

Beware of unbelief

'A lord on whose hand the king leaned answered the man of God, and said, Behold, if the LORD *would make windows in heaven, might this thing be?'* 2 Kings 7:2
SUGGESTED FURTHER READING: Isaiah 42:5–16

This is many a man's notion of revival—'If you could get Mr Eloquent to come and hold a course of services in our town he would wake us up, but I do not see any other way.' Do you not call that unbelief? God calls it so. If the Lord wished to feed Samaria, he could have done it by multiplying the food that was there, just as he multiplied the widow's oil; or he could have continued the quantity of food undiminished, just as he did the barley cake and the little oil of the widow of Zarephath. God has a thousand ways of accomplishing his purposes. He might have turned every stone in Samaria into a loaf and made the dust of its streets into flour, if so he willed. If in the wilderness he sent food without harvests and water without wind and rain, he can do as he wills and perform his own work in his own way. Do not let us think of limiting the Holy One of Israel to any special mode of action. When we hear of men being led into new ways of going to work, do not let us feel, 'This must be wrong;' rather let us hope that it is very probably right, for we need to escape from these horrid ruts and wretched conventionalisms, which are rather hindrances than helps. Some very stereotyped brethren judge it to be a crime for an evangelist to sing the gospel, and as to that American organ—dreadful! One of these days another set of conservative souls will hardly endure a service without such things, for the horror of one age is the idol of the next. Every man in his own order, and God using them all; if there happens to be some peculiarity, some idiosyncrasy, so much the better. God does not make his servants by the score as men run iron into moulds; he has a separate work for each man.

FOR MEDITATION: The omnipotent God is bound neither by his own precedents nor by our narrow ways and thoughts (Isaiah 55:8–9; Ephesians 3:19–20). Regardless of the means he chooses to use, his word will accomplish his purposes (Isaiah 55:11).

N.B. This sermon was subtitled 'A watchword for Messrs Moody and Sankey's campaign in South London.' See also no.1239 (16 May).

SERMON NO. 1238

Fearful of coming short

'Let us therefore fear, lest, a promise being left us of entering into his rest, any of you should seem to come short of it. For unto us was the gospel preached, as well as unto them: but the word preached did not profit them, not being mixed with faith in them that heard it.' Hebrews 4:1–2

SUGGESTED FURTHER READING: Galatians 2:11–21

Let us examine ourselves with great anxiety, for on many points we may come short. We may fail in reference to the object of our faith. A man may say, 'I have faith,' but another question arises, 'In what have you faith?' 'I have faith in what I have felt.' Then get rid of it, for what you have felt is not an object of faith, nor to be trusted in at all. 'I have faith,' says another, 'in the doctrines which I have been taught.' I am glad you believe them, but doctrines are not the Saviour, and a man may believe all the doctrines of truth, and yet may be lost; a creed cannot save, neither can a dogma redeem. What is the object of faith, then? It is a living, divine, appointed person. And who is that person? He is none other than Jesus the Nazarene, the Son of God, 'over all, God blessed for ever', and yet the son of Mary, born into this world for our sakes. No faith will save a man which does not rest upon Jesus Christ as God; we must depend upon a whole Christ, or else our faith is not the faith of God's elect. We must believe in his proper humanity and rejoice in the sufferings which he endured: we must believe in his assured Deity and rejoice in the merit which that Deity imparted to his sufferings. We must believe in Christ as a substitute for us, suffering that we might not suffer, making atonement on our behalf to the broken law of God, so that God 'might be just, and the justifier of him which believeth in Jesus'. If we do not fix our faith upon this basis, our faith is not the work of the Holy Spirit, for his work always tends to glorify Christ. Let us be very careful here.

FOR MEDITATION: (*Our Own Hymn Book* no.666 v.4—John Newton, 1779)

> 'Beyond a doubt, I rest assured
> Thou art the Christ of God;
> Who hast eternal life secured
> By promise and by blood.'

SERMON NO. 1177

Medicine for the distracted

'In the multitude of my thoughts within me thy comforts delight my soul.' Psalm 94:19
SUGGESTED FURTHER READING: Psalm 119:49–56

What did David do when beset with thoughts of trouble and distress? He went to the Lord and delighted in the comforts of his God. This is an age of care. We live too fast by half, do too much and accomplish, therefore, too little. Our sires could afford time for lengthened family devotions of a character which seem impossible to us. They could listen to sermons which would tire us and snap the bonds of our patience, because their minds were more solid and their lives were vexed with fewer cares. We are all hurry, ride the whirlwind, and are scarcely satisfied with the speed of lightning. Christians cannot rush at this pace without serious injury to themselves unless they often refresh themselves with the comforts of God. The Sabbath is the great safeguard for the sanity of merchants and business men, and those who break it to bring business cares into the one day in seven act a suicidal part. If oftener in the other six days Christians would get alone with God, pour out their hearts before him, tell him their cares, and unveil to him their souls, they would have more ease of mind, be stronger for the struggles of life, and less likely to fail through an over-wrought brain. 'In the multitude of my thoughts within me thy comforts delight my soul.' Londoners used to go into the fields on May Day morning to bathe their faces in the dew, for they thought it made them fair; if every morning we bathed our faces in the dew of heaven, we would be comelier to look upon when mingling with men in the business of the day. If every night before we went to sleep we dipped our foot in the ocean of divine love, our sleep would be more sweet, and care would not eat into the heart and even the bodily constitution, as it does in many cases in this weary age. Get away to your God, O Christian!

FOR MEDITATION: (*Our Own Hymn Book* no.685 v.5—Augustus M.Toplady, 1772)
'When we in darkness walk,
Nor feel the heavenly flame;
Then is the time to trust our God,
And rest upon His name.'

The hold fast

'Take fast hold of instruction; let her not go: keep her; for she is thy life.'
Proverbs 4:13
SUGGESTED FURTHER READING: Psalm 119:92–105

Mr Arnot, in his beautiful book upon the Proverbs, tells a story to illustrate this text. In the Southern seas an American vessel was attacked by a wounded whale. The huge monster ran out a mile from the ship, then turned round, and with the whole force of its acquired speed struck the ship and made it leak at every timber, so that it began to go down. The sailors got out all their boats, filled them as quickly as they could with the necessaries of life, and began to pull away from the ship. Just then two strong men could be seen leaping into the water; they swam to the vessel, leaped on board, disappeared for a moment, and then came up, bringing something in their hands. Just as they sprang into the sea down went the vessel, and they were carried round in the vortex, but were both observed to be swimming, not as if struggling to get away, but as if looking for something, which at last they both seized and carried to the boats. What was this treasure? What could be so valued as to lead them to risk their lives? It was the ship's compass, which had been left behind and without which they could not have found their way out of those lonely southern seas into the high road of commerce. That compass was life to them, and the gospel of the living God is the same to us. You and I must venture all for the gospel: this infallible word of God must be guarded to the death. Men may tell us what they please and say what they will, but we will risk everything sooner than give up those eternal principles by which we have been saved. The Lord give us all abundant grace that we may 'take fast hold of' divine instruction.

FOR MEDITATION: (*Our Own Hymn Book* no.684 v.4—John Andrew Rothe, 1728; tr. John Wesley, 1740)
    'Though waves and storms go o'er my head,
    Though strength, and health, and friends be gone,
    Though joys be withered all, and dead,
    Though every comfort be withdrawn;
    On this my steadfast soul relies,
    Father, Thy mercy never dies.'

SERMON NO. 1418

Happiness the privilege and duty of Christians

'Happy art thou, O Israel: who is like unto thee, O people saved by the LORD, *the shield of thy help, and who is the sword of thy excellency!'*
Deuteronomy 33:29
SUGGESTED FURTHER READING: Matthew 5:1–12

If we are not as happy as the days are long in these summer months, it is entirely our own fault, for there is plenty of reason for being so. Christians, why are you cast down? Why are you so disquieted? Have you not forgotten your redemption, adoption, justification and safety in Christ? Have you not also somewhat neglected to survey your hopes? What if you have little of this world: see what is laid up in store for you hereafter. Within a few years you are to be with the angels, where no dust of toil shall ever stain your garments again, where no sweat of labour shall stand upon your brow, where no care shall scourge the heart, and no sorrow dim the eye. Grief, loss, bereavement or want shall never approach you there. You are of the blood imperial and you are soon to be acknowledged as a peer of heaven's own realm; the day of your accession to sacred honours hastens on. It may be but a week or two that the bliss will tarry; even a few hours may be the only interval, and we shall stand beatified amongst the perfected ones who see God's face without a veil between. We have every reason to be happy, and if we are not so, it must be because we fail to remember the privileges which our Lord has bestowed upon us.

'Why should the children of a King go mourning all their days?
Come, cease to groan, and loudly sing a psalm of gladsome praise.'

How highly favoured are you to be exhorted to so delicious a privilege. When happiness becomes a duty who will not be glad?

FOR MEDITATION: (*Our Own Hymn Book* no.758 v.1—John Kent, 1803)
'What cheering words are these!
Their sweetness who can tell?
In time and to eternal days,
'Tis with the righteous well.'

SERMON NO. 1359

Love's birth and parentage

'We love him, because he first loved us.' 1 John 4:19
SUGGESTED FURTHER READING: Psalm 139:1–18

It is notable that the older a believer becomes and the more deeply he searches into divine truth, the more inclined he is to give the whole of the praise for his salvation to the grace of God and to believe in those precious truths which magnify, not the free will of man, but the free grace of the Ever Blessed. I want no better statement of my own doctrinal belief than this—'We love him, because he first loved us.' I know it has been said that he loved us on the foresight of our faith, love and holiness. Of course the Lord had a clear foresight of all these, but remember that he had also the foresight of our lack of love, our lack of faith, our wanderings and our sins, and surely his foresight in one direction must be supposed to operate as well as his foresight in the other direction. Recollect also that God himself did not foresee that there would be any love to him arising out of ourselves, for there never has been any, and there never will be; he only foresaw that we should believe because he gave us faith; he foresaw that we should repent because his Spirit would work repentance in us; he foresaw that we should love, because he wrought that love within us; and is there anything in the foresight that he means to give us such things that can account for his giving us such things? The case is self-evident—his foresight of what he means to do cannot be his reason for doing it. His own eternal purpose has made the gracious difference between the saved and those who wilfully perish in sin. Let us give all the glory to his holy name, for to him all the glory belongs.

FOR MEDITATION: (*Our Own Hymn Book* no.248 v.6—Julia Anne Elliott, 1835)
   'Because, when we were heirs of wrath,
   Thou gav'st us hope of heaven;
   We love because we much have sinned,
   And much have been forgiven.'

SERMON NO. 1299

Eyes opened

'And God opened her eyes.' Genesis 21:19
SUGGESTED FURTHER READING: Psalm 8:1–9

God has been pleased to open the natural eyes of mankind by the invention of optical instruments. What a discovery it was when first of all certain pieces of glass were arranged in connection with each other and men began to peer into the stars! What a change has come over the knowledge of our race by the invention of the telescope! How much of truly devout, adoring thought, and of deep, intense, unutterable reverence has been born into the world by the Lord's having in this sense opened men's eyes! When he turned his telescope upon the nebulae and discovered that these were innumerable stars, what a hymn of praise must have burst from the reverent astronomer's heart. How infinite thou art, most gracious Lord! What wonders hast thou created! Let thy name be held in reverence for ever and ever. Equally marvellous was the effect upon human knowledge when the microscope was invented. We could never have imagined what wonders of skill and of taste would be revealed by the magnifying glass, and what marvels of beauty would be found compressed within a space too small to measure. Who dreamed that a butterfly's wing would display art, wisdom and a delicacy never to be rivalled by human workmanship? The most delicate work of art is rough, crude and raw compared with the commonest object in nature; the one is the production of man, the other the handiwork of God. Spend an evening with the microscope and, if your heart be right, you will lift your eye away from the glass to heaven and exclaim, 'Great God, thou art as wonderful in the little as thou art in the great, and as much to be praised for the minute as for the magnificent.' While we say, 'Great art thou, O God, for thou madest the great and wide sea, and the leviathan whose lot it is to play therein', we feel that we must also say, 'Great art thou, O Lord, for thou madest the drop of water and hast filled it with living things innumerable.'

FOR MEDITATION: Glory in God's creative wisdom, seen in all creatures great and small (Psalm 104:24–25). By wisdom he made the vast heavens (Psalm 136:5) and he has bestowed wisdom upon even the smallest of his creatures (Proverbs 30:24). 'O the depths of the riches both of the wisdom and knowledge of God' (Romans 11:33).

SERMON NO. 1461(B)

The song of songs

'Sing, O ye heavens; for the LORD *hath done it: shout, ye lower parts of the earth: break forth into singing, ye mountains, O forest, and every tree therein: for the* LORD *hath redeemed Jacob, and glorified himself in Israel.' Isaiah 44:23*
SUGGESTED FURTHER READING: Psalm 150:1–6

The meaning of the whole seems to be this, that wherever saints are they ought to praise God for redeeming love, whether they climb the Alps or descend into the plains, whether they dwell in the cities or walk in the quietude of the woods. In whatever state of mind they feel themselves they still should praise redeeming grace and dying love, whether on the mountain top of communion or in the valley of humiliation, whether lifted up by prosperity or cast down by adversity. They should leave a shining trail of praise behind them in their daily course even as does the vessel when it ploughs the sea. The text calls upon all classes and conditions of men to praise God for redemption. You that are lifted up like mountains—magistrates, princes, kings and emperors—and you who lie beneath like plains, you who eat bread in the sweat of your faces, you children of poverty and toil, rejoice in redeeming love. You who dwell in the midst of sin as in a tangled forest, you who have transgressed against God and plunged into the deep places of vice, be glad, for you may be restored. All you of woman born, together praise the Redeemer of Israel, for he has accomplished the salvation of his people! Let us join in this song. Mr Sankey is now behind me, but he cannot sing sweetly enough to set forth to the full the majesty of this song, nor could the choicest choir of singing men and singing women; this task exceeds the reach of the seraphim themselves. Praise is silenced, O Lord, by the glory of thy love. Yet, brethren, let us give forth such music as we have.

FOR MEDITATION: (*Our Own Hymn Book* no.428 v.5—Isaac Watts, 1709)
   'Oh, for this love let rocks and hills
   Their lasting silence break,
   And all harmonious human tongues
   The Saviour's praises speak.'

SERMON NO. 1240

Forty years

'For the LORD *thy God hath blessed thee in all the works of thy hand: he knoweth thy walking through this great wilderness: these forty years the* LORD *thy God hath been with thee; thou hast lacked nothing.'*
Deuteronomy 2:7
SUGGESTED FURTHER READING (Spurgeon): Deuteronomy 8:1–10

Having reached forty years, we are bound to feel a powerful influence upon us as to the future. How? Read in Deuteronomy 2:2–3 'And the LORD spake unto me, saying, Ye have compassed this mountain long enough: turn you northward.' What way was northward? Why, towards Canaan. Forty years wandering up and down in the wilderness is enough; now turn your faces towards Canaan and march heavenward. It is time we all had our faces turned heavenward more completely. We have not always had our conversation in heaven as we should have done. Some of our faculties have been taken up with inferior things and we have looked towards Egypt, but we have 'compassed this mountain long enough': it is time that we concentrated all our powers and turned them all straight away to the Zion which is above, and to the 'innumerable company of angels … and to the spirits of just men made perfect'. Our window should now be open 'toward Jerusalem'. Forty years of the world is forty years of banishment! As we are soon to have done with it, let us up and away 'to the hill of frankincense'. They tell me that years ago when sailors used to go to India they would give as a toast when they left, 'To our friends astern', but when they had reached half way on the voyage, they changed it to, 'To our friends ahead.' When we get to forty we may reckon we are probably more than mid-way on our voyage: we are bound, therefore, to remember our friends ahead. We have a large company waiting for us of dear ones that have gone before: indeed, the aged have a majority of their friends 'on the other side Jordan'. Let us salute them.

FOR MEDITATION: (*Our Own Hymn Book* no.214 v.7—Joseph Addison, 1712)
'Through every period of my life Thy goodness I'll pursue;
And after death, in distant worlds, the glorious theme renew.'

N.B. This was preached five days before Spurgeon's fortieth birthday.

Good cheer for outcasts

'He gathereth together the outcasts of Israel.' Psalm 147:2
SUGGESTED FURTHER READING: Psalm 40:1–17

If Jesus Christ received some of us when we felt ourselves to be outcasts, how we ought to love him! It does you good to look back 'to the hole of the pit whence ye are digged'. We get to be very top-lofty at times, my brethren. We are wonderfully big, are we not? Are we not experienced Christians now? Why, we have known the Lord these five-and-twenty years. Dear me, how important we are! Perhaps we are deacons of churches, or, at any rate, we have a class in the Sunday-school, and we pray in the prayer-meeting: considerable importance attaches to us, and we are high and mighty on that account. I have heard say of a man worth his thousands that once he had not a shirt to his back, and, if he recollected from what he sprang, he would not carry his head so high. I do not see much in that, but I do see something in this—if we recollected the time when we 'were dead in trespasses and sins', when we had not a rag to cover us, when we were under God's frown and heirs 'of wrath, even as others', if we recollected our lost and ruined state by nature, I am sure that we should not lift our heads so very loftily, and want to have respect paid to us in the church, or think that God ought not to deal so very hardly with us, as if we had cause for complaint. Dear friends, let us remember what we used to be, and that will keep us low in our own esteem. But how it will fire us with zeal to remember from what a depth he has lifted us up. Did Jesus save such a wretch as I was? Then for him would I live and for him would I die. This ought to be the utterance of us all. We ought to live in that spirit. God grant we may!

FOR MEDITATION: When Christians begin to glory in their own characters and achievements, they are thinking like unbelievers and forgetting the ground on which they stand before God (Ephesians 2:8–9). The apostle Paul knew how to burst the pride of arrogant Christians. Consider some of the questions he asked one proud church (1 Corinthians 4:6–7; 5:1–2,6). He had to remind them of the various pits from which God had lifted them (1 Corinthians 1:26–29; 6:9–11).

SERMON NO. 1302

Encouragement to trust and pray

'He will be very gracious unto thee at the voice of thy cry; when he shall hear it, he will answer thee.' Isaiah 30:19
SUGGESTED FURTHER READING: Matthew 26:69–27:5

Refuse despair. When a man sees that his confidences are broken up like a potter's vessel till, to use the expressive figure of the prophet, there is not a piece left large enough 'to take fire from the hearth, or to take water withal out of the pit', then he is apt to exclaim, 'Now it is all over with me and I must perish.' You loved your wife; she was all the world to you, but alas, she is dead, and you cry, 'Let me die also.' You hugged your wealth; it has melted; that speculation has dissolved it and left you a beggar: and now you cry, 'What is there worth living for?' Beware of dark thoughts which may beset you just now. In your worst moment, should Satan whisper in your ear a suggestion concerning rope, or knife, or poison bowl, or sullen stream, flee from it with all your soul. Obey the apostolic word, 'Do thyself no harm'.' Nothing could be worse for you than to break the law, which says expressly, 'Thou shalt do no murder.' Self-destruction, if done by a man in his senses, is a daring defiance of God and the sealing of damnation. This is to leap from measured trouble into infinite woe, the depth of which none can guess. Why should you do this? Turn unto your God; that is a wiser thing for a man to do than to destroy his own life; there is something braver for a man to do than to rush upon the pikes of the foe because the battle waxes too hot for him. Go to your great Captain, even to him whom God has given to be a witness, a leader and a commander to the people, and he will make you more than a conqueror. There are brighter days in store for you yet.

FOR MEDITATION: Suicide is generally the ultimate act of despair in a life of disobedience to God, as in the cases of Saul (1 Samuel 31:4), Ahithophel (2 Samuel 17:23), Zimri (1 Kings 16:18–19) and Judas (Matthew 27:5). Samson is the exception which proves the rule (Judges 16:28–30). The Jews thought that the Lord Jesus Christ was going to commit suicide (John 8:21–22), but even he, in laying down his life for our sins (John 10:17–18), did not crucify himself. The Philippian jailer was spared to discover the best answer to despair (Acts 16:27–34).

SERMON NO. 1419

The good Samaritan

'Go, and do thou likewise.' Luke 10:37
SUGGESTED FURTHER READING: Mark 12:28–34

I have often wondered which way the priest was going, whether he was going up to the temple and was in a hurry to be in time for fear of keeping the congregation waiting, or whether he had fulfilled his duty, had finished his month's course at the temple and was going home. I conclude that he was going from Jerusalem to Jericho, because Luke 10:31 says, 'by chance there came down a certain priest that way'. To the metropolis it is always 'going up', going up to London, or up to Jerusalem; as this priest was coming down, he was going to Jericho. It was quite literally going down, for Jericho lies very low. I conclude that he was going home to Jericho, after having fulfilled his month's engagements at the temple, where he had been familiar with the worship of the Most High, as near to God as man could be, serving amidst sacrifices, holy psalms and solemn prayers; and yet he had not learned how to make a sacrifice himself. He had heard those prophetic words which say, 'I desired mercy, and not sacrifice', but he was entirely forgetful of such teaching: he had often read that law, 'Thou shalt love thy neighbour as thyself', but he regarded it not. The Levite had not been quite so closely engaged in the sanctuary as the priest, but he had taken his share in holy work, and yet he came away from it with a hard heart. This is a sad fact. They had been near to God, but were not like him. Dear people, you may spend Sabbath after Sabbath in the worship of God, or what you think to be so, you may behold Christ Jesus 'evidently set forth, crucified among you', and themes which ought to turn a heart of stone to flesh may pass before your minds, nevertheless you may return into the world to be as miserly as ever, and to have as little feeling towards your fellow men as before. It ought not to be so.

FOR MEDITATION: (*Our Own Hymn Book* no.92 part 1 v.1—Isaac Watts, 1719)
    'Sweet is the work, my God, my King,
    To praise Thy name, give thanks, and sing,
    To show Thy love by morning light,
    And talk of all Thy truth at night.'

SERMON NO. 1360

Life's need and maintenance

'None can keep alive his own soul.' Psalm 22:29
SUGGESTED FURTHER READING: Nehemiah 8:1–18

We should diligently use all those means whereby the Lord communicates fresh support to our life. A man does not say, 'Well, I was born on such and such a day; that is enough for me.' No, the good man needs his daily meals to maintain him in existence. Being alive, his next consideration is to keep alive, and therefore he does not neglect eating, nor any operation which is essential to life. So you, dear friends, must labour 'for that meat which endureth unto everlasting life'; you must feed on the 'bread from heaven'. Study the Scriptures daily—I hope you do not neglect that. Be much in private prayer; your life cannot be healthy if the mercy seat be neglected. We must not forsake 'the assembling of ourselves together, as the manner of some is'. Be eager to hear the word; endeavour both to understand and practise it. Gather with God's people in their more spiritual meetings, when they join in prayer and praise, for these are healthful means of sustaining the inner life. If you neglect these, you cannot expect that grace will be strong within you; you may even question if there be any life at all. Still, remember that even if a man should eat and drink, that would not keep him alive without the power of God, and many die with whom there is no lack either of air or food. You must, therefore, look beyond the outward means to God himself to preserve your soul; be this your daily prayer, 'O Saviour, by whom I began to live, daily enable me to look to thee that I may draw continuous life from thy wounds, and live because thou livest.' Take these things home and practise them.

FOR MEDITATION: (*Our Own Hymn Book* no.407 v.3—Augustus M.Toplady, 1771)
 'I can do nothing without Thee;
 My strength is wholly Thine:
 Withered and barren should I be,
 If severed from the vine.'

SERMON NO. 1300

Every man's necessity

'*Ye must be born again.*' John 3:7
SUGGESTED FURTHER READING: 1 Peter 1:22–2:2

Every soul that is born again *repents of its sin*. If a man lives in his sin as he used to do, he must not pretend that he is a twice-born man, or he will mightily deceive himself. If he can look upon sin in the same light as he did before, if he can find pleasure in it, and if he does not sincerely turn from it with loathing and seek the mercy of God to blot it out, he knows nothing of what regeneration is. Again all the regenerate *have faith:* they all agree in finding all the sole ground of their hope in the blood and merit of Jesus. Meet them anywhere and they will tell you they have no confidence except in the Saviour's precious blood; he is all their salvation and all their desire. They rest upon this rock, every one of them; and no matter what high professors they may be, nor what lofty offices they hold in the church, if Christ is not their one and only trust, they know not what it is to be born again. In addition to all this all that have passed from death unto life *pray*. If it really rises from the heart, prayer is an infallible mark of the new birth, and if it can be said of a man, 'He does not pray,' then he is still dead in his sins; the Spirit of God has not renewed his soul. I might mention some other holy signs which are invariable accompaniments of the new birth, but these three will suffice for all practical purposes. You can test yourselves, beloved, by them. Have you repented? Have you faith towards God? Do you rejoice to draw near to God in prayer? If these things are in you they are marks of the new life, for they were never yet found in the spiritually dead.

FOR MEDITATION: Consider some of the evidences of the new birth—faith in the Lord Jesus Christ (John 1:12–13; 1 John 5:1), spiritual hunger (1 Peter 2:2), righteous living (1 John 2:29), repentance from sin (1 John 3:9; 5:18), brotherly love (1 John 4:7), unworldliness (1 John 5:4). While none of us will be perfect in any of these areas, they should all be seen in us to some degree. Do you still need to be born again?

SERMON NO. 1455

Honest dealing with God

'If we say that we have no sin, we deceive ourselves, and the truth is not in us. If we confess our sins, he is faithful and just to forgive us our sins, and to cleanse us from all unrighteousness. If we say that we have not sinned, we make him a liar, and his word is not in us.' 1 John 1:8–10
SUGGESTED FURTHER READING: Isaiah 28:7–18

Our tendency to be false is illustrated in 1 John 1, where we find three grades of it. There is first *the man who lies:* 'If we say that we have fellowship with him, and walk in darkness, we lie, and do not the truth'. We say and do that which is untrue, if, while abiding under the influence of sin and falsehood, we claim to have fellowship with God. If this tendency is left unchecked, you will find the man growing worse and doing according to the eighth verse, where it is written, 'we deceive ourselves'. Here the utterer of the falsehood has come to *believe his own lie;* he has blinded his understanding and befooled his conscience till he has become his own dupe. Falsehood has saturated his nature, so that he puts 'darkness for light, and light for darkness'. This is at once his sin and his punishment; he closed his eyes so long that at length he has become stone blind. He will soon reach the complete development of his sin, which is described in the tenth verse, when the man, who first lied, and then deceived himself, becomes so audacious in his falseness as to blaspheme the Most Holy by *making him a liar.* It is impossible to say where sin will end; the beginning of it is as a little water in which a bird may wash and scatter half the pool in drops, but in its progress sin, like the brook, swells into a torrent deep and broad. We must judge ourselves very severely, lest our natural tendency to falseness should lead us to false assertion as to ourselves, and then urge us on till we delude ourselves into the foolish belief that we are what we proudly represent ourselves to be, and dare in the desperation of our pride to think God himself untrue.

FOR MEDITATION: (*Our Own Hymn Book* no.551 v.3b—Charles Wesley, 1740)
    'Just and holy is Thy name,
    I am all unrighteousness,
    False and full of sin I am;
    Thou art full of truth and grace.'

SERMON NO. 1241

The sieve

'Not every one that saith unto me, Lord, Lord, shall enter into the kingdom of heaven; but he that doeth the will of my Father which is in heaven.' Matthew 7:21
SUGGESTED FURTHER READING: Matthew 6:1–6

Some say, 'Lord, Lord,' but not in sincerity. They are very busy, always ready to do anything, and are not happy unless they have something to do. I blame them not for being busy; I wish sincere people were half as busy; but I detect in them this vice—they are fondest of doing that which will be most seen; they prefer to serve God in those places where the most honour will be gained. To speak in public is to them infinitely preferable to the visitation of a poor, sick woman. To work or to give where the deed will be blazoned abroad is after their minds. To take the chair at a public meeting and receive a vote of thanks is delightful to them; but to go into a back street and look after the poor, or plod on in the Sunday School in some inferior class, is not according to their taste. It may seem harsh, but it is nevertheless true that many are serving themselves under the pretence of serving Christ; they labour to advance the cause in order that they themselves may be advanced; they push themselves forward in the church for the glory of place and position, that everybody may say, 'What a good man he is, how much influence he has, and how well he serves his Master!' If you and I do anything nominally for God, and at the bottom are doing it for the sake of praise, it is not for God; we are doing it for ourselves. I would like your conscience to ask you, 'Do I really serve the Lord, or do I work in the church in order that I may be considered to be an industrious, praiseworthy minister, seeking the good of my fellow-men?' Shun the desire of human praise and never let it pollute your motives. May the Holy Spirit purify you from so base a motive. Seek the praise of God, to have him say, 'Well done, good and faithful servant', but avoid honour from men as you would a viper.

FOR MEDITATION: Those whose aim is to receive glory from others (John 5:44) obtain a temporary reward (Matthew 6:2,5,16), but rob God of the glory which belongs to him (Matthew 5:16) and rob themselves of any reward they would have received from him (Matthew 6:1). Such treasures laid up on earth will get stolen (Matthew 6:19).

SERMON NO. 1158

A sacred solo

'The LORD *is my strength and my shield; my heart trusted in him, and I am helped: therefore my heart greatly rejoiceth; and with my song will I praise him.' Psalm 28:7*
SUGGESTED FURTHER READING: Psalm 43:1–5

Some people's rejoicing is skin deep. They laugh; their face is surfaced over with smiles and their mouth bubbles up with silly glee. There is hardly anything more sad than the frequent laughter which exposes a vacant mind. The moment company has gone this volatile mirthfulness subsides, and the jolly companions resolve into solitary individuals, each one dull and dreary, far from any of them being happy. You may have heard of Carlini, one of the most celebrated clowns at the beginning of this century, a man whose wit and humour kept all Paris in a roar of laughter; but he himself had little share of the cheerfulness he simulated so well and stimulated so much. His comedies brought him no comfort. Though a professor of mirth, he was a victim of melancholy. He consulted a physician and asked for a prescription to relieve his lowness of spirits and habitual despondency. His physician gave him some medicine, but advised him by way of recreation to go to the theatre and hear Carlini, whose fun and frolic were of such repute. 'If he does not fetch the blues out of you, nobody will.' 'Alas!' said he, 'I am Carlini.' Often men make glee for others when they are full of gloom themselves. The face smiles like summer, but the heart is freezing with the cold of winter. Not so the man who has laid hold on God; 'my heart greatly rejoiceth', he says, as if it were as full of joy as it could be, as though it throbbed and danced joyously with a fulness of delight. Christians can say this whenever they lay hold on God, even though they are surrounded with a world of trouble. We sometimes know what it is to wear a sad face with a glad heart, just as others wear a glad face with a sad heart. Blessed is the man whom God has taught greatly to rejoice.

FOR MEDITATION: Trying to be what we are not is a futile exercise. Putting on a show of superficial jollity is no more spiritual than putting on a hypocritical display of looking miserable (Matthew 6:16). Remember that, while man looks on the outward appearance, God looks on the heart (1 Samuel 16:7).

SERMON NO. 1423

The head stone of the corner

'The stone which the builders refused is become the head stone of the corner. This is the LORD's doing; it is marvellous in our eyes. This is the day which the LORD hath made; we will rejoice and be glad in it.' Psalm 118:23–24
SUGGESTED FURTHER READING: Mark 2:23–3:6

What day is this 'which the LORD hath made'? Why, it is a Sabbath day, the beginning of a long line of Sabbaths. The day in which our Lord Jesus rose from the dead is now sacred to rest and holy joy. Let us keep it with reverent love, and bless God for making it. The world calls the Sabbath Sun-day; do not let us turn it into Cloud-day. Certain good Christian people look upon the Lord's day as a season so solemn that it can only be properly kept by being as dreary as possible. Draw down the blinds, darken the room, chide the children, banish every smile: now we are getting sabbatic. Let us go up to the house of prayer like convicts exercising in the prison yard, and there let us be as decorously miserable as possible; let the preacher be as dull and monotonous as though he had no subject to preach about but death and destruction and must preserve an air of melancholy, or none would think him gracious. Such is not the teaching of our Master, nor is it according to his mind and spirit. Herbert well says of the Sabbath, 'Thou art a day of mirth, and where the week-days trail on ground, thy flight is higher, as thy birth.' It should be 'a day most calm, most bright', fit to be called 'the endorsement of supreme delight'. It is a time of the singing of birds, for the winter of our Lord's humiliation is over and he has risen from the dead; today we celebrate the glory of Christ in the highest heavens, as the elect of God and the corner stone of his church: surely it ill becomes us to go about with our hands upon our loins as if we mourned his victory and grudged his honour.

FOR MEDITATION: While it may not be appropriate to turn Sunday into fun-day, we should never forget that it is a good day. On the day when the Lord Jesus Christ rose from the dead the fearful obtained great joy (Matthew 28:5–8; Luke 24:37–41; John 20:19–20) and the sad acquired great zeal and purpose (Luke 24:17,31–33; John 20:11–18). Whether on Sunday or any other day, we should take care to avoid giving the false impression that the Lord Jesus Christ is still dead in the tomb.

SERMON NO. 1420

The final perseverance of the saints

'The righteous also shall hold on his way.' Job 17:9
SUGGESTED FURTHER READING (Spurgeon): John 10:1–30

Scripture does not teach that a man will reach his journey's end without continuing to travel along the road; it is not true that one act of faith is all, and that nothing else is needed of daily faith, prayer and watchfulness. Our doctrine is the very opposite, namely, that the righteous 'shall hold on his way', continuing in faith, repentance and prayer, and under the influence of the grace of God. We do not believe in salvation by a physical force which treats a man as a dead log and carries him towards heaven whether he wills it or not. No, he holds on, he is personally active about the matter, and plods on up hill and down dale till he reaches his journey's end. We never dreamed that, because a man supposes that he once entered on this way, he may conclude that he is certain of salvation, even if he leaves the way immediately. No, but we say that he who truly receives the Holy Spirit, so that he believes in the Lord Jesus Christ, shall not go back, but persevere in the way of faith. It is written, 'He that believeth and is baptized shall be saved'; this cannot be if he is left to go back and delight in sin as before; therefore, he shall be kept by the power of God through faith unto salvation. Though the believer to his grief will commit many a sin, yet the tenor of his life will be holiness to the Lord, and he will hold on in the way of obedience. We detest the doctrine that a man who has once believed in Jesus will be saved even if he altogether forsakes the path of obedience. We deny that such a turning aside is possible to the true believer.

FOR MEDITATION: Consider some of the references quoted by Spurgeon. Apostasy is a danger (1 John 2:19), but the final perseverance of the saints is supported by (a) the nature of the life imparted at regeneration (John 4:14; 1 Peter 1:23), (b) our Lord's own express declarations (John 3:14–16,36; 6:47,51; 10:28), (c) our Lord's intercession (Luke 22:31–32; John 17:11–12; Hebrews 7:25), (d) the character and work of Christ (John 13:1; 2 Timothy 1:12), (e) the tenor of the covenant of grace (Isaiah 54:10; 55:3), (f) the faithfulness of God (Malachi 3:6; John 6:39; Romans 11:29; 1 Corinthians 1:8), and (g) what has already been done in us (Jeremiah 31:3; Romans 5:9–10; 8:29,33–35,38–39; Ephesians 1:13–14; Philippians 1:6).

SERMON NO. 1361

A Prince and a Saviour

'Him hath God exalted with his right hand to be a Prince and a Saviour, for to give repentance to Israel, and forgiveness of sins.' Acts 5:31
SUGGESTED FURTHER READING: Matthew 1:18–2:6

If he be a Saviour, this shows to trembling hearts how approachable he is. You might be ashamed at coming to a prince, but you may be encouraged in coming to a Saviour. You that would be rid of your sin, do you fear the Prince? Well may you, for he can punish you. But fear not, for the Saviour will forgive you. Diseased with sin, do you think yourself unworthy of his princely presence? Yet he is Physician as well as Prince: therefore come where the glance of his eye, or the touch of his hand will make you perfectly whole. I wish I knew how to put my Lord before you in the best of words and describe him so sweetly that you would all fall in love with him: but, indeed, I believe him to be so beautiful that, if I can only convey to you the faintest idea of him, you must be enamoured of him, if you love that which is good and fair. While I am describing him, I feel I only put a mist about him; but, then, he is the sun, and he can break through my cloudy language and cause your hearts to see him in all his glory. 'A Prince and a Saviour'; suppose I put the words together and say, a Prince-saviour, one who is lordly and kingly in the salvation which he brings, and deals out no stinted grace, but makes us to receive 'of his fulness ... grace for grace'. Turn the titles the other way and reverse the order, and truly he is a Saviour-prince whose glory it is to save, whose kingdom, power and dominion are all turned in full force to achieve the work of rescuing his people from destruction. 'A Prince and a Saviour'; this is the Christ to whom you must come, you who would be delivered from your sins. Look to him and live.

FOR MEDITATION: At his birth the Lord Jesus Christ was announced as Prince and King by virtue of who he had been for all eternity (Matthew 2:2,6; John 18:37); he was also prophesied as Saviour by virtue of what he was going to do by his death on the cross (Matthew 1:21; Mark 10:45; Luke 2:11; 1 Timothy 1:15). Have you accepted him in both joint-roles?

The recorders

'To record, and to thank and praise the LORD *God of Israel.'*
1 Chronicles 16:4
SUGGESTED FURTHER READING: Exodus 17:8–16

We should not allow the mercies of the Lord to lie forgotten in unthankfulness and die without praises, if we can help it. How can we strengthen memory? I conceive that sometimes it is a good thing to make an actual record of God's mercy, literally to write it down in your pocket-book, so as to look at it another day. I am sure it is a proper thing to do, and often it will prove to be a very useful momento. I do not believe in keeping diaries and putting down every day what you feel, or what you think you feel but never did feel. I fear it would become a mere formality, or an exercise of imagination to most of us, for when I read very pious people's diaries, they always seem to me to have had an eye to the people who would read them, and to have put down both more and less than the truth; I am a little frightened at the artificial style of experience to which it must lead. The fact is that we have not a great deal to put down every day if we lead an ordinary life; but there are days which ought to have a memorial, days of sore trouble and of great deliverance, days of sharp temptation and of wonderful help: these ought to be chronicled. Some days of brilliant mercy are like seven days in one. There are days which seem like chips of heaven, fragments of eternity, stray days of delight which have broken loose from the days of heaven and wandered down to earth. Make a note of the favoured day. Put the event down in black and white just as it occurred. Never mind if nobody else ever reads it: you will read it one of these days and thank God that it stands recorded for the strengthening of your faith. Therefore make a record.

FOR MEDITATION: Memory of the past can be a great help in the present (2 Timothy 1:3–7; Hebrews 10:32–36). But we all too easily and all too quickly forget what we ought to remember (Genesis 40:9–15,20–23; James 1:23–24). Could you do with a spiritual 'aide-memoire'?

Abraham's prompt obedience to the call of God

'By faith Abraham, when he was called to go out into a place which he should after receive for an inheritance, obeyed; and he went out, not knowing whither he went.' Hebrews 11:8
SUGGESTED FURTHER READING (Spurgeon): Genesis 12:1–9

Abraham probably heard a voice from heaven speaking audibly to him, 'Get thee out of thy country, and from thy kindred, and from thy father's house.' We have had many calls, but perhaps we have said, 'If I heard a voice speaking from the sky, I would obey it'; but the form in which your call has come has been better than that, for Peter in his second epistle tells us that he himself heard a voice 'from the excellent glory' when he was with our Lord 'in the holy mount', but adds, 'We have also a more sure word of prophecy', as if the testimony which is written, the 'light that shineth in a dark place', which beams forth from the word of God, was even more sure than the voice which he heard from heaven. I will show you that it is so, for, if I should hear a voice, how am I to know that it is divine? Even if it were, might it not be suggested to me that I was mistaken, that it was most unlikely that God should speak to a man at all, and more unlikely still that he should speak to me. Might not a hundred difficulties and doubts be suggested to lead me to question whether God had spoken to me at all? But most of you believe the Bible to be inspired by the Spirit of God and to be the voice of God. In it you have the call, 'Come out from among them, and be ye separate … and touch not the unclean thing; and I will receive you, and will be a Father unto you, and ye shall be my sons and daughters.' Do not say that you would accept that call if it were spoken with a voice rather than written; you know that it is not so in daily life. If a man receives a letter from his father or a friend, dos he attach less importance to it than he would have done to a spoken communication? By no means!

FOR MEDITATION: It took Samuel three audible calls from God and a word of guidance from Eli before he realised who was calling him (1 Samuel 3:4–10). It took Peter three visions from God and a word of direction from the Holy Spirit before he got the message (Acts 10:9–21). How many times does God have to speak to you through his written word before you pay proper attention (Hebrews 2:1–3; 2 Peter 1:19)?

SERMON NO. 1242

Jacob worshipping on his staff

'By faith Jacob, when he was a dying, blessed both the sons of Joseph; and worshipped, leaning upon the top of his staff.' Hebrews 11:21
SUGGESTED FURTHER READING: Genesis 49:28–33

That expression, 'when he was a dying,' reminds me of many deathbeds, but I shall not speak of them now, for I desire each one of you to rehearse the scene of your own departure, for soon of every one a tale will be told, commencing 'when he was a dying'. I want each one to project his mind a little forward to the time when he must gather up his feet in the bed, pronounce his last farewell and yield up the ghost. Before your actual departure there may be allotted to you, unless you are carried away with a sudden stroke, a little time in which it shall be said, 'he was a dying'. Perhaps it is a desirable thing to occupy some weeks in departure, till the mind seems to have passed through the gate and to be already in the glory, while yet the body lingers here; but as we have had no experience, we are scarcely able to form a judgment. Very much might be said in favour of that sudden death which is sudden glory, but yet one might prefer to have enough time and sufficient clearness of mind to gaze into eternity, and so to become familiar with the thought of departing out of the body. It would seem desirable to lose the dread and first surprise of the chill torrent, and to become fully at ease on the banks of Jordan, sitting with your feet up to the ankles in its stream, and by degrees descending into the greater depths, singing and beginning even on earth the everlasting song which is heard for ever on the other side of the mysterious river. Such dying is a fit ending to a life of genuine piety, and both displays and proves its truthfulness. Jacob 'was a dying' and in his dying we see the man.

FOR MEDITATION: (*Our Own Hymn Book* no.821 v.3—William Williams, 1773)
  'When I tread the verge of Jordan,
  Bid my anxious fears subside;
  Death of deaths, and hell's destruction,
  Land me safe on Canaan's side:
  Songs of praises
  I will ever give to Thee.'

SERMON NO. 1401

The hiding of Moses by faith

'By faith Moses, when he was born, was hid three months of his parents, because they saw he was a proper child; and they were not afraid of the king's commandment.' Hebrews 11:23
SUGGESTED FURTHER READING (Spurgeon): Exodus 1:22–2:10

The mother of Moses had to hide her child. I have no doubt if she and her husband were here, they would have a long story to tell of the things that happened, how often their hearts were in their mouths, how frequently poor Amram was in a cold sweat because one of his companions with whom he worked talked of going home with him, how that prying neighbour of theirs, who always wanted to put her finger into everybody's dish, tried to find out what there was that made Mrs Jochebed keep at home so much, how they were afraid even of their own little children lest they might in their play talk of their little brother. What fear was upon the whole family, lest discovery should lead to destruction, we may guess from their hiding the baby. The mother was put to great shifts to hide her child, and she used all her wits and commonsense. She did not put her child in the front room, or carry it into the street, or sit at the open door and nurse it, but she was prudent and acted as if all depended upon her concealing the baby. Some people suppose that if you have faith you may act like a fool. But faith makes a person wise. It is one of the notable points about faith that it is sanctified commonsense. That is not at all a bad definition of faith. It is not fanaticism or absurdity; it is making God the grandest asset in our account, and then reckoning according to the soundest logic. It is not putting my hands into boiling water with the impression that it will not scald me; it is not doing foolish and absurd things. Faith is believing in God and acting towards God as we ought to do.

FOR MEDITATION: Seeing that folly is at the heart of unbelief (Psalm 14:1; 53:1) and the opposite of faith in God and his word (Luke 24:25), it should be no surprise that it has no place in the Christian life. The Christian's life and behaviour should display wisdom and understanding, not folly (Ephesians 5:15–17).

The chief physician and the centurion's servant

'Jesus saith unto him, I will come and heal him.' 'And Jesus said unto the centurion, Go thy way; and as thou hast believed, so be it done unto thee.' Matthew 8:7,13
SUGGESTED FURTHER READING (Spurgeon): Luke 7:1–10

If I were pleading for the conversion of a sinner, I should feel hampered by my own unworthiness if I believed that salvation necessitated a bodily manifestation of my Lord or some extraordinary display of power before men's eyes: but if my Lord will save by his word only, then I venture to ask with confidence. Here is no parade of power, but quiet divine energy, and this the meek of the earth delight in. I am sure that it pleases faith better than any other way. O my Lord, how I desire of thee that thou wouldst save thousands, and I would be glad if it were done without me or any of thy servants, if thou wouldst only say a word and by thy Holy Spirit cause a nation to be born in a day! Certain professors pine for a great stir: they will not believe that the kingdom of God prospers unless thousands crowd into our assemblies, great excitement reigns and all the papers are ringing with the names of famous preachers. They like it all the better if they hear of people being thrown into fits during the meeting, or read of men and women falling down, or screaming under excitement. They can believe in Christ's power if there are signs and wonders, but not otherwise. That is going back to 'come and heal him'. But we are content to abide by the second mode. Can you not believe that by each one of us making the gospel of God to have free course, our Lord can effectually save men by his word? Quietly, without observation, sign or wonder, Jesus will bless believing testimonies and answer believing prayers. Strong faith is well content with the Lord's settled and usual mode of action, and rejoices to see him save men by his word in answer to the prayer of faith.

FOR MEDITATION: If faith is the 'evidence of things not seen' (Hebrews 11:1) and if Christians claim to 'walk by faith, not by sight' (2 Corinthians 5:7), we can look like unbelievers and liars when we demand visible proof that God is at work. Thomas was at least being honest when he equated his unbelief with his not having seen the risen Christ (John 20:25); Jesus taught him the better way (John 20:29).

SERMON NO. 1422

Mourning for Christ

'I will pour upon the house of David, and upon the inhabitants of Jerusalem, the spirit of grace and of supplications: and they shall look upon me whom they have pierced, and they shall mourn for him, as one mourneth for his only son, and shall be in bitterness for him, as one that is in bitterness for his firstborn.' Zechariah 12:10

SUGGESTED FURTHER READING: James 4:1–10

I pray the Spirit of God to enable you to mourn over the past, but what shall we say as to the present? Take stock now of last week. Did you make any survey of the days as they passed? If so I think you might have said with Dr Watts—

'What have I done for him that died to save my wretched soul?
How are my follies multiplied fast as my minutes roll.'

Has it been a week of real service for Christ? You have done something; did you do your best? Did you throw your heart into it? When you were trying to bring others to Christ, did you feel that tenderness which a Christian ought to feel? You had some little contention with another; did you act in a Christian spirit? Did you show the mildness and gentleness of Jesus? You were offended; did you forgive freely? For his dear sake did you cast it all behind your back? You have been somewhat in trouble; did you take your burden to him as naturally as a little child runs to its mother with a cut finger? Did you tell him all and leave it all to him? You had a loss; did you voluntarily resign all to his will? Has there been no pride this week? Pride grieves him very much, for he is not a proud Master and is not pleased with a proud disciple. Has there not been much to mourn over? And now at this very moment, what is the state of our feeling towards him? Must we not confess that, though there is a work of grace in our souls, yet there is much about us at this moment which should make us bow down in grief before the Lord?

FOR MEDITATION: The only decent response to sin is to mourn over it (Ezra 10:6). To be arrogant about it (1 Corinthians 5:1–2) or to laugh it off (James 4:8–9) must be the height of spiritual indecency.

SERMON NO. 1362

The believer in the body and out of the body

'We are confident, I say, and willing rather to be absent from the body, and to be present with the Lord.' 2 Corinthians 5:8
SUGGESTED FURTHER READING: Philippians 1:21–26

The spirits of those saints who have left their bodies in the grave are not annihilated; they live on. Paul could not have counted it better to be annihilated than to lead a life of holy confidence. The saints are not dead; our Lord gave a conclusive answer to that error when he said, 'Now that the dead are raised, even Moses shewed at the bush, when he calleth the Lord the God of Abraham, and the God of Isaac, and the God of Jacob. For he is not a God of the dead, but of the living: for all live unto him.' Those who have departed this life are still alive: we are sure of that, or else Paul would not have preferred that state. Neither are they unconscious, as some say, for who would prefer torpor to active confidence? Whatever trials there may be in the Christian life here below, the man of faith does really enjoy life and could not prefer unconsciousness. Neither are the saints in purgatorial fires, for nobody would desire to be tormented, and we may be sure that the apostle Paul would not have been willing to be in purgatory rather than to live here and serve his Lord. The saints live in consciousness and happiness. Moses came and talked with Christ on the mount of Transfiguration, though he had no body, just as readily as Elijah, though that mighty prophet carried his body with him when he ascended in a chariot of fire. The body is not necessary to consciousness or to happiness. The best of all is that the spirits of the departed are with Christ; 'to be with Christ; which is far better', said the apostle. For 'ever with the Lord', their portion is allotted them. It is the Lord's own prayer: 'I will that they also, whom thou hast given me, be with me where I am; that they may behold my glory,' and the prayer is fulfilled in them.

FOR MEDITATION: (*Our Own Hymn Book* no.865 v.1—Samuel Crossman, 1664)

'Jerusalem on high my song and city is,
My home whene'er I die, the centre of my bliss.
O happy place! When shall I be,
My God, with Thee, and see Thy face?'

SERMON NO. 1303

The final separation

'And before him shall be gathered all nations: and he shall separate them one from another, as a shepherd divideth his sheep from the goats.'
Matthew 25:32
SUGGESTED FURTHER READING: John 5:19–29

There are in this world nowhere any other sort of people beside those who are dead in sin and those who are alive unto God. There is no state between. A man either lives or is dead; you cannot find a neutral condition. A man may be in a swoon or asleep, but he is alive; no state is there that is not within the boundary of either life or death. Is this not clear enough? There is no state between converted and unconverted, between being quickened and being dead in sin. There is no condition between being pardoned and having our sins upon us. There is no state between dwelling in darkness and being brought into marvellous light. One or the other must always be our condition; and this is the great folly of mankind in all times—they will dream of a middle state and try to loiter in it. It was for this cause that Elijah, standing on Carmel's brow, said, 'How long halt ye between two opinions? if the LORD be God, follow him: but if Baal, then follow him.' It is for this reason that we have constantly to call the attention of mankind to the great declaration of the gospel—'He that believeth and is baptized shall be saved; but he that believeth not shall be damned.' Be not deceived about it; you are either in the way to heaven or on the road to hell. There is no purgatory or middle condition in the next world. Purgatory is an invention of the Pope for the filling of his cellar and his larder; and no more profitable speculation has ever been set agoing than the saying of masses and the robbing of dupes, under the pretence of altering that state which is fixed for ever. Purgatory Pickpurse was the name the first reformers gave it. You will go to heaven or to hell, and you will remain in one place or the other.

FOR MEDITATION: The only alternative to heaven and hell is earth (Matthew 16:18–19) and that is why we must ensure that we pass from spiritual death to spiritual life while we are still here (John 5:24), otherwise after death it will be too late to escape from God's wrath and judgment (Luke 16:22–26; John 5:28–29; Hebrews 9:27).

SERMON NO. 1234

The danger of unconfessed sin

'When I kept silence, my bones waxed old through my roaring all the day long.' Psalm 32:3
SUGGESTED FURTHER READING: James 3:5–18

I find it good to look all round sometimes and think, 'I am a father; there are my sins against my children. Have I trained them up for God as I should? I am a husband; there are sins in that relationship. I am a master; there are sins in that position: how have I acted towards my servants? I am a pastor; how many sins occur in that relationship?' You will not look around you, if God opens your eyes, without being helped to see what you ought to confess. Take the very limbs of your body and they will accuse you: sins of the brain in evil thoughts, sins of the eye in idle glances, sins of this little naughty member, the tongue, which does more mischief than all the rest. There is no member without its own special sins. There are sins of the ear—how often have we heard the gospel, but heard it in vain? On the other hand, have we not too often lent a willing ear to unholy words and to wicked stories against our neighbours? I need not read over the calendar of our offences; go and write it out in the closet and pour out a flood of tears over it. If you are willing to confess, everything will help you to confession, and there is good reason for doing it at once. May the Holy Spirit work with his tenderest influences to melt your heart into contrition. While you are confessing, remember that each one of your sins has a world of evil in it. There is a mine of sin in every little sin. You have taken up a spider's nest sometimes—one of those little money-spinner's nests—and you have opened it. What thousands of spiders you find hanging down and hastening away in various directions. So in every sin there is a host of sins. There is a conglomeration of many kinds of evil in every transgression; therefore be humbled on account of each one.

FOR MEDITATION: (*Our Own Hymn Book* no.51 version 3 v.1—Isaac Watts, 1719)
  'O Thou that hear'st when sinners cry,
  Though all my crimes before Thee lie,
  Behold them not with angry look,
  But blot their memory from Thy book.'

Thinking and turning

'I thought on my ways, and turned my feet unto thy testimonies.' Psalm
119:59
SUGGESTED FURTHER READING: James 3:1–5

Think of the best things you have ever done; does the flush of self-
congratulation colour your cheek? So far as I am concerned, far from me
be every thought of glorying in anything which I have done for my Lord.
Upon no sermon I have ever preached, though God knows I have
preached my very soul out, am I able to look back without a measure of
shame and confusion of face. I know I have preached the gospel, but the
manner of my preaching does not satisfy me. I would wash every
discourse in the tears of repentance, for in each one there are faults and
failures that betray the weakness of a man, the infirmity of a creature
and the unprofitableness of a servant. Upon no deed of charity or act of
devotion that I have performed can I look back with unmixed feelings. I
wish that my best had been a thousand times better, and had not been so
sadly spoiled, as it often has been, by unbelief at the outset, or pride at
the end, or flagging zeal in the middle. This confession is no insincere
regret, or a spurious attempt to appear humble—I mean what I say—and
I believe that in the like confession the most devout of men would the
most heartily concur. The sins of our holy things; how grievous they are!
It is only because our consciences are so blind that we do not shudder at
the sight of them. Do you ever think you have done well? In that very
thinking you have done ill. When I hear any of my brethren talk of being
perfect, I wonder what they mean. Do they use the English language? Do
they know themselves or their God? In perfect ignorance they surely
must be held captive. As to their own nature and its workings they can
have no knowledge, or else such boastful expressions could not come
from their lips. Brethren, the saints are sinners still.

FOR MEDITATION: (*Our Own Hymn Book* no.605 v.1—John Morrison,
1781)
> 'Come, let us to the Lord our God
> With contrite hearts return;
> Our God is gracious, nor will leave
> The desolate to mourn.'

SERMON NO. 1181

The apple tree in the wood

'As the apple tree among the trees of the wood, so is my beloved among the sons.' Song of Solomon 2:3

SUGGESTED FURTHER READING: John 6:47–59

We can say with great propriety, if we love the Lord Jesus Christ, 'As the apple tree among the trees of the wood, so is my beloved among the sons.' The point of the metaphor is this. There are many trees of the forest and they all have their uses, but when one is hungry, faint and thirsty, the forest trees yield no succour, and we must look elsewhere; they yield shelter, but not refreshing nutriment. If, however, in the midst of the wood one discovers an apple tree, he there finds the refreshment which he needs; his thirst is alleviated and his hunger removed. Even so the church here means to say that there are many things in the world which yield us a kind of satisfaction—many men, many truths, many institutions, many earthly comforts—but there are none which yield us the full solace which the soul requires, none which can give to the heart the spiritual food for which it hungers; Jesus Christ alone supplies the needs of the sons of men. As the apple tree is the exception to the forest trees in bearing its fruit, as it stands on that account in contrast to the trees of the wood, so does Jesus our beloved contrast with all others and transcendently excel them. Wandering, as I have been during the last few days, up and down in the New Forest, the only real forest of our country, and finding rest in its vast solitudes, often has this text occurred to me, and therefore I can do no other than speak of it to you—'As the apple tree among the trees of the wood, so is my beloved among the sons.'

FOR MEDITATION: (*Our Own Hymn Book* no.805 v.1—William Cowper, 1779)

'I thirst, but not as once I did,
The vain delights of earth to share;
Thy wounds, Immanuel, all forbid
That I should seek my pleasures there.'

N.B. Spurgeon's visits to the New Forest formed part of a touring holiday in Southern England (mainly Surrey and Hampshire) during June 1873.

SERMON NO. 1120

The trees in God's courts

'Those that be planted in the house of the LORD *shall flourish in the courts of our God. They shall still bring forth fruit in old age; they shall be fat and flourishing; to shew that the* LORD *is upright: he is my rock, and there is no unrighteousness in him.'* Psalm 92:13–15

SUGGESTED FURTHER READING: Hebrews 12:5–11

Little do you and I know what special attention God has paid to us personally and individually. There are some of us upon whom the Lord has been long accustomed to look with a tender but jealous eye. If he has seen a little wrong about us, he has grieved at it and felt, 'I must put it away.' When he has seen us getting a little cold, he has begun at once to rouse us up, for he has loved us too well to leave us exposed to even a little spiritual sickness. He has sometimes said, 'There is my servant, and he will get proud of his service or his success; I must bring him down.' High looks and haughty thoughts are an abomination in his sight. Another time he has said, 'Such-and-such a man is increasing in wealth; he will get worldly-minded. I must take away some of his worldly goods that he may take more account of his treasures laid up in heaven and set his heart more on me.' 'The LORD thy God is a jealous God'. Where there is love there is often a sensitiveness which stirs up jealousy. The greatness of God's love makes him very zealous for us and very jealous of us. If he sees those whom he very much loves with the slightest evil thing about them, he is quick to observe it and prompt to purge it away. You know that you do not like to see a spot on your dear child's face. You will have it washed off as soon as possible. So will the Lord cleanse his people, both without and within. The care and the trouble he has had with us, as I have already said, none of us can tell. We ought to bring forth fruit to the profit of the husbandman, to the glory of God. Branches that bring forth fruit he purges.

FOR MEDITATION: (*Our Own Hymn Book* no.732 v.5—George Keith, 1787)
    'When through fiery trials thy pathway shall lie,
    My grace all-sufficient shall be thy supply;
    The flame shall not hurt thee; I only design
    Thy dross to consume, and thy gold to refine.'

SERMON NO. 1365

Sudden sorrow

'Suddenly are my tents spoiled, and my curtains in a moment.' 'And when thou art spoiled, what wilt thou do?' Jeremiah 4:20,30
SUGGESTED FURTHER READING: Job 1:13–22

All that we possess here below is God's property; he has only loaned it out to us, and what he lends he has a right to take back again. We hold our possessions and our friends not upon freehold, but upon lease terminable at the Supreme Owner's option. Do you wonder when the holding ceases? Do you know the parable of the wise Jewish woman? When her husband, the Rabbi, had gone out to teach his disciples, certain neighbours in great sorrow brought home to her the corpses of her only two children, two sweet boys, who had been drowned. She took them upstairs, laid them upon the bed, covered them with a sheet and waited in her deep affliction until her husband came home, grieving most of all for the sorrow which would overwhelm him. She stood at the door and mournfully said, 'My husband, do you know that a great tribulation has happened to me? A friend had lent me a treasure and, while I have had it, it has been a great joy to me, but this day he has taken it back again, and I know not what to do.' 'My beloved,' said the Rabbi, 'Speak not so. Can it be a sorrow to you to return that which you have borrowed? O daughter of Abraham, you cannot harbour dishonesty in your soul. If the treasure has been lent, be grateful to him who permitted you the loan, and send it back with cheerfulness.' 'Do you say so?' she said; 'Come here.' Then she turned back the coverlet; he gazed upon the cold faces of his two children and said, 'You have spoken wisely, O woman, for I understand that God has lent these children to me, and that I must not complain because he has taken back his own.' Do you see how natural it is that loans should be returned to their lender in due season?

FOR MEDITATION: If all that we possess is only on short-term loan from the Lord, we ought to hold our possessions lightly (1 Corinthians 7:29–31; Hebrews 10:34). This applies equally to our very lives (Mark 8:35–36) which can be recalled whenever God chooses (Luke 12:19–20). The Christian's body belongs to God both by creation and by redemption (1 Corinthians 6:19–20).

SERMON NO. 1363

Enquire of the Lord

'I will yet for this be enquired of by the house of Israel, to do it for them;
I will increase them with men like a flock. As the holy flock, as the flock
of Jerusalem in her solemn feasts; so shall the waste cities be filled with
flocks of men: and they shall know that I am the LORD.*' Ezekiel 36:37–38*
SUGGESTED FURTHER READING: 2 Chronicles 7:11–22

Prayer must be offered by an anxious, observant, enterprising church. The expression 'I will ... be enquired of' implies that the people must think, ask questions, argue and plead with God. It is well to ask him why he has not given the blessing and to urge strong reasons why he should now do so. We should quote his promise to him, tell him of our undesert and great need, and then come back again to asking, enquiring and pleading our cause. Such a church, pleading, will win a blessing beyond all doubt. It must be a church which remembers the waste places; the text puts it in the promise and it must not be forgotten in the prayer—'so shall the waste cities be filled with flocks of men'. A church which anxiously remembers the departments of service which are not succeeding, casts a friendly eye over other churches which may be failing, takes careful notice of those places where the Spirit of God does not seem to be at work, and mentions all those in prayer, is the church to which the promise is made. May the Lord give you heartbreak over sinners whose hearts do not break, and painful anxiety for those who are not anxious; may God make you all anxious enquirers; when the saved ones are anxious enquirers themselves, there will be plenty of anxious enquirers brought from the world. The way to have enquiring sinners is for us to become enquiring saints. When the saints enquire of the Lord, the sinners will ask their way to Zion. Every prayer meeting ought to be an enquirers' meeting, where true hearts 'behold the beauty of the LORD, and ... enquire in his temple'.

FOR MEDITATION: Some of the Psalms begin with asking God serious heartfelt questions—why (Psalm 10:1; 22:1; 74:1), how long (Psalm 13:1), who (Psalm 15:1)? Other godly believers such as Abraham (Genesis 18:23–25), Moses (Exodus 5:22–23; 32:11–12), Joshua (Joshua 7:7–9), Gideon (Judges 6:12–15) and Habakkuk (Habakkuk 1:2–3) have done the same. How much of this does the Lord hear in your prayers?

SERMON NO. 1304

The rising sun

'But unto you that fear my name shall the Sun of righteousness arise with healing in his wings; and ye shall go forth, and grow up as calves of the stall.' Malachi 4:2
SUGGESTED FURTHER READING: Jonah 1:7–16

Jonah in the ship was in a very sinful state of mind and was fleeing away from God, yet he did not hesitate to say, 'I am an Hebrew; and I fear the LORD.' This is the abiding character of the saints in their worst state. If they backslide, they still fear the name of the Lord. They fear it at times very slavishly with the spirit of bondage, but they do fear it. They lose the evidence of their sonship and cease to walk in the light, but still have a fear of the Most High: they do not treat him lightly; they could not sin against him cheaply; there is still within their hearts a sense of his greatness. It generally assumes the form of a reverence of his person. They know there is a God; they are sure that he made the heavens and the earth; they are equally clear that he is everywhere present, marking the ways of men. Others may blaspheme, but they cannot; others may sin and make merry with it, but sin costs them dear; others may feast themselves without apprehension, but they cannot, for they fear the Lord. I know that this expresses all true religion and has a very comprehensive meaning, but it suits my purpose just now to view it as a description of believers, which is true of them all, into whatever state they may come. They still fear the Lord. Do you tremble before God? There is something in that. I do not ask you whether you tremble at hell. That is no sign of grace, for what thief will not tremble at the gallows? I do not ask if you are afraid of death. What mortal man is not, unless he has a good hope through grace? But do you tremble in the presence of God because you have offended him, and do you tremble in the presence of sin lest you should again offend him?

FOR MEDITATION: As in Jonah's case, the Psalmist's fear of God was shown not only by his profession (Psalm 119:63,120) but also by his concern at having gone astray from God (Psalm 119:176). How fearful a situation it is when rebellious sinners have no concern about fearing God and when God himself has to raise the matter with them (Jeremiah 5:22–24).

SERMON NO. 1463(B)

Rivers of water in a dry place

'As rivers of water in a dry place.' Isaiah 32:2
SUGGESTED FURTHER READING: Psalm 63:1–11

Do not many of you find your outward circumstances very dry places?
Are you rich? Wealthy society is generally as dry a place as the granite
hills. 'Gold and the gospel seldom do agree.' Are you poor? Poverty is a
dry place to those who are not rich in faith. Are you engaged in business
from day to day? How often do its cares parch the soul, like the hot
sand-wind of the desert! To rise up early and to toil late amid losses and
crosses is to dwell in a dry place. O to feel the love of Christ flowing
then! This is to have 'rivers of water'. To have Christ near when you are
losing your money, when bills are being dishonoured and commercial
houses falling, this is true religion. To rejoice in Christ when you are out
of work, to have Christ when the wife is sick, Christ when the darling
child has to be buried, Christ when the head is aching, Christ when the
poor body is half starved, this is sweetness. You will never know the
sweetness of Christ until you know the bitterness of trial. You cannot
know his fulness until you see your emptiness; I pray that it may be our
experience always to feel ourselves going down and Christ going up,
ourselves getting poorer and poorer apart from him, while we know
more and more of the priceless riches which are ours in Christ Jesus our
Lord. The point of the whole seems to me to be this, that Christ is a river
of abounding grace, but he is most so to those who are most dry. Alms
are sought only by the poor, the physician is esteemed only by the sick,
the lifeboat is valued only by the man who is drowning; so, Christ will be
dearer and dearer to you just in proportion as you have less and less
esteem of yourself.

FOR MEDITATION: (*Our Own Hymn Book* no.488 vv.4&5—Isaac Watts,
1706)
> 'Ho, ye that pant for living streams, and pine away and die,
> Here you may quench your raging thirst with springs that never dry.
> Rivers of love and mercy here in a rich ocean join;
> Salvation in abundance flows, like floods of milk and wine.'

SERMON NO. 1243

A singular title and a special favour

'The God of my mercy shall prevent me.' Psalm 59:10
SUGGESTED FURTHER READING: John 1:9–18

I want you all to pause a moment and ask whether you really have appropriated by faith the mercy of God and the God of the mercy. Why did not that unhappy artiste fly the other day? Why did he fall to the ground a mangled mess? Because his wings were not his own or a part of himself. The smallest bat which ventures out in the evening twilight can fly because it has its own wings, and the tiniest humming-bird which dives into a flower bell can fly because its wings belong to it; but this man had only a borrowed contrivance, a mechanical invention, which he could not appropriate to his own being; another might use it as well as he, if indeed it could be used at all. If you wish to fly, you must have wings of your own. Many religious professors have a mechanical religion; they have the baptism of babyhood and the priestly efficacy of sacraments—a mere flying machine! It will not serve their turn; they must have faith and grace of their own, personal faith in a personal God. Those who have such appropriating faith 'shall mount up with wings as eagles', but no others can. Wings which are not your own wings will be of no use to you, but ensure your destruction; but if you are the humblest, weakest and most obscure of all God's children, if you have a real faith of your own, so that you can say, 'My God, my Saviour!' and can cry 'Abba, Father', you shall mount aloft to his abode and make your nest for ever by the throne of love. God grant us power to appropriate his precious things and call him 'The God of my mercy.'

FOR MEDITATION: Saving faith has to dwell in individual members even of a 'Christian' family (2 Timothy 1:5). Only faith in the Lord Jesus Christ counts for anything; reliance on material or fleshly things achieves nothing (1 Peter 1:18–19,23–25).

N.B. Vincent de Groof, the 'flying-man', died on 9 July 1874 when he fell with his newly-invented parachute, made in imitation of a bat's wings, from a balloon which had ascended from Cremorne Gardens, Chelsea. The balloon landed in Essex in front of a train which stopped just in time to avoid a collision.

SERMON NO. 1182

Christ asleep in the vessel

'Master, carest thou not that we perish?' Mark 4:38
SUGGESTED FURTHER READING: Romans 5:6–11

Do you think that Christ came from heaven to earth to save you, and is now indifferent about you? Do you think that he lived here thirty years of toil and weariness for your redemption, and will now cast you away? Do you believe that he went up to the cross for you, having endured Gethsemane's terrible garden, and yet has no concern about you? Do you think he bore all the wrath of God on your behalf, and now thinks your salvation such a trifling thing that he cares not whether you perish or not? Do you believe that he slept in the grave for you, rose again for you, went within the veil for you and pleads before God for you, but is, after all, a hypocrite and has no real love to you? If what Christ has done does not convince you, what can? Many waters could not quench his love, neither could the floods drown it; will you not confide in him for the present and the future after what he has done for you? Consider, yet again, what he has wrought upon you personally and what you have known and felt within yourself. Years ago you were his enemy, but he saved you and made you his friend. Do you remember when, in the agony of your soul, you cried to him as from the lowest pit and he came to your rescue? Will he leave you now? If God had not done so much for us already, we might question his intentions concerning us; but after the goodness and the mercy he has manifested, surely he will go through with it and perfect the work which he has begun. He has spent too much upon his work to relinquish it now.

FOR MEDITATION: (*Our Own Hymn Book* no.981 v.6—John Newton, 1779—not sung during the service, but quoted by Spurgeon within the above sermon extract)

    'Thou hast helped in every need,
    This emboldens me to plead;
    After so much mercy past,
    Canst Thou let me sink at last?'

The lifting up of the bowed down

'*And, behold, there was a woman which had a spirit of infirmity eighteen years, and was bowed down together, and could in no wise lift up herself. And when Jesus saw her, he called her to him, and said unto her, Woman, thou art loosed from thine infirmity. And he laid his hands on her: and immediately she was made straight, and glorified God.' Luke 13:11–13*
SUGGESTED FURTHER READING: Job 1:6–12 & 2:1–7

Satan had done a good deal to the poor woman, but he had done all he could do. You may rest assured that whenever Satan smites a child of God he never spares his strength. He knows nothing of mercy, neither does any other consideration restrain him. When the Lord delivered Job into Satan's hand for a time, what destruction and havoc he made with Job's property. He did not save him chick, child, sheep, goat, camel or ox, but he smote him right and left, and caused ruin to his whole estate. When, under a second permit, he came to touch him in his bone and in his flesh, nothing would satisfy the devil but covering him from the sole of his foot to the crown of his head with sore boils and blisters. He might have pained him quite sufficiently by torturing one part of his body, but this would not suffice; he must glut himself with vengeance. The devil would do all he could and therefore he covered him with running sores. Yet, as there was a limit in Job's case, so was there here; Satan had bound this woman, but he had not killed her. He might bend her towards the grave, but he could not bend her into it; he might make her droop over till she was bent double, but he could not take away her poor feeble life: with all his infernal craft he could not make her die before her time. Moreover, she was still a woman and he could not make a beast of her, notwithstanding that she was thus bowed down into the form of the brute. Even so the devil cannot destroy you, child of God. He can smite you, but he cannot slay you.

FOR MEDITATION: While we should not underestimate Satan's powers, we must not exaggerate them either. In Peter's experience we see the devil roaring (Luke 22:31), the disciple resisting (Luke 22:33,49–50,54–56) but failing (Luke 22:45–46,56–60) and the deity restoring (Luke 22:32,61–62; 24:34). Meditate on these three points as passed on to us by Peter in 1 Peter 5:8–10.

SERMON NO. 1426

Strong faith

'But was strong in faith, giving glory to God.' Romans 4:20
SUGGESTED FURTHER READING: 1 Timothy 5:17–22

We who are teachers of others ought to have strong faith in God. I think we may at times profitably mention our own doubts and fears for the encouragement of those who are terribly downcast, but it ought always to be done with very great prudence and much regret. I recollect once speaking of my own tremblings, when preaching, and a venerable brother said to me afterwards. 'I do not think, dear pastor, that you were right in speaking of your own transgressions so freely. You encouraged the people certainly by what you said about yourself, but I hardly think they ought to be encouraged. Now, suppose you were to go into the pulpit and say, "there are some of you who are thieves; it is very wrong of you, but still do not despair, for I thieve a little myself." Why, you know you would not be doing any good, but harm; and yet thieving is not more truly a sin than doubting God; in fact there is the utmost sin in unbelief.' I replied to my good brother that he was right and I thanked him for the correction. Whenever, dear hearers, you catch any of us who are teachers doubting and fearing, do not pity us, but scold us. We have no right to be in Doubting Castle. Do not visit us there. Follow us as far as we follow Christ, but if we get into the horrible Slough of Despond, come and pull us out by the hair of our heads if necessary, but do not fall into it yourselves. Never say, 'My beloved pastor went there, and therefore I may go there.' No, but say, 'Even our minister fell into that error, and therefore I will keep as far from it as ever I can, for if the teacher slips, the disciple may easily do so, and therefore I must very carefully watch against unbelief.'

FOR MEDITATION: The truly spiritual leader will not be a man who behaves in a domineering manner (1 Peter 5:1–3), but one who will be well aware that he is capable of making many mistakes (James 3:1–2). Even an apostle needed rebuking (Galatians 2:11–14). But none of this exempts us from honouring and respecting those who are over us in the Lord (1 Thessalonians 5:12–13; Hebrews 13:17; 1 Peter 5:5).

SERMON NO. 1367

Aeneas

'As Peter passed throughout all quarters, he came down also to the saints which dwelt at Lydda. And there he found a certain man named Aeneas, which had kept his bed eight years, and was sick of the palsy. And Peter said unto him, Aeneas, Jesus Christ maketh thee whole: arise and make thy bed. And he arose immediately.' Acts 9:32–34
SUGGESTED FURTHER READING (Spurgeon): Isaiah 55:1–7

Somebody says, 'I wish I had Christ!' Soul, why not have him at once? 'Oh, but I am not fit.' You never will be fit; you cannot be fit, except in the sense in which you are fit even now. What is fitness for washing? Why, being dirty. What is fitness for alms? Why, being in distress. What is fitness for a doctor? Why, being ill. This is all the fitness that a man wants for trusting in Christ to save him. Christ's mercy is to be had for nothing; bribe or purchase is out the question. I have heard of a woman whose child was in a fever and needed grapes; there was a prince who lived near, in whose hothouse there were some of the rarest grapes that had ever been grown. She scraped together the little money she could earn, went to the gardener and offered to buy a bunch of the royal fruit. Of course he repulsed her and said they were not to be sold. Did she imagine that the prince grew grapes to sell like a market-gardener? He sent her on her way, much grieved. She came again; she came several times, for a mother's importunity is great, but no offer of hers would be accepted. At last the princess heard of it and wished to see the woman; when she came the princess said, 'The prince does not sell the fruit of his garden:' but, snipping off a bunch of grapes and dropping them into a little bag, she said, 'He is always ready to give it away to the poor.' Now, here is the rich cluster of gospel salvation from the true vine. My Lord will not sell it, but he is always ready to give it away to all who humbly ask for it; if you want it, come and take it now by believing in Jesus.

FOR MEDITATION: Because God has purchased the salvation of sinners (1 Corinthians 6:20; 7:23) by means of Christ's blood (Acts 20:28), the blessings of the gospel can be received for free (Romans 3:24; 5:15–16; Revelation 21:6). But we each have to obey the command to receive the free gift of salvation (Revelation 22:17).

SERMON NO. 1315

The secret of a happy life

'I have set the LORD always before me: because he is at my right hand, I shall not be moved.' Psalm 16:8
SUGGESTED FURTHER READING: Acts 14:8–18

I beseech you to pray that you may have this text wrought into your very souls: 'I have set the LORD always before me'. Refuse to see anything without seeing God in it. Regard the creatures as the mirror of the great Creator. Do not imagine that you have understood his works until you have felt the presence of the great worker himself. Do not reckon that you know anything until you know that of God which lies within it, for that is the kernel which it contains. Wake in the morning and recognise God in your chamber, for his goodness has drawn back the curtain of the night and taken from your eyelids the seal of sleep: put on your garments and perceive the divine care which provides you with raiment from the herb of the field and the sheep of the fold. Go to the breakfast room and bless the God whose bounty has again provided for you 'a table in the wilderness': go out to business and feel God with you in all the engagements of the day: perpetually remember that you are dwelling in his house when you are toiling for your bread or engaged in merchandise. At length, after a well-spent day, go back to your family and see the Lord in each one of the members of it; own his goodness in preserving life and health; look for his presence at the family altar, making the house to be a very palace wherein king's children dwell. At last, fall asleep at night as in the embraces of your God or on your Saviour's breast. This is happy living. The worldling forgets God, the sinner dishonours him, the atheist denies him, but the Christian lives in him; 'in him we live, and move, and have our being ... we are also his offspring.'

FOR MEDITATION: (*Our Own Hymn Book* no.708 v.3—Ann Letitia Waring, 1850)
    'I thirst for springs of heavenly life,
    And here all day they rise;
    I seek the treasure of Thy love,
    And close at hand it lies.'

Faith's ultimatum

'Though he slay me, yet will I trust in him.' Job 13:15
SUGGESTED FURTHER READING (Spurgeon): Psalm 73:1–28

I have been putting a little riddle to myself. Here it is. Is it easier to trust God when you have nothing, or when you have all things? Is it easier to say, 'Though he slay me, yet will I trust in him', or to say, 'Though he make me alive, I will trust in him'? Will you think it over? Shall I help you? Here is a man without a penny in the world: his cupboard is bare, his flocks are cut off from the field, and his herds from the stall; is it hard for that man to trust in God? If you say so, I will not dispute with you. But here is another man who has a bank full of gold; his meadows are covered with flocks and herds, his barns are ready to burst with corn, and his trade prospers on all hands. Now, is it easy for that man to trust God? Do you say 'Yes'? I say 'No'. I say that he has a very hard task indeed to live by faith, and the probabilities are that when he says 'I trust God,' he is trusting his barn or his bank. All things considered, it occurs to me that it is easier to trust God in adversity than in prosperity, because whatever trust there is in adversity is real trust, but a good deal of the faith we have in prosperity is a kind of trust which you will have to take upon trust, and whether it is faith or not is a matter of serious question. Where is the room for faith when you can already see all that you want? A full barn has no room for faith if she be any bigger than a mouse, but in an empty barn faith has scope and liberty. When the brook Cherith is dried up, when the poor widow has nothing left but a handful of meal and a little oil, then there is room for the prophet to exercise faith.

FOR MEDITATION: (*Our Own Hymn Book* no.689 v.1—Thomas Kelly, 1815)
> 'When we cannot see our way,
> Let us trust and still obey;
> He who bids us forward go,
> Cannot fail the way to show.'

Is conversion necessary?

'Therefore if any man be in Christ, he is a new creature: old things are passed away; behold, all things are become new.' 2 Corinthians 5:17
SUGGESTED FURTHER READING (Spurgeon): John 3:16–36

Everywhere in Scripture men are divided into two classes with a very sharp line of distinction between them. Read in the gospels and you shall find continual mention of sheep lost and sheep found, guests refusing the invitation and guests feasting at the table, the wise virgins and the foolish, the sheep and the goats. In the epistles we read of those who are 'dead in trespasses and sins' and of others to whom it is said, 'And you hath he quickened', so that some are alive to God and others are in their natural state of spiritual death. We find men spoken of as being either in darkness or in light, and the phrase is used of being called 'out of darkness into his marvellous light'. Some are spoken of as having been formerly aliens and strangers, but having been made fellow-citizens and brethren. We read of 'children of God' in opposition to 'children of wrath'. We read of believers who are not condemned, and of those who are condemned already because they have not believed. We read of those who have 'gone astray' and of those who have 'returned unto the Shepherd and Bishop of' their souls. We read that those 'that are in the flesh cannot please God', and of those who are chosen, called and justified, whom the whole universe is challenged to condemn. The apostle speaks of 'us which are saved' as if there are some saved while upon others 'the wrath of God abideth'. 'Enemies' are continually placed in contrast with those who are 'reconciled to God by the death of his Son'. There are those that are 'far off' from God 'by wicked works', and those who are 'made nigh by the blood of Christ'. I could continue till I wearied you. The distinction between the two classes runs through the whole of Scripture; never do we find a hint that there are some that are naturally good and do not need to be removed from one class into the other.

FOR MEDITATION: Consider some other terms used to describe conversion—'passed from death unto life' (John 5:24); 'delivered us from the power of darkness, and hath translated us into the kingdom of his dear Son' (Colossians 1:13); 'bring us to God' (1 Peter 3:18). Has this transformation occurred in your life?

SERMON NO. 1183

Fresh grace confidently expected

'I shall be anointed with fresh oil.' Psalm 92:10
SUGGESTED FURTHER READING (Spurgeon): Isaiah 40:27–31

Changes are appointed us as long as we are here. Men may promise themselves they shall never see a change, but they are greatly mistaken. David said, 'I shall never be moved', but in a very little time he sang another hymn. When I hear brethren so very confident that they shall never doubt again, I am reminded of a story I have heard of the olden times. A young gentleman who had never travelled before went over Hounslow Heath, and was accosted by another gentleman who rode by his side and joined in an interesting conversation. Our friend said at last, 'I have always been told by my father that this is a very dangerous heath, but the old gentleman was, I think, exceedingly nervous, for we have come all this way without being molested by highwaymen.' 'Yes,' said the other, 'but now is the time for you to stop and deliver'; and he clapped his pistol to his ear. It often happens, when we say, 'I shall have no more temptations,' that our very confidence is in itself a temptation. Yes, there have been times of sore trial, but the Lord has appeared for us. Up to this moment not one good thing has failed of all that the Lord God has promised.

> 'Thus far we prove that promise good
> Which Jesus ratified with blood.'

We have no fault to find with our God. Jehovah Jireh, the Lord, has provided to this day; in the mount of the Lord shall it be seen. 'Ebenezer … Hitherto hath the LORD helped us.' If he has done so up till now, so will he, for he is an unchangeable God; let us be assured that we 'shall be anointed with fresh oil'.

FOR MEDITATION: (*Our Own Hymn Book* no.676 v.4—Isaac Watts, 1709)
> 'From Thee, the overflowing spring,
> Our souls shall drink a fresh supply,
> While such as trust their native strength,
> Shall melt away, and droop, and die.'

SERMON NO. 1122

A vile weed and a fair flower

'He hath said, I will never leave thee, nor forsake thee. So that we may boldly say, The Lord is my helper.' Hebrews 13:5–6
SUGGESTED FURTHER READING: 1 Kings 17:1–16

A promise from the mouth of God is better than a bond signed and sealed by the wealthiest of men. No negotiable securities can be comparable in value to this declaration of the Lord, 'I will never leave thee, nor forsake thee.' It is put very strongly. In the original there are five negatives, as in this verse:—

> 'The soul that on Jesus hath leaned for repose,
> I will not, I will not desert to his foes;
> That soul, though all hell should endeavour to shake,
> I'll never, no never, no never forsake!'

The five negatives in the last line correspond with the five in the Greek text—'I will never leave thee, nor forsake thee.' In no single instance, nor in any particular, nor for any reason will he leave you. If you have cast yourself upon his infinite power and grace, he will carry you to the end. Not only will he not desert you altogether, but he will not leave you even for a little while. He may seem for a small moment to hide his face from you, but he will still love you and supply your needs. Behind the wall he will pour oil upon the flame, if in front of it he permits Satan to throw water upon it. He will feed you somehow by the back door if not by the front, by the ravens if not by the doves. If the brook Cherith fails, he will find a widow, even in a distant land, who in all her straits shall nevertheless feed the servant of God. 'I will never leave thee, nor forsake thee.' Surely we cannot fail to be contented if we get fast hold of this promise.

FOR MEDITATION: A double negative in the Greek text may not mean much in a mere man's mouth (Matthew 26:35), but can be trusted when the Lord is the speaker. The possibilities of a Christian thirsting (John 6:35), being cast out (John 6:37), perishing (John 10:28), having sins remembered (Hebrews 8:12) and being blotted out of the book of life (Revelation 3:5) are strongly denied by double negatives.

SERMON NO. 1449

The covenant pleaded

'Have respect unto the covenant.' Psalm 74:20
SUGGESTED FURTHER READING: Psalm 25:1–14

I might take you through all the various needs of God's people, and show that in seeking to have them supplied they may fitly cry, 'Have respect unto the covenant.' For instance, suppose you were in great distress of mind and needed special comfort, you could go to him with that covenant promise, 'As one whom his mother comforteth, so will I comfort you.' Go to him with that and say, 'Lord, comfort thy servant.' Or if there should happen to be a trouble upon us, not for ourselves, but for the church, how sweet it is to go to the Lord and say, 'Thy covenant runs thus—"the gates of hell shall not prevail against it." O Lord, it seems as though they would prevail. Interpose thy strength and save thy church.' If it ever should happen that you are looking for the conversion of the ungodly and desiring to see sinners saved, and the world seems so dark, look at our text again, the whole verse—'Have respect unto the covenant: for the dark places of the earth are full of the habitations of cruelty.' To this you may add, 'but thou hast said that "the earth shall be filled with the knowledge of the glory of the LORD" and that "all flesh shall see the salvation of God." Lord, have respect unto thy covenant. Help our missionaries, speed thy gospel, bid the mighty "angel fly in the midst of heaven, having the everlasting gospel to preach" to every creature.' Why, it is a grand missionary prayer—'Have respect unto the covenant'. Beloved, it is a two-edged sword to be used in all conditions of strife, and it is a holy balm of Gilead that will heal in all conditions of suffering.

FOR MEDITATION: (*Our Own Hymn Book* no.228 v.1—Philip Doddridge, 1755)
   'My God, the covenant of Thy love
   Abides for ever sure;
   And in its matchless grace I feel
   My happiness secure.'

Fat things, full of marrow

'This is as the waters of Noah unto me: for as I have sworn that the waters of Noah should no more go over the earth; so have I sworn that I would not be wroth with thee, nor rebuke thee.' Isaiah 54:9
SUGGESTED FURTHER READING: Genesis 8:18–9:17

Until God drowns the whole world again, he never can let out his great wrath against his people. Many centuries have gone by since Noah was saved in the ark, and there has been no other universal flood. There have been partial floods here and there, but the earth has never been completely destroyed with water. I should not wonder that the first shower of rain that fell after he came out of the ark frightened Noah, and if it had not been that he saw the bow of God in the cloud, he would have trembled lest once again the world would be buried in the deeps: but his fears were all in vain; generations have followed generations in perfect safety from a deluge, and I do not suppose that there is a man existing who is afraid of a general flood. Child of God, you must once for all get rid of all fear that God's great wrath can ever be let loose upon you, for it can never come upon the justified. Be sure that as 'the waters of Noah should no more go over the earth', so, if you believe in the Lord Jesus Christ, the Lord will never be angry with you, nor rebuke you, so as to destroy you or count you his enemy. His great wrath is over. The flood lasted twelve months and more, and during that time there was neither sowing nor reaping, but the Lord said that never again shall a flood interrupt the operations of nature. 'Seedtime and harvest ... and summer and winter ... shall not cease', and they have not. Go now into the fields and see how loaded they are with the fruits of the earth, ripening for the sickle. As God has not allowed the seasons to be suspended by another flood, though thousands of years have passed, so certain is it that he will not suspend your spiritual life.

FOR MEDITATION: (*Our Own Hymn Book* no.738 v.1(b)—Augustus M.Toplady, 1771)
    'The terrors of law, and of God,
    With me can have nothing to do;
    My Saviour's obedience and blood
    Hide all my transgressions from view.'

The royal prerogative

See now that I, even I, am he, and there is no god with me: I kill, and I make alive; I wound, and I heal.' Deuteronomy 32:39
SUGGESTED FURTHER READING: Isaiah 44:6–20

There is only one God: Jehovah is his name—the 'I AM'. That one God will not endure a rival. Why should he? He made all things and sustains all things. Should a creature that his own hands have made set up in rivalry with him? If it be a great man like Nebuchadnezzar who says, 'Is not this great Babylon, that I have built?' God will send him to grass among the bullocks and make him to know that no man is great in the sight of God. What a provocation it must be to God to see men bowing down before idols fashioned by their own hands! What a degradation to man that he should worship gold, silver, wood or stone; but what a grievous dishonour to the great God of all! And it seems to me to be the worst of all dishonours when God sees the image of his own dear Son made into an idol, and the representation of the cross, on which redemption was made, lifted on high that before it men may prostrate themselves in worship. This must touch his sacred soul and vex him even to the uttermost, for God is God alone and beside him there is none else: his glory will he not give to another, neither his praise to graven images. The Lord says, 'I, even I.' That 'I' is so great that it fills all places, and, therefore, there can be no room for another. 'I, even I, am he, and there is no god with me.' In another place he says, 'I am the LORD, and there is none else, there is no God beside me.' Oh to have such lofty thoughts of God that we can have no consideration for anything that would rob him of the glory which is so exclusively his own. May we burn with a holy jealousy which abhors the idea of a rival god, and casts the name of Baal out of its mouth with utter loathing.

FOR MEDITATION: 'Jealous' is not only a description of God; it is also his name (Exodus 34:14)! His righteous jealousy is rightly aroused by man's worship of idols (Exodus 20:4–5) and false gods (Deuteronomy 6:14–15; Joshua 24:19–20). Even if you feel that you are not in danger of doing this, remember that God is also jealous when we fall in love with the world (James 4:4–5).

SERMON NO. 1465

The special prayer-meeting

'When he had considered the thing, he came to the house of Mary the mother of John, whose surname was Mark; where many were gathered together praying.' Acts 12:12
SUGGESTED FURTHER READING: Acts 1:12–14

Peter 'considered the thing': I fancy that he thought 'Where shall I go?' and recollected that it was prayer meeting night at John Mark's mother's house; there he would go, because he felt that he should meet with true brethren. In those days they did things by plan and order according to the text, 'Let all things be done decently and in order.' I have no doubt that it had been duly arranged that the meeting should be held that evening at the house of John Mark's mother; therefore Peter went there and found, as he probably expected, that there was a prayer meeting going on. They were not met to hear a sermon. It is most proper that we should very frequently assemble for that purpose, but this was distinctly a prayer meeting 'where many were gathered together praying'. Prayer was the business on hand. I do not know that they even had an address, though some will come to the prayer meeting if the pastor is present to speak; James, who is generally thought to have been pastor of the church at Jerusalem, was not there, for Peter said, 'Go shew these things unto James', and most probably none of the apostles were there, because he added, 'and to the brethren'; I suppose he meant the brethren of the apostolic college. The eminent speaking brethren all seem to have been away, and perhaps no one expounded or exhorted that night, nor was there any need, for they were all too much engrossed in the common intercession. The meeting was convened for praying; this was a regular institution of the Christian church and ought always to be kept up. There should be meetings wholly devoted to prayer, and there is a serious flaw in the arrangements of a church when such gatherings are omitted or placed in a secondary position.

FOR MEDITATION: Meeting for corporate prayer was a priority in the early church (Acts 1:14; 2:42; 12:5,12; 1 Timothy 2:1,8). How high is it on the agenda of your church or on your own personal agenda?

N.B. Spurgeon selected this topic to call for follow-up prayer after the departure from London of the evangelists Moody and Sankey.

SERMON NO. 1247

An earnest warning against lukewarmness

'Because thou art lukewarm, and neither cold nor hot, I will spue thee out of my mouth.' Revelation 3:16
SUGGESTED FURTHER READING: Malachi 3:6–18

The condition in our text is one of mournful indifference and carelessness. They were not cold, but they were not hot; they were not infidels, yet they were not earnest believers; they did not oppose the gospel, neither did they defend it; they were not working mischief, neither were they doing any great good; they were not disreputable in moral character, but they were not distinguished for holiness; they were not irreligious, but they were not enthusiastic in piety nor eminent for zeal; they were what the world calls 'Moderates'; they were of the Broad-church school, neither bigots nor Puritans; they were prudent and avoided fanaticism, respectable and averse to excitement. Good things were maintained among them, but they did not make too much of them; they had prayer meetings, but there were few present, for they liked quiet evenings at home: when more attended the meetings were still very dull, for they did their praying very deliberately and were afraid of being too excited. They were content to have all things 'done decently and in order', but vigour and zeal they considered to be vulgar. Such churches have schools, Bible-classes, preaching rooms and all sorts of agencies, but they might as well be without them, for no energy is displayed and no good comes of them. They have deacons and elders who are excellent pillars of the church, if the chief quality of pillars is to stand still and exhibit no motion or emotion. They have ministers who may be the angels of the churches, but if so they have their wings closely clipped, for they do not fly very far in preaching the everlasting gospel, and they are not flames of fire: they may be shining lights of eloquence, but they are not burning lights of grace, setting men's hearts on fire. In such communities everything is done in an half-hearted, listless, dead-and-alive way, as if it did not matter much whether it was done or not.

FOR MEDITATION: Christians should not only 'abstain from all appearance of evil' (1 Thessalonians 5:22), but also beware of glorying in the mere outward appearance of good (2 Corinthians 5:12), because the Lord looks on the heart (1 Samuel 16:7).

SERMON NO. 1185

God beseeching sinners by his ministers

'And all things are of God, who hath reconciled us to himself by Jesus Christ, and hath given to us the ministry of reconciliation.' 2 Corinthians 5:18

SUGGESTED FURTHER READING: Colossians 1:11–23

Man became God's enemy wantonly, without the slightest offence given on God's part, but man did not make advances towards reconciliation, or express regret because peace was broken. The first overtures for peace are not made by man the offender, but by our aggrieved and offended God. Hence our text begins 'all things are of God'. Reconciliation of man to his Maker is never achieved by man, but is the work of God from first to last, and to God must be all the glory. The passage (2 Corinthians 5:18–21) enforces this truth by giving us a brief summary. The Lord first finds the messengers of reconciliation by reconciling some men to himself. He chooses his ministers, having called them into a state of reconciliation. The ambassador is sent not from man to God, but from God to man. Then the matter of the ambassador's message is altogether from God, for it is God who has reconciled 'the world unto himself' through Jesus Christ. He gave his Son to be the atoning sacrifice by the ordained method of substitution; thus it is he alone who has made a way of access between fallen man and himself. Furthermore, the method by which this atonement is applied to the reconciling of men is also of God. It is not man who beseeches God, but God who beseeches man to be reconciled. It is not man who cries to Christ, but Christ through his ministers, whom he places in his stead, prays man to be reconciled to God. So from the first thought of reconciliation, right on through the provision of the atonement, to the conclusion of the solemn league and covenant between the heart and God, 'all things are of God'.

FOR MEDITATION: (*Our Own Hymn Book* no.202 v.2—Samuel Davies, 1769)

'Crimes of such horror to forgive,
Such guilty, daring worms to spare;
This is Thy grand prerogative,
And none shall in the honour share:
Who is a pardoning God like Thee?
Or who has grace so rich and free?'

To souls in agony

'The sorrows of death compassed me, and the pains of hell gat hold upon me: I found trouble and sorrow. Then called I upon the name of the LORD; *O* LORD, *I beseech thee, deliver my soul.' 'Thou hast delivered my soul from death, mine eyes from tears, and my feet from falling.' Psalm 116:3–4,8*
SUGGESTED FURTHER READING: Matthew 6:7–13

'O LORD, I beseech thee, deliver my soul.' A very *natural prayer,* was it not? He just said what he meant and meant what he said; that is the way to pray. It was a very *short prayer.* Many a prayer is twenty times too long. It is smothered under a bed-full of words. There are times when a Christian man can pray from hour to hour, but it is a great mistake when brethren measure their supplications by the clock. The great matter is not how long you pray, but how earnestly you pray. Consider the life of the prayer rather than the length of the prayer. If your prayer reaches to heaven it is long enough. What longer can it need to be? If it does not reach the Lord, though it occupied you for a week, it would not be long enough to be of use. It was a *humble prayer:* 'O LORD, I beseech thee.' It is the language of one who is bowed into the dust. It was an *intense prayer:* 'O LORD, I *beseech* thee, deliver my soul.' But I want you most of all to notice that it was a *scriptural prayer.* There are three great little prayers in Scripture—'O LORD, I beseech thee, deliver my soul', 'God be merciful to me a sinner', and 'Lord, remember me when thou comest into thy kingdom.' These are all contained in the Lord's prayer. 'O LORD, I beseech thee, deliver my soul' is 'deliver us from evil'. 'God be merciful to me a sinner'—what is that but 'forgive us our sins'? And what is the prayer 'Lord, remember me when thou comest into thy kingdom', but that grand petition, 'Thy kingdom come'? How wonderfully comprehensive is that prayer which our Lord Jesus has given us for a model. All prayers may be condensed into it or distilled from it.

FOR MEDITATION: The 'Lord's Prayer' was taught by Jesus both as a set prayer (Luke 11:2) and as a suggested pattern (Matthew 6:9). Consider the prayers of some Old Testament saints who did not know the 'Lord's Prayer' but who certainly shared its spirit (1 Chronicles 29:10–11; Proverbs 30:7–9)

SERMON NO. 1216

The turning of Job's captivity

'The LORD *turned the captivity of Job, when he prayed for his friends: also the* LORD *gave Job twice as much as he had before.' Job 42:10*
SUGGESTED FURTHER READING: Luke 6:27–37

In Job's case the Lord turned his captivity 'when he prayed for his friends'. Prayer for ourselves is blessed work, but for the child of God it is a higher exercise to become an intercessor and to pray for others. Prayer for ourselves, good as it is, has just a touch of selfishness about it: prayer for others is delivered from that ingredient. Herein is love, the love which God the Holy Spirit delights to foster in the heart, when a man's prayers go up for others. And what a Christlike form of prayer it is when you are praying for those who have ill-treated you and despitefully used you. Then are you like your Master. Praying for yourselves, you are like those for whom Jesus died; but praying for your enemies, you are like the dying Jesus himself. 'Father, forgive them; for they know not what they do' has more of heaven in it than the songs of seraphs, and your prayer, when offered for those who have treated you ill, is somewhat akin to the expiring prayer of your Lord. Job was permitted to take a noble revenge, I am sure the only one he desired, when he became the means of bringing his friends back to God. God would not hear them, he said, for they had spoken so wrongly of his servant Job, and now Job is set to be a mediator or intercessor on their behalf: thus the contempt poured upon the patriarch was turned into honour. If the Lord will only spare the opposer's soul through your prayer, it will be a splendid way of returning bitter speeches. If many unkind insinuations have been thrown out and wicked words said, if you can pray for those who used such words, and God hears you and brings them to Jesus, it will be such a triumph as an angel might envy you. Never use any other weapon of retaliation than the weapon of love.

FOR MEDITATION: The Bible teaches us to love our enemies and pray for them (Matthew 5:44), and to give them assistance when they need it (Romans 12:20). If this sounds unreasonable, remember that God in his common grace practises what he preaches (Matthew 5:45; Luke 6:35). If you are a Christian, never forget how kindly God treated you when you were his enemy (Romans 5:10).

SERMON NO. 1262

Enoch

'Enoch walked with God: and he was not; for God took him.' Genesis 5:24
'By faith Enoch was translated that he should not see death; and was not found, because God had translated him.' Hebrews 11:5
SUGGESTED FURTHER READING: 1 Corinthians 15:50–58

We are told that 'he was not'. Those who believe that the word to 'die' means to be annihilated, would have been still more confirmed in their views if the words 'he was not' had been applied to all the departed, for if any expression might mean annihilation, this is the one. 'He was not' does not, however, mean that he was annihilated, and neither does the feebler term of dying signify anything of the kind. 'He was not' means he was not *here,* that is all. He was gone from earth, but he was *there,* where God had translated him. He was, he is, with God. Do not grudge him his avoidance of death. It was a favour, but not by any means as great as some would think, for those who do not die must undergo a change and Enoch was changed. 'We shall not all sleep, but we shall all be changed.' The flesh and blood of Enoch could not 'inherit the kingdom of God': in a moment he underwent a transformation which we will have to undergo in the day of the resurrection; and so, though he was not on earth, he was translated or transplanted from the gardens of earth to the Paradise above. If there is any man in the world that shall never die, it is he who walks with God. If there is any man to whom death will be as nothing, it is he who has looked to the second advent of Christ and gloried in it; if there is any man who, though he pass through the iron gates of death, shall never feel the terror of the grim foe, it is he whose life below has been perpetual communion with God. Go not about by any other way to escape the pangs of death, but walk with God, and you will be able to say, 'O death, where is thy sting? O grave, where is thy victory?'

FOR MEDITATION: Enoch's faith started somewhere (Genesis 5:22), showed somehow (Genesis 5:22,24), said something (Jude 14) and satisfied someone (Hebrews 11:5–6). Such a life's outcome should be noted and such faith followed (Hebrews 13:7).

N.B. Spurgeon's 'good brother Verdon', his youngest elder, had just been buried.

Three crosses

'But God forbid that I should glory, save in the cross of our Lord Jesus Christ, by which the world is crucified unto me, and I unto the world.'
Galatians 6:14
SUGGESTED FURTHER READING: Galatians 1:3–11

There are a great many people who could hardly endure to live if they should happen to be misjudged by the world or what is called 'society'. Oh yes, we must be respectable. We must have every man's good word or we are ready to faint. Paul was of another mind. What cared he for anything the world might say? How could he wish to please a world so abominable that it had put his Lord to death? He would sooner have its bad opinion than its good. It is better to be frowned at than to be smiled upon by a world that crucified Christ. Certainly its condemnation is more worth having than its approbation if it can put Christ to death: so Paul utterly despised its judgment, and it was crucified to him. We are told to think a great deal about 'public opinion', 'popular belief', 'the growing feeling of the age', 'the sentiment of the period' and 'the spirit of the age'. I should like Paul to read some of our religious newspapers; and yet I could not wish the good man so distasteful a task, for I dare say he would sooner pine in prison than do so; but, still, I should like to see how he would look after he had read some of those expressions about the necessity of keeping ourselves abreast with the sentiment of the period. 'What', he would say, 'the sentiment of the world! It is crucified to me! What can it matter what its opinion is? "We are of God, and the whole world lieth in wickedness." Would you heed what the world, that is lying in the wicked one, thinks of you or of the truth of your Lord? Are you going to smooth your tongue and soften your speech to please the world that lieth in the wicked one?' Paul would be indignant with such a proposition. He said, 'the world is crucified unto me'.

FOR MEDITATION: (*Our Own Hymn Book* no.805 v.2—William Cowper, 1779)
'It was the sight of Thy dear cross
First weaned my soul from earthly things;
And taught me to esteem as dross
The mirth of fools and pomp of kings.'

The choice of a leader

'And he spake a parable unto them, Can the blind lead the blind? Shall they not both fall into the ditch? The disciple is not above his master: but every one that is perfect shall be as his master.' Luke 6:39–40
SUGGESTED FURTHER READING: Matthew 23:1–26

If we are agreed that we need a guide, it is clear that the most important thing is to examine the claims of those who aspire to the office. Some take a guide because he is appointed by authority; he happens to be the parson of the parish or the family minister, and he is at once accepted without consideration. He would be a very foolish person who, in climbing the mountains of Switzerland, would take a guide merely because he professed to be one and carried the usual certificates, if upon looking at him it was clear that the man was stone blind. Would you say that does not matter, since he says he is appointed by authority? Would you go to the top of Mont Blanc with him? If so, he would soon conduct you into a crevasse, and there would be an end to your folly. Yet multitudes resolve upon taking their religion by prescription, feeling confident that what is patronised by the great, and established and endowed by the nation, must of course be right. Whether the guide can see or not seems to be a trifle, but he must have been properly ordained and duly inducted; if that be settled, the unthinking many ask no more. For my part, I like to look at my guide's eyes; I like to know whether he has ever traversed the country and whether he has had experience of the way; if he cannot satisfy me on those points, I look elsewhere to one who is all sight and has had all experience, even the Lord Jesus. His authority I cannot question; I take for granted all that he teaches me. I am glad to be a seeing man following a seeing leader, and I endeavour to be an intelligent scholar learning of a wise and sympathetic teacher.

FOR MEDITATION: (*Our Own Hymn Book* no.852 v.5—Isaac Watts, 1709)
'Our glorious Leader claims our praise
For His own pattern given,
While the long cloud of witnesses
Show the same path to heaven.'

SERMON NO. 1248

The blood of the covenant

'Now the God of peace, that brought again from the dead our Lord Jesus, that great Shepherd of the sheep, through the blood of the everlasting covenant, make you perfect in every good work to do his will.' Hebrews 13:20–21
SUGGESTED FURTHER READING: Ezekiel 34:11–31

It is very beautiful to trace the shepherds through the Old Testament, and to see Christ as Abel, the witnessing shepherd, pouring out that blood which cries from the ground; as Abraham, the separating shepherd, leading out his flock into the strange country where they dwelt alone; as Isaac, the quiet shepherd, digging wells for his flock and feeding them in peace in the midst of the enemies; as Jacob, the shepherd who is surety for the sheep, who by long toils and weariness earns them all, separates them, and walks in the middle of them to Canaan, preserving them by his own lone midnight prayers. There, too, we see our Lord as Joseph, the shepherd who is head over Egypt for the sake of Israel, of whom his dying father said, 'From thence is the shepherd, the stone of Israel'—head over all things for his church, the King who governs all the world for the sake of his elect, the 'great Shepherd of the sheep', who for their sakes has all power committed unto his hands. Then follows Moses, the chosen shepherd, who led his people through the wilderness up to the Promised Land, feeding them with manna and giving them drink from the smitten rock—what a wide theme for reflection here! And then there is David, the type of Jesus, as reigning in the covenanted inheritance over his own people, as a glorious king in the midst of them all. All these together enable us to see the varied glories of 'that great Shepherd of the sheep'. Let us rejoice that our Shepherd is great, because he with his great flock will be able to preserve them from all the great dangers into which they are brought, and to perform for them the great transactions with the great God which are demanded of a Shepherd of such a flock as that which Jesus calls his own.

FOR MEDITATION: Read about the great shepherd and his care for his sheep as prophesied in Isaiah 40:10–11. Look back to what he has already done as the good shepherd (John 10:11,14–15) and look forward to one of the things he is going to do on his return as the chief shepherd (1 Peter 5:4).

SERMON NO. 1186

The world on fire

'Seeing then that all these things shall be dissolved, what manner of persons ought ye to be in all holy conversation and godliness.' 2 Peter 3:11
SUGGESTED FURTHER READING: Psalm 90:1–17

I saw yesterday with much solemnity of mind the spot where the Bishop of Winchester met with sudden death. A cross is cut in the turf to mark the place. The spot is in the midst of the most lovely scenery conceivable. I have often walked hard by, full of delight at the fair prospect. It is a spot too fair to be darkened by so dark a cloud; death seems hardly congruous with the beauty which everywhere charms the eye. I could only imagine, if anyone knew that he should die at that moment, what would be his conversation. What would be the conversation of a man of God riding over the downs, who expected to die in the valley below? Such ought to be our constant conversation. We should live always as if we might die in a moment. Mr Wesley once said, 'Now, if I knew I should die tomorrow morning, I would do exactly what I have planned to do. I should take the class-meeting at such an hour, preach at such an hour and be up at such a time in the morning to pray.' That good man's life was spent in prospect of sudden departure, and it was therefore active and holy. Is ours the same? The motive for holiness becomes stronger still if the thought is not merely that I shall die, but that 'all these things' around me 'shall be dissolved'. That breezy down, that towering hill, yonder lofty trees, this overhanging cliff, these rich meadows, the ripening harvest, all will in a moment be in a blaze. Am I ready to be caught away to be with my Lord in the air? Or shall I be left to perish amidst the conflagration? How ought I to live? How ought I to stand as it were on tip-toe, ready when he shall call me, to be away up into the glory, far off from this perishing world!

FOR MEDITATION: 'Prepare to meet thy God' (Amos 4:12); it may happen out of the blue (Luke 12:40). Peter presumed he was ready before he was (Luke 22:33–34), but Paul knew when he was ready (Acts 21:13).

N.B. Samuel Wilberforce (born 1805 the third son of William Wilberforce the emancipator, and Bishop of Winchester from 1869) fell from his horse and broke his neck at Abinger in the Surrey Hills on 19 July 1873.

SERMON NO. 1125

A wilderness cry

'O God, thou art my God; early will I seek thee: my soul thirsteth for thee, my flesh longeth for thee in a dry and thirsty land, where no water is; to see thy power and thy glory, so as I have seen thee in the sanctuary.' Psalm 63:1–2
SUGGESTED FURTHER READING: Psalm 107:33–43

We may have been so unwatchful as to have brought ourselves into this condition by actual faults of life and conduct. I would make it a matter of personal enquiry by asking a few questions. Have you restrained prayer? Do you wonder that the land grows dry? Has the word of God been neglected? Have you left off its study of late through pressure of other concerns? If you have left the streams, do you wonder that your soul thirsts? Have you been overmuch engaged in hunting after temporal gain, and has the hot desert wind of worldliness parched your heart? Has there been anything about your spiritual life that has grieved the Holy Spirit? Have you been idle as a Christian? Have you been content to eat the fat and drink the sweet, and to do nothing to win souls? Or have you, while you have fed upon the word of God, taken the sweet things of the gospel as a matter of course and not blessed the Lord for them? Has there been a lack of humility or a deficiency of gratitude? If so, can you wonder that you are 'in a dry and thirsty land'? Have you been careless in your walk? Has sin been permitted in the family? Have you been condoning evil in your children? Have you permitted it in yourself? If so, remember it is written, 'He turneth rivers into a wilderness, and the watersprings into dry ground; a fruitful land into barrenness, for the wickedness of them that dwell therein.' You may have fallen into a parched condition of spirit because you have forgotten him of whom in happier days you sang, 'All my springs are in thee.' Because you have walked contrary to God, God is walking contrary to you; it is your duty to repent and return at once to your Lord.

FOR MEDITATION: Ezekiel's vision of the valley of dry bones and its application to the people of Israel both teach us that spiritual life is dependent upon the word of God (Ezekiel 37:4–7) and the Spirit of God (Ezekiel 37:8–10,14). In our spiritual hunger and thirst we still need the word of God (1 Peter 1:23–2:2) and the Spirit of God (John 7:37–39). We cannot ignore them and still expect to grow.

SERMON NO. 1427

The God of peace and our sanctification

'The God of peace … make you perfect.' Hebrews 13:20–21
SUGGESTED FURTHER READING: Psalm 23:1–6

The title 'the God of peace' sheds a light over the whole passage (Hebrews 13:20–21) and is beautifully in harmony with every word of the prayer. Let us read it line by line. 'Now the God of peace, that brought again from the dead our Lord Jesus.' War drives men down to the dead and is the great jackal of the grave. How sadly the nations see this exemplified in the East at this moment. War brings down to death, but 'the God of peace' brings back 'from the dead'. The restoration of the Lord Jesus from the grave was a peaceful act and was meant to be the guarantee of peace accomplished for ever. 'That great Shepherd of the sheep'—sheep are peaceful creatures and a shepherd's occupation has nothing to do with blood-red fields of strife. We always couple with the idea of peace the quietness and repose of the sheepfold and the simple restfulness of flocks in green pastures. Peace is the very atmosphere of pastoral scenes. 'Through the blood of the everlasting covenant'. The very word 'covenant' is also full of peace: especially is it so when we remember that it is a covenant of peace which eternal love has established between God and man. Where no covenant or league exists war may break out at any time, but where a covenant is once established there is peace and rest. The apostle goes on to pray, 'make you perfect in every good work to do his will'. If God's will is done by us, then there must be peace, for no ground of difference can exist. 'Working in you that which is well pleasing in his sight'—when all in us is well pleasing to God, then indeed is he the God of peace to us. The final doxology is also very significant, for in effect it proclaims the universal and eternal reign of peace: 'To whom be glory for ever and ever. Amen.' What can there be to disturb the universe when the Lord God omnipotent shall reign and all nations shall glorify and extol the Ever Blessed, world without end?

FOR MEDITATION: 'The God of peace' can also be with us (Romans 15:33; 2 Corinthians 13:11; Philippians 4:9), bruise Satan under our feet (Romans 16:20) and sanctify us wholly (1 Thessalonians 5:23). 'Now the God of peace himself give you peace always by all means' (2 Thessalonians 3:16).

SERMON NO. 1368

The little dogs

'But he answered and said, It is not meet to take the children's bread, and to cast it to dogs. And she said, Truth, Lord: yet the dogs eat of the crumbs which fall from their masters' table.' Matthew 15:26–27 (see also Mark 7:27–28)
SUGGESTED FURTHER READING: Jeremiah 29:10–14

This poor woman is a lesson to all outsiders, who think themselves beyond the pale of hope, who were not brought up to attend the house of God. She was a Sidonian; she came of a race that had been condemned to die many centuries before, one of the accursed seed of Canaan, and yet she became great in the kingdom of heaven because she believed, and there is no reason why those who are reckoned to be quite outside the church of God should not be in the very centre of it, the most shining lights of the whole. Poor outcasts and far off ones, take heart and comfort, come to Jesus Christ and trust yourselves in his hands. This woman is next an example to those who think they have been repulsed in their endeavours after salvation. Have you been praying and not succeeded? Have you sought the Lord and seem to be more unhappy than ever? Have you made attempts at reformation and believed that you made them in the divine strength, but they have failed? Trust in him whose blood has not lost its efficacy, whose promise has not lost its truth, and whose arm has not lost its power to save. Cling to the cross, sinner. If the earth sinks beneath you, cling on; if storms should rage, all the floods be out, and even God himself seems to be against you, cling to the cross. There is your hope. You cannot perish there. This is a lesson, next, to every intercessor. This woman was not pleading for herself, but asking for another. When you plead for a fellow sinner, do not do it in a cold-hearted manner; plead as for your own life. That man will prevail with God as an intercessor who solemnly bears the matter upon his own heart, makes it his own, and with tears entreats an answer of peace.

FOR MEDITATION: (*Our Own Hymn Book* no.551 v.2—Charles Wesley, 1740)

'Other refuge have I none, hangs my helpless soul on Thee!
Leave, ah! leave me not alone, still support and comfort me!
All my trust on Thee is stayed, all my help from Thee I bring;
Cover my defenceless head with the shadow of Thy wing.'

SERMON NO. 1309

Girding on the harness

'And the king of Israel answered and said, Tell him, Let not him that girdeth on his harness boast himself as he that putteth it off.' 1 Kings 20:11

SUGGESTED FURTHER READING: 1 Timothy 3:1–7

The devil whispers, 'Ah, now we are somebody.' We have commenced to teach in the Sunday school and feel pleased to think we are to be teachers of the young: is it not a noble work? Nobody will be able to say now that we are mere babes in grace. Why, we are getting to be quite defenders of the faith and bold servants of Christ; surely we may be allowed a little self-respect! If we have begun to preach and have been praised by many of our hearers, it is probable that we scarcely know whether we are in the body or out of it; we think we are Whitefields already and apostles in embryo. What preachers we are going to be and what wonders we shall certainly accomplish! Satan has patted us with his black paw and told us that we have done amazingly well and deserve great credit, and we fully believe him. It is well known that even in natural things Jack in office is bound to be proud, and the like thing will occur even to good young men when they are put a little forward. They can scarcely be trusted even to open the door of the Lord's house or to sweep a crossing in the streets of the New Jerusalem, but straightway they become important. It is much easier to be puffed up than to be built up, much easier to grow in self-conceit than in vital godliness; a little advancement turns many brains. Baruch was employed by the prophet Jeremiah to write the roll, and straightway he had high ideas of what Baruch must be and needed the message, 'seekest thou great things for thyself? seek them not'. We are always up in the air unless God in his infinite mercy chains us down to the rock and keeps us there, for pride is like the eagle and delights to soar on high.

FOR MEDITATION: At first sight pride may appear to have its attractions, but God opposes it (James 4:6) and if God be against us, who can be for us? In the light of this, pride is actually exposed as an extremely unattractive proposition indeed (Proverbs 11:2; 16:5; 29:23).

Saints in heaven and earth one family

'The whole family in heaven and earth.' Ephesians 3:15
SUGGESTED FURTHER READING: Hebrews 12:18–24

'The whole family in heaven and earth', not the two families nor the divided family. It appears at first sight as if we were effectually divided by the hand of death. Can it be that we are one family when some of us labour on and others sleep beneath the ground? There was a great truth in the sentence which Wordsworth put into the mouth of the little child when she said, 'O master! we are seven':—

> '"But they are dead: those two are dead!
> Their spirits are in heaven!"
> 'Twas throwing words away; for still
> The little maid would have her will,
> And said "Nay, we are seven."'

Should we not thus speak of the divine family, for death has no separating power in the household of God. We are 'persuaded that' death cannot 'separate us from the love of God'. The breach caused by the grave is only apparent; the family is still united. When there is a loss in a family, the father is bereaved, but you cannot conceive of our heavenly Father being bereaved. 'Our Father which art in heaven', thou hast lost none of thy children. We wept and went to the grave, but thou didst not, for thy child is not dead, but has come closer to thee to receive a sweeter caress and to know more fully the infinity of thy love! When a child is lost, the elder brother is a mourner, but our Elder Brother is not bereaved; Jesus has lost none of his; has he not rather brought home to himself his own redeemed?

FOR MEDITATION: (*Our Own Hymn Book* no.859 v.3—Charles Wesley, 1759)
'One family we dwell in Him, one church above, beneath,
Though now divided by the stream, the narrow stream of death.'

N.B. The much-loved Mrs Bartlett, 'president of the female class at the Tabernacle' had just died on 2 August 1875 and is buried in Nunhead Cemetery.

SERMON NO. 1249

The three witnesses

'There are three that bear witness on earth, the Spirit, and the water, and the blood: and these three agree in one.' 1 John 5:8
SUGGESTED FURTHER READING: John 3:1–15

'These three agree in one.' Therefore, every true believer should have the witness of each one, and if each one does not witness in due time, there is a cause for grave suspicion. For instance, people have arisen who have said that the Spirit of God has led them to do this and that. Of them we inquire, what are your lives? Does the water bear witness? Does the blood testify for you? If these questions cannot be answered, they may rave as they like about the Spirit of God, but the witness to their salvation is open to the gravest suspicion. We have known some who will say, 'Look at my life; I am very different from what I was. I am a sober, honest, excellent man.' Yes, but do you rest in the blood of Jesus? Practical evidence is good, but it must arise out of faith. If you do not believe in Jesus, you have not the essential witness and your case is not proved. Many also say to us, 'I believe that Jesus died for me,' but we must ask them concerning their lives. Are you cleansed in act? Are you an altered man? For remember, unless the water speaks with the blood, you have not the three-fold testimony. There may be some who say, 'Well, we believe in Jesus and our lives are changed': but remember, you may say that, but is it so? If so, the Spirit of God changed you: if you have merely excited yourself into the belief that it is so, or if you were born by your own free will, you have not the witness, because the truly saved are 'born, not of blood, nor of the will of the flesh, nor of the will of man, but of' the Spirit of God. The three witnesses 'agree in one'.

FOR MEDITATION: Consider the futility of self-righteousness which bypasses the blood of Jesus (John 6:53; Hebrews 9:22; 10:29), antinomianism which bypasses the call to holiness (Romans 6:14–15; 2 Peter 2:19–21) and supposed Christianity which bypasses the work of the Holy Spirit (John 3:5; Acts 19:1–4; Romans 8:9).

SERMON NO. 1187

A song concerning lovingkindnesses

'I will mention the lovingkindnesses of the LORD, and the praises of the LORD, according to all that the LORD hath bestowed on us.' Isaiah 63:7
SUGGESTED FURTHER READING (Spurgeon): Psalm 106:1–12

Do you not use much idle talk? I am afraid we all do. Do you not often complain when there is nothing to complain of? Do you not murmur? Are you not far too ready to break forth in words of lamentation? Waste not your breath on such base uses, but consecrate it all to praise. Tell what God's hand has given, what his lip has spoken. Tell how he has blessed you with countless mercies; it will make the daughters of despondency rejoice and the sons of mourning lift up their heads. Make mention of the lovingkindnesses of God, because it will glorify him, and this should always be your master motive. The Christian lives to honour God. Tell what the Lord has done, that men may praise him. The sons of men are apt enough to forget him; keep them in remembrance of him. They are apt enough to speak hard things concerning him; tell them of his lovingkindnesses and make them know what a good master he is whom you serve. Din it into their ears, make them hear it, tell them again and again of the great goodness of the Lord to you. Can you give me any reason why you should not 'mention the lovingkindnesses of the LORD'? Can you tell me any company in which you ought to be, in which you could not 'mention the lovingkindnesses of the LORD'? I know some people who ride hobbies; you cannot be long with them before they will introduce them. They may be very inappropriate but somehow or other they bring the conversation round to their favourite theme. I would have you ride this hobby without fear. Rather I would have you take this noble steed and ride it through all companies; make them feel that it is your manner and habit to tell of God's goodness and that you cannot help it. Bring it in somehow. You never need be short of reasons for praise.

FOR MEDITATION: Consider how the Psalmists took steps to escape from a spirit of complaining. Asaph meditated upon God's great deeds (Psalm 77:1–14), David looked forward to giving thanks to God (Psalm 142:1–7), but an anonymous Psalmist (see title of Psalm 102) went one stage further. He not only sought to praise God in his affliction, but also wanted others to join in (Psalm 102:12–22).

SERMON NO. 1126

The true position of the witness within

'He that believeth on the Son of God hath the witness in himself.' 1 John
5:10
SUGGESTED FURTHER READING: Ephesians 1:11–19

What is this witness within? It may be seen as follows: take the verses
that precede my text and you will get one form of it. Jesus Christ is the
Son of God and the Saviour of sinners—that is the main point to be
witnessed. First *the Spirit,* after we have believed, bears witness in our
soul that it is so, because we perceive that the Spirit has led us to believe
in Jesus and has given us repentance; the Spirit has renewed us, the Spirit
has made us different from what we were, the Spirit helps us in prayer,
the Spirit lifts us up upon the wings of praise, the Spirit works upon us
wondrously, and so we gather that this comes to us through believing in
Jesus; he is indeed the Saviour of sinners, for we are saved. Then *the
water* bears witness within us—that is to say, we feel a new life, we feel
the living waters in our hearts, and we are conscious of being alive to
things to which we were once dead. We find that now there is within us a
new nature which we never possessed before. All this becomes
comfortable evidence that what we have believed is true; we have proved
it to be true, for we have the life which was promised to us upon our
believing in Jesus. Thirdly, *the precious blood* within our souls bears
further witness, for when it gives us peace, we sing as sinners bought
with blood, we rejoice before God as cleansed by the blood from all sin
and as having access into that which is within the veil by the sprinkled
blood, and we feel deep peace within our souls through the voice of the
blood. This is a witness sweet and clear within us, proving that what we
received upon God's word without any other evidence is certainly true.
Now we have confirmatory evidence within our spirits, given not
because we demanded it, but as a sweet reward and gracious privilege.
We should never have received it if we had not believed first on the
naked word of God, but after that the witness flows naturally into the
heart.

FOR MEDITATION: Read Hebrews 10:15–22 and consider the contributions
made by the Holy Spirit (vv.15–17), the blood of Jesus (vv.19–20) and the
water (v.22) towards a full assurance of faith (v.22).

SERMON NO. 1428

Proclamation of acceptance and vengeance

'To proclaim the acceptable year of the LORD, and the day of vengeance of our God; to comfort all that mourn.' Isaiah 61:2
SUGGESTED FURTHER READING: Luke 4:14–30

You may have noticed that when our Lord read this passage at Nazareth he stopped short; he did not read it all; he read down as far as 'to proclaim the acceptable year of the LORD', then 'he closed the book, and he gave it again to the minister, and sat down.' I suppose that at the commencement of his ministry, before he had been rejected by the nation and before he had suffered for sin, he wisely chose to allude to the gentler topics rather than to those more stern and terrible ones; but he did not conclude his ministry without referring to the stern words which followed those which he had read. If you turn to Luke 21:21–22 you will find him saying, 'Then let them which are in Judæa flee to the mountains; and let them which are in the midst of it depart out; and let not them that are in the countries enter thereinto. For these be the days of vengeance, that all things which are written may be fulfilled.' You know the story of the siege of Jerusalem, the most harrowing of all narratives, for the anger of God was concentrated upon that wicked city beyond all precedent. It was because they rejected Christ that vengeance came upon them. They filled up the measure of their iniquity when at last they disowned their king and cried out, 'Away with him, away with him, crucify him.' Mark you then, that if you have heard the gospel and rejected it, you have incurred great guilt, and you can never sin so cheaply as you did before; for you there will be a 'day of vengeance' above the men of Sodom or Gomorrah, because you have perpetrated a crime which they were not capable of committing—you have rejected the Christ of God. The year of acceptance to believers will be a day of vengeance to those who obey not his gospel.

FOR MEDITATION: Vengeance belongs to God (Deuteronomy 32:35,41,43; Psalm 94:1). That being the case, God warns us that he will repay (Romans 12:19; Hebrews 10:30). If you do not know him yet and continue to disobey the gospel, be warned that God will inflict eternal vengeance upon you (2 Thessalonians 1:7–10).

SERMON NO. 1369

Jesus, the stumbling stone of unbelievers

'*Unto them which be disobedient, the stone which the builders disallowed, the same is made the head of the corner, and a stone of stumbling, and a rock of offence, even to them which stumble at the word, being disobedient.*' 1 Peter 2:7–8
SUGGESTED FURTHER READING: 1 Corinthians 1:18–24

Some stumble at Christ's teaching because it is too holy. 'Christ is too puritanical; he cuts off our pleasures.' But he denies us no pleasure which is not sinful; he multiplies our joys. The things which he denies to us are joyous only in appearance, while his commands are real bliss. 'His teachings are too severe,' say some. Yet from others I hear the opposite accusation, for when we preach free grace, objectors cry, 'You encourage men in sin.' There is little chance of pleasing men, for what gratifies some offends others; but there is no just reason on either ground to stumble at the gospel, for though it places good works where they should be, as fruits of the Spirit and not things of merit, yet it is a gospel according to holiness, as those who have proved its power know. Some object to the teachings of Christ because they are too humbling. He destroys self-confidence and presents salvation to none but those who are lost. 'This lays us too low,' says one. Yet have I heard an objection to the gospel because it makes men proud, for say some, 'How dare you speak of being certain that you are saved. That is boastful and ill befits a lowly mind.' Do not stumble at blessed truth, for believers are certainly saved and may know it, yet be all the humbler for the knowledge. You are humbled by Christ and laid low, but when in due time he exalts you by his grace there is no fear of boasting, for it is excluded by grace. Others object that the gospel is too mysterious; they cannot understand it. Again I have heard the objection that it is too plain. Being saved by believing in Christ is too plain for many and too hard for others. Do not cavil at it for either reason.

FOR MEDITATION: (*Our Own Hymn Book* no.2 v.1—William Goode, 1811)

'Though sinners boldly join, against the Lord to rise,
Against his Christ combine, th' Anointed to despise;
Though earth disdain, and hell engage,
Vain is their rage, their counsel vain.'

SERMON NO. 1224

A distinction with a difference

'And Zacharias said unto the angel, Whereby shall I know this?' 'Then said Mary unto the angel, How shall this be?' Luke 1:18,34
SUGGESTED FURTHER READING: Titus 1:5–16

Brother ministers, if we are unbelieving, we in our unbelief do not sin so cheaply as our people: we have more time to study the word and therefore have, or ought to have, more acquaintance with it. We are more familiar with divine things and ought to be more richly filled with their faith-creating spirit. If the Lord has been pleased to make us under-shepherds over his people, we are bound to be examples to the flock. Our high position demands of us the exhibition of a greater degree of grace than we can expect from common believers who are God's dear people, but not set apart to be leaders. The same argument will apply in due proportion to each servant of our Lord Jesus: according to their measure of grace more is expected of some than of others. You, dear sisters, who teach young people, should remember that they watch you and expect to see in you a bright example; what is more, God, who has placed you in the position of teachers or mothers, intends that there should be in you, by his grace, something that others may look up to, that the young beginners may learn from you. Take heed that they never learn unbelief from your doubtings. Let them never see in you that worry, anxiety and fretfulness which denotes the absence of a calm reliance upon God, but let them, whatever they gather from you, learn that which is worth knowing. And what can be a better lesson than that of faith in God? You who are in the church, preachers, elders, deacons and instructors of others, see that your lives and words do not breed unbelief. Let those of us who are guides of others see that we do not dishonour God by mistrust and questioning, for unbelief in us is a glaring fault, and God will visit it upon us, even if he winks at it in the weak ones of the flock.

FOR MEDITATION: The Lord Jesus Christ supremely exemplified faith during his sufferings (1 Peter 2:21–23). Faith is among the most important examples to be set by church leaders (1 Timothy 4:12) and imitated by church members (Hebrews 6:11–12; 13:7). The disobedience of unbelief is a fearful example to set or copy (Hebrews 3:18–4:2,11).

SERMON NO. 1405

The priest dispensed with

'He that believeth on the Son of God hath the witness in himself.' 1 John
5:10
SUGGESTED FURTHER READING: Hebrews 8:1–13

'There is one God, and one mediator between God and men, the man
Christ Jesus.' Why should we set up other mediators and go to them for
absolution, when our Lord Jesus receives all who come to him? Do you
see in the New Testament any trace of such assumptions on the part of
God's ministers? Does the gospel say, 'He that believeth and is baptized
shall be saved, if absolved by a priest'? That interpolation is foreign to
the gospel. 'Believe on the Lord Jesus Christ, and thou shalt be saved' is
the gospel according to the Scriptures: 'confess to the priest and thou
shalt be forgiven' is the gospel according to the Vatican. Everywhere the
Scripture calls man to come into personal contact with his reconciled
God in Christ Jesus. The first resolution of the awakened sinner is not, 'I
will arise and go to the authorised minister who stands between me and
my Father'; it is not, 'I will resort to sacraments and ceremonies', but 'I
will arise and go to my father'. In fact the whole object of the gospel is to
bring us near to God in Christ Jesus and to put down every interposing
medium. He who rent the veil of the temple has ended this priestly
business. There is no need of a certificate from any man as to our being
forgiven, for 'He that believeth on the Son of God hath the witness in
himself'. He does not need a new revelation; he does not need to wait
until the day of judgment: he is forgiven; he knows it, and knows it
infallibly too, by a witness within himself. May the Spirit of God help us
to get at the real truth. I would to God that all who hear me this day
would believe in our Lord Jesus Christ and have the witness of his
salvation in themselves.

FOR MEDITATION: The 'one mediator between God and men, the man Christ
Jesus' (1 Timothy 2:5) does not take kindly to those who try to usurp or
share his unique role; the only 'rock' on which the church is built is 'Christ,
the Son of the living God' (Matthew 16:16–18). Read the sharp words he
had to say about some who have since been placed on unscriptural
pedestals, notably Peter (Matthew 16:21–23; John 13:6–8) and Mary (Luke
11:27–28; John 2:3–4), when they tried to interfere with his work.

SERMON NO. 1250

A word for the persecuted

'What if thy father answer thee roughly?' 1 Samuel 20:10
SUGGESTED FURTHER READING: John 15:18–16:4

The large proportion of Christians find themselves opposed by those of their own family, or by those with whom they labour or trade. Is it not likely to be so? Was it not so from the beginning? Is there not enmity between the seed of the serpent and the seed of the woman? Did not Cain slay his brother Abel because he was accepted by the Lord? In the family of Abraham was there not an Ishmael born after the flesh, who persecuted Isaac, who was born after the Spirit? Was not Joseph hated by his brethren? Was not David persecuted by Saul, Daniel by the Persian princes, and Jeremiah by the kings of Israel? Has it not ever been so? Did not the Lord Jesus Christ himself meet with slander, cruelty and death, and did he not tell us that we must not look for favour where he found rejection? He said plainly, 'I came not to send peace, but a sword', and he declared that the immediate result of the preaching of the gospel would be to set the son against the father and the father against the son, so that 'a man's foes shall be they of his own household'. Did he not carefully enquire of every recruit who wished to enlist in his army, 'Have you counted the cost'? Have you not admired his perfect honesty and admirable caution in dealing with men, when he bids them remember that if they follow him they must deny themselves, take up their cross daily and be content to be hated by all men for his sake? He warns us not to expect that the disciple will be above his Master, for if men 'have called the master of the house Beelzebub,' they will assuredly confer no sweet titles upon his household. Since our Lord has forewarned us, it is well for us to stand ready for the trial which he predicts, and to ask ourselves whether we are ready to bear oppression for Christ's sake.

FOR MEDITATION: Suffering for Christ ought never to come to us as a surprise (1 Peter 4:12–13). When he spoke to his followers about persecution, he said 'when', not 'if' (Matthew 5:11; 10:23) and promised it to them all (Mark 10:29–30; John 15:20). Those who fall away because of persecution cannot accuse him of misleading them; the fault lies within themselves (Mark 4:17).

SERMON NO. 1188

Harvest men wanted

'Then saith he unto his disciples, The harvest truly is plenteous, but the labourers are few; pray ye therefore the Lord of the harvest, that he will send forth labourers into his harvest.' Matthew 9:37–38
SUGGESTED FURTHER READING: John 4:28–42

The harvest in our own country is just now ripe and ready for the sickle; but suppose the owner of some large estate should walk through his broad acres and say, 'I have a great harvest—look at those far-reaching fields: but the country has become depopulated, the people have emigrated and I have no labourers. There are one or two yonder; they are reaping with all their might, make long days, and toil till they faint; but over yonder there are vast ranges of my farm unreaped and I have not a sickle to thrust in. The corn is being wasted and it grieves me sorely. See how the birds are gathering in troops to prey upon the precious ears! Meanwhile the season is far advanced, the autumn damps are already upon us, and the chill, frosty nights which are winter's vanguard are on their way. Mildew is spoiling the grain, and what remains sound will shell out upon the ground or swell with the moisture and become of no service.' Behold in this picture the Redeemer. He looks upon the world today and says, 'All these multitudes of precious souls will be lost, for there are so few reapers to gather them in. Here and there are men who with prodigious energy are reaping all they can and all but fainting as they reap; I am with them and blessed sheaves are taken home, but what are these among so many?' Look, can your eye see it? Can even an eagle's wing fly over the vast fields, unreaped plains, without growing weary in the flight? There are the precious ears; they decay, rot, perish and are ruined to the loss of God and to their own eternal injury, and it grieves the Great Husbandman. That is still the case today and it ought to grieve us, for his sake and for the sake of our fellow men. A multitude of precious souls were perishing, and this the Saviour lamented.

FOR MEDITATION: The Lord Jesus Christ first calls labourers to down tools and come to him (Matthew 11:28; Romans 4:5), then sends them back to work with his tools (Matthew 10:1,5–7; Ephesians 2:10). There is no place for early retirement before the Christian dies (Revelation 14:13). Are you working for the Lord or on strike?

Faith's sure foundation

'He that believeth on him shall not be confounded.' 1 Peter 2:6
SUGGESTED FURTHER READING: Luke 6:46–49

If you want to know what it is to believe on Jesus, it is to lie upon him as a stone lies upon a foundation when the mason puts it there. There is the foundation firm and strong, 'a precious corner stone,' tried and sure. Here is a smaller stone, quarried from the pit, and the builder places it upon the foundation. Its lying on the foundation represents faith. Our souls' eternal interests are laid on Christ. The foundation bears up the stone and holds it in its place; so Christ bears up our souls and holds them in their position, so that they fall not to the ground. The stone presses with all its weight upon the foundation and that is what the believer does with his Lord; he casts all his care upon him. Faith is leaning, depending, relying. As the key hangs on the nail, so hang we on Jesus. Faith is the giving up of self-reliance and self-dependence, and the resting of the soul upon him whom God has laid 'in Zion for a foundation'. A stone thrown about from hand to hand is self-contained and independent, but when the mason puts it on the foundation it is dependent; it leans on the corner-stone upon which it is placed. Poor tempted soul, that is just what you have to do: you must not be a loose stone resting on yourself and tossed hither and thither upon the earth, but you must lie still upon Christ and let him bear your whole weight upon himself. A stone rests wholly on the foundation. If a wall is well built, it is not shored up with timber so that the stones have two supports, but the whole structure rests on a common basis. There is a good foundation and each stone lies upon it. It can do no more, for it could not keep its place for an instant if the foundation were removed. If the foundation fails the stone falls, but while the foundation stands the stone remains secure. That is faith: resting upon Christ wholly and entirely.

FOR MEDITATION: It is a mark of man's perversity that he tries to usurp God's unique role as foundation-layer by trying to lay a new foundation of his own making. The Lord Jesus Christ is the only foundation we need (1 Corinthians 3:11; Ephesians 2:19–20). He cannot be bettered; all we need to do is to trust ourselves to him (Isaiah 28:16).

SERMON NO. 1429

Sheep among wolves

'Behold, I send you forth as sheep in the midst of wolves: be ye therefore wise as serpents, and harmless as doves.' Matthew 10:16
SUGGESTED FURTHER READING (Spurgeon): Luke 10:1–12

It is well to get out of the society of ungodly men, and let them see that their habits and modes of conversation are not ours. Seek to benefit them, but do not seek their society. Their wolfish propensities are most seen in their leisure time, drinking and revelling; therefore keep far from these. You have no business in their gay parties, frivolous assemblies, drinking bouts and places of lascivious song. Do not accept their invitations when you know they will be under no restraint; do not linger near them when they are talking lewdly or profanely; your moving off will be your most telling protest. You must be with them in your business, indeed you are sent to them, but while you are *with* them you must not be *of* them; you should discreetly avoid them when you know that you can do no good. You younger ones should get out of the way of old blasphemers and scoffers as much as you can, for they delight to worry the lambs. Do not attempt to answer them, but keep out of their way. Do not court quarrelling and controversy, but avoid all disputing about the gospel. Your workmates will tease you, and no doubt you will receive many opprobrious epithets, but neither provoke this treatment nor resent it. Do not cast 'pearls before swine'; hold your principles firmly, but when you know a man will only blaspheme if he hears you name the name of Jesus, do not give him the occasion. Stand up for Jesus when the time is fit, but do not exercise zeal without knowledge. When a man is half drunk or in a passion, leave him to himself and thus escape many a brawl. At another opportunity, when the occasion is more favourable, then endeavour to instruct and persuade, but not when failure is certain. Be very prudent and hold your peace when silence is better than speech.

FOR MEDITATION: There were times when the Lord Jesus Christ was wary not only of a fox like Herod (Luke 13:31–32), but also of people who appeared to support him (John 2:23–25; 6:15). Christians also need to take care over relationships with the worldly—whether we surprise (1 Peter 4:3–4) or silence them (Titus 2:7–8; 1 Peter 2:15), our behaviour and speech should above all be different from their's.

SERMON NO. 1370

A gospel sermon to outsiders

'Be of good comfort, rise; he calleth thee.' Mark 10:49
SUGGESTED FURTHER READING: 1 Peter 2:18–25

When you go to a foreign city for the first time and stay at an inn, it may be that you miss your way when you go out and are not able to get back again as easily as you wish; it is generally expedient, therefore, for travellers to learn the main streets of every town which they visit. In Rome we come to know which way the Corso runs, and when we get an idea of the run of that main thoroughfare we by and by are able to pick our way through the city. Now, the main street of the gospel is substitution. He 'made him to be sin for us, who knew no sin; that we might be made the righteousness of God in him.' The main street of the gospel runs crosswise; follow it and you will know the ins and outs of the other great streets before long. This is the High Street of the City of Grace—'Christ hath redeemed us from the curse of the law, being made a curse for us'. Christ stood in our stead and suffered that we might not suffer. He died 'the just for the unjust, that he might bring us to God'. Whosoever believes in Christ is saved from the damning power of sin and delivered from the wrath to come. Take this fact in all its breadth and length, and never doubt it, and you have the key of the gospel. Whosoever trusts his soul with the Lord Jesus Christ, relying on that sacrifice which he offered and that death which he endured, is saved. Let him not doubt it. He has God's word for it; let him believe it and rejoice in it. 'He that believeth on him is not condemned', for 'as Moses lifted up the serpent in the wilderness, even so must the Son of man be lifted up: that whosoever believeth in him should not perish, but have eternal life'.

FOR MEDITATION: (*Our Own Hymn Book* no.427 v.3—James Montgomery, 1853)

'To Him who suffered on the tree,
Our souls, at His soul's price, to gain,
Blessing, and praise, and glory be:
"Worthy the Lamb, for He was slain!"'

Jesus, the delight of heaven

'And they sung a new song, saying, Thou art worthy to take the book, and to open the seals thereof: for thou wast slain, and hast redeemed us to God by thy blood out of every kindred, and tongue, and people, and nation; and hast made us unto our God kings and priests: and we shall reign on the earth.' Revelation 5:9–10
SUGGESTED FURTHER READING: Revelation 14:1–7

The redemption they sing about in heaven is not general redemption. It is particular redemption: 'thou ... hast redeemed *us* to God by thy blood *out of* every kindred, and tongue, and people, and nation.' They do not speak of the redemption of every tongue, people and nation, but of a redemption *out of* every tongue, people and nation. I thank God I do not believe that I was redeemed in the same way that Judas was, and no more. If so I shall go to hell as Judas did. General redemption is not worth anything to anybody, for of itself it secures to no one a place in heaven: but the special redemption, which does redeem men *out of* the rest of mankind, is the redemption that is to be prayed for, and for which we shall praise God for ever and ever. We are redeemed from among men. 'Christ also loved the church, and gave himself for it.' He 'is the Saviour of all men,'—let us never deny that—but 'specially of those that believe.' There is a wide far-reaching sacrificial atonement which brings untold blessings to all mankind, but by that atonement a special divine object was aimed at, which will be carried out, and that object is the actual redemption of his own elect from the bondage of their sins, the price being the blood of Jesus Christ. May we have a share in this particular, efficient redemption, for this alone can bring us where they sing the new song. This redemption is one which is personally realised. Redemption is sweet but 'thou ... hast redeemed *us*' is sweeter still. If I can only believe he 'loved me, and gave himself for me', that will tune my tongue to sing Jehovah's praise.

FOR MEDITATION: (*Our Own Hymn Book* no.412 v.7—Isaac Watts, 1709)
'Thou hast redeemed our souls with blood,
Hast set the prisoners free;
Hast made us kings and priests to God,
And we shall reign with Thee.'

The sacred love-token

'And the blood shall be to you for a token.' Exodus 12:13
SUGGESTED FURTHER READING: Hebrews 10:15–23

We read in Revelation (13:16 & 14:1) that those who received the mark of the beast sometimes bore it 'in their foreheads', but sometimes also 'in their right hand', while he who had the mark of God always received it in his forehead, never in his right hand where it could be hidden within the palm. It has been well remarked that there is a back door to hell, but not to heaven. The way to heaven is the king's highway, a way which is not made for concealment, but for honest travellers who have nothing to hide. Believers must be seen, for they are the lights of the world; yet there are some who try to go to heaven up the back stairs and serve the Lord only by night. It must not be. Strike the blood where all can see it, and let men know that you are a believer in the Lord Jesus Christ's atoning sacrifice: whether they like it or not, let them know that this is all your salvation and all your desire. I had the pleasure of riding into the Leonine city in Rome a short time after the Italian troops had taken possession, and I noticed that every house had marked up most conspicuously the arms of the kingdom of Italy and the name of Victor Emmanuel. They were not content to have it over their doors, but all over the front of the houses you read 'Victor Emmanuel, King of Italy', showing that they were very glad to escape from the dominion of the Pope, and to avow their allegiance to a constitutional king. Surely, if for a human monarch and the earthly freedom which he brought men could thus set up his ensign everywhere, you and I who believe in Jesus are bound to exhibit the blood-red token and to keep it always conspicuous. Let others believe the priest; we believe Jesus. Let others trust their works; we trust the sprinkled blood.

FOR MEDITATION: (*Our Own Hymn Book* no.549 v.1—Edward Mote, 1825—not sung during the service, but quoted by Spurgeon after the above sermon extract)
   'My hope is built on nothing less than Jesus' blood and righteousness;
   I dare not trust the sweetest frame; but wholly lean on Jesus' name:
   On Christ the solid rock I stand, all other ground is sinking sand.'

SERMON NO. 1251

The turning point

'And he arose, and came to his father.' Luke 15:20
SUGGESTED FURTHER READING: Matthew 21:28–32

The prodigal pressed beyond mere resolving. That is a sweet verse which says, 'I will arise', but that is far better which says, 'And he arose'. Resolves are good, like blossoms, but actions are better, for they are the fruits. We are glad to hear from you the resolution, 'I will turn to God,' but holy angels in heaven do not rejoice over resolutions; they reserve their music for sinners who actually repent. Many of you, like the son in the parable, have said, 'I go, sir', but you have not gone. You are as ready at forgetting as you are at resolving. Every earnest sermon, every death in your family, every funeral knell for a neighbour, every pricking of conscience, and every touch of sickness sets you resolving to amend, but your promissory notes are never honoured; your repentance ends in words. Your goodness is as the dew, which at early dawn hangs each blade of grass with gems, but leaves the fields all parched and dry when the sun's burning heat is poured upon the pasture. You mock your friends and trifle with your own souls. You have often said, 'Let me reach my chamber and I will fall upon my knees,' but on the way home you have forgotten what manner of men you were and sin has confirmed its tottering throne. Have you not dallied long enough? Have you not lied unto God sufficiently? Should you not now give up resolving and proceed to the solemn business of your souls like men of common sense? You are in a sinking vessel and the lifeboat is near, but your mere resolve to enter it will not prevent you going down with the sinking craft; as sure as you are a living man, you will drown unless you take the actual leap for life. 'He arose, and came to his father.'

FOR MEDITATION: Matthew 'arose and followed' Jesus as soon as he was told to (Matthew 9:9). Contrast his obedient action with the futile and unfulfilled resolutions of Felix over a two-year period (Acts 24:24–27). Which of the two did the will of God (Matthew 21:31)? And which of the two are you like?

SERMON NO. 1189

Love's crowning deed

'Greater love hath no man than this, that a man lay down his life for his friends.' John 15:13
SUGGESTED FURTHER READING: Ephesians 3:14–21

The atmosphere around the cross of Christ is bracing to the soul: think much of his love and you will grow strong and vigorous in grace. As dwellers in the low-lying Alpine valleys become weak and full of disease in the close, damp atmosphere, but soon recover health and strength if they climb the hill-side and tarry there, so in this world of selfishness, where the mean spirit of caring only for one's own self reigns predominant, the saints become weak and diseased, even as worldlings are; but up on the hill-sides, where we learn Christ's self-denying affection to the sons of men, we are braced to nobler and better lives. If men are to be truly great they must be nurtured beneath the wing of free grace and dying love. The grandeur of the Redeemer's example calls his disciples to make their own lives sublime, and furnishes them both with motives for so doing and with forces to constrain them thereto. We may well tarry in the region of the love of Christ, because not only is it full of bracing influences, but it has an outlook towards the better shore. Shipwrecked mariners upon a desert island have been known to linger most of the day upon that headland which pushes furthest out into the main ocean, in the hope that, if they cannot catch a glimpse of their own country across the waves, they may possibly discern a sail which has left one of the ports of the well-beloved land; so it is that while we are sitting on the headlands of divine love we look across to heaven and become familiar with the spirits of the just. If ever we are to see heaven while tarrying here, it must surely be from Cape Cross or Mount Fellowship, from that jutting piece of holy experience which runs away from the ordinary thoughts of men and approaches the heart of Christ.

FOR MEDITATION: (*Our Own Hymn Book* no.250 v.4—Thomas Kelly, 1809)
'Constrained by this, they walk with Him,
His love their most delightful theme;
To glorify Him here, their aim,
Their hope, in heaven to praise His name.'

SERMON NO. 1128

The matchless mystery

'For we are members of his body, of his flesh, and of his bones.'
Ephesians 5:30
SUGGESTED FURTHER READING: 1 Corinthians 12:12–27

'No man ever yet hated his own flesh.' Surely 'the man Christ Jesus' never yet hated his own flesh. If 'we are members of his body, of his flesh, and of his bones', he may chasten, correct, lay on heavy strokes, give sharp twinges and make us cry out; he may even thrust us in the fire and heat the furnace seven times hotter, but he can never neglect and abhor his own flesh. Still is there love in his heart. I hate no part of my body, not even when it aches. I hate it not, but love it still; it is part of myself; and so does Jesus love his people. You, poor sinners, who feel that you are not worthy to be called his people, nevertheless his love goes out to you despite your imperfections. 'Having loved his own which were in the world, he loved them unto the end', and he has left it upon record, 'As the Father hath loved me, so have I loved you: continue ye in my love.' Another most enchanting thought arises from our subject. The apostle goes on to say, 'no man ever yet hated his own flesh; but nourisheth and cherisheth it, even as the Lord the church'. Are you living in a district where you do not get the gospel? Well then, go to the gospel's Lord and say to him, 'Lord, hate not thine own flesh, but nourish me.' Have you been for a while without visits from Christ? Have you lost the light of his countenance? Do not be satisfied with nourishing: go further and plead for cherishing. Ask for those love tokens, for those gentle words, for those secret blandishments, known to saints and none but saints, for 'The secret of the LORD is with them that fear him; and he will shew them his covenant.' Go and ask for both these forms of love, and you shall be nourished and cherished.

FOR MEDITATION: (*Our Own Hymn Book* no.762 v.5—James George Deck, 1837)
'Oh teach us Lord, to know and own
This wondrous mystery,
That Thou with us art truly ONE,
And we are ONE with Thee!'

SERMON NO. 1153

Brave waiting

'Wait on the LORD: *be of good courage, and he shall strengthen thy heart: wait, I say, on the* LORD.' *Psalm 27:14*
SUGGESTED FURTHER READING: Psalm 37:1–9

Waiting upon God strengthens the heart by lessening the causes of fear. And then it inflames the heart with love. Nothing can give us greater courage than a sincere affection for our Lord and his work. Courage is sure to abound where love is fervent. Look among the mild and gentle creatures of the animal creation and see how bold they are when once they become mothers and have to defend their offspring. A hen will fight for her chicks, though at another time she is one of the most timid of birds. Gilbert White, in his book on Selborne, tells of a raven that was hatching her young in a tree. The woodman began to fell it, but there she sat; the blows of the axe shook the tree, but she never moved, and when it fell she was still upon her nest. Love will make the most timid creature strong; if you love Christ you will defy all fear and count all hazards undergone for him to be your joy. In this sense also, 'perfect love casteth out fear'; it 'hopeth all things, endureth all things', and continues still to wait upon the Lord. To have more love we must more continually wait upon the Lord, and this will mightily renew the strength of our heart. Again, waiting upon the Lord breeds peace within the soul, and when a man is perfectly at rest within, he cares little for trials or foes. It is conscience that makes cowards of us all, but let conscience be pacified through the atoning blood of Jesus, and you can smile when others spit their venom at you, and, like your blessed Master, you can bear their taunts without reply, for there is a heavenly calm within. A heart unsettled towards God is sure to be afraid of men, but when the soul waits on the Lord in glad serenity it stoops not to fear.

FOR MEDITATION: Waiting upon God is always a worthwhile activity for it is from him that all the blessings we need come (Isaiah 30:18), including help (Psalm 33:20), salvation (Psalm 62:1), expectation (Psalm 62:5) and renewed strength (Isaiah 40:31). Waiting upon him will never leave us feeling ashamed (Psalm 25:3; 69:6; Isaiah 49:23).

SERMON NO. 1371

God of the hills and God of the valleys

'And there came a man of God, and spake unto the king of Israel, and said, Thus saith the LORD, Because the Syrians have said, The LORD is God of the hills, but he is not God of the valleys, therefore will I deliver all this great multitude into thine hand, and ye shall know that I am the LORD.' 1 Kings 20:28

SUGGESTED FURTHER READING: 1 Samuel 2:1–10

There is no trial or temptation, though it be low, degrading, base, in which the Lord cannot as much assist you, when labouring under it, as in the sublimer struggles of the most noble life. Commit yourself to God and entertain no fears as to his all-sufficiency and faithfulness. But you say, 'I would not entertain any of those fears if I were like eminent saints, but I am far inferior to the godly men of whom I read and hear. I am obscure and insignificant; I have little talent and even less grace. I am a nobody.' But is our God the 'God of the hills' and not the 'God of the valleys'? Will God help Oliver Cromwell and not a private soldier who trusts in God and keeps his powder dry? Will God aid a Whitefield and not help a poor local preacher holding forth upon the green? Will he assist the earnest minister who addresses thousands, and desert the simple girl who teaches a dozen little children the old, old story of the cross? Is this after the fashion of God, to patronise the eminent and neglect the lowly? Does Jesus despise 'the day of small things'? Surely you have misread the Scriptures if you think so, for the Christ of the gospels took note of a widow's small coins, and was pleased with the hosannas of boys and girls. He rejoiced that his Father revealed his great things not to the wise and prudent, but to babes, and he called to his work not the high priests and philosophers, but the fishermen and tax-collectors. So, because you see a difference between yourself and others, and a change in the circumstances of your trial, do not begin to think that the Heavenly Father will desert you, or I shall again have to tell you that he is God of the valleys as well as the hills.

FOR MEDITATION: The Lord can 'save by many or by few' (1 Samuel 14:6), by small as well as great. To stop us taking the credit (Judges 7:2), he uses us when we feel weak. Moses (Exodus 4:10–12), Gideon (Judges 6:14–16), David (1 Samuel 17:33–37), Solomon (1 Kings 3:7–9) and Jeremiah (Jeremiah 1:4–8) all proved this early on.

SERMON NO. 1311

A holy and homely resolve

'I will behave myself wisely in a perfect way. O when wilt thou come unto me? I will walk within my house with a perfect heart.' Psalm 101:2
SUGGESTED FURTHER READING: 2 Samuel 12:1–12

The man is what he is at home. This is a simple but crucial test of character. If a man does not make his family happy, and if his example is not that of holiness in the domestic circle, he may make what pretension of godliness he likes, but his religion is base, worthless, mischievous. The sooner he gets rid of such a profession the better for himself, for then he may begin to know what he is and where he is, and seek the Lord in spirit and in truth. It is at home that the lack of true religion will do most damage. If you are a hypocrite and go out into the world, you will soon be found out and the people who observe you will not be much influenced by your example. They will come to the conclusion that you are what you are, they will treat you as such and there will be an end of it. But that will not be so with little Master Johnny who sees his father's actions. He is not able to criticise, but he has a wonderful faculty for imitation. And, mother, it is not likely that little Polly will begin to say, 'Mother is inconsistent.' She does not know that, but she will take it for granted that mother is right. Her character will be fashioned upon your pattern, and you will be injuring her for life unless the grace of God wonderfully intervenes. At home to our children, especially when they are young, we are like little gods; they take their law from us and their conduct is shaped according to the pattern we set before them. Round the hearth holiness ought to be conspicuous, for there it is most beautiful, most useful and most productive. It is a blessed thing for some of us that we can look back upon a father's and a mother's example with nothing but pure gratitude to God for both.

FOR MEDITATION: Godliness at home can be a great influence for good (Deuteronomy 11:18–21; Ephesians 6:1–4; 2 Timothy 1:5), but even a godly parent cannot be guaranteed godly children (1 Samuel 8:1–3). This warns us of the dire consequences that a lack of discipline (1 Samuel 3:12–14) or an ungodly example (2 Chronicles 33:21–22) may have. Then even a parent's repentance is unlikely to redirect children already set in their ways (1 Samuel 2:22–25; 2 Chronicles 33:23).

SERMON NO. 1230

The first day of creation

'And God saw the light that it was good.' Genesis 1:4
SUGGESTED FURTHER READING: Acts 15:36–16:3

Older Christian people, if the Lord says that his work on the first day is good, I want you to say so too. Do not wait until you see the second, third, fourth, fifth or sixth day before you feel confidence in the convert and offer him fellowship. If God speaks encouragingly so soon, I want you to do the same. A few words to a young Christian will be very greatly helpful to him, and his weakness craves them. Those of us who have been a long while in the Lord's ways ought to be ashamed if we are gruff, sour and critical. You know it was the elder brother, not one of the younger people, who said, 'this thy son was come, which hath devoured thy living with harlots' and so on. Do not degenerate into the elder brother's spirit. You must grow older in years, but endeavour to remain young at heart. There is a tendency to look for too much in young converts and to expect in them a great deal more than we shall ever see. This is wrong. We shall not do them much good by criticising them, but we may greatly benefit them by encouraging them. We have all read in the papers this week about Captain Webb's swimming across the channel, and we noticed that every now and then his friends gave him a cheer. Would that help him? No doubt it did. There is nothing like a cheer to a fellow when he feels faint and fagged. Give the weak brother a cheer, I say. When you meet with a young believer who is tossed about, give him a hearty cheer. Tell him some choice promise; tell him how the Lord helped you. Your few words may not be much to you, but they will be very much to him, whereas the hard look, which perhaps you really did not mean, may chill him to the very marrow of his bones. Many a poor young Christian has been frostbitten by the coldness of stern professors.

FOR MEDITATION: Even young people can struggle and need renewed strength (Isaiah 40:30). Consider the wisdom of Elisha and David when dealing with weak or immature young people (2 Kings 6:15–17; 1 Chronicles 22:5; 29:1–2). Paul told Timothy to treat younger Christians as brothers and sisters (1 Timothy 5:1–2).

N.B. On 25 August 1875 Captain Matthew Webb was the first to swim the English Channel.

SERMON NO. 1252

A song among the lilies

'My beloved is mine, and I am his: he feedeth among the lilies.' Song of
Solomon 2:16
SUGGESTED FURTHER READING: 2 Samuel 22:1–7

'My beloved is mine.' He is altogether mine, his Godhead and his
manhood, his life, his death, his attributes and prerogatives, yes, all he is,
all he was, all he ever will be, all he has done and all he ever will do, is
mine. I possess not a portion in Christ, but the whole of him. All his
saints own him, but I own him as much as if there were never another
saint to claim him. Child of God, do you see this? In other inheritances if
there are many heirs, there is so much the less for each, but in this great
possession every one who has Christ has a whole Christ all to himself
from the head of 'most fine gold' down to his legs which 'are as pillars of
marble'. The whole of his boundless heart of love, his whole arm of
infinite might and his whole head of matchless wisdom, all is for you.
Whoever you may be, if you do indeed trust in Jesus, he is all your own.
My beloved is all mine and absolutely mine, not mine merely to look at
and talk about, but mine to trust in, to speak to, to depend upon, to fly
to in every troubled hour, yes, mine to feed upon, for his 'flesh is meat
indeed' and his 'blood is drink indeed'. Our beloved is not ours to use
only in certain ways, but ours outright, without restriction. I may draw
what I will from him, and both what I take and what I leave are mine.
He himself in his ever glorious person is mine, and mine always, mine
when I know it and mine when I do not know it, mine when I am sure of
it and mine when I doubt it, mine by day and mine by night, mine when I
walk in holiness, yes, and mine when I sin, for 'if any man sin, we have
an advocate with the Father, Jesus Christ the righteous'.

FOR MEDITATION: (*Our Own Hymn Book* no.660 v.6—John S.B.Monsell,
1863)
  'For I am His, and He is mine,
  The God whom I adore!
  My Father, Saviour, Comforter,
  Now and for evermore!'

SERMON NO. 1190

The heart of flesh

'I will take away the stony heart out of your flesh, and I will give you an heart of flesh.' Ezekiel 36:26
SUGGESTED FURTHER READING: Isaiah 66:1–5

The man who has a heart of flesh given to him becomes sensitive to fear. He trembles at the thought of a holy God in arms against him. He no longer objects about hell and eternity, as so many do, but he says, 'my heart standeth in awe of thy word' 'and I am afraid of thy judgments.' He no longer argues that the Lord is too severe, but owns that he is just when he judges and clear when he condemns. The renewed heart is afraid of what others call little sins, and flees from them as from a serpent. The regenerate man knows that there is death in every drop of sin's wine and he will not venture to sip thereof, nor taste a mouthful of sin's most royal dainties. He fears the Lord and dreads to offend, because he is made alive, so as to know the Lord's holiness and perceive his justice. The stony heart neither knows nor fears, and therefore abides in death. I have little fear for a soul that fears, but I tremble for those who never tremble. I have sometimes wished that certain very assured Christians, as they think themselves, who are, I fear, in very truth presumptuous pretenders, could and would have a dash of fear about them. Fear of the kind we now mean is a holy salt to a man's character. Fear and trembling will befit even the most eminent saint. 'God is greatly to be feared in the assembly of the saints.' 'Serve the LORD with fear, and rejoice with trembling.' 'Work out your own salvation with fear and trembling.' Though I greatly deplore all doubts of God's truthfulness, I do not equally deprecate doubts concerning our own condition, for there is such a thing as holy anxiety and I charge you never to think little of it.

FOR MEDITATION: Those who know the fear of the Lord enjoy great blessings (Proverbs 1:7; 10:27; 14:26–27; 16:6; 19:23), but those who choose to carry on without any fear of God place themselves in great danger (Proverbs 1:29–32; Jeremiah 2:19; Jude 12–13).

The message from the Lord's mouth

'Son of man, I have made thee a watchman unto the house of Israel: therefore hear the word at my mouth, and give them warning from me.'
Ezekiel 3:17
SUGGESTED FURTHER READING: Acts 4:5–31

There are several ways of speaking. I was trying to illustrate differences of speaking when addressing my students the other day. I said, 'Suppose you saw by the look of my face, while I was sitting here, that I was in a terrible state of indignation when I arose to address you; you would say, "Now we shall have it; we can see by the look of him that he will drive at us."' Just so when a man preaches or warns others; it ought to be in a living style which indicates that something is coming. The man should be full of emotion, moved not by anger but by a sacred passion which arouses him and makes the people feel that he is in awful earnest, carried out of himself, not delivering set phrases and words from his mouth outwardly, but speaking from his inmost heart. If we were to meet our Lord Jesus himself and were then to speak of him in the state of mind in which his presence left us, what a style of speech that would be. I think I hear a mother, who has been with Jesus, talking to her girl. She says, 'Dear child, there is such joy in loving Jesus that I pant for you to know it. He is so great and good that my dear little daughter must not forget him.' I can imagine that a father has met with the Lord Jesus and felt God's truth sent into his own soul by the Holy Spirit, and I am sure that when he gets his boy alone, he pleads with him in deep and tender earnestness, which commands the boy's ear and heart. He does not know what has happened to his father; he is so earnest and pleads so seriously, but the secret reason is that father has listened to the Lord himself and is himself the echo of that voice. Facts vividly brought before the mind greatly influence a speaker. A sinner seen as lost touches the heart. Jesus seen as crucified affects the speech.

FOR MEDITATION: (*Our Own Hymn Book* no.972 v.2—James Montgomery, 1825)
    'Give tongues of fire and hearts of love
    To preach the reconciling word;
    Give power and unction from above,
    Whene'er the joyful sound is heard.'

SERMON NO. 1431

God our portion and his word our treasure

'Thou art my portion, O LORD: I have said that I would keep thy words.'
Psalm 119:57
SUGGESTED FURTHER READING: 2 Timothy 2:8–19

'I have said that I would keep thy words'—'I will believe thy *doctrines*. When I cannot comprehend the great mysteries I will still believe them. Though others dispute, I will believe! Despite the insinuations of crafty men I will hold to the doctrines of grace, believing them as long as reason holds her throne. What I see in God's word I will not dare to doubt or neglect.' The doctrines of grace are the backbone of the Christian life. Keep to them for your comfort and you shall never be ashamed of them. If you willingly tamper with any of the doctrines, there is no knowing where you will drift. Cast out more anchors; never drift. 'I have said that I would keep thy words'—thy *precepts*. 'What thou biddest me, I will delight to do. I will not merely rejoice in the doctrines, but in the commands also, and will ask for grace to obey them all. I will keep thine *ordinances* too, for they are a part of thy word and are to be kept as delivered, without addition or diminution. I will not say, "This is non-essential and this is unimportant," but I have said that I would keep thy words, and keep them I will, through thy grace, in every particular. I will do what thou biddest me, as and when thou biddest me.' So much evil has grown out of slight departures from Scripture that Christians ought to be very scrupulous and carefully observe every ordinance as set forth in the word. 'I have said that I would keep thy words'—'I will keep thy *promises* in my heart to comfort me, in my faith, expecting their fulfilment, in my mind, for daily use and solace, and on my tongue, that I may encourage others.' Since God keeps his promises by fulfilling them, we ought to keep them by remembering them.

FOR MEDITATION: The writer of Psalm 119 longed to keep God's statutes (vv.5,8,33,145), word (vv.17,67,101), testimonies (vv.22,88,129,146,167–168), law (vv.34,44,55), precepts (vv.56,63,69,100,134,168), commandments (vv.60,115), and righteous judgments (v.106). Those who failed to do this grieved him (vv.136,158). God commands us to keep his precepts diligently (v.4) and blesses those 'that keep his testimonies' (v.2). How much concern do you have about these things?

SERMON NO. 1372

Good news for seekers

'They shall praise the LORD that seek him.' Psalm 22:26
SUGGESTED FURTHER READING: Nehemiah 9:1–5

Without knowing it, the humble seeker is already praising God. That confession of sin which he made with so many tears was a glorifying of God by bearing witness to the justice of God's law and the truth of the charges which it brings against our fallen nature. 'My son,' said Joshua even to Achan, 'give, I pray thee, glory to the LORD God of Israel, and make confession unto him.' There is a measure of true praise in confession, and it is as pure and real as that which angels present before the sapphire throne. The seeker, when he acknowledges that he deserves to be sent to hell, is in fact praising justice—he is adoring the Judge of all. Even though in so doing there is a mixture of unbelief and a forgetfulness of other attributes, yet there is a firm belief in divine justice, and a suppliant adoration of it which is far from being unacceptable. There is also in the seeker a measure of delight in God's mercy, for while the poor sin-smitten soul is craving for pardon, it confesses heartily how sweet mercy is in itself, if it might obtain it, how gracious forgiveness is and how precious lovingkindness is, if it might be favoured with it. No living man has so keen an eye to the tender attributes of God as he whose soul is covered all over with wounds, bruises and putrefying sores through a sense of sin. Meanwhile the seeking soul is really praising the Lord Jesus by appreciating the preciousness of his love and the value of his blood, and saying within itself, 'Oh that I might know the value of these in my own case! Oh that I could but touch the hem of his garment for myself! Would God I knew what it is to be washed in his blood and to be covered with his righteousness!' There is in all these emotions a measure of latent praise.

FOR MEDITATION: Seeking the Lord leads not only to praising him, but also to rejoicing in him (Psalm 70:4; 105:2–4). Look again at the suggested further reading and trace how what began as a mournful confession of sin ended in joyful praise of God. Truly God does turn sincere and genuine mourning into gladness (Psalm 30:11; Jeremiah 31:13; Luke 6:21).

SERMON NO. 1372

An anxious enquiry for a beloved son

'And the king said, Is the young man Absalom safe?' 2 Samuel 18:29
SUGGESTED FURTHER READING: Acts 27:9–44

If one day the shadow of a disaster should cross your path, and you should fear that your beloved ones are lost, exercise faith at such a time, if you are Christian people, and stay yourselves upon God. If you become so anxious as to lose your clearness of mind, you will not be fit for the emergency. By retaining calmness of soul you may be of service; but by giving up the very helm of your mind and allowing yourself to drift before the torrent of anxiety, you will become useless and helpless. 'In your patience possess ye your souls.' The world is in God's hand after all. The young man Absalom will not die without the appointment of heaven. Your children are not out of the keeping of the Most High. However dear they are to you and however great their peril, there is One that rules and overrules; quiet prayer has more power with him than impatient fretfulness. If your dear ones are dead you cannot restore them to life by your unbelief; and if they survive, it will be a pity to be downcast and unbelieving when there is no occasion for it. Your strength is to sit still. Remember that a Christian is expected to be more self-possessed than those who have no God to fly to. The holy self-composedness of faith is one of the things which recommend it to the outside world, and men who see Christians calm, when others are beside themselves, are led to ask, 'What is this?' and unconsciously to own, 'This is the finger of God.'

FOR MEDITATION: (Flowers and fruits no.25 v.2—F.J.Crosby, 1868)
    'Safe in the arms of Jesus, safe from corroding care,
    Safe from the world's temptations, sin cannot harm me there,
    Free from the blight of sorrow, free from my doubts and fears;
    Only a few more trials, only a few more tears.'

N.B. On the evening of 3 September 1878 there occurred the worst marine disaster in British waters. The pleasure steamer *Princess Alice* was cut in two during a collision on the River Thames near Woolwich and sank with the loss of 640 of the 800 or so on board. At least five members of the Metropolitan Tabernacle died.

SERMON NO. 1433

The lion-slayer, the giant-killer

'Thy servant slew both the lion and the bear: and this uncircumcised Philistine shall be as one of them, seeing he hath defied the armies of the living God. David said moreover, the LORD that delivered me out of the paw of the lion and out of the paw of the bear, he will deliver me out of the hand of this Philistine.' 1 Samuel 17:36–37
SUGGESTED FURTHER READING: 2 Timothy 4:1–5

The vessel of the church has such an awful lot of top-hamper that I wonder how she can be navigated at all; if a tempest were to come on, she would have to cut herself free from nearly all of it. When shall we get at the work? If there should ever come a day when brethren will go forth preaching the gospel, simply resting in faith upon the Lord alone, I expect to see grand results; but at present Saul's armour is everywhere. When we get rid of formality in preaching we shall see great results, but the churches are locked up in irons which they call armour. If we are to have a special service, one brother must have it conducted on the Moody method and another can only have Sankey hymns. Who are we that we must follow others? Do not talk to us about innovations and all that. Let us serve God with all our hearts and preach Jesus Christ to sinners with our whole souls, and the mode is of no consequence. To preach down priestcraft and error, and do it in the simplest possible manner by preaching up Christ, is the way of wisdom. We must preach, not after the manners of doctors of divinity, but after the manner of those 'unlearned and ignorant men' in the olden time who 'had been with Jesus' and learned of him. Some of you have too much armour on. Put it off: be simple, artless, plain-spoken, trustful in the living God, and you will succeed. Less of the artificer's brass and more of heaven-anointed manhood is wanted, more sanctified naturalness and less of studied artificialness. O Lord, send us this, for Christ's sake.

FOR MEDITATION: (*Our Own Hymn Book* no.681 v.2—Isaac Watts, 1709)
'I glory in infirmity,
That Christ's own power may rest on me:
When I am weak, then am I strong,
Grace is my shield, and Christ my song.'

SERMON NO. 1253

For whom did Christ die?

'Christ died for the ungodly.' Romans 5:6
SUGGESTED FURTHER READING: Luke 15:1–24

I see the Good Shepherd in all the energy of his mighty love going forth into the dreadful wilderness. For whom is he gone forth? For the ninety and nine who feed at home? No, but into the desert his love sends him, over hill and dale, to seek the one lost sheep which has gone astray. Behold, I see him arousing his church, like a good housewife, to cleanse her house. With the broom of the law she sweeps and with the candle of the word she searches. For what? For those bright new coined pieces fresh from the mint, which glitter safely in her purse? Assuredly not, but for that lost piece which has rolled away into the dust and lies hidden in the dark corner. And lo, the grandest of all visions, I see the Eternal Father himself, in the infinity of his love, going forth in haste to meet a returning child. And whom does he go to meet? The elder brother returning from the field, bringing his sheaves with him? An Esau, who has brought him savoury meat such as his soul loves? A Joseph whose godly life has made him lord over all Egypt? No, the Father leaves his home to meet a returning prodigal, who has companied with harlots and grovelled among swine, and who comes back to him in disgraceful rags and disgusting filthiness! It is on a sinner's neck that the Father weeps; it is on a guilty cheek that he sets his kisses; it is for an unworthy one that the fatted calf is killed, the best robe is worn and the house is made merry with music and dancing. Yes, tell it, and let it ring round heaven and earth—'Christ died for the ungodly.' Mercy seeks the guilty, and grace has to do with the impious, the irreligious and the wicked. The physician has not come to heal the healthy, but to heal the sick.

FOR MEDITATION: (*Our Own Hymn Book* no.553 v.2—William Hiley Bathurst, 1831)
    'How can a soul condemned to die
    Escape the just decree?
    A vile, unworthy wretch am I,
    But Jesus died for me.'

The Christian's great business

'Restore unto me the joy of thy salvation; and uphold me with thy free spirit. Then will I teach transgressors thy ways; and sinners shall be converted unto thee.' Psalm 51:12–13
SUGGESTED FURTHER READING: Ezekiel 33:1–9

If we do not try to bring sinners to Christ, where is our humanity? If I believed that sinners could be annihilated, I should have no particular reason for preaching to them; in fact, I should have a very urgent reason for never doing anything of the kind. Certain heretics teach that if men do not hear the gospel at all they will be annihilated at death, but if they hear it and reject it, they will live and be punished for a time; then, I say, let them die; they will be better without hearing the gospel, and he is a traitor who preaches it to them and makes them run so great a risk. But, beloved, we who believe the solemn truth, which has often made us tremble from head to foot, that the wrath of God abides upon the ungodly for ever, we, if we do not attempt their salvation, are demons! That was a harsh word, but I will not correct it; I will leave it where it stands. I care not what pretensions you are making to Christianity, if you are doing nothing in any way for the souls of men, you act like demons! If there is a wreck at sea and a mariner refuses to aid in saving when he is strong and able, men cry shame of him. A man is dying for want of bread at your door, and if you have plenty, but refuse to give him a crust and let him die on your doorstep, the whole neighbourhood will censure you. But a soul perishing for lack of knowledge, for lack of the bread of life, and you have it, but do not hand it to him—'how dwelleth the love of God' in you? Is there a spark left? You are without grace, for you have fallen below the humanity of nature.

FOR MEDITATION: (*Our Own Hymn Book* no.473 v.4—Philip Doddridge, 1755)
    'My God, I feel the mournful scene;
    My bowels yearn o'er dying men;
    And fain my pity would reclaim,
    And snatch the firebrands from the flame.'

SERMON NO. 1130

Divine interpositions

'He sent from above, he took me, he drew me out of many waters.'
Psalm 18:16
SUGGESTED FURTHER READING: Isaiah 45:1–13

We do not believe in two co-existent forces, each supreme, one creating disasters, and the other distributing blessings. The prince of evil is, according to our faith, subordinate to the great Lord of all. Thus says Jehovah, by the mouth of his servant Isaiah, 'I form the light, and create darkness: I make peace, and create evil: I the LORD do all these things.' He reigns in the calm summer's day and gives us the precious fruits of harvest, but he is equally present and reigning in the hurricane which destroys or the blight which desolates. His providence speeds the ship to its desired haven, but equally sinks the boat to the bottom of the sea. His power looses 'the bands of Orion' and binds 'the sweet influences of Pleiades'; his are the lightnings as well as the sunbeams, the thunderbolts as well as the raindrops. He is able to make the 'heaven as iron' and the 'earth as brass', so that our 'land shall not yield her increase'; he can call for a famine and break the whole 'staff of your bread', for famine, pestilence and war are as rods in his hand. Everywhere is God and in all things his hand is present: in things which seem evil as well as in events which appear good, God is at work. He does no wrong, 'for God cannot be tempted with evil, neither tempteth he any man', but we speak of physical evil which causes sorrow, pain and death among men, and we say that certainly God is there. If not a sparrow 'fall on the ground without your Father', we are sure that no great calamity can befall us apart from him. He is not far from us in our deepest sorrow, and however we may trace a calamity to the carelessness or the mistake of men, these are only the second causes, and we see behind all mere detail the permit of the Lord.

FOR MEDITATION: Isaiah 45:7 shows God in creating: 'I form the light' (see Genesis 1:3), in concealing: 'and create darkness' (see Job 9:7), in common grace: 'I make peace' (see Psalm 145:9; Matthew 5:45), and in condemning: 'and create evil' (see Amos 3:6), all consistent with his character—'I the LORD do all these things.'

N.B. The text was 'suggested by the loss of the *Princess Alice*' (see 4 September).

SERMON NO. 1432

Our last journey

'When a few years are come, then I shall go the way whence I shall not return.' Job 16:22
SUGGESTED FURTHER READING: 2 Corinthians 5:6–10

Can you picture the spirit of a man as it leaves the body? I confess my imagination does not enable me to picture it to myself, and certainly my words are not competent to convey to you what little I can realise to my mind. The soul finds itself rid of materialism; how will it feel when it has shaken itself loose of its shell of clay? I cannot tell. We all love 'our earthly house of this tabernacle' and leave it with reluctance. But it does not matter what lingering looks we cast; our soul will have done with the body in its present fashion, and it must for a while dwell apart from all materialism. At once it must come before God. Its state will immediately after death be known to it. In a moment it will know beyond all doubt whether it is accepted before God, and beyond all hope whether it is reprobate and condemned. That knowledge will at once commence its happiness, which will increase as ages roll on, or will at once commence its misery, which will deepen evermore. The soul will abide in the disembodied state for a while, and then will come the clarion note of the resurrection trumpet, and the body shall rise again to be again inhabited by the soul. What will the meeting be? What will be the sensation of the remarriage of mind with matter, of soul with body? We know not. The resurrection is the blessed hope of the Christian, but it is a terrible dread to the ungodly. The soul shall never more return to the world's cares, nor to the world at all as the world is now, but it shall again inhabit the body and stand before the judgment seat of Christ to receive the verdict from the lips of him who is appointed Judge of all mankind.

FOR MEDITATION: The earthly body is a tent which will be taken down one day (2 Corinthians 5:1; 2 Peter 1:13–14). The Christian looks forward to putting on something infinitely better in the resurrection (2 Corinthians 5:1–4), but an entirely different prospect awaits the unbeliever (John 5:28–29).

N.B. This sermon followed the recent deaths of a child in Spurgeon's orphanage and of both a past and a present student of the Pastor's College.

SERMON NO. 1373

A second word to seekers (see title of 3 September)

'And ye shall seek me, and find me, when ye shall search for me with all your heart.' Jeremiah 29:13

SUGGESTED FURTHER READING: Acts 17:16–34

How ought a man to seek after heaven and eternal life? Should it not be with all his heart? Poor seeker, recollect that every one you have to do with in this matter is in earnest. Look down on hell's domain and see how earnest Satan is to hold you and ruin you! How diligently the enemy baits his hooks and sets his traps to catch the souls of men! How does he compass sea and land to hold his captives lest they escape. On the other hand see how earnest Christ is! He proved his earnestness by a life of toil by day and of prayer by night, by hunger, thirst, faintness and sweat. The zeal of God's house had eaten him up; he was earnest even to the death for sinners. And God is in earnest: there is no mockery with him, or carelessness or indifference about human souls. When he speaks of sinners perishing, he cries out with a solemn oath that he has no pleasure in their death, but if they to the last refuse his love and defy his justice, he will not trifle with them, but will judge in earnest and punish in earnest. Has he not said, 'Consider this, ye that forget God, lest I tear you in pieces, and there be none to deliver'? The majesty of his power is revealed in flaming wrath against transgressors; hell is no trifle and his wrath is no small matter. Heaven and hell, then, are in earnest, and so must you be if you would find salvation. Shall we, who have to tell you to escape from the wrath to come, pray to be in earnest, and shall we never feel earnest enough, but always cry that we may be seized with a yet more intense passion for your welfare, and shall it seem to you to be a common-place affair, a thing that you may let alone and let happen as it may?

FOR MEDITATION: (*Our Own Hymn Book* no.594 v.1—John S.B.Monsell, 1863)

'Mercy, mercy, God the Father!
God the Son, be Thou my plea!
God the Holy Spirit, comfort!
Triune God, deliver me!'

SERMON NO. 1313

Ejaculatory prayer

'*So I prayed to the God of heaven.*' *Nehemiah 2:4*
SUGGESTED FURTHER READING: Nehemiah 13:14–31

When you have got any arduous undertaking on hand or a heavy piece of business, do not touch it until you have breathed your soul out in a short prayer. When you have a difficulty before you and are seriously perplexed, when business has got into a tangle or a confusion which you cannot unravel or arrange, breathe a prayer. It need not occupy a minute, but it is wonderful how many knots come loose after just a word of prayer. Are the children particularly troublesome to you, good woman? Does it seem as if your patience was almost worn out with the worry? Now for an ejaculatory prayer. You will manage them all the better, and you will bear with their naughty tempers all the more quietly. At any rate your own mind will be the less ruffled. Do you think that there is a temptation before you? Do you begin to suspect that somebody is plotting against you? Now for a prayer—'lead me in a plain path, because of mine enemies.' Are you at work at the bench, or in a shop or a warehouse, where lewd conversation and shameful blasphemies assail your ears? Now for a short prayer. Have you noticed some sin that grieves you? Let it move you to prayer. Do you feel your own heart going off the rails? Does sin begin to fascinate you? Now for a prayer, a warm, earnest, passionate cry—'Hold thou me up'. Did you see something with your eye and did that eye infect your heart? Do you feel 'my feet were almost gone: my steps had well nigh slipped'? Now for a prayer—'hold "me by my right hand."' Has something quite unlooked for happened? Has a friend treated you badly? Then like David say, 'O LORD, I pray thee, turn the counsel of Ahithophel into foolishness.' Breathe a prayer now. Are you anxious to do some good? Be sure to have a prayer over it.

FOR MEDITATION: (*Our Own Hymn Book* no.181 v.5—Josiah Conder, 1824)

'Come, make your wants, your burdens known;
He will present them at the throne;
And angel-bands are waiting there,
His messages of love to bear.'

Jesus in our midst

'Then the same day at evening, being the first day of the week, when the doors were shut where the disciples were assembled for fear of the Jews, came Jesus and stood in the midst, and saith unto them, Peace be unto you.' John 20:19
SUGGESTED FURTHER READING: John 14:18–24

Probably there is no statement of human history which is better sustained by evidence than this fact, that Jesus of Nazareth who hung upon the cross and died, did afterwards rise again from the dead. The time of eye-witnesses is now over; more evidence would be superfluous and we are now in the mid-ocean of faith. The Lord knows that sight interferes with faith, and therefore he does not give us a mixture of the two. We do not walk by sight and faith, but 'we walk by faith, not by sight'. To let us see occasionally would in fact remove us out of the realm of faith and bring us down from the high position of believers to the low platform of sightseers. Adieu, therefore, for a while, O sight! Yet, dear brethren, there are spiritual visits from Jesus, which are more than sufficient substitutes for his bodily presence, and these we may still desire and expect. Christ may be really present where he is not materially present. There is a discerning of the presence of Christ which we must all have, especially when we come to the communion table, for we are told that he that is 'not discerning the Lord's body' 'eateth and drinketh unworthily'. There is a discerning of the Lord's presence in the midst of his people which is essential to the power of our assemblies, and if we have this, we shall not be behind those who saw Jesus with their eyes and heard him with their ears. I do not think there is any privilege which the actual bodily presence of Christ could bestow, which we may not obtain at this moment by the actual spiritual presence of Christ, if we exercise faith in him as being in the midst of us. He has said, 'lo, I am with you alway.'

FOR MEDITATION: (*Our Own Hymn Book* no.785 v.2—Ray Palmer, 1858)
'I see Thee not, I hear Thee not,
Yet art Thou oft with me;
And earth hath ne'er so dear a spot,
As where I meet with Thee.'

SERMON NO. 1254

Hindrances to prayer

'That your prayers be not hindered.' 1 Peter 3:7
SUGGESTED FURTHER READING: Colossians 4:2–12

If prayer is to speed, there must be *fervour and importunity*. It is written, 'The effectual fervent prayer of a righteous man availeth much', not the dead-and-alive prayer of the mere professor, nor the prayer of one who does not care whether he is answered or not. There must be eagerness and intensity, the pouring out of the heart before God. The arrow must be put on the bow string and the bow must be drawn with all our might. The best bow is of no use until you draw it, and if you draw the bow of faith and shoot at the target up there in heaven, you will get what you want; only you must resolve to have it with this boundary—'The will of the Lord be done', and you will succeed. There must be, next, a *desire for God's glory,* for that is the white of the target, and if we do not shoot towards that, the arrow will avail nothing. We must earnestly desire what we ask, because we believe it will glorify God to give it to us. If we are wholly living unto God, our prayers will run side by side with his purposes, and none of them will fall to the ground. 'Delight thyself also in the LORD; and he shall give thee the desires of thine heart.' We must also have *holy expectancy,* or we shall hinder prayer. The man who shoots must look to see where his arrow goes. We must direct our prayer unto God and look up. Eyeing the Lord Jesus in all, we must look to succeed through the merits of the Redeemer; 'if we know that he hear us … we know that we have the petitions that we desired of him.' Presumption in prayer shoots with the bow of self-confidence, not for God's glory but for the gratification of itself, and therefore it fails.

FOR MEDITATION: (*Our Own Hymn Book* no.994 v.2—William Cowper, 1779)

> 'Prayer makes the darkened cloud withdraw,
> Prayer climbs the ladder Jacob saw,
> Gives exercise to faith and love,
> Brings every blessing from above.'

The seed upon stony ground

'And some fell on stony ground, where it had not much earth; and immediately it sprang up, because it had no depth of earth: but when the sun was up, it was scorched; and because it had no root, it withered away.' Mark 4:5–6
SUGGESTED FURTHER READING: Matthew 13:18–23

The parable does not refer to ground with stones in it, such as we commonly call stony ground, for that will grow corn well enough, but to soil where there was a hard rock underneath and only a very thin covering of earth. A hard pan of iron rock was at the bottom, and it was barely hidden by a little mould created by the lichens and mosses, enough to catch the seed and make it germinate, but not enough to feed its roots for any length of time. In these people their hearts have never been broken. 'Is not my word ... like a hammer?' says the Lord. They do not know, for it never hammered them. They got their joy and peace without a blow. What is to be done with a piece of ground which has the rock so close to the surface? Nothing can be done with it by man. The only thing that can be done is for God to come in, and when God in his infinite mercy changes the rock into good soil, then the wheat will grow, but not till then. 'A new heart also will I give you, and a new spirit will I put within you: and I will take away the stony heart out of your flesh, and I will give you an heart of flesh.' There must be a work of the Holy Spirit by which the natural rock of nature shall be turned into the good soil of grace, or else all the sowing in the world will never produce a harvest. These people skipped over that and in fact they did not like to hear of it. They liked preachers who always preached simple faith in the work of Jesus, but never mentioned the work of the Holy Spirit, lopsided preachers, messengers whose legs are not equal, who deliver half God's message and no more: under such teaching they found peace without soul-trouble and comfort without the new birth.

FOR MEDITATION: Superficiality is no substitute for genuine and thorough conversion. Those who profess conversion but turn out to be like rootless seeds will share the same sad fate as others who have been compared to waterless wells (2 Peter 2:17), waterless clouds and fruitless trees (Jude 12–13). False assurance does nobody any favours.

SERMON NO. 1132

Jesus

'And she shall bring forth a son, and thou shalt call his name Jesus: for he shall save his people from their sins.' Matthew 1:21
SUGGESTED FURTHER READING: Hebrews 4:1–16

Jesus and Joshua are the same word; Joshua is the Hebrew form and Jesus the Greek form. There was one of old who bore this famous name and who was a type of our Jesus. What did Joshua do? When Moses could not lead the people into Canaan, Joshua did it; and so our Jesus accomplishes what the law could never have done. Joshua overcame the enemies of God's people: though they were very many and very strong, and had cities walled to heaven and chariots of iron, yet in the name of Jehovah, as captain of the Lord's host, Joshua smote them. Even so does our glorious Joshua smite our sins and all the powers of darkness, and utterly destroys our spiritual enemies. Before him Amalek is smitten, Jericho falls and Canaanites are put to rout, while he gives us triumph in every place. Moreover Joshua conquered an inheritance for Israel, took them across the Jordan, settled them in a land that flowed with milk and honey, and placed each tribe and each man in the lot which God had ordained for him. Precisely this is what our Jesus does, only our inheritance is more divine, and on each of us it is more surely entailed. Joshua could not give the people the heavenly *Sabbatismos*, or rest of the highest kind, yet he gave them rest most pleasant, so that every man sat 'under his vine and under his fig tree', none making him afraid; but our glorious Joshua has given us infinite, eternal rest, for 'he is our peace', and they that know him have entered into rest. Joshua, the son of Nun, caused the people to serve the Lord all his days, but he could not save the nation from their sins, for after his death they grievously went astray: our Joshua preserves to himself a 'people, zealous of good works', for 'he ever liveth' and 'is able to keep' them 'from falling'.

FOR MEDITATION: (*Our Own Hymn Book* no.331 v.3—Charles Wesley, 1749)
    'Jesus the prisoner's fetters breaks,
    And bruises Satan's head;
    Power into strengthless souls it speaks,
    And life into the dead.'

SERMON NO. 1434

'For ever with the Lord'

'So shall we ever be with the Lord.' 1 Thessalonians 4:17
SUGGESTED FURTHER READING: John 13:36–14:6

For ever with the Lord—what will it mean? I remember a sermon upon this text by a notable preacher, of which the heads were as follows:- 'For ever life, for ever light, for ever love, for ever peace, for ever rest, for ever joy.' What a chain of delights! What more can heart imagine or hope desire? Carry those things in your mind and you will get, if you can drink into them, some idea of the blessedness which is contained in being for ever with the Lord; but still recollect these are only the fruits and not the root of the joy. Jesus is better than all these. His company is more than the joy which comes out of it. I do not care so much for 'life for ever', nor for 'light for ever', as I do for 'for ever with the Lord'. To be with him! I ask no other bliss and cannot imagine anything more heavenly. Why, the touch of the hem of his garment healed the sick woman; the sight of him was enough to give life to us when we were dead! What, then, must it be to be with him actually, consciously and always, to be with him no more by faith, but in very deed with him for ever? My soul is ready to swoon away with too much joy as she drinks even in her shallow measure into the meaning of this thought, and I dare not venture further. I must leave you to muse your souls into it, for it needs quiet thought and room for free indulgence of holy imagination until you cause your soul to dream of this excess of joy. 'Eye hath not seen, nor ear heard, neither have entered into the heart of man, the things which God hath prepared for them that love him. But God hath revealed them unto us by his Spirit'.

FOR MEDITATION: (*Our Own Hymn Book* no.846 v.1—James Montgomery, 1835)

> '"For ever with the Lord!"
> Amen! so let it be!
> Life from the dead is in that word,
> 'Tis immortality!'

SERMON NO. 1374

The mighty arm

'Thou hast a mighty arm: strong is thy hand, and high is thy right hand.'
Psalm 89:13
SUGGESTED FURTHER READING: Psalm 68:28–35

'Trust ye in the LORD for ever: for in the LORD JEHOVAH is everlasting strength.' If he is so strong, then trust him in everything. You that are his people, never dare to distrust him. Is his arm shortened? Cannot the Lord deliver you? Bring your burdens, your troubles, your wants and your griefs; pour them out like water before him and let them flow forth at the foot of the Almighty, and they shall pass away and you shall sing, 'the LORD JEHOVAH is my strength and my song; he also is become my salvation.' If God is so strong, then shake off all fear of man. Who are you that you should be afraid of a man who shall die? Man is but grass, withered in an hour; why should you tremble at his frown? He is 'crushed before the moth'; why then fear him? Let not the faces of proud men confound you. Trust in God and fear not, for the mighty God of Jacob is with us, and greater is he that is for us than all they who can be against us. And now as to your service to which you are called by the Lord. If he is so strong, do not think of your own weakness any longer, except as being a platform for his strength. Have you only one talent? God's Holy Spirit is not limited in power. He can make your one talent as fruitful as another man's ten. Are you weak as water? Then rejoice this day and glory in infirmity, because the power of God shall rest upon you. Think not of what you can do—that is a very small affair—but consider what he can do by you. He can strengthen the feeble against the strong.

FOR MEDITATION: If we claim to know the God who is so strong, we should seek him diligently (1 Chronicles 16:11; Psalm 105:4), rejoice in him (Nehemiah 8:10; Psalm 21:1), trust in him (Psalm 18:2), not be afraid of men (Psalm 27:1), cry to him for help (Psalm 31:4; 80:2), run to him for refuge (Psalm 46:1; Proverbs 18:10) and always take great care not to provoke him (1 Corinthians 10:22).

SERMON NO. 1314

Faith and its attendant privileges

'But as many as received him, to them gave he power to become the sons of God, even to them which believe on his name.' John 1:12
SUGGESTED FURTHER READING (Spurgeon): 1 John 3:1–10

If you are a son of God, you must act like it. If I hear of a man who says, 'I am a child of God,' but he gives short weight and is hard in his bargains, I am ashamed of him. He a son of God? He who must make money, hold it and keep it? He a son of God? He is not very like his Father. Son of God? And yet sharp, quick-tempered, angry and spiteful! He is not very like his Father. A child of God and do a mean thing? My dear brethren, what are you at? A son of God and tell a lie? A son of God and be afraid of anybody? A son of God and not look your fellow-man in the face without a blush? A son of God and at home a tyrant? Such conduct will never bear a thought, and he who is guilty of it gravely offends. When the great Emperor Napoleon was in his power, if a member of his family married below his rank, he was made to know the emperor's anger, for members of the imperial house were under bonds of honour to keep up their dignity. You girls, who are daughters of God, dare you marry out of the imperial family? Never do that. Take care that you are not unequally yoked. When a king was taken prisoner, Alexander asked him how he would be treated, and he said, 'Like a king.' Christian, act like a king. When a quarrelsome person offends us, we should say in our heart, 'I would have quarrelled with you, but I could not stoop to it; I am a child of God.' I read a bitter remark of Guizot's to his enemies the other day, which ran something like this: 'Come up the steps, and mount as high as you can, and when you reach the top, you will be beneath my contempt.' So may the child of God think of the world and all the shams and temptations which are in it: 'I have a great work; how can I come down to you? I am a son of God; my conversation is in heaven. I cannot leave my position to come down to you.' 'Walk as children of light.'

FOR MEDITATION: If we claim to be God's 'dear children' (Ephesians 5:1), we ought to prove it by behaving as God's 'obedient children' (1 Peter 1:14), otherwise we may prove not to be his children at all (John 8:42–44; Hebrews 12:8; 1 John 3:10).

How to converse with God

'Then call thou, and I will answer: or let me speak, and answer thou me.'
Job 13:22
SUGGESTED FURTHER READING: Daniel 9:1–19

Dear Mr Muller, who is a man living near to God and whose every word is like a pearl, said the other day, 'Sometimes when I go into my closet to pray, I find I cannot pray as I would. What do I then? Why, since I cannot speak to the Lord, I beg the Lord to speak to me, and therefore I open the Scriptures and read my portion; and then I find the Lord gives me matter for prayer.' Is not this a suggestion of much weight? Does it not commend itself to your spiritual judgment? Have you not observed that when somebody calls to see you, you may not be in a fit condition to start a profitable conversation, but if your friend will lead, your mind takes fire, and you have no difficulty in following him? Frequently it will be best to ask the Lord to lead the sacred converse, or wait awhile till he does so. It is a blessed thing to wait at the posts of his doors, expecting a word of love from his throne. It is generally best in communion with God to begin with hearing his voice, because it is due to his sacred majesty that we should first hear what he has to say to us; and it will especially be best for us to do so when we feel out of order for communion. If the flesh in its weakness hampers the spirit, then let the Bible reading come before the praying that the soul may be awakened thereby. Still, there are times when it will be better to speak to our heavenly Father at once. For instance, if a child has done wrong, it is very wise of him to run straight away to his father, before his father has said anything to him, and say, 'Father, I have sinned.' The prodigal had the first word, and so should our penitence seek for speedy audience and pour itself out like water before the Lord. Sometimes too, when our heart is very full of thankfulness, we should allow praise to burst forth at once.

FOR MEDITATION: Bible reading ought to affect us in a variety of ways (2 Timothy 3:16), which should be reflected in our praying. Note how the reading of God's word has been followed by prayers of commitment (2 Chronicles 34:30–31), praise (Nehemiah 8:1–6), confession (Nehemiah 9:3) and supplication (Daniel 9:1–3).

SERMON NO. 1255

'I and the children'

'Behold, I and the children whom the LORD *hath given me are for signs and for wonders in Israel from the* LORD *of hosts, which dwelleth in Mount Zion.' Isaiah 8:18*
SUGGESTED FURTHER READING (Spurgeon): Isaiah 9:1–7

The text has in it very clearly the idea of charge and responsibility. Children are a charge always, a comfort sometimes. No parent has a child without lying under obligations to God to take care of it and to nurse it for him. Sometimes the responsibility becomes very heavy and involves us in much anxiety. Wherever conscience is lively, fatherhood is regarded as a solemn thing. Now, Jesus Christ, when looking upon his people, calls them 'the children which God hath given me', as if he recognised the charge laid upon him to keep, instruct and perfect his own people. Remember his last words to his Father before he went to his passion: 'I have manifested thy name unto the men which thou gavest me out of the world: thine they were, and thou gavest them me; and they have kept thy word.' 'While I was with them in the world, I kept them in thy name: those that thou gavest me I have kept, and none of them is lost, but the son of perdition; that the scripture might be fulfilled.' Like Jacob with Laban's sheep, our Lord looked upon his elect as a charge for which he was responsible, and before he departed out of this life he rendered in an account to his heavenly Father. Even now 'that great shepherd of the sheep' charges himself with the preservation of his own ransomed ones, and when he, at the last, shall gather all his redeemed people around him, there will not be one missing and he will say, 'Behold, I and the children which God hath given me.' We call him Father, then, because as a father has charge of his family and is responsible before God for their training and upbringing, so Christ himself is surety for his people and is under bond to bring the 'many sons unto glory'.

FOR MEDITATION: Earthly parents do fall down on their responsibilities (Isaiah 49:15) and need reminding of them (Ephesians 6:4), but the Lord Jesus Christ will never let his own people down (John 14:18; Hebrews 2:10–18).

N.B. Spurgeon preached this sermon on the eighteenth birthday of his twin sons, Thomas and Charles.

SERMON NO. 1194

A fatal deficiency

'If any man have not the Spirit of Christ, he is none of his.' Romans 8:9
SUGGESTED FURTHER READING: Luke 13:22–30

'He that believeth not is condemned already, because he hath not believed in the name of the only begotten Son of God.' If you were set up for an instant upon the top of St Paul's Cathedral, poised in the air upon the cross with none to hold you up, how dreadful would be your feelings as you looked beneath you and knew that the next gust of wind would sweep you down to sure destruction! Sinner, you are now in a similar position. If you are 'none of his', you are now in awful peril. You stand over the mouth of hell upon a single plank, and that plank is rotten. You hang over the jaws of perdition by a slender thread, and the angel of justice is ready to cut that thread in sunder now. 'None of his'! How dreadful to live 'none of his', to die 'none of his' and to have this for your epitaph—'NONE OF HIS'! And then to wake up on the resurrection morning and see the King in his beauty on the throne, and to know that you are 'none of his'! To cry to the rocks to hide you and to the hills to cover you, for you are 'none of his'! Then to be brought out before the great white throne resplendent in its holiness and hear the fact announced, so that all may hear, that there is a Saviour, but you are 'none of his'! What it will be to see the pit open her mouth to devour you, and, descending for ever, to understand that you are 'none of his'!

> 'Ye sinners, seek His grace,
> Whose wrath ye cannot bear;
> Fly to the shelter of His cross,
> And find salvation there.'

If you look to Jesus by faith, the Spirit is with you as you look; there is life in a look at the crucified Redeemer. Trust him!

FOR MEDITATION: It is a comfort to the Christian that 'The Lord knoweth them that are his' (2 Timothy 2:19), but a warning to the unbeliever that the Lord is also well aware of all those who are not his. See the stark contrast in John 10:26–27.

SERMON NO. 1133

Adoption—the Spirit and the cry

And because ye are sons, God hath sent forth the Spirit of his Son into your hearts, crying, Abba, Father.' Galatians 4:6
SUGGESTED FURTHER READING: John 16:5–15

Note the style and title under which the Holy Spirit comes to us: he comes as the Spirit of Jesus. The words are 'the Spirit of his Son', by which is not meant the character and disposition of Christ, though that were quite true, for God sends this to his people, but it means the Holy Spirit. Why, then, is he called 'the Spirit of his Son', or 'the Spirit of Christ'? May we not give these reasons? It was by the Holy Spirit that the human nature of Christ was born of the virgin. By the Spirit our Lord was attested at his baptism, when the Holy Spirit descended upon him like a dove and abode upon him. In him the Holy Spirit dwelt without measure, anointing him for his great work, and by the Spirit he was anointed 'with the oil of gladness above' his fellows. The Spirit was also with him, attesting his ministry by signs and wonders. The Holy Spirit is our Lord's great gift to the church; it was after his ascension that he bestowed the gifts of Pentecost, and the Holy Spirit descended upon the church to abide with the people of God for ever. The Holy Spirit is 'the Spirit of Christ' because he is also Christ's witness here below, for 'there are three that bear witness on earth, the Spirit, and the water, and the blood'. For these and many other reasons he is called 'the Spirit of his Son', and it is he who comes to dwell in believers. I would urge you very solemnly and gratefully to consider the wondrous condescension which is here displayed. God himself, the Holy Spirit, takes up his residence in believers. I never know which is the more wonderful, the incarnation of Christ or the indwelling of the Holy Spirit.

FOR MEDITATION: The Holy Spirit was uniquely associated with the revelation of the Lord Jesus Christ as the Son of God (Luke 1:35; 3:22). How wonderful it is that he is also specially associated with every individual Christian in their position as an adopted son or daughter of God (Romans 8:14–16; Galatians 4:5–6).

SERMON NO. 1435

'Now then do it'

'Ye sought for David in times past to be king over you: now then do it: for the LORD *hath spoken of David, saying, By the hand of my servant David I will save my people Israel out of the hand of the Philistines, and out of the hand of all their enemies.'* 2 Samuel 3:17–18
SUGGESTED FURTHER READING: Genesis 19:12–28

You were more impressionable years ago than you are now, and, speaking after the manner of men, you are now far less likely to be saved. You know it is so, and yet you did at that time, after a fashion, pray, and, after a sort, you were in earnest: but what of all that? Nothing has come of it. Will anything ever come of it? The Israelites might talk about making David king, but that would not crown him. They might meet together and say they wished it were so, but that would not do it. It might be generally admitted that he ought to be monarch and it might even be earnestly hoped that one day he would be so, but that would not do it: something more decided must be done. And am I not hitting the very centre of the target, when I say of some of you that you have scores of times given up the whole question as a matter of argument? Yes, and your heart has submitted that it was wrong of you to continue as you are, and you have been moved with strong resolutions towards repentance and faith, and yet you are the same as ever and not one inch more forward. Still you are in darkness, still under the dominion of Satan, still the slave of sin, and so you will be in ten years' more time, I fear; and so you will be to the end of life, and so for ever and for ever! May God grant that my words may not be prophetic concerning any one of you, but that you may this very day be moved by the Eternal Spirit to take decided action through his grace; 'now then do it'.

FOR MEDITATION: (*Our Own Hymn Book* no.658 v.2—Philip Doddridge, 1755)
  ''Tis done! the great transaction's done:
  I am my Lord's, and He is mine:
  He drew me, and I followed on,
  Charmed to confess the voice divine.'

SERMON NO. 1375

Why the heavenly robes are white

'These are they which came out of great tribulation, and have washed their robes, and made them white in the blood of the Lamb.' Revelation 7:14
SUGGESTED FURTHER READING: 1 Thessalonians 2:13–3:5

I do not think that the text refers to some one great persecution, but to the great conflict of the ages in which the seed of the serpent perpetually molests and oppresses the seed of the woman. The strife began at the gates of Eden when the Lord said to the serpent, 'I will put enmity between thee and the woman, and between thy seed and her seed; it shall bruise thy head, and thou shalt bruise his heel.' Satan takes care to nibble at the heel, though his own head has been broken by our great Lord. There is an hereditary conflict, a great tribulation, always to be suffered by the saints below, for 'as then he that was born after the flesh persecuted him that was born after the Spirit, even so it is now.' The enmity takes all sorts of shapes, but from the beginning even until now it is in the world. The white robed ones had come out of that continuous and general conflict uninjured, like the three holy children who came out of the furnace with not so much as the smell of fire upon them. Some of them had been slandered: men of the world had thrown handfuls of the foulest mud upon them, but they 'washed their robes and made them white'. Others of them had come out of remarkable temptations from men and devils: Satan himself had poured his blasphemies into their ears, so that they truly thought they should themselves blaspheme; they were tried by the most defiling of temptations, but 'they overcame … by the blood of the Lamb', and were delivered from every polluting trace of the temptation by the efficacy of the atoning sacrifice. Some of them were cruelly persecuted and trodden down as mire in the streets, yet they rose to glory white as snow. They went through fire and water, wandered without a certain dwelling-place, and were made to be as 'the offscouring of all things', but they came uninjured and unspotted out of it all.

FOR MEDITATION: Tribulation cannot separate Christians from Christ's love, but in it we through him can be 'more than conquerors' (Romans 8:35,37). It is unnatural to seek tribulation, but in it the Christian can glory (Romans 5:3), be patient (Romans 12:12), be comforted (2 Corinthians 1:4) and rejoice (2 Corinthians 7:4).

SERMON NO. 1316

There go the ships

'There go the ships.' Psalm 104:26
SUGGESTED FURTHER READING: Matthew 6:25–34

What is your cargo? 'There go the ships', but what do they carry? You cannot tell from looking at them far out at sea, except that you can be pretty sure that some of them do not carry much. Look at that showy vessel! You can tell by the look of her that she has not much on board; from the fact of her floating so high it is clear that her cargo is light. Big men, very important individuals, very high-floating people are common, but there is nothing in them. If they had more on board they would sink deeper in the water. The more grace a man has the lower he lies before God. Well, brethren, what cargo have you got? I am afraid some of you who lie down in the water are not kept down by any very precious cargo, but I fear you are in ballast. I have gone aboard some Christians; I thought there was a good deal in them, but I have not been able to find it. They have a deal of trouble and they always tell you about it. There is a good old soul I call in to see sometimes: I begin to converse with her, and her conversation is always about rheumatism, nothing else: you cannot get beyond rheumatism: that good sister is in ballast. There is another friend of mine, a farmer; if you talk with him, it is always about the badness of the times: that brother is in ballast too. There are many tradesmen who, though they are Christians, cannot be made to talk of anything but the present dulness of business. I wish they could get that ballast out and fill up with something better, for it is not worth carrying. You must have it sometimes, I suppose, but it is infinitely better to carry a load of praises, prayers, good wishes, holy doctrines, charitable actions and generous encouragements.

FOR MEDITATION: (*Our Own Hymn Book* no.686 v.1—Paul Gerhardt, 1659; tr. by John Wesley, 1739)
'Give to the winds thy fears;
Hope, and be undismayed;
God hears thy sighs, and counts thy tears:
God shall lift up thy head.'

SERMON NO. 1259

The old man's sermon

'O God, thou hast taught me from my youth: and hitherto have I declared thy wondrous works. Now also when I am old and greyheaded, O God, forsake me not.' Psalm 71:17–18
SUGGESTED FURTHER READING: Isaiah 45:22–46:4

You who are feeling your strength fail through old age have been praying, 'O God, forsake me not': will the Lord answer your prayer? It is not possible for him to do otherwise. Is it like our Lord to leave a man because he is growing old? Would you cast off your father because he totters about the house? Would you leave your elder brother because he is now aged and infirm? Do any of us, as long as we have human hearts, pitilessly desert the aged? God is far better than we are, and he will not despise his worn-out servants. The feeble moanings of the most afflicted and infirm are heard by him, not with weariness, but with pity. Will the Lord turn off his old servants? Among men it is common enough to leave poor old people to manage for themselves. The soldier who has spent the prime of his life in his country's service has been left to beg by the roadside or die of want. Even the saviours of a nation have been allowed in old age to pine in poverty. How often have kings cast off their most faithful servants and left them to their enemies? When time has wrinkled the handsome face and bowed the erect figure, the old man has no longer found a place in the throng of courtiers. But the King of kings does not cast off his veteran soldiers, nor his old courtiers, but indulges them with peculiar favours. We have a proverb that old wine and old friends are best, and we need not look far to see that the oldest saints are frequently the best esteemed by the Lord. He did not forsake Abraham when he was well stricken in years, nor Isaac when he was blind, nor Jacob when he worshipped upon the top of his staff.

FOR MEDITATION: (*Our Own Hymn Book* no. 71 song 2 v.3—Isaac Watts, 1719)
   'Cast me not off when strength declines, when hoary hairs arise;
   And round me let Thy glory shine, whene'er Thy servant dies.'

N.B. Spurgeon was shortly to celebrate a century of ministry in Kettering by Mr Toller (c.55 years) and Mr Toller's father (45 years) before him.

SERMON NO. 1256

Abundant pardon

'He will abundantly pardon.' Isaiah 55:7
SUGGESTED FURTHER READING: 1 John 1:5–2:2

That there is abundant pardon may be clearly seen from the fact that the substitute was not an angel, nor a creature of limited power and merit; but he who came to save us was none other than God himself, 'very God of very God'. The fountain filled for us to wash in is not a fountain which can only cleanse a little and then will be exhausted of its virtues. The Son of God has filled it from his pierced heart, and the merit of the atoning blood is without limit. There was a limit to the purpose for which it was shed, for he 'loved the church and gave himself for it', but it is blasphemous to imagine that there is any boundary to the merit of the atonement itself. There is in the sacrifice of the Son of God a degree of power which seraphim cannot conceive. Were all the stars worlds, all filled with myriads of inhabitants who had revolted against God, if an atonement had been wanted for them all, it is not within my power to conceive that a greater atonement could be required for the whole host of creatures than that which Christ presented upon the cross. The boundless merit of it, therefore, makes us rejoice, for our God 'will abundantly pardon'. Sinner, if there had been a little saviour, you might have despaired; if the Saviour had offered a small sacrifice, or if there had been a narrow degree of merit in his agonies and cries, I might have spoken to you with bated breath; but now I know that 'he is able also to save them to the uttermost that come unto God by him', and, therefore, I am warranted to declare to you that our God in Christ Jesus 'will abundantly pardon'. May God send these things home to the hearts of those who are labouring under a sense of guilt.

FOR MEDITATION: (*Our Own Hymn Book* no.202 v.3—Samuel Davies, 1769)
> 'In wonder lost, with trembling joy
> We take the pardon of our God;
> Pardon for crimes of deepest dye;
> A pardon bought with Jesus' blood:
> Who is a pardoning God like Thee?
> Or who has grace so rich and free?'

SERMON NO. 1195

Paved with love

'The midst thereof being paved with love, for the daughters of Jerusalem.' Song of Solomon 3:10
SUGGESTED FURTHER READING: 1 John 4:7–12

The text does not say that the exterior part of this chariot was adorned with self-apparent love, but that love was in the midst. If you stand examining the exterior of providence and the mere letter of the word, and begin to judge and try your God, I should not wonder if little enough of love should be conspicuous to you. Look into the heart of God and read what he has written there. When faith takes a step upward and mounts to the inside of the chariot of grace, she finds that it is 'paved with love, for the daughters of Jerusalem'. Come and sit side by side with Jesus in his chariot of grace, his bed of rest. Come and recline with him in hallowed fellowship. There is room enough for you and strength enough to bear your weight. Come now and be carried with him who carried all your cross. Sit down with him who on his hands and on his side bears the memorials of his dying love to you. What company you have and what royal accommodation is provided for you! I seem to sit in the chariot with the Beloved now and I begin to look around me. I catch a glimpse of the purple above my head and remember the unspeakable love which bled and died for sinners; I look at the silver pillars which support the covering, and consider how infinite holiness stands fast and in love to me secures my perfection; I place my foot on the golden bottom of the chariot, and know that divine power is pledged by love to preserve and bear me through; I see above me, around me and beneath me nothing but love, the free unbounded love of God. Now, indulge yourselves with a glance around you.

FOR MEDITATION: (*Our Own Hymn Book* no.421 v.2—Samuel Stennett, 1787)
'Survey the beauties of His face,
And on His glories dwell;
Think of the wonders of His grace,
And all His triumphs tell.'

SERMON NO. 1134

What the church should be

'That thou mayest know how thou oughtest to behave thyself in the house of God, which is the church of the living God, the pillar and ground of the truth.' 1 Timothy 3:15

SUGGESTED FURTHER READING (Spurgeon): 1 Timothy 4:1–16

How holy should all members of Christian churches be! 'Holiness becometh thine house.' An unholy member of a church! What shall I say? Let that black stone be wet with tears of penitence this day, and then may it be washed in the blood of Jesus. O member of the church, is your conduct inconsistent with your profession? Judge yourself, be zealous and repent. All of us may well humble ourselves in the sight of God and ask him to cleanse us that we may be fit for him to dwell in. *How obedient* also should we be, for if we are a part of the house of God, let it be our joy to submit ourselves to the Master. When we were children in the home of a loving father, his rule was not irksome to us, and with such a Father as our God we own that 'his commandments are not grievous'. Let us obey carefully and joyfully, each one of us. *How struck with awe* ought every church-member to be to think that he is built into God's house. Truly, as I enter among the people of God, I feel bound to cry with Jacob, 'How dreadful is this place! This is none other but the house of God.' Take not lightly upon yourselves a profession of Christianity, and when you have been baptized into the name of Christ and are united with his church, 'see then that ye walk circumspectly' and 'adorn the doctrine of God our Saviour in all things'. At the same time, *how full of love* ought we to be, for 'God is love'. A house is no home if love is absent, and a church is unchurchly if there is division among the brethren. Is it not written, 'the Father himself loveth you'; 'love one another'; 'God is love; and he that dwelleth in love dwelleth in God, and God in him'?

FOR MEDITATION: Christians are not to be seen as members of a social club, but as members of Christ's body, the church. Local churches ought to be characterised by holiness (1 Corinthians 6:15–20; Ephesians 4:24–25), obedience (Ephesians 5:24; 1 Peter 1:14–16), awe (Acts 5:11; 9:31) and love (1 Corinthians 12:25–27). Is your church like that? Are you?

SERMON NO. 1436

The true priesthood, temple and sacrifice

'Ye also, as lively stones, are built up a spiritual house, an holy priesthood, to offer up spiritual sacrifices, acceptable to God by Jesus Christ.' 1 Peter 2:5
SUGGESTED FURTHER READING: Ephesians 2:11–22

While real, the temple of God in the saints is spiritual: a church is made up of spiritual people and her temple form is spiritual. Your eye cannot as yet see the church in which God dwells. Words have come to be so misused nowadays that they call a steeple and a building made of stone or brick and mortar a church, which cannot possibly be correct, for a church is a company of faithful people. Alas, they have yet further perverted language, and they make a company of ecclesiastics, whether regenerated or not, to be 'the church'. 'Going into the church' is a current phrase which shows the ignorance of those who use it. Nor is this all; there is no one visible church which can claim to be *the* church. The Church of Jesus Christ differs greatly from those associations which are called churches. The visible church contains a large part of the true church of Christ, but it is not identical with it. Like its Lord, the church is as yet hidden, and the creation itself 'waiteth for the manifestation of the sons of God'. The Lord has a people scattered abroad everywhere, whose lives are 'hid with Christ in God', and these make up the real temple of God in which the Lord dwells. Men of every name, region and age are quickened into life, made living stones and then laid upon Christ, and these constitute the true temple which God and not man has built, for he 'dwelleth not in temples made with hands', that is to say of man's building, but in a temple which he himself has built for his habitation for ever, saying, 'This is my rest for ever: here will I dwell; for I have desired it.'

FOR MEDITATION: When speaking of worship, Jesus drew attention away from physical places towards spiritual people (John 4:21–24). As a body of spiritual people the church can be told things and heard (Matthew 18:17), fed (Acts 20:28), edified (1 Corinthians 14:4–5,12), nourished and cherished (Ephesians 5:29), but also persecuted (Acts 8:1; 1 Corinthians 15:9; Galatians 1:13; Philippians 3:6), vexed (Acts 12:1), offended (1 Corinthians 10:32) and despised (1 Corinthians 11:22). Are you a member of it through faith in the Lord Jesus Christ?

SERMON NO. 1376

The sinner's Saviour

'And when they saw it, they all murmured, saying, That he was gone to be a guest with a man that is a sinner.' Luke 19:7
SUGGESTED FURTHER READING: Acts 9:10–31

I remember a sailor, who used to swear and rattle it out volley after volley. He got converted and when he prayed it was much in the same fashion. How he woke everybody up the first time he opened his mouth at the prayer-meeting; the little church had quite a revival, for their old jog-trot pace would not do for the newcomer, so full of love and zeal. The prayers offered in the meetings had become quite stereotyped, and so had everything else. There were the same sleepy people, long prayers and dreary addresses; but Jack's conversion was like an earthquake and startled everybody, and their zeal revived. They even began to think that sailors might be saved, started a service on the quay and did many other good things. The conversion of a great sinner is the best medicine for a sick church. In all churches you good people who are settled on your lees need stirring up every now and then, and one of the best stirrings you can have is to open the door of the church and see a Saul of Tarsus standing there to be admitted. The porter enquires, 'Who is this that seeks admission here?' 'A recruit,' says he and we look at him. Why, he is one of the devil's most famous soldiers, one who carried the black flag in the battle and ridiculed us most! We are apt to look a little askance at him, for we feel dubious, and we refer him to the elders that they may enquire and sift him to see whether he is really a changed character. Perhaps these earnest men are not quite sure and hesitate till they see more of him, and they are quite right to do so; but if the Lord has really called the sinner by his grace, no sooner does the church receive such a man than they find that he has brought with him fresh fire and throws a fresh impetus into the whole work.

FOR MEDITATION: After the unexpected conversion and reception of Saul of Tarsus there was much growth and expansion (Acts 9:26–31), the name 'Christians' was adopted (Acts 11:25–26), God was glorified (Galatians 1:22–24) and a great example of God's grace towards repentant sinners was established (1 Timothy 1:12–16). Should we be praying for unlikely conversions in these spiritually barren times?

SERMON NO. 1319

The word of a king

'Where the word of a king is, there is power.' Ecclesiastes 8:4
SUGGESTED FURTHER READING (Spurgeon): Psalm 19:7–14

Some have thought it necessary, in order to have power among 'the masses', that there should be fine music. An organ is nowadays thought to be the power of God and a choir is a fine substitute for the Holy Spirit. They have tried that kind of thing in America, where solos and quartets enable singers to divide their services between the church and the theatre. Some churches have paid more attention to the choir than to the preaching. I do not believe in it. If God had meant people to be converted in that way, he would have sent them a command to attend the music-halls and operas, for there they will get far better music than we can hope to give them. If there be charms in music to change the souls of men from sin to holiness, and if the preaching of the gospel will not do it, let us be done with Peter, Paul, Chalmers and Chrysostom, let us exalt Mozart and Haydn into their places, and let the great singers of the day take the places of the pleaders for the Lord. Even this would not content the maniacs of this age, for with the music-room they crave the frippery of the theatre. Combine with philosophy the sweet flowers of oratory and those of the Covent Garden, adding thereto the man-millinery and ornaments of Rome, and then you can exclaim with the idolaters of old, 'These be thy gods, O Israel'. Men are now looking for omnipotence in toys. But we do not believe it. We come back to this—'Where the word of a king is, there is power', and while we are prepared to admit that all and everything that has to do with us can be the vehicle of spiritual power if God so wills, we are more than ever convinced that God has spiritual power to give by his word alone. We must keep to the King's word if we desire to have this spiritual power for the Lord's work.

FOR MEDITATION: Paul's determination to concentrate on preaching the gospel instead of trying to flatter or entertain his hearers (1 Thessalonians 2:1–6) bore abundant fruit in their clear conversions (1 Thessalonians 1:5,9). Is it any wonder that so many of our churches make so little lasting impact, when we rely on ourselves rather than upon God and seek to attract unbelievers by means of fun and entertainment instead of sticking to God's word? Why should God bless any of this?

SERMON NO. 1697

Love to Jesus the great test

'Jesus said unto them, If God were your Father, ye would love me: for I proceeded forth and came from God; neither came I of myself, but he sent me.' John 8:42
SUGGESTED FURTHER READING: 1 John 2:15–24

Love to Christ is the test of sonship. Certain modern teachers have asserted that God is the Father of all mankind, and the doctrine of Universal Fatherhood is, I am told, exceedingly prevalent in certain quarters. That God is the Creator of all men, and that in this sense men are the offspring of God, is undoubtedly true, but that unregenerate men are the sons of God is undoubtedly false. How that flesh-pleasing doctrine can be supported I do not know, for certainly my text gives it no assistance whatever, but rather strikes it a deadly blow. 'If God were your Father, ye would love me'; consequently God is not the Father of those who do not love Christ. What do these teachers make out of the privilege of adoption? Why are men adopted if children by nature? How is it that it is a special promise, 'I will be a Father unto you, and ye shall be my sons and daughters'? What need is there of a promise of that which they have already? 'But as many as received him, to them gave he power to become the sons of God, even to them that believe on his name.' What does that mean if everybody is already a child of God? How do they understand that God 'hath begotten us again unto a lively hope by the resurrection of Jesus Christ'? Were we sons already? How were we 'by nature the children of wrath, even as others', if all men are in the family of God? They make use of an expression which bears two renderings to set up a theory which is destructive of the gospel. I leave those to defend that statement who care to do so; I believe it to be altogether untenable if we keep to the word of God. The Fatherhood of God is to a special people, 'chosen … before the foundation of the world', and adopted and regenerated in due time through his grace.

FOR MEDITATION: We cannot honour, know and abide in God the Father, unless we honour (John 5:23), know (John 8:19; 14:7) and abide in (1 John 2:24; 2 John 9) God the Son. If we hate (John 15:23–24) or deny (1 John 2:22–23) God the Son, we also hate and deny God the Father. We cannot pick and choose which persons of the Trinity to accept.

SERMON NO. 1257

The moral of a miracle

'Jesus answering saith unto them, Have faith in God.' Mark 11:22
SUGGESTED FURTHER READING: Psalm 65:1–13

We ought, I think, to have our eyes open constantly to see the power of God in renewing the face of the earth. I like to observe it in the seasons. What a wonderful power was that which, on a sudden, called up all sleeping bulbs and flowers from their graves, and caused that which had been black soil suddenly to blossom into a golden garden, or to bloom into beds bespangled with many colours. Have you not seen lone places in the wood and nooks among the trees so glorious in colour that it seemed as though the Lord had rent pieces of the robe of the sky and flung them down among the trees in the wood? We have seen the hyacinths on a sudden in their deepest azure standing where all before had been black mould or sere leaf. We see it every year, but it is a marvellous thing, and we might stand and say, 'How soon has the winter passed away! How speedily has earth put on her youth again!' Do you see no power of God in all this? These creations and resurrections of spring, are they nothing? And now at this season of the year when the leaves are falling all around us, though the trees are not withering away, how rapidly they are undergoing their wonderful process of disrobing. The other day you passed by a tree which was green, and you delighted to be beneath its foliage; and now in the setting sun of this afternoon it seemed as though it were blazing with golden fire: every leaf has turned yellow by the touch of autumn. How has God wrought all this? Silently and quietly, without sound of trumpet, from year to year these miracles of nature proceed, of which I am speaking very roughly now, but he that looks into them and studies them shall be filled with amazement at the extraordinary power of God.

FOR MEDITATION: Marvel at the power of God as displayed in creating (Jeremiah 10:12–13; Romans 1:20) and in sustaining (Hebrews 1:2–3) the universe. Even this takes no more than his voice (Jeremiah 10:13) and the 'word of his power' (Hebrews 1:3). Tremble at the display of his power which is still to come if you do not yet know him as your God and Saviour (Matthew 24:29–31).

SERMON NO. 1444

Signs of the times

'When ye see a cloud rise out of the west, straightway ye say, There cometh a shower; and so it is. And when ye see the south wind blow, ye say, There will be heat; and it cometh to pass. Ye hypocrites, ye can discern the face of the sky and of the earth; but how is it that ye do not discern this time?' Luke 12:54–56
SUGGESTED FURTHER READING: Jeremiah 8:7–20

If you were in the fields during the past week, you must have marked the waning year. The leaves are fading, clothing the departing year with a wonderful beauty. As they fade, they preach, 'You too will soon fall to earth and wither.' Have you heard the sermons of the falling leaves? You say, 'Winter will soon be here.' You begin to lay in your stocks of fuel to meet the coming cold; do you not see those gray hairs upon your head? Are they not wintry tokens too? Do you not note your decaying teeth, trembling limbs, loosened sinews and furrowed brow? Do these not show that your winter is hastening on? Have you made no provision for eternity? Will you be driven for ever away where there shall be no hope? Have you laid by no stores of comfort for another world? Let the birds of the air rebuke you. The other day I saw the swallows assembling; then, away they flew across the sea to sunnier climes. They did not wait till all their food was gone and they must famish, but took to themselves wings and followed the sun. Has all the wisdom entered into birds and have men none left? 'The stork in the heaven knoweth her appointed times; and the turtle and the crane and the swallow observe the time of their coming; but my people know not the judgment of the LORD.' You will linger in this world amongst its dying joys till you die and perish for ever. Take the wings of faith and fly where the Sun of Righteousness points the way. There, where the cross is the guiding constellation, steer your course, and you will reach the land of everlasting summer, where fading flowers and withering leaves are never known.

FOR MEDITATION: Human mortality is likened to shadows that disappear (1 Chronicles 29:15; Psalm 102:11), wind that passes away (Psalm 78:39), grass that withers (Psalm 90:5–6; Isaiah 40:6–8; James 1:11) and vapour that vanishes (James 4:14). These temporary things all say to us, 'Prepare to meet thy God' (Amos 4:12).

SERMON NO. 1135

Others to be gathered

'The Lord GOD which gathereth the outcasts of Israel saith, Yet will I gather others to him, beside those that are gathered unto him.' Isaiah 56:8

SUGGESTED FURTHER READING: 1 Corinthians 10:1–13

Just as our Lord delivered Mary of Magdalene from seven devils, so can he deliver any of you who are sore beset by temptation. Do the devils within you arise from habit? Such spirits are very powerful, but Jesus is more than a match for them. Habit becomes second nature to a man, but Jesus is greater than either first or second nature. Habits begin to bind us as with spiders' webs, but they thicken and harden into meshes of iron: our Lord can with a breath remove the iron net and set the prisoner free. Or are you tempted by constitutional sin, some evil which has entrenched itself within the peculiarities of your being, finding, as it were, a rest within the special texture of your mind and fashion of your body? Jesus can dislodge the subtle foe and make this body of yours, which has been a cage of unclean birds, to become a temple of the Holy Spirit. Or are your surroundings very unfavourable? Does the devil molest you through the place where you dwell and the people among whom you reside? Jesus can help you there and make you fair 'as the curtains of Solomon' even while you dwell in 'the tents of Kedar'. Or is your case of another kind? Are you beset with doubts and infidelities innumerable? Do you question this and question that? Has your mind a sceptical bias? My Master can gather you also and make you stronger in faith than your brethren, even as Thomas, who doubted, became a firm and adoring believer. Unbelief is a very tormenting spirit and causes much distress of soul, but the Lord can gather unbelievers and misbelievers, and bring them to the true faith and to the peace which comes of it.

FOR MEDITATION: Temptations arise from self (Mark 7:21–23; James 1:13–15), society (1 Corinthians 15:33) and Satan (1 Peter 5:8) and we by nature follow all three sources of temptation (Ephesians 2:1–3). But deliverance from temptation is available from the Saviour (Hebrews 2:18), whether the source is self (Romans 7:24–25), society (Galatians 1:3–5) or Satan (John 17:15; Hebrews 2:14–15).

SERMON NO. 1437

Taking hold upon God

'There is none that calleth upon thy name, that stirreth up himself to take hold of thee.' Isaiah 64:7
SUGGESTED FURTHER READING (Spurgeon): Isaiah 65:1–10

I do not know that the condition of the church of God at the present time is quite as bad as that which is here described. It would be wrong to boast of our condition, but it would be worse to despair of it. It would not be honest to apply the words of our text to the church of the present day. Blessed be God, we could not say, 'there is none that calleth upon thy name, that stirreth up himself to take hold of thee', for there are many who plead day and night for the prosperity of Zion. Yet in a measure we are somewhat in the same plight as that which is described by the prophet, and there is much to mourn over. Prayer languishes in many churches, power in intercession is by no means a common attainment, and meetings for prayer are, as a rule, thinly attended and not much thought of. Sin abounds, empty profession is common, hypocrisy is plentiful, and the life of God in the soul is little esteemed. Notice carefully that according to our text the prophet traces much of the evil which he deplored to the lack of prayer. After he has compared their righteousness to filthy rags, he adds, 'there is none that calleth upon thy name, that stirreth up himself to take hold of thee'. When there is a degeneracy of public manners, you may be sure that there has also occurred a serious decline of secret devotion. When the outward service of the church begins to flag and her holiness declines, you may be sure that her communion with God has been sadly suspended. Devotion to God will be found to be the basis of holiness and the buttress of integrity. If you backslide in secret before God, you will soon err in public before men. You may judge yourselves as to your spiritual state by the condition of your hearts in the matter of prayer.

FOR MEDITATION: (*Our Own Hymn Book* no.674 v.3—George Duffield, 1858)

    'Stand up! Stand up for Jesus! Stand in His strength alone:
    The arm of flesh will fail you; ye dare not trust your own:
    Put on the gospel armour, and watching unto prayer,
    Where duty calls, or danger, be never wanting there.'

SERMON NO. 1377

Overcome evil with good

'Be not overcome of evil, but overcome evil with good.' Romans 12:21
SUGGESTED FURTHER READING: John 18:1–24

Whatever is Christlike is manly, and whatsoever you think to be manly which is not Christlike, is really unmanly, as judged by the highest style of man. The Lord Jesus draws near to a Samaritan village, but they will not receive him, though he was always kind to Samaritans. Good, gentle John becomes highly indignant and cries, 'Lord, wilt thou that we command fire to come down from heaven, and consume them?' Jesus meekly answers, 'Ye know not what manner of spirit ye are of. For the Son of man is not come to destroy men's lives, but to save them.' See him on another occasion: your Master has risen from his knees, with the blood and sweat still on his face; Judas comes and betrays him, and they begin to handle him very roughly, and therefore, being highly provoked, brave Peter draws out his sword; and just to flesh it a little he cuts off the ear of Malchus. Hear how gently Jesus says, 'Put up again thy sword into his place: for all they that take the sword shall perish with the sword.' And so he heals that ear at once. Was that manly, do you think? Was it manly to refuse to call fire from heaven, and to touch and heal the wounded ear? To me it seems superlatively manly, and may such be my manliness and yours. Look at our Lord again before the high priest, when an officer of the court, incensed by his gentle answers, smites him on the cheek; what does Jesus say? Observe the difference between Christ and Paul. Paul says, 'God shall smite thee, thou whited wall'. Bravo, Paul, that is speaking up for yourself! We cannot blame you, for who are we to censure an apostle? But look at Paul's Master and hear his words: 'If I have spoken evil, bear witness of the evil: but if well, why smitest thou me?' Is not the example of Jesus the more noble, the more Godlike?

FOR MEDITATION: (*Our Own Hymn Book* no.706 v.4—Thomas Cotterill, 1812)
> 'Oh may that mind in us be formed
> Which shone so bright in Thee;
> May we be humble, lowly, meek,
> From pride and envy free.'

SERMON NO. 1317

Faith, and the witness upon which it is founded

'He that believeth on the Son of God hath the witness in himself: he that believeth not God hath made him a liar; because he believeth not the witness that God witnessed of his Son.' 1 John 5:10
SUGGESTED FURTHER READING: John 5:30–38

Wash and be clean, believe and live, trust and find it true. May the Lord grant that this simple matter may be clear to you, that you may accept it eagerly and lay hold upon it earnestly; then, having believed, you shall have the witness in yourself which will prove it to be true. 'Doctor,' say you, 'will your medicine heal me?' 'Yes,' says he. 'But doctor,' say you, 'I cannot believe till I have the witness in myself, that it will make me well.' 'But,' says he, 'you won't be able to take my medicine on those terms, because you cannot have that witness till you have taken it. Will you have it on my witness that I have prescribed this dose in many similar cases, and I know, from what I understand of the anatomy of the body, that the drugs suit your disease and will remove it?' 'No, doctor,' say you, 'I must feel better before I can have confidence in you.' 'What, feel the power of the medicine before you take it?' 'Yes.' 'Then your demand is preposterous; you must surely be weak in your intellect.' Moved by this reproof, you take the dose. He comes the next day; you feel relieved from the pain, a new tone is given to your system, and you cheerfully exclaim, 'Now, doctor, I have the witness in myself.' If you had been foolish enough not to take the medicine till you had proved it, and yet you could not prove it till you took it, you would have behaved like an idiot; the man who will not take God at his word, but wants something else besides the Lord's witness, not only insults God, but plays the part of an insane suicide and deserves to perish. God give you grace to accept the gospel; then you shall have the witness in yourself; he shall have the praise and you the comfort.

FOR MEDITATION: (*Our Own Hymn Book* no.486 v.3—Isaac Watts, 1709)
'In vain the trembling conscience seeks
Some solid ground to rest upon;
With long despair the spirit breaks,
Till we apply to Christ alone.'

The hand of God in the history of a man

'Is there not an appointed time to man upon earth? Are not his days also like the days of an hireling?' Job 7:1
SUGGESTED FURTHER READING: Psalm 13:1–6

If our griefs were the offspring of chance, we might pine to have them ended, but if the loving Lord appoints, we would not hurry him in his processes of love. Let the Lord do what seems good to him. Here is good cheer for those who have lain so long upon the bed of pain and who are apt to ask, 'Will it never end? O Lord, will the chariots of salvation never come? Have the angels forgotten thy servant in his sickness? Must he for ever remain a prisoner under his infirmity, loneliness and decay? Hast thou placed me as a sentinel to stand upon my watch-tower through a night which will never end, and shall I never be relieved from my weary guard? Shall I never know rest? Must I for ever peer into the dark with these eyes so red with weeping?' Courage, brother, sister! The ever merciful Lord has appointed every moment of your sorrow and every pang of your suffering. If he ordains the number ten, it can never rise to eleven, neither should you desire it to shrink to nine. The Lord's time is best: to a hair's breadth your span of life is rightly measured. God ordains all: therefore peace, restless spirit, and let the Lord have his way. So too has he fixed life's termination. 'Is there not an appointed time to man upon earth?' a time in which the pulse must cease, the blood stagnate and the eye be closed. It is of no use for us to indulge any idle dream of living for ever here; a time of departure must come to every one of us, unless the Lord himself should appear on a sudden, and then we shall not die, but be changed.

FOR MEDITATION: (*Our Own Hymn Book* no.90 v.7—Isaac Watts, 1719)
  'Our God, our help in ages past,
  Our hope for years to come;
  Be Thou our guard while troubles last,
  And our eternal home!'

N.B. Spurgeon's text was prompted by the sudden death of his 'beloved brother, Henry Olney' the previous afternoon after returning home from work in the City.

SERMON NO. 1258

The claims of God

'Know ye that the LORD *he is God: it is he that hath made us, and not we ourselves; we are his people, and the sheep of his pasture. Enter into his gates with thanksgiving, and into his courts with praise: be thankful unto him, and bless his name. For the* LORD *is good; his mercy is everlasting: and his truth endureth to all generations.' Psalm 100:3–5*
SUGGESTED FURTHER READING: 1 Samuel 15:10–31

If ever this drivelling age of little men is to be lifted up into something like respectability and redeemed from the morass of falsehood in which it lies festering, we must breed a race of men who mean to serve God come what may, and to make no reckoning but this: 'Is this right? It shall be done. Is this wrong? Then it shall cease.' There must be no compromise, no talk about marring our usefulness and spoiling our position by being too exact. Usefulness and position! Let them be marred and spoiled if truth comes in the way, for God is to be followed into the jungle and down the wild beasts' throats and into the jaws of hell, if he leads the way. God must be the guide, and if we follow God it shall be well with us. But if we do not, that which man thinks easiest is after all the hardest. He thinks it easiest to be as near right as you can, but to run no risks; he thinks it best to keep peace at home, to yield many points, and not to be too puritanic and too precise. That is the easy way, the way which God abhors, and the way which will end in a festering conscience at last and in being shut out of heaven. But the way to serve God is to be washed in the blood of Jesus, and then to obey the Lord without reserve and seek his honour only. This is the way to heaven, and when we reach those blissful seats we shall be all in tune with the perfected, for they serve the Lord day and night and find it bliss to do so. This preparation and service on earth is absolutely essential to the enjoyment of heaven above.

FOR MEDITATION: (*Our Own Hymn Book* no.187 v.3—Isaac Watts, 1709)
    'God is a King of power unknown;
    Firm are the orders of His throne;
    If He resolves, who dare oppose,
    Or ask Him why, or what He does?'

'For ever with the Lord'

'To be with Christ; which is far better.' Philippians 1:23
SUGGESTED FURTHER READING: 2 Timothy 4:6–18

Picture yourself sitting in a gloomy dungeon, a captive of the cruel tyrant Nero, and under the supervision of the infamous prefect Tigellinus, the most detestable of Nero's attendants. Conceive yourself as expecting soon to be taken out perhaps to such a horrible death as the refined cruelty of the monster had often devised, as, for instance, to be smeared with bituminous matter and burned in the despot's garden to adorn a holiday. What would be your feelings? If you were not a Christian I should expect you to tremble with the fear of death, and even if you were a believer, I should not marvel if the flesh shrunk from the prospect. Paul was an utter stranger to any feeling of the kind. He had not the slightest dread of martyrdom. He calls his expected death a departure, a loosing of the cable which holds his ship to the shore, and a putting forth upon the main ocean. So far from being afraid to die, he stands fully prepared, waits patiently, and even anticipates joyfully the hour when his change shall come. On the other hand, I can imagine that amidst the miseries of a wretched prison, subject to frequent insults from a rude soldiery, you might be seized with a desire to escape from life. Good men have felt the power of that feeling. Elijah said, 'take away my life; for I am not better than my fathers.' Job sighed to be hidden in the grave, and often, under far less afflictions than those which vexed the apostle, good men have said, 'Would God this life were at an end and these miseries over; I am weary; when will death release me?' I see nothing of that in the apostle; he is not restive under the chain; there is not a trace of impatience about him. He joyfully admits that to be with Christ is far better, but sees reasons for remaining here and therefore cheerfully submits to whatever may be the Lord's will. His mind is so wrapped up with God and free from self that he cannot choose. What a blessed state to be in!

FOR MEDITATION: Consider the words which sum up Paul's state of mind as he faced difficult circumstances and an uncertain future—ready (Acts 21:13), expectation and hope (Philippians 1:20), content (Philippians 4:11). His secret is surely to be found in Isaiah 26:3 and Philippians 4:6–7.

The hope laid up in heaven

'For the hope which is laid up for you in heaven, whereof ye heard before in the word of the truth of the gospel.' Colossians 1:5
SUGGESTED FURTHER READING: Romans 13:8–14

From the form of the language it is clear that the apostle intended to state that his readers' love to the saints was very much produced in them by the hope which was laid up in heaven. You noticed the word 'for' which stands there: 'the love which ye have to all the saints, for', or on account of, or because of 'the hope which is laid up for you in heaven'. There can be no doubt that the hope of heaven tends greatly to foster love to all the saints of God. We have a common hope; let us have a common affection: we are on our way to God; let us march in loving company: we are to be one in heaven; let us be one on earth. One is our Master and one is our service; one is our way and one is our end; let us be knit together as one man. We all expect to see our Well-beloved face to face, and to be like him; why should we not even now love all those in whom there is anything of Christ? Brethren, we are to live for ever in heaven; it is a pity we should quarrel. We are for ever to be with Jesus Christ, partakers of the same joy, of the same glory and of the same love; why should be we scant in our love to each other? On the way to Canaan we have to fight the same enemy, to publish the same testimony, to bear the same trials and to fly to the same helper: therefore let us love one another. It would not be difficult to show that the hope which is laid up in heaven should be productive of love among the saints on earth.

FOR MEDITATION: (*Our Own Hymn Book* no.203 v.5—James Montgomery, 1819)
    'Saints below, with heart and voice,
    Still in songs of praise rejoice;
    Learning here, by faith and love,
    Songs of praise to sing above.'

SERMON NO. 1438

The righteous Father known and loved

'*O righteous Father, the world hath not known thee: but I have known thee, and these have known that thou hast sent me. And I have declared unto them thy name, and will declare it: that the love wherewith thou hast loved me may be in them, and I in them.*' John 17:25–26
SUGGESTED FURTHER READING: 1 John 2:23–3:1

In verse 25 there is a testing name given to God, by which we may decide whether we know the name of the Lord or not. It is this: 'righteous Father'. I do not know that in any other portion of Scripture God is called by that name. In this prayer Jesus had not addressed the Father by that title before. He had spoken of him as 'Father' and also as 'Holy Father', but here alone it is—'righteous Father'. I say that the knowledge of this name may serve as a test as to whether you do truly and spiritually know God, or have only a notional and outward idea of him. If you know him aright you know and understand what is comprehended under those two simple words, which are so remarkable when found in combination—'righteous Father'. He is 'righteous', having the attributes of a judge and ruler, just and impartial, by no means sparing the guilty. He is 'Father', near of kin, loving, tender and forgiving. In his character and in his dealings with his people he blends the two as they were never combined before. How can a judge and a father be found in one? Where guilty men are concerned, how can both characters be carried out to the full? How is it possible? There is only one answer and that is found in the sacrifice of Jesus which has joined the two in one. In the atonement of our Lord Jesus 'Mercy and truth are met together; righteousness and peace have kissed each other.' In the sacred substitution we see declared how God is 'righteous' and yet 'Father': in the sublime transactions of Calvary he manifests all the love of a tender father's heart and all the justice of an impartial ruler's sword.

FOR MEDITATION: Rejoice in some of the other combined attributes of 'our Father in heaven'. He is 'a just God and a Saviour' (Isaiah 45:21), 'just, and the justifier of him which believeth in Jesus' (Romans 3:26) and 'faithful and just to forgive us our sins and to cleanse us from all unrighteousness' (1 John 1:9), if we confess to him our ungodliness and sinfulness.

SERMON NO. 1378

Increased faith the strength of peace principles

'The apostles said unto the Lord, increase our faith.' Luke 17:5
SUGGESTED FURTHER READING (Spurgeon): Matthew 18:19–35

When our Lord preached about forgiving others, his disciples were so astonished that the apostles exclaimed in surprise, 'Lord, increase our faith.' It is most important in this case to see the connection of the text, or you will fail to see its drift and bearings. It was not for the sake of working miracles that the apostles sought increased faith, nor in order to bear their present or future trials, neither was it to enable them to receive some mysterious article of the faith, but their prayer referred to a common everyday duty enjoined by the gospel, the forgiving of those who do us wrong; for the previous verses are to this effect: 'Take heed to yourselves: If thy brother trespass against thee, rebuke him; and if he repent forgive him. And if he trespass against thee seven times in a day, and seven times in a day turn again to thee, saying, I repent; thou shalt forgive him.' It was upon hearing this that the apostles cried, 'Increase our faith.' If you have been surprised at the high standard of Christian duty which my Lord has laid down for you, I only trust your surprise may drive you to the same resort as it did those first servants of the Lord, and compel you to appeal for help to him who issued the command. Will he not help us in walking in his own ways? When we feel that his 'commandment is exceeding broad', to whom should we appeal for aid but to him who is our leader in all holy conversation and godliness? He will not set you the task and refuse you his assistance in performing it.

FOR MEDITATION: It takes the obedience of faith for us to receive the forgiveness of sins (Luke 7:47–50; Acts 13:38–39; Romans 4:5–7). It also takes obedience as well as faith for us to forgive others (Matthew 18:21–22; Mark 11:25; Luke 6:37; 2 Corinthians 2:7; Ephesians 4:32; Colossians 3:13).

SERMON NO. 1318

Receiving the kingdom of God as a little child

'Verily I say unto you, Whosoever shall not receive the kingdom of God as a little child shall in no wise enter therein.' Luke 18:17
SUGGESTED FURTHER READING: 1 Corinthians 3:18–4:17

To put the thought of the apostles into one or two words, they thought that the children must not come to Christ because they were not like themselves; they were not men and women. A child not big enough, tall enough, grown enough, great enough to be blessed by Jesus! So they half thought. The child must not come to the Master because he is not like the man. How the blessed Saviour turns the tables and says, 'Do not say the child may not come till he is like a man, but know that you cannot come till you are like the child. It is no difficulty in the child's way that he is not like you; the difficulty is with you, that you are not like the child.' Instead of the child needing to wait until he grows up and becomes a man, it is the man who must grow down and become like a child. 'Whosoever shall not receive the kingdom of God as a little child shall in no wise enter therein.' Our Lord's words are a complete and all-sufficient answer to the thought of his disciples, and as we read them we may each one learn wisdom. Let us not say, 'Would to God my child were grown up like myself that he might come to Christ', but rather may we almost wish that we were little children again, could forget much that we now know, could be washed clean from habit and prejudice, and could begin again with a child's freshness, simplicity and eagerness. As we pray for spiritual childhood, Scripture sets its seal upon the prayer, for it is written, 'Except a man be born again, he cannot see the kingdom of God' and again, 'Except ye be converted, and become as little children, ye shall not enter into the kingdom of heaven.'

FOR MEDITATION: Paul rejoiced in being able to call the Corinthians beloved children (1 Corinthians 4:14; 2 Corinthians 6:13). But though he was glad about their childlike reception of the gospel (1 Corinthians 4:15), he was none too pleased with their childish behaviour (1 Corinthians 3:1–3). We must receive the gospel like boys and girls, but afterwards we are also supposed to mature into Christian men and women (1 Corinthians 13:11; 14:20; 16:13).

SERMON NO. 1439

The unbroken line of true nobles

'Instead of thy fathers shall be thy children, whom thou mayest make princes in all the earth.' Psalm 45:16
SUGGESTED FURTHER READING: 1 Samuel 3:1–20

If we are to have good successors, our young friends must acquire a noble carriage from their childhood. That is a great word, 'whom thou mayest make princes in all the earth', and we must not be content to come short of it. What, make our young converts princes? Yes, so says the text, and it is to be done, by God's grace, if they are imbued with heavenly principles by the Holy Spirit, if we set before them the example of our princely Saviour, and if each one of us shall try to make his own life right royal in dignity of purpose and aim. The nobility of the text is of a rare sort—'princes in all the earth'. Why, a man may be a prince in his own country and have no power out of it; but a man of high Christian character is a prince in all the earth, and we would have all our children such. That ancient schoolmaster, Jacob Trebonius, whenever he went into his school, was accustomed to take off his hat to his boys, and when asked why he did so, replied, 'Because, sir, I do not know what learned doctors and great men I may be teaching.' He was quite right, for Martin Luther was one of the boys in his school, and I would have taken off my hat to Martin Luther if I had been his schoolmaster, perhaps chastised him as well, but taken off my hat at any rate, out of respect to the man concealed in such a boy. Who knows, but amongst those whom we teach for Jesus, right royal spirits may be concealed; it is ours to try, by the grace of God, to train those choice spirits that they may be yet more noble.

FOR MEDITATION: Pray that God will raise up in these days godly men who will far surpass their teachers, as did the Psalmist (Psalm 119:99) and the apostle Paul (Acts 22:3).

N.B. The text Spurgeon chose related both to the recent death of Henry Olney (see 10 October) and to the start of a week of prayer for the young.

The agony in Gethsemane

'*And being in an agony he prayed more earnestly: and his sweat was as it were great drops of blood falling down to the ground.*' *Luke* 22:44
SUGGESTED FURTHER READING: Matthew 26:36–46

I dread to the last degree that kind of theology so common nowadays, which seeks to depreciate and diminish our estimate of the sufferings of our Lord Jesus Christ. That was no trifling suffering which made recompense to the justice of God for the sins of men. I am never afraid of exaggeration when I speak of what my Lord endured. All hell was distilled into that cup of which our God and Saviour Jesus Christ was made to drink. It was not eternal suffering, but since he was divine he could in a short time offer unto God a vindication of his justice which sinners in hell could not have offered had they been left to suffer in their own persons for ever. The woe that broke over the Saviour's spirit, the great and fathomless ocean of inexpressible anguish which dashed over the Saviour's soul when he died, is so inconceivable, that I must not venture far, lest I be accused of a vain attempt to express the unutterable; but this I will say, the very spray from that great tempestuous deep, as it fell on Christ, baptized him in a sweat of blood. He had not yet come to the raging billows of the penalty itself, but even standing on the shore, as he heard the awful surf breaking at his feet, his soul was sore amazed and very heavy. It was the shadow of the coming tempest, the prelude of the dread desertion which he had to endure, when he stood where we ought to have stood, and paid to his Father's justice the debt which was due from us; it was this which laid him low. To be treated and smitten as a sinner, though in him was no sin, this it was which caused him the agony of which our text speaks.

FOR MEDITATION: (*Our Own Hymn Book* no.271 v.3—Joseph Hart, 1759)
'There my God bore all my guilt;
This through grace can be believed;
But the horrors which He felt
Are too vast to be conceived.
None can penetrate through thee,
Doleful, dark Gethsemane!'

To Sabbath-school teachers and other soul-winners

'Brethren, if any of you do err from the truth, and one convert him; let him know, that he which converteth the sinner from the error of his way shall save a soul from death, and shall hide a multitude of sins.' James 5:19–20

SUGGESTED FURTHER READING: 2 Peter 1:19–2:3

Modern thinkers treat revealed truth with entire indifference; though they may feel sorry that wilder spirits go too far in free thinking, and wish they would be more moderate, yet so large is their liberality that they are not sure enough of anything to be able to condemn the reverse of it as a deadly error. To them black and white are terms which may be applied to the same colour as you view it from different standpoints. Yes and no are equally true in their esteem. Their theology shifts like the Goodwin Sands, and they regard all firmness as bigotry. Errors and truths are equally comprehensible within the circle of their charity. It was not in this way that the apostles regarded error. They did not prescribe large-hearted charity towards falsehood, or hold up the errorist as a man of deep thought, whose views were 'refreshingly original'; far less did they utter some wicked nonsense about the probability of more faith living in honest doubts than in half the creeds. They did not believe in justification by doubting, but set about the conversion of the erring brother, treated him as a person who needed conversion, and viewed him as a man who, if he were not converted, would suffer the death of his soul and be covered with a multitude of sins. They were not such easy-going people as our cultured friends of the school of 'modern thought', who have learned that the deity of Christ may be denied, the work of the Holy Spirit ignored, the inspiration of Scripture rejected, the atonement disbelieved, and regeneration dispensed with, and yet the man who does all this may be as good a Christian as the most devout believer! O God, deliver us from their deceitful infidelity, which, while it damages the erring man and often prevents his being reclaimed, does yet more mischief to our own hearts by teaching us that truth is unimportant.

FOR MEDITATION: 'To utter error against the LORD' (Isaiah 32:6) is foolish, sinful and punishable by God (Romans 1:24–27). We must carefully discern error (1 John 4:1–6), otherwise we may get led astray and destabilised by it (2 Peter 3:17).

Pressing questions of an awakened mind

'Who art thou, Lord? ... what wilt thou have me to do?' Acts 9:5–6
SUGGESTED FURTHER READING: Psalm 143:1–12

The apostle here puts himself into the position of a soldier waiting for orders. He will not stir until he has received his officer's command. 'Lord, what wilt thou have me to do?' He stands quite ready to do it, but he wants to know what the order may be, and therefore he looks up and prays, 'Lord, direct me. What wouldst thou have me to do?' It is the Lord's will alone that he now means to do. 'Lord, what wilt *thou* have me to do?' Before it used to be, 'What will Moses have me to do?' And with some now present it has been 'What should I like to do?' for whatsoever their soul lusts after they have done, and whatsoever new pleasure, no matter how sinful it might be, if it were within their reach, they followed greedily after it; but he that would be saved must yield up his own will to his Lord. Take heed unto yourselves that Christ be your Master, and nobody else. It would never do to say, 'What would the church have me to do?' As far as the church teaches what Christ taught, obey her, but no further. It would not even be right to say, 'What would an apostle have me to do?' Paul said, 'Be ye followers of me, even as I also am of Christ.' But if Paul does not follow Christ, we must not follow Paul. He says, 'though we, or an angel from heaven, preach any other gospel ... let him be accursed.' I count it to be a sad lowering of a Christian's standard when he takes any mortal man living, or even any man now in heaven, to be his guide and master. 'One is your Master, even Christ', and your question should be, 'Lord, what wilt thou have me to do?'

FOR MEDITATION: A good soldier of Jesus Christ seeks to satisfy the one who enlisted him (2 Timothy 2:3–4). A good servant of Jesus Christ seeks his Master's favour rather than that of men (Galatians 1:10). A good student of Jesus Christ seeks to live in such a way as pleases God (1 Thessalonians 4:1–2).

SERMON NO. 1520

The magnanimity of God

'Behold, God is mighty, and despiseth not any: he is mighty in strength and wisdom.' Job 36:5
SUGGESTED FURTHER READING: Mark 10:35–45

The truly great are courteous, tender and considerate. The strong have no reason to be suspicious and jealous; therefore they are free from envy; they are void of fear of the power of others; therefore they become anxious that their own power should not oppress the weak ones around them. They become considerate of others because this furnishes a fit sphere for the use of their strength. The man who is strong only in appearance, but is really feeble, despises others because he dreads them; knowing how much he deserves to be despised himself, he pretends to look down upon his neighbours. It is the half-educated man who sneers, the pretender to gentility who gives himself airs. Wherever anything is mere pretence, it endeavours to shield itself from criticism by casting sarcasms upon its rivals. It is said that the Pharisees 'trusted in themselves that they were righteous, and despised others': had they been truly righteous they would not have despised others, but because they had a mere veneer of religion, a superficial varnish or gilding of righteousness, or something looking like righteousness, they affected to look down with scorn upon all who did not make the same show as themselves. God is so great that he despises none: he has no rivals and no need to sustain himself by lowering the good name of others. He is supremely real, so true and thorough, that in him there can never be a thought of despising any in order to guard himself. His power is not so soon aroused to war, because it has no opposition to fear; his might is associated with gentleness, and fury is not in him, because it is such great might that once it is in action it devours his adversaries as flame consumes stubble. God is too great to be contemptuous, too mighty to be haughty.

FOR MEDITATION: God will not despise the afflicted (Psalm 22:24), the contrite (Psalm 51:17) or the destitute (Psalm 102:17), but will oppose all who despise neighbours (Proverbs 11:12; 14:21), parents (Proverbs 15:5,20; 30:17), children (Matthew 18:10) or the poor (James 2:6). Despising others can actually amount to despising God himself (Luke 10:16).

SERMON NO. 1379

Rest for the labouring

'Come unto me, all ye that labour and are heavy laden, and I will give you rest. Take my yoke upon you, and learn of me; for I am meek and lowly in heart: and ye shall find rest unto your souls.' Matthew 11:28–29
SUGGESTED FURTHER READING: Ecclesiastes 1:12–2:11

Some of you are labouring after *happiness*. You think to find it in gain, hoarding up your pounds and seeking for rest in the abundance of your beloved wealth. You will never have enough till you get Christ, but then you will be full to the brim. Contentment is the peculiar jewel of the beloved of the Lord Jesus. All the Indies could not fill a human heart: the soul is insatiable till it finds the Saviour; then it leans on him and enters into perfect peace. Perhaps you are labouring after *fame*. You despise gold, but long to obtain a great name. Alas, ambition's ways are very weary, and he who climbs to the loftiest peak of honour finds that it is a slippery place where rest is quite unknown. Take a friend's advice and care no longer for man's praise, for it is mere wind. If you would rise to a great name, become a Christian, for the name of Christ is the 'name which is above every name', and it is bliss to be hidden beneath it and overshadowed by it. Christ will not make you great among men, but he will make you so little in your own esteem that the lowest place at his table will more than satisfy you. He will give you rest from that delirious dream of ambition, and fire you with a higher ambition than ever. What are you labouring for? Is it *knowledge?* I commend you: it is a good possession and a choice treasure. Search for it as for silver. But all the knowledge that is to be had from the zenith to the centre of the earth will never satisfy your understanding, till you know Christ and are found in him. He can give rest to your soul by giving you the knowledge of God and a sense of his love. Whatever it is you labour after, come to Jesus and he will give you rest.

FOR MEDITATION: No one had as much happiness, fame and knowledge as Solomon (1 Kings 4:29–34; 10:1–8), but he received earthly blessings for seeking God and his wisdom instead of them (1 Kings 3:7–14). In Proverbs 3 he tells us to admit the lack of wisdom (vv.5&7), approach the Lord of wisdom (vv.5–7,19) and avoid the loss of wisdom (v.21). This will bring true happiness, gain and honour (vv.13–18).

SERMON NO. 1322

Wherefore should I weep?

'And there followed him a great company of people, and of women, which also bewailed and lamented him. But Jesus turning unto them said, Daughters of Jerusalem, weep not for me, but weep for yourselves, and for your children.' Luke 23:27–28
SUGGESTED FURTHER READING: Zechariah 12:10–13:1

Jesus would not have these women weep for one thing, because they were to weep for another thing which far more seriously demanded their weeping. You need not weep because Christ died one tenth so much as because your sins rendered it necessary that he should die. You need not weep over the crucifixion, but weep over your transgression, for your sins nailed the Redeemer to the accursed tree. To weep over a dying Saviour is to lament the remedy; it would be wiser to bewail the disease. To weep over the dying Saviour is to wet the surgeon's knife with tears; it would be better to bewail that spreading tumour which that knife must cut away. To weep over the Lord Jesus as he goes to the cross is to weep over that which is the subject of the highest joy that heaven and earth have ever known; your tears are scarcely needed there; they are natural, but a deeper wisdom will make you brush them all away and chant with joy his victory over death and the grave. If we must continue our sad emotions, let us lament that we should have broken the law which he thus painfully vindicated and let us mourn that we should have incurred the penalty which even he to the death was made to endure. Jesus wished them not so much to look at his outward sufferings as at the secret inward cause of that outward sorrow, namely, the transgression and the iniquity of his people, which had laid the cross upon his shoulders and surrounded him with enemies.

FOR MEDITATION: (*Our Own Hymn Book* no.265 v.1—Benjamin Beddome, 1818)
  'Did Christ o'er sinners weep,
  And shall our cheeks be dry?
  Let floods of penitential grief
  Burst forth from every eye.'

Sow to yourselves

'Sow to yourselves in righteousness, reap in mercy.' Hosea 10:12
SUGGESTED FURTHER READING (Spurgeon): Ephesians 4:17–32

'Sow to yourselves', and see that in your soul there is repentance of sin. Do not fall under the notion that the necessity for repentance is over. I have heard it said that repentance is 'merely a change of mind'. I wish that those who so speak had undergone that change. It is a sad sign of a faulty ministry when men can depreciate that precious grace. Mark you, no sinner will ever enter into heaven who has not repented of his sins. No promise can be found in the inspired page of eternal life to men who live and die without repentance. It is an old-fashioned virtue, I know, but it is in fashion with the angels, who rejoice over sinners who possess it. Know that sin is an evil and bitter thing, and the language to be used about it is such as David employed in Psalm 51. Pray to God to convince you of your guilt, and ask him to enable you to flee from every false way. Seek grace to detect sin, and as soon as you discern its presence fly from it as you would from a deadly serpent. May there be wrought in you an inward abhorrence of sin, and a loathing of yourself because of your tendency to transgress. 'Ye that love the LORD, hate evil:' 'hating even the garment spotted by the flesh.' May you also have a full conviction that in you, that is in your flesh, there 'dwelleth no good thing', and that your nature is empty, void and waste, like the chaos of old, unless the blessed Spirit shall brood over you, and the everlasting God shall new create you. There needs to be in your soul a deep sense of its ruin, or you will not prize redemption, and much of the godly sorrow of repentance, or you will not know the ecstasy of forgiveness. O for a plentiful sowing in tears, that we may reap in joy.

FOR MEDITATION: (*Our Own Hymn Book* no.119 song 2 v.5—Isaac Watts, 1719)
   'My soul hath gone too far astray,
   My feet too often slip;
   Yet since I've not forgot Thy way
   Restore Thy wandering sheep.'

SERMON NO. 1261

The power of the risen Saviour

'And Jesus came and spake unto them, saying, All power is given unto me in heaven and in earth. Go ye therefore, and teach all nations, baptizing them in the name of the Father, and of the Son, and of the Holy Ghost, teaching them to observe all things whatsoever I have commanded you: and lo, I am with you alway, even unto the end of the world. Amen.' Matthew 28:18–20
SUGGESTED FURTHER READING: Acts 14:19–28

We are to teach or, as the Greek word has it, to make disciples. Our business is, each according to the grace given, to tell our fellow men the gospel and to try and disciple them to Jesus. When they become disciples, our next duty is to give them the sign of discipleship by 'baptizing them'. That symbolic burial sets forth their death in Jesus to their former selves and their resurrection to newness of life through him. Baptism enrols and seals the disciples, and we must not omit or misplace it. When the disciple is enrolled, the missionary is to become the pastor, 'teaching them to observe all things whatsoever I have commanded you'. The disciple is admitted into the school by obeying the Saviour's command as to baptism, and then he goes on to learn, and as he learns he teaches others also. He is taught obedience not to some, but to all things which Christ has commanded. He is put into the church not to become a legislator or deviser of new doctrines and ceremonies, but to believe what Christ tells him, and to do what Christ bids him. Thus our Lord intends to set up a kingdom which shall break in pieces every other; those who know him are to teach others; and so the wondrous power which Christ brought from heaven shall spread from land to land. See, then, your high calling and also the support you have in pursuing it. At the front behold 'all power' going forth from Christ! In the rear behold the Lord himself—'lo, I am with you alway, even unto the end of the world.' If you are enlisted in this army, be faithful to your great captain, do his work carefully in the way which he has prescribed for you, and expect to see his power displayed to his own glory.

FOR MEDITATION: See the Great Commission in action in 1 Thessalonians 1:5–8. God's methods to encourage the spread of discipleship include imitation (1 Corinthians 11:1) and instruction (2 Timothy 2:2). What part are you playing in the process?

A family sermon

'And the LORD said unto Noah, Come thou and all thy house into the ark
... And Noah went in, and his sons, and his wife, and his sons' wives
with him, into the ark, because of the waters of the flood.' Genesis 7: 1,7
SUGGESTED FURTHER READING: Colossians 3:11–17

From the time of Noah's entrance he is to find all his *pleasure* in the ark.
There are no outdoor amusements for him or his family; he cannot even
find pleasure in the scenery, for that is blotted out by the deluges of rain;
the valleys have vanished and even the hills have disappeared as the
deluge has increased. If he is to find any pleasure, he must find it inside
the ark. It was a melancholy prospect indeed, if he could look out from
the window, but his joy and delight lay within the chambers of the ark,
for there was he saved and there he dwelt with God. All his *food* also to
supply his necessities he must find inside the ark. He had no barn nor
warehouse to look to, and there was no port at which he could take in
cargo. Whatever need might arise must be met by the stores within the
ark, for there was nothing outside but death. All his *work* was inside the
ark too. He had nothing to do now except within that vessel, no fields to
plough, no shops to keep, nothing to do but what was inside the ark.
Now, when a soul comes to Christ, it commits itself to him for
everything: Christ must feed it; you must no longer eat for your soul
anything but the bread of heaven; Jesus must become meat and drink to
you for his 'flesh is meat indeed' and his 'blood is drink indeed'. Now
you are to find your pleasure in him, your choicest delights, your
sweetest joys, all in Christ Jesus, who is our hope, crown, delight and
heaven. Henceforth your service must be to him only. 'Ye are not your
own. For ye are bought with a price', and all that you have to do in this
world now lies within the circumference of Christ's will. The commonest
duties of life are now to be brought within the sacred circle. You have
nothing to do outside in the waters of sin, self and Satan. You need
neither fish in the waters of sin, nor go boating upon the waves of
worldliness; you are in danger if you do.

FOR MEDITATION: (*Our Own Hymn Book* no.489 v.1—Isaac Watts, 1709)
   'In vain we lavish out our lives to gather empty wind,
    The choicest blessings earth can yield will starve a hungry mind.'

SERMON NO. 1336

The prosperous man's reminder

'I did know thee in the wilderness, in the land of great drought. According to their pasture, so were they filled; they were filled, and their heart was exalted; therefore have they forgotten me.' Hosea 13:5–6
SUGGESTED FURTHER READING (Spurgeon): Deuteronomy 8:11–20

I will put to you one question. Can you find in the word of God one instance of a man of God who was injured by his troubles? Do they not all, like Job, come out of the furnace of affliction much profited thereby? Let me then ask another question. Is it not almost a rule with us, though it ought not to be, that our prosperity is our loss? David, when hunted like a partridge on the mountains, glorified the Lord his God, but David, when he abode in a palace, sinned again and again, so that the Holy Spirit draws a distinction between his earlier and his latter life, for it is written of Jehoshaphat that he walked before the Lord 'in the first ways of his father David'. Solomon, the wisest man that ever lived, was not proof against prosperity. He had all he could desire, and then his earthly loves stole away his heart. Take one case which will give both sides of the matter. See Hezekiah with Sennacherib's letter, spreading it before the Lord in faith: he is then an example in history, a man of God to be envied for his prayer of faith. He is far fallen when his realm is at peace and his riches are multiplied, for he becomes boastful and displays to the Babylonian ambassadors all his treasures, and provokes the Lord his God. I wish you great prosperity, but far more do I wish you great peace, that you may carry a full cup with a steady hand. There is need to pray for men who are going uphill lest they fall upon their high places. In our low estate grace will surely be given, for the Lord pities us, but when we are rising we have double need to pray, for 'God resisteth the proud'.

FOR MEDITATION: (*Our Own Hymn Book* no.809 vv.2&3—John S.B. Monsell, 1863)
  'I knew Thee when the world was waste, and Thou alone wast fair,
  On Thee my heart its fondness placed, my soul reposed its care.
  And if Thine altered hand doth now my sky with sunshine fill,
  Who amid all so fair as Thou? Oh let me know Thee still.'

SERMON NO. 1441

A Sabbath-school sermon

'He shall gather the lambs with his arm, and carry them in his bosom.'
Isaiah 40:11
SUGGESTED FURTHER READING: Matthew 18:1–10

I read the other day a pleasing anecdote of what one lamb may come to. A ewe brought forth three lambs, and the brutal shepherd threw the third into the hedge that there might be the more milk for the other two. A poor woman passing by begged for the thrown away lamb, employed her utmost care in nursing it by means of a sucking bottle, and reared it till it could eat grass for itself. She turned it upon the common and in due course it produced twins: by care she at length raised a whole flock of sheep from the single ewe and in process of time she became a woman of considerable estate. See what one poor half-dead lamb may yet produce. Who knows what one poor trembling soul may yet bring forth? Jesus knows that perhaps a boy may be here who will be the spiritual father of scores and hundreds of thousands before he dies. There may be in the congregation of today a Chrysostom or an Augustine. Right among us may sit a little Whitefield, a young Luther, or some other of honourable character who shall lead many to Christ. There was a dreadful snow-storm one Sunday morning when Dr Tyng of New York set out to preach; when he reached the church there was only one poor little girl there. Most preachers would have gone home when one child made up the whole of the congregation, but Dr Tyng went through the service as earnestly as if the pews had been crowded. He preached to the little girl; God gave him that girl's soul and never was he better repaid. To his knowledge she had been the means of bringing some twenty-five to the Lord Jesus, and among them was one of his own sons. The greatest orator, the most spiritual teacher, the most useful evangelist may not dare to despise one of Christ's little ones.

FOR MEDITATION: Some of the godliest people in the Bible came to know the Lord as children (1 Samuel 3:1–10,19–21; 2 Chronicles 34:1–3; Jeremiah 1:4–7; Luke 1:13–15,80; 2 Timothy 1:5; 3:15). Early conversion is preferable (Ecclesiastes 12:1).

N.B. The Sunday-school Union had asked ministers to encourage prayer for Sabbath-schools on this day.

SERMON NO. 1381

Why may I rejoice?

'Notwithstanding in this rejoice not, that the spirits are subject unto you; but rather rejoice, because your names are written in heaven.' Luke 10:20
SUGGESTED FURTHER READING: Philippians 2:17–3:3

God may have given you many gifts for use in the kingdom of heaven; he may also have given you influence in his church and power among men of the world; moreover, your gifts and power have not been used in vain, but have been made useful in many ways, so that your course has been one of honour and success. The kingdom of God has come near to many through you, and the enemy's kingdom has suffered injury by your means. Because of this you are greatly cheered. Is this wrong? Ought you not to be full of joy? I say yes, you are bound to be glad. We should all be grateful for gifts, influence and success; a gratitude which is not attended with joy can scarcely be called gratitude at all. Would you have gratitude lament the possession of the blessing for which she is grateful? There must be joy in the thing received, or else one can hardly be imagined to be thankful. If gratitude for these things be a duty, then surely a measure of joy concerning them must also be a duty. You may rejoice that to you 'is this grace given' to 'preach among the Gentiles the unsearchable riches of Christ'; and you may be glad that from you the word of God has sounded forth throughout all the region in which you dwell. Thus far we go, but we must not exceed due bounds, lest we become transgressors: this joy must be held within its own lines and never suffered to run riot. Let us see how our Lord puts a restraining 'notwithstanding' and a repressing negative upon this joy, when he judges that it is danger of passing due bounds; and let us also note how he replaces this joy by something higher and better when he says, 'Notwithstanding in this rejoice not, that the spirits are subject unto you; but rather rejoice, because your names are written in heaven.'

FOR MEDITATION: Christians have many reasons for rejoicing that their names are written in heaven. There will be great rewards for the persecuted (Matthew 5:12), we will share the glory of God (Romans 5:2), our completed salvation and Christ's glory will be revealed (1 Peter 1:5–6; 4:13) and we will be presented faultless before the presence of his glory (Jude 24). Are you able to share in this joy?

SERMON NO. 1321

A question for hard-hearted hearers

'Shall horses run upon the rock? Will one plough there with oxen?' Amos
6:12
SUGGESTED FURTHER READING: 2 Corinthians 7:2–12

A farmer who is too tender-hearted to tear up and harrow the land will
never see a harvest. Here is the failing of certain divines; they are afraid of
hurting anyone's feelings, and so they keep clear of all the truths which
are likely to excite fear or grief. They have not a sharp ploughshare on
their premises and are never likely to have a stack in their rickyard. They
angle without hooks for fear of hurting the fish, and fire without bullets
out of respect to the feelings of the birds. This kind of love is real cruelty
to men's souls. It is much the same as if a surgeon should permit a patient
to die because he would pain him with the lancet or by the necessary
removal of a limb. It is a terrible tenderness which leaves men to sink into
hell rather than distress their minds. It is a diabolical love which denies
the eternal danger which assuredly exists and argues the soul into
presumption, because it thinks it a pity to excite terror, and so much the
more pleasant to prophesy smooth things. Is this the spirit of Christ? Did
he conceal the sinner's peril? Did he cast doubts upon the unquenchable
fire and the undying worm? Did he lull souls into slumber by dulcet notes
of flattery? No, but with honest love and anxious concern he warned men
of the wrath to come and bade them repent or perish. Let the servant of
the Lord Jesus in this thing follow his Master, and plough deep with a
sharp ploughshare, which will not be balked by the hardest clods. This we
must school ourselves to do. It may be contrary to our impulses and
painful to our feelings, but it must not be left undone to gratify our love
of ease and our desire to please our hearers. If we really love the souls of
men, let us prove it by honest speech.

FOR MEDITATION: Disturbing the sinner is an essential function of God's
word (2 Timothy 3:16) and an essential role for God's messenger
(2 Timothy 4:2). The sinner may ignore the message (Isaiah 6:9–10;
Ezekiel 33:30–32) and even resent it (Micah 2:6), but that is no excuse for
the preacher to disobey God and soft-pedal God's truth (Jeremiah 1:16–
17).

SERMON NO. 1470

The man of one subject

'For I determined not to know anything among you, save Jesus Christ, and him crucified.' 1 Corinthians 2:2
SUGGESTED FURTHER READING: 1 Thessalonians 2:1–8

If the wisest plans for spreading the Redeemer's kingdom would have been to have opened his ministry at Corinth by proclaiming the unity of the Godhead, or by philosophically working out the possibilities of God's becoming incarnate, Paul would have adopted them. But, having examined them with all care, he could not see that anything was to be got by indirect preaching or by keeping back a part of the truth; therefore he determined to go straight forward and promote the gospel by proclaiming the gospel. Whether men would hear or forbear, he resolved to come to the point at once and preach the cross in its naked simplicity. Instead of knowing a great many things which might have led up to the main subject, he would not know anything in Corinth 'save Jesus Christ, and him crucified'. Paul might have said, 'I had better beat about the bush and educate the people up to a certain mark before I come to my main point; to lay bare my ultimate intent at the first might be to spread the net in the sight of the birds and frighten them away. I will be cautious and reticent and take them with guile, enticing them on in pursuit of truth.' But not so: looking at the matter all round as a prudent man should, he came to this resolve, that he would know nothing among them 'save Jesus Christ, and him crucified'. I would to God that the 'culture' we hear of in these days, and all this boasted 'modern thought' would come to the same conclusion. This most renowned and scholarly divine after reading, marking, learning and inwardly digesting everything as few men could do, came to this as the issue of it all: 'I determined not to know anything among you, save Jesus Christ, and him crucified.'

FOR MEDITATION: (*Our Own Hymn Book* no.483 vv.1&2—Isaac Watts, 1709)
'Christ and His cross is all our theme; the mysteries that we speak
Are scandal in the Jew's esteem, and folly to the Greek.
But souls enlightened from above with joy receive the Word;
They see what wisdom, power, and love, shine in their dying Lord.'

SERMON NO. 1264

With the King for his work!

'These were the potters, and those that dwelt among plants and hedges: there they dwelt with the king for his work.' 1 Chronicles 4:23
SUGGESTED FURTHER READING: Mark 3:7–19

I offer to Sunday-school teachers a motto which may last them for life: 'with the king for his work.' Put that up now over your mantelpieces: 'with the king for his work.' Work by all means, because you are 'with the king', but get 'with the king' by all means, because you want to do his work. How important it is that every good servant of our heavenly Master should be with him. Why? Do you ask me, why? Because you cannot know his will if you do not live with him. He that lives with Christ gets his orders every day, and often from moment to moment he gets guidance from his great Lord's eye. He says, 'I will guide thee with mine eye.' You know how a servant in the house watches her mistress. The mistress does not always need to speak. Perhaps it is at a dinner. There are a number of guests. She does not keep calling, 'Mary', and instructing her in measured sentences to attend to the various requirements, but by a simple movement of her head or a quiet glance of her eye, Mary can understand all her mistress means. Now, those that live with Jesus Christ have a sort of secret alphabet between themselves and him. Often when a Christian does the right thing, you read as a story or as an anecdote that enlivens a book, how strangely wise he was, how he dropped the fit word at the fitting moment, how he had a knack of giving the right answer to one who wrongly assailed him. Do you know why he had that knack? He lived with his Master, so he knew what you knew not. He knew the meaning of his Master's eye, and it guided him. I believe that, if Sunday-school teachers and ministers live with their Lord, they will be made wise to win souls.

FOR MEDITATION: When we draw near to God, he draws near to us (John 14:22–23; James 4:8). A desire to stay close to God will often bring with it a clear indication of what is right and what is wrong (John 7:17; 1 John 2:26–27). More than once Jesus promised that his apostles would be given the right things to say when they found themselves in difficulties (Luke 12:11–12; 21:12–15).

SERMON NO. 1400

Unwillingness to come to Christ

'And ye will not come to me, that ye might have life.' John 5:40
SUGGESTED FURTHER READING: Isaiah 53:1–12

How is it that any man can be so base as not to come to my Lord Jesus Christ? Look at him: let me portray him to you as he completed your redemption. He hangs upon his cross: his face is all distained with the bruises and the spittle of the rough soldiers, and down it trickle the red drops that have been started from his temples by the crown of thorns. His eyes are red with weeping and watching, and 'his visage was so marred more than any man'. You can tell all his bones; his body is emaciated and worn with anguish. His hands the cruel nails have dragged and torn till you see the wide gaping wounds from which the blood distils. His feet are the same; they are both founts of blood: and then behold his side, from which gushed blood and water from the deep wound made by the spear. It is he who thus redeemed mankind. The Lord of glory hangs there! The only begotten Son of the Highest, the Prince of the kings of the earth, has emptied himself of all glory for you and has given up himself to bleed and to die a felon's death for you. And what is your attitude towards him? You turn your backs upon him! Is it nothing to you that Jesus should die? Is it nothing to you that Jesus should bleed to redeem men? Do you mean to refuse a share in that redemption? Do you utterly reject the ransom price he paid upon the cross? If it be so, then put it down in black and white in plain English and sign your name to it—'I refuse Christ's blood'. To write it down is the very best thing you can do, because, perhaps, when you have read the dreadful lines, your conscience may be lashed into something like life, and you may begin to look at him whom you have pierced, and mourn because of him. Do think of this, you that will not come unto him that you might have life.

FOR MEDITATION: (*Our Own Hymn Book* no.515 vv.1&2—Joseph Grigg, 1765)

'Behold! a stranger's at the door! He gently knocks, has knocked before;
Has waited long; is waiting still; you treat no other friend so ill.
But will He prove a friend indeed? He will; the very friend you need:
The Man of Nazareth, 'tis He, with garments dyed at Calvary.'

SERMON NO. 1324

Sorrow at the cross turned into joy

'Ye shall weep and lament, but the world shall rejoice: and ye shall be sorrowful, but your sorrow shall be turned into joy.' John 16:20
SUGGESTED FURTHER READING: Luke 24:13–43

Let us mourn by all means, for Jesus died; but by no means let us make mourning the prominent thought in connection with his death if we have obtained thereby the pardon of our sins. The language of our text allowed and yet forbade sorrow; it gave permission to weep, but only for a little while, and then it forbade all further weeping by the promise to turn the sorrow into joy: 'ye shall weep and lament,' that is, his disciples, while he was dying, dead and buried, would be sorely distressed: 'and ye shall be sorrowful, but your sorrow shall be turned into joy'; their grief would end when they saw him risen from the dead, and so it did, for we read, 'Then were the disciples glad, when they saw the Lord.' The sight of the cross to their unbelief was sadness only, but now to the eye of faith it is the gladdest sight that the human eye can rest upon: the cross is as the light of the morning, which ends the long and dreary darkness which covered the nations. Wounds of Jesus, you are as stars, breaking the night of man's despair. Spear, you have opened the fountain of healing for human woe. Crown of thorns, you are a constellation of promises. Eyes that were red with weeping sparkle with hope at the sight of thee, O bleeding Lord. As for thy tortured body, O Emmanuel, the blood which dropped from it cried from the ground and proclaimed peace, pardon and Paradise to all believers. Though laid in the grave by thy weeping friends, thy body, O divine Saviour, is no longer in Joseph's tomb, for thou art risen from the dead, and we find in the songs of resurrection and ascension an abundant solace for the griefs of thy death.

FOR MEDITATION: (*Our Own Hymn Book* no.301 vv.1&2—Hymns & Poetry for Schools, 1840).
   '"It is finished;" shall we raise songs of sorrow or of praise?
   Mourn to see the Saviour die, or proclaim His victory?
   If of Calvary we tell, how can songs of triumph swell?
   If of man redeemed from woe, how shall notes of mourning flow?'

SERMON NO. 1442

The touch

'She said, If I may touch but his clothes, I shall be whole.' Mark 5:28
SUGGESTED FURTHER READING: 1 John 4:13–18

This woman did not obtain assurance until she made an open confession. She felt in herself that she was whole, but there was more comfort in reserve for her. The Lord Jesus Christ would have those who follow him come forward and no longer hide in the crowd. Those who believe ought to be baptized on confession of their faith. He who in his heart believes should with his mouth make confession of him. So Christ turned round and said, 'Who touched my clothes?' At that the newly-kindled flame of her joy began to damp under the fear of losing what she had stolen. Down went her spirits. Then the officious disciples said, 'Thou seest the multitude thronging thee, and sayest thou, Who touched me?' But Jesus said, as he looked around again, 'Somebody hath touched me', for not his clothes alone, but he himself, had been touched by somebody. That poor 'somebody' wanted to sink into the earth. She trembled as Jesus looked for her. Those blessed eyes looked around and lighted upon her, and as she gazed upon them she did not feel so much alarmed as before; but, still afraid and trembling, she came, fell down before him, and told him the truth. Then he gently raised her up and said, 'Daughter, thy faith hath made thee whole; go in peace, and be whole of thy plague.' Now she knew her cure from Christ's lips as well as from her own consciousness. She had now the divine witness bearing witness with her spirit that she was indeed healed. Those of you who desire to obtain the witness of the Spirit should come forward, confess your faith and tell what the Lord has done for you: then shall you receive the sealing witness of the Spirit with your spirit that you are indeed born of God.

FOR MEDITATION: (*Our Own Hymn Book* no.603 vv.4–6—William Cowper, 1779)
'She too, who touched Thee in the press, and healing virtue stole,
Was answered, "Daughter, go in peace, Thy faith hath made thee whole."
Concealed amid the gathering throng, she would have shunned Thy view,
And if her faith was firm and strong, had strong misgivings too.
Like her, with hopes and fears, we come to touch Thee if we may;
Oh! send us not despairing home, send none unhealed away.'

SERMON NO. 1382

Providence—as seen in the book of Esther

'Though it was turned to the contrary, that the Jews had rule over them that hated them.' Esther 9:1
SUGGESTED FURTHER READING (Spurgeon): Esther 5:9–7:10

You are probably aware that some have denied the inspiration of the Book of Esther because the name of God does not occur in it. They might with equal justice deny the inspiration of a great number of chapters in the Bible and of a far greater number of verses. Although the name of God does not occur in the Book of Esther, the Lord himself is there most conspicuously in every incident which it relates. I have seen portraits bearing the names of persons for whom they were intended, and they certainly needed them, but we have all seen others which required no name, because they were such striking likenesses that the moment you looked upon them you knew them. In the Book of Esther, as much as in any other part of the word of God, the hand of Providence is manifestly to be seen. 'All scripture is given by inspiration of God, and is profitable' whether it be history or doctrine. God never meant the Book of Esther to lie dumb, and whatever it seemed good to him to teach us by it, it ought to be our earnest endeavour to learn. The Lord intended by the narrative of Esther's history to set before us a wonderful instance of his providence, that when we had viewed it with interest and pleasure, we might praise his name and then go on to acquire the habit of observing his hand in other histories and especially in our own lives. Well does Flavel say that he who observes providence will never be long without a providence to observe. The man who can walk through the world and see no God, is said upon inspired authority to be a fool, but the wise man's eyes are in his head; he sees with an inner sight and discovers God everywhere at work. It is his joy to perceive that the Lord is working according to his will in heaven and earth and in all deep places.

FOR MEDITATION: (*Our Own Hymn Book* no.251 v.4—Robert Robinson, 1774)

'For Thy providence, that governs
Through Thine empire's wide domain,
Wings an angel, guides a sparrow;
Blessed be Thy gentle reign.'

SERMON NO. 1201

The minister's plea

'Through your prayer, and the supply of the Spirit of Jesus Christ.'
Philippians 1:19
SUGGESTED FURTHER READING: Romans 14:17–15:6

'The supply of the Spirit' is essential to the edification of the church of God. What if the ministry should be the best that ever was produced, its outward form and fashion orthodox and ardent? What if it should be continued with persevering consistency? Yet the church will never be built up without the Holy Spirit. To build up a church life is needed: we are living stones of a living temple. Where is the life to come from but from the breath of God? To build up a church there is needed light, but where is the light to come from but from him who said, 'Let there be light'? To build up a church there is needed love, for this is the cement which binds the living stones together; but whence comes true genuine love but from the Spirit, who sheds abroad in the heart the love of Jesus? To build up a church we must have holiness, for an unholy church would be a den for the devil and not a temple for God; but whence comes holiness but from the Holy Spirit? There must be zeal, too, for God will not dwell in a cold house; the church of God must be warm with love; but whence comes the fire except it be the fire from heaven? We must have the Holy Spirit, for to build up the church there must be joy; a joyous temple God's temple must always be: but the Spirit of God alone produces the fruit of heavenly joy. There must be spirituality in the members, but we cannot have a spiritual people if the Spirit of God himself be not there. For the edification of the saints, then, we must have beyond everything else 'the supply of the Spirit'.

FOR MEDITATION: (*Our Own Hymn Book* no.454 v.1—Isaac Watts, 1709)
  'Come, Holy Spirit, heavenly Dove,
  With all Thy quickening powers,
  Kindle a flame of sacred love
  In these cold hearts of ours.'

Paul's doxology

'Now unto him that is able to do exceeding abundantly above all that we ask or think, according to the power that worketh in us, unto him be glory in the church by Christ Jesus throughout all ages, world without end. Amen.' Ephesians 3:20–21
SUGGESTED FURTHER READING: Psalm 19:1–6

In our text we have adoration, not prayer; the apostle had done with that; adoration—not even so much the act of praise as the full sense that praise is due, and far more of it than we can render. I hardly know how to describe adoration. Praise is a river flowing on joyously in its own channel, banked up on either side that it may run towards its one object, but adoration is the same river overflowing all banks, flooding the soul and covering the entire nature with its great waters, and these not so much moving and stirring as standing still in profound repose, mirroring the glory which shines down upon it, like a summer's sun upon a sea of glass, not seeking the divine presence, but conscious of it to an unutterable degree, and therefore full of awe and peace, like the sea of Galilee when its waves felt the touch of the sacred feet. Adoration is the fulness, the height and depth, the length and breadth of praise. Adoration seems to me to be as the starry heavens, which are always telling the glory of God, and yet 'There is no speech nor language, where their voice is not heard.' It is the eloquent silence of a soul that is too full for language. To prostrate yourself in the dust in humility, and yet to soar aloft in sublime thought, to sink into nothing, and yet to be so enlarged as to be filled with all the fulness of God, to have no thought and yet to be all thought, to lose yourself in God, this is adoration. This should be the frequent state of the renewed mind. We ought to set apart far longer time for this sacred engagement.

FOR MEDITATION: (*Our Own Hymn Book* no.166 v.5—Charles Wesley, 1757)
   'To the Great One in Three
   Eternal praises be, hence evermore:
   His sovereign majesty,
   May we in glory see,
   And to eternity love and adore.'

SERMON NO. 1266

The cause and cure of weariness in Sabbath-school teachers

'Let us not be weary in well doing: for in due season we shall reap, if we faint not.' Galatians 6:9
SUGGESTED FURTHER READING: Mark 10:13–16

Sunday-school work is 'well doing'. How can it be otherwise, for it is an act of obedience? I trust you have entered upon it because you call Jesus your Master and Lord, and you wish to fulfil the great command, 'Go ye into all the world, and preach the gospel to every creature.' You find children to be creatures, fallen creatures, but still lovable little things, full of vigour, life and glee. You see them to be a component part of the race, and you conclude at once that your Master's command applies to them. You are not like the disciples who would put them back, for you have learned from their mistake, and you remember the words of their Master and yours, 'Suffer the little children to come unto me, and forbid them not'. You know, too, that 'Out of the mouth of babes and sucklings' he has 'ordained strength because of' the adversary, so that you are sure that he included the little ones in the general commission when he said, 'preach the gospel to every creature.' You are doubly sure that you are obeying his will because you have certain special precepts which relate to the little ones, such as 'Feed my lambs', and 'Train up a child in the way he should go: and when he is old, he will not depart from it.' You know that it is our duty to preserve alive a testimony in the world, and therefore you are anxious to teach the word to your children that they may teach it to their children, that so, from generation to generation, the word of the Lord may be made known. Be the task pleasant or irksome to you, it is not yours to hesitate but to obey. The love which has redeemed you also constrains you.

FOR MEDITATION: The Lord Jesus Christ 'went about doing good' (Acts 10:38). This included giving quality time to little children (Luke 8:41–42,49–56; 9:46–48; 18:15–17) and delighting in their praises (Matthew 21:15–16). If he was not weary in such well-doing, neither should his followers be.

N.B. This sermon was preached 'at a convention of the Sunday-school Union'.

SERMON NO. 1383

Good news for the destitute

'He will regard the prayer of the destitute, and not despise their prayer.'
Psalm 102:17
SUGGESTED FURTHER READING: Revelation 3:14–22

The whole of this verse is connected with the building up of Zion. Hence there must be some connection between the two, and it is just this: the church of God must never expect to see great revivals, nor to see the world converted to Christ, until she comes before the Lord as destitute. I am afraid that when we plead most with God, we still feel we are a very respectable community of Christians, with a large number of ministers, a number of wealthy laymen, a large amount of chapel property, and a good deal of power and influence: 'thou sayest, I am rich, and increased with goods'. It may be that all this is the ensign of our poverty, and we may be 'miserable, and poor, and blind, and naked'. But when we get right down, and feel we are nothing and nobody, that we could not save a soul if our lives depended upon it, that we are weak as water and must come to God as utterly impotent apart from the power of the Spirit of God, then will the Lord appear in his glory, and his destitute church shall become rich in his riches, strong in his strength and victorious in his might. We must be brought down. I see among the various denominations too much emulation as to their position; we stand in this position, and we in the other, and the voluntaries are doing such wonders. But, brethren, we are just a lot of poor unworthy sinners, who owe everything we have to the sovereign grace of God, and what we are to do for God must be accomplished 'Not by might, nor by power, but by' his Spirit. When we feel this, the building of Zion will come, and not till then. The Lord send it!

FOR MEDITATION: Self-congratulation on the part of a church invited ridicule from the apostle Paul (1 Corinthians 4:8) and disgusts the Lord Jesus Christ (Revelation 3:16–17). It is a mark of folly when expressed by an unbeliever (Luke 12:19–20), but how much worse when seen in Christians, who really ought to know a good deal better.

N.B. Voluntaries—those who support the system of maintaining church institutions by voluntary contributions rather than by State aid.

SERMON NO. 1141

Holy water

'Whosoever drinketh of the water that I shall give him shall never thirst, but the water that I shall give him shall be in him a well of water springing up into everlasting life.' John 4:14
SUGGESTED FURTHER READING: Philippians 3:12–16

Satisfied with Christ the Christian always is, but altogether and entirely satisfied with his own realisation of the blessings which Jesus brings, so as to desire no more, I think he never will be till he gets to heaven. Have you never heard of that great painter who one day, breaking his palette and putting aside his brush, said to a friend that he should paint no more, for his day was over? When his friend inquired why he had come to that singular conclusion, he said, 'Because the last painting which I executed perfectly contented me, and therefore I feel that the high ideal which led me on has departed and I shall succeed no more.' It is so. There is in every man who is a master of his art a high ideal after which he strains, and the fact that he has that ideal ever above him is one of the tokens of his lofty genius. I suppose that Milton as a poet never reached the 'height of that great argument' as he desired to reach it: when he had composed a portion of his wondrous epic, he would feel that his thoughts were above his words, and that he had an inner unshaped conception towering higher than his actually formed and shapen thoughts. He was a poet because that was the case, and other rhymesters are not poets because their verses please them. That man is holy who mourns the unholiness of his holiest deeds, and that man is no longer holy who conceives himself to be without sin and to have reached the highest attainable excellence. The mariner who dreams that he has cast anchor hard by earth's utmost bound where the universe comes to an end, will never be a Columbus. Up with your anchor, my brother, for there are wide seas beyond and a land of gold across the main. Self-satisfaction is the grave of progress; he who thinks himself perfect is never likely to be so. Brethren, shun the spirit of self-content.

FOR MEDITATION: Contentment with our material possessions is a virtue to be sought (Luke 3:14; Philippians 4:11; 1 Timothy 6:6–8; Hebrews 13:5), but self-contentment with our spiritual attainments is a vice to be shunned.

SERMON NO. 1202

A round of delights

'Now the God of hope fill you with all joy and peace in believing, that ye may abound in hope, through the power of the Holy Ghost.' Romans 15:13
SUGGESTED FURTHER READING: Philippians 4:4–9

Sometimes the believer is full of joy. Joy is active and expressive; it sparkles and flashes like a diamond; it sings and dances like David before the ark. To be filled with holy joy is a delicious excitement of the sweetest kind; may you often experience it, until strangers are compelled to infer that the Lord has done great things for you. Nevertheless, the flesh is weak and might hardly endure continuous delight, and so there comes a relief in the lovely form of peace, in which the heart is really joyous, but after a calm and quiet manner. I have seen the ringers make the pinnacles of a church tower reel to and fro while they have made the joy bells sound out to the full, and then they have played quietly and let the fabric settle down again. Even thus does joy strain the man, but peace comes in to give him rest. In this peace there is not much to exhilarate, not much which could fittingly be spoken out in song, but silence, full of infinite meaning, becomes the floodgate of the soul. You seek not the exulting assembly, but the calm shade and the quiet chamber. You are as happy as you were in your joy, but not so stirred and moved. Peace is joy resting, and joy is peace dancing. Joy cries hosanna before the Well-beloved, but peace leans her head upon him. In the midst of bereavements and sickness we may scarcely be able to rejoice, but we may be at peace. When faith cannot break through a troop with her sacred joy, she stands still and sees the salvation of God in hallowed peace. We work with joy and rest with peace. What a blessing it is that when we come to die, if we cannot depart with the banners of triumphant joy all flying in the breeze, we can yet fall asleep safely in the arms of peace.

FOR MEDITATION: God's 'joy and peace' which can fill believers is no ordinary joy and peace. The joy he gives is full (Psalm 16:11), exceeding (Psalm 43:4), everlasting (Isaiah 35:10), abundant (2 Corinthians 8:2), unspeakable and full of glory (1 Peter 1:8), while his peace is great (Psalm 119:165), perfect (Isaiah 26:3) and passes all understanding (Philippians 4:7). Do you know them both?

SERMON NO. 1384

And why not?

'And he said unto the disciples, The days will come, when ye shall desire to see one of the days of the Son of man, and ye shall not see it.' Luke 17:22

SUGGESTED FURTHER READING: Job 29:1–6

When our spiritual spring is with us we are fearful of its March winds and April showers, but when it is gone and we are parched with summer heat, we wish we had the winds and showers back again. So, too, when autumn comes, we mistake ripening for decaying and mournfully wish the roses of summer would return, while all through winter we are sighing for those summer hours we once enjoyed and those mellow autumn fruits which were so sweet to our taste. Thus, brethren, we continue, if we permit ourselves to do so, to judge each state in which we have been to be better than that in which we are, and to shed useless tears of regret over times and seasons which are gone past recall. While they are with us we see their deficiencies: when they are gone we remember only their excellencies. It would be wiser if we took each time and season, each state and experience, while yet it was on the wing, turned it to the best account for God's glory, and rejoiced in its mercy while we enjoyed it. While we have the light let us walk in it. While the bridegroom is with us let us keep the feast; it will be time enough to mourn when he is gone from us. After all, each season has its fruits, and it would be a pity to wither them with idle regrets. Let us turn to good account the old wordling's motto, and live while we live. Let us live one day at a time, enjoy the present good, and leave yesterday with our pardoning God. The days of the Son of man, of which the apostles thought comparatively little, they afterwards sighed for, and these present days, of which we are complaining, may yet come to be regarded as among the choicest portions of our lives.

FOR MEDITATION: Yesterday is past (Psalm 90:4) and should be treated as such (Philippians 3:13). Tomorrow is something about which we should neither boast (Proverbs 27:1; James 4:13–16) nor worry (Matthew 6:34). Today is the time to hear God's voice, to avoid hardening our hearts, and to exhort one another to do likewise (Hebrews 3:7,13,15).

SERMON NO. 1323

Vanities and verities

'We look not at the things which are seen, but at the things which are not seen: for the things which are seen are temporal; but the things which are not seen are eternal.' 2 Corinthians 4:18
SUGGESTED FURTHER READING: Romans 8:18–25

The present is so soon to be over that Paul does not care to look at it. There is so little of it and it lasts such a brief time, that he does not even deign to give it a glance. Here he is persecuted, despised, forsaken. 'It will not last long', says he. 'It is but a pin's prick; it will soon be over, and I shall be with the goodly fellowship above and behold my Master's face.' He ignores it. Thus it behoves us to do if surrounded with trials, troubles and present sorrows: we should not think so much of them as to fix our attention or rivet our gaze on them. Rather let us treat them with indifference and say, 'It is really a very small matter whether I am in wealth or in poverty, in health or in sickness, whether I am enjoying comforts or am robbed of them. The present will so soon be gone that I do not care to look at it. I am like a man who stays at an inn for a night while on a journey. Is the room uncomfortable? When the morning breaks it is no use making a complaint, and so he merely chronicles the fact and moves on. He says to himself, "Never mind, I am up and away directly; it is no use fretting about trifles."' If a person is going a long distance in a railway carriage, he may be a little particular as to where he shall sit to see the country, and as to which way he likes to ride, but if it is only a short stage—between, say, the Borough Road and the Elephant and Castle—he does not think about it or care in whose company he may be; it is only for a few minutes; he is hardly in before he is out again; it is not worth thinking about. That is how the apostle regarded it.

FOR MEDITATION: There is a proper way for the Christian to regard the present (Titus 2:12). In one sense it is to be enjoyed (1 Corinthians 3:22; 1 Timothy 4:4) and poses no threat to our security in Christ (Romans 8:38–39), despite the suffering and distress it may bring (Romans 8:18; 1 Corinthians 7:26). But in another sense it is full of spiritual evil from which Christ died to deliver us (Galatians 1:3–4) and of traps into which we may still fall (2 Timothy 4:10).

SERMON NO. 1380

The miracle of the loaves

'They considered not the miracle of the loaves.' Mark 6:52
SUGGESTED FURTHER READING: 1 Corinthians 16:1–18

There must be a clearing up after every banquet. The disciples went round, gathered up the fragments that remained, and found twelve baskets full. This, as has often been remarked, teaches us economy in everything that we do for God, not economy as to giving to him, but as to the use of the Lord's money. Break your alabaster boxes and pour out the sacred nard with blessed wastefulness, for that very wastefulness is the sweetness of the gift, but when God entrusts you with any means to use for him, use those means with discretion. When we have money given to us for use in God's cause, we should be more careful with it than if it were our own; the same rule applies in other matters. Ministers, when God gives them a good time in their studies, and they read the Word and it opens up before them, should keep notes of what comes to them. The wind does not always blow alike, and it is well to grind your wheat when the mill will work. You should put up your sails and let your vessel fly along when you have a good, favouring breeze, and this may make up for dead calms. Economically put by the fragments that remain after you have fed next Sunday's congregation, that there may be something for hard times when your head aches, and you are dull and heavy in pulpit preparations. But I think the beauty of it was this, that after they had all been fed, there was something left. Did I hear a heavy heart complain, 'I hear of a great revival and a great blessing, but I was not there; I was just gone out of the town when that blessing came. Woe's me; I am too late'? Ah, there is plenty left. No penitent sinner is too late. Sometimes friends come in at the end of a meal and there is nothing left beyond the bare bones, but here is quite enough for you. Here are twelve baskets full to the brim. You are not too late. Come and welcome.

FOR MEDITATION: (*Our Own Hymn Book* no.500 v.5—Baptist Psalmist, 1843)
'There's room around thy Father's board
For thee and thousands more;
Oh, come and welcome to the Lord;
Yes, come this very hour.'

SERMON NO. 1218

The consecration of priests

'This is the thing that thou shalt do unto them to hallow them, to minister unto me in the priest's office.' Exodus 29:1
SUGGESTED FURTHER READING: Revelation 5:6–14

Under the law only one family could serve God in the priest's office, but under the gospel all the saints are 'a chosen generation, a royal priesthood' (1 Peter 2:9). In the Christian church no persons whatsoever are set apart to the priesthood above the rest of their brethren, for in us is fulfilled the promise which Israel by reason of her sin failed to obtain— 'ye shall be unto me a kingdom of priests'. Paul, in addressing all the saints, bids them present their 'bodies a living sacrifice, holy, acceptable unto God, which is' their 'reasonable service'. It is the grand design of all the works of divine grace, both for us and in us, to fit us for the office of the spiritual priesthood, and it will be the crown of our perfection when with all our brethren we shall sing unto the Lord Jesus the new song, 'Unto him that loved us, and washed us from our sins in his own blood, and hath made us kings and priests unto God and his Father; to him be glory and dominion for ever and ever.' This honour have all the saints: according to Peter (1 Peter 2:2–5) it belongs even to 'newborn babes' in grace, for even such are spoken of as forming part of 'an holy priesthood, to offer up spiritual sacrifices'. Nor is this confined to men as was the Aaronic priesthood, for in Christ Jesus 'there is neither male nor female'. It does not refer exclusively or even specially to persons called clergymen or ministers, but to all of you who believe in Jesus, for you are God's clergy, that is, his inheritance, and you should all be ministers, ministering 'according to the grace that is given to' you.

FOR MEDITATION: All believers are expected to make living sacrifices to God (Romans 12:1). In Hebrews 13:15–16 we learn that these ongoing sacrifices should include our praises (Psalm 69:30–31), our prayers (Revelation 5:8), our practices (Micah 6:6–8) and our presents (Philippians 4:18).

Death for sin, and death to sin

'Who his own self bare our sins in his own body on the tree, that we, being dead to sins, should live unto righteousness: by whose stripes ye were healed.' 1 Peter 2:24

SUGGESTED FURTHER READING: Romans 6:1–14

Sin appears to us now to be too mean and trivial a thing for us to care about. Picture Paul going along the Appian way towards Rome, met by some Christians far away at Puteoli and afterwards by others at the Three Taverns. Can you imagine what was their conversation as Paul walked chained along the highway? Why, they would commune concerning Jesus, the resurrection, the Spirit, saints converted and souls in heaven. I can conceive that the soldiers and others who would come up with them along the Roman road, stopping at the taverns, and so on, would have many things to talk of. One of them would say, 'There will be a grand fight at the amphitheatre next week.' Another would say, 'Oh, but over at such a theatre there is a splendid show; a hundred beasts are to be slain in a single night, and the famous German gladiator is to exhibit his prowess tomorrow evening.' Others would ask, 'Who is to be commander in Spain next year?' or 'Who is appointed over the Praetorian Guard?' and the babble would be about a thousand things, but the apostle would be supremely indifferent to it all. Not a topic that any one of those soldiers, or any one of the people around him, could bring before him could interest him. He was dead to the things to which they were alive, and alive to the things to which they were dead. So is the Christian. The cross has killed him and the cross has quickened him. We are 'dead to sins' that we 'should live unto righteousness', and now our very power to enjoy sin, if indeed we are resting in Christ, is gone from us. We have lost now, by God's grace, the faculty which once was gratified with these things.

FOR MEDITATION: In their blindness to the things of God (2 Corinthians 4:4) it is only natural that the unconverted have their minds set on earthly things (Philippians 3:18–19). But Christians have received a different outlook and should lift their eyes accordingly from earthly things to heavenly things (Philippians 3:20–21; Colossians 3:1–2). What are you looking at?

SERMON NO. 1143

Our Lord's humanity a sweet source of comfort

'Then there came again and touched me one like the appearance of a man, and he strengthened me.' Daniel 10:18
SUGGESTED FURTHER READING: Hebrews 9:15–28

Do you feel yourselves guilty before God? Do you wish for mercy? Come, then, and come directly, for Jesus Christ, a man like yourselves, invites you. Remember, you cannot go to God without a mediator, but you may go to Christ without one: you may go just as you are. You need no introduction to Jesus. I know that you can go and tell another man like yourself your sin, for some are so foolish as to do so. They confess their sins to the priests, like Judas did, but you know Judas then went and hanged himself, which was a very likely thing to do after such a confession. But if you will go and tell your sins to Jesus, who is a man and something more than a man, he will hear your story, and it will not pollute his ear. He will listen to it and do more; he will absolve you effectually. Have you not felt, now that you have grown up, that you wished you were boys again, so that you could go at night and tell mother all that you had done wrong during the day, so that mother might kiss you and you would go to bed feeling that everything was right again? Well, there is no mortal to whom you can go for such forgiveness now, but the Lord Jesus Christ will be to you all that your mother was to you when you were a child. Go and tell him all about it, and ask him to wash you in his blood and cover you with his righteousness, and he will forgive you as freely as your own kind mother would have done. Jesus Christ will feel for you, for he knows all your temptations and weaknesses. If there is any sort of excuse to be made for you, he will make it: he did that for his murderers when he said, 'Father, forgive them; for they know not what they do.' For that which cannot be mitigated at all he has something a great deal better than an excuse, namely his own atoning sacrifice.

FOR MEDITATION: By virtue of his atoning sacrifice upon the cross the Lord Jesus Christ is fully equipped and qualified to act as our intercessor (Romans 8:34; Hebrews 7:25–27), mediator (1 Timothy 2:5–6; Hebrews 9:14–15; 12:24) and advocate with the Father (1 John 1:7–2:1). He does not require the assistance of human priestly 'confessors'.

SERMON NO. 1295

Jesus interceding for transgressors

'And made intercession for the transgressors.' Isaiah 53:12
SUGGESTED FURTHER READING: 1 Timothy 2:1–8

If Christ appears in heaven for us, let us be glad to appear on earth for him. He owns us before God and the holy angels; let us not be ashamed to confess him before men and devils. If Christ pleads with God for men, let us not be backward to plead with men for God. If he by his intercession saves us to the uttermost, let us hasten to serve him to the uttermost. If he spends eternity in intercession for us, let us spend our time in intercession for his cause. If he thinks of us, we ought also to think of his people and especially supplicate for his afflicted. If he watches our cases and adapts his prayers to our necessities, let us observe the needs of his people and plead for them with understanding. Alas, how soon do men weary of pleading for the Lord. If a whole day is set apart for prayer and the meeting is not carefully managed, it readily becomes a weariness of the flesh. Prayer-meetings very easily lose their flame and burn low. Shame on these laggard spirits and this heavy flesh of ours, which needs to be pampered with liveliness and brevity, or we go to sleep at our devotions. For ever is not too long for him to plead, and yet an hour tries us here. On and on and on through all the ages, still his intercession rises to the throne, and yet we flag and our prayers are half dead in a short season. See, Moses lets his hands hang down, and Amalek is defeating Joshua in the plain! Can we endure to be thus losing victories and causing the enemy to triumph? If your ministers are unsuccessful, if your labourers for Christ in foreign lands make little headway, and if the work of Christ drags, is it not because in the secret place of intercession we have but little strength? The restraining of prayer is the weakening of the church.

FOR MEDITATION: Although we are unable to match the everlasting nature of Christ's intercession for us (Hebrews 7:25), our intercessions on behalf of others are supposed to be wide-ranging (1 Timothy 2:1–2). Giving up is not an option, because the Holy Spirit is ever-present to help us in our weakness (Romans 8:26–27).

Christ the end of the law

'For Christ is the end of the law for righteousness to every one that believeth.' Romans 10:4
SUGGESTED FURTHER READING: Galatians 3:23–4:7

'Christ is the end of the law' in the sense that he is the termination of it. His people are not under it as a covenant of life. We 'are not under the law, but under grace'. The old covenant as it stood with father Adam was, 'This do and thou shalt live'; its command he did not keep and consequently he did not live, nor do we live in him, since in Adam all died. The old covenant was broken and we became condemned thereby, but now, having suffered death in Christ, we are no more under it, but are dead to it. Brethren, at this present moment, although we rejoice to do good works, we are not seeking life through them; we are not hoping to obtain divine favour by our own goodness, nor even to keep ourselves in the love of God by any merit of our own. Chosen, not for our works, but according to the eternal will and good pleasure of God, and called, not of works, but by the Spirit of God, we desire to continue in this grace and return no more to the bondage of the old covenant. Since we have put our trust in an atonement provided and applied by grace through Jesus Christ, we are no longer slaves but children, not working to be saved, but saved already and working because we are saved. Neither that which we do, nor even that which the Spirit of God works in us, is to us the ground and basis of the love of God toward us, since he loved us from the first, because he would love us, unworthy though we were; and he loves us still in Christ and looks upon us not as we are in ourselves, but as we are in him, washed in his blood and covered in his righteousness; 'ye are not under the law'.

FOR MEDITATION: (*Our Own Hymn Book* no.647 v.4—William Cowper, 1779)

'Then all my servile works were done
A righteousness to raise;
Now, freely chosen in the Son,
I freely choose His ways.'

SERMON NO. 1325

The stern pedagogue

'Wherefore the law was our schoolmaster to bring us unto Christ, that we might be justified by faith. But after that faith is come, we are no longer under a schoolmaster.' Galatians 3:24–25
SUGGESTED FURTHER READING: Romans 3:9–20

Many transgressors argue, 'I have not done worse than other people,' to which the law replies, 'What have you to do with other people? Each individual must stand or fall on his account before the law. The law is to *you*. If another has broken it, he shall be punished even as you shall, inasmuch as you have broken it.' Then the man cries, 'But I have been better than others.' But the law says, 'If you have not walked perfectly in all the ways of the Lord your God to do them, I have nothing to do with comparing you with others: for this is my sentence, "Cursed is every one that continueth not in all things which are written in the book of the law to do them."' Now, these are not my words, but the words of God by his servant Moses, and there they stand like a flaming sword, turning every way and blocking up the legal road to the tree of life. Conscience, when it is really awakened by the law, confesses herself condemned and ceases to uphold her plea of innocence. How can it be otherwise when the law is so stern? Then perhaps the man will say, 'I mean to do better in the future,' to which the law replies, 'What have I to do with that? It is already due that you should be perfect in the future, and if you should be perfect, in what way would that wipe out your old offences? You will only have done what you ought to have done.' But the man cries, 'I do repent of having done wrong.' 'Yes,' says the law, 'but I have nothing to do with repentance.' There is no provision in the ten commandments for repentance. Cursed is the man that breaks the law; and that is all that the law has to say to him.

FOR MEDITATION: (*Our Own Hymn Book* no.647 v.2—William Cowper, 1779)
> 'How long beneath the law I lay
> In bondage and distress!
> I toiled the precept to obey,
> But toiled without success.'

The story of a runaway slave

'Perhaps he therefore departed for a season, that thou shouldest receive him for ever.' Philemon 15

SUGGESTED FURTHER READING: Colossians 3:18–4:1

Rowland Hill used to say that he would not give a halfpenny for a man's piety if his dog and his cat were not better off after he was converted. There was much weight in that remark. Everything in the house goes better when grace oils the wheels. The mistress is, perhaps, rather sharp and quick; well she gets a little sugar into her constitution when she receives the grace of God. The servant may be apt to loiter, be late up of a morning, very slovenly and fond of a gossip at the door, but, if she is truly converted, all that kind of thing ends. She is conscientious and attends to her duty as she ought. The master—well, he is the master, and you know it. But when he is a truly Christian man, he has a gentleness, a suavity, a considerateness about him. The husband is the head of the wife, but when renewed by grace he is not at all the head of the wife as some husbands are. The wife also keeps her place and seeks by all gentleness and wisdom to make the house as happy as she can. I do not believe in your religion, dear friend, if it belongs to the Tabernacle and the prayer-meeting, but not to your home. The best religion in the world is that which smiles at the table, works at the sewing-machine, and is amiable in the drawing-room. Give me the religion which blacks boots and does them well, which cooks the food and cooks it so that it can be eaten, which measures out yards of cloth and does not make them half-an-inch short, and which sells a hundred yards of an article and does not label ninety a hundred, as many tradespeople do. That is the true Christianity which affects the whole of life. If we are truly Christians we shall be changed in all our relationships to our fellow men.

FOR MEDITATION: It is right and proper that 'all things be done decently and in order' at church (1 Corinthians 14:40), but this should be equally true of the Christian's life at home, whether as husband (Ephesians 5:25,28,33; 1 Peter 3:7), wife (Ephesians 5:22–24; Titus 2:4–5; 1 Peter 3:1–6), parent (Ephesians 6:4; Titus 2:4) or child (Ephesians 6:1–3; 1 Timothy 5:4).

SERMON NO. 1268

The reception of sinners

'But the father said to his servants, Bring forth the best robe, and put it on him; and put a ring on his hand, and shoes on his feet: And bring hither the fatted calf, and kill it; and let us eat and be merry.' Luke 15:22–23

SUGGESTED FURTHER READING: Acts 16:11–34

It is not the Lord's desire that sinners should tarry long in the state of unbelieving conviction of sin; it is something wrong in themselves which keeps them there; either they are ignorant of the freeness and fulness of Christ, or they harbour self-righteous hopes or cling to their sins. 'Sin lieth at the door'; it is no work of God which blocks the way. He delights in their delight and joys in their joy. It is the Father's will that the penitent sinner should at once believe in Jesus, find complete forgiveness, and enter into rest. If any of you came to Jesus without the dreary interval of terror which is so frequent, do not judge yourselves as though your conversions were dubious; they are all the more instead of all the less genuine because they bear the marks of the gospel rather than of the law. The weeping of Peter, which in a few days turns to joy, is far better than the horror of Judas, which ends in suicide. Conversions, as recorded in Scripture, are for the most part exceedingly rapid. People were pricked in the heart at Pentecost, and the same day were baptized and added to the church, because they had found peace with God through Jesus Christ. Paul was smitten down with conviction, and in three days was a baptized believer. Sometimes God's power is so very near us that the lightning flash of conviction is often attended at the very same moment by the deep thunder of the Lord's voice, which drives away our fears and proclaims peace and pardon to the soul. In many cases the sharp needle of the law is immediately followed by the silken thread of the gospel; the showers of repentance are succeeded at once by the sunshine of faith.

FOR MEDITATION: (*Our Own Hymn Book* no.548 v.2—Mary Jane Deck, 1847)

'Though clothed with shame, by sin defiled,
The Father hath embraced His child;
And I am pardoned, reconciled,
O Lamb of God, in Thee!'

SERMON NO. 1204

A mighty plea

'*Thou has been my help; leave me not, neither forsake me.*' *Psalm* 27:9
SUGGESTED FURTHER READING: Psalm 62:1–12

In times of distress it is somewhat a difficulty to have a choice of helpers, because while we are making our selection, the danger may have overtaken us. While the fox was considering which way to run, the hounds had seized him; while the sick man was selecting the physician and judging of the medicine, his disease carried him off. It is well to be shut up to one sole help, if that help is all we need; it is for our good, in such a case, to have no alternative, but to have, as the old proverb has it, Hobson's choice—that or none. The believer is exactly in that condition; he must trust in his God or remain without hope. He dares not look to others as he once did, for he has discovered their incompetence; he cannot rely upon himself as he was once foolish enough to do, for he has learned by bitter experience the folly of self-confidence. He is compelled to look to the Lord alone. Blessed is that wind which drives the ship into the harbour; blessed is that wave which washes the mariner upon the rock of safety; and blessed is that distress which forces a man to rest only in his God. Such was the condition of the psalmist when he wrote the text; his spirit looked to God alone; in his past experience the goodness of the Lord shone forth as the pole star of his life's voyage, and, therefore, as to the future, he fixed his eye steadily on that one sure guiding light, and trusted in the God of his salvation.

FOR MEDITATION: (*Our Own Hymn Book* no.734 v.3—John Newton, 1779)
  'His love in time past forbids me to think
  He'll leave me at last in trouble to sink;
  Each sweet Ebenezer I have in review,
  Confirms His good pleasure to help me quite through.'

For the sick and afflicted

'Surely it is meet to be said unto God, I have borne chastisement, I will not offend any more: that which I see not teach thou me: if I have done iniquity, I will do no more.' Job 34:31–32
SUGGESTED FURTHER READING: Hebrews 12:1–4

Do you find in the law that any sin is excused upon the ground that it is constitutional? Do you find anything in the example of Christ, or in the precepts of the gospel, to justify a man in saying, 'I must be treated with indulgence, for my nature is so inclined to a certain sin that I cannot help yielding to it'? You must not talk such nonsense. Your first business is to conquer the sin you love best; against it all your efforts and all the grace you can get must be levelled. Jericho must be first besieged, for it is the strongest fort of the enemy, and until it is taken nothing can be done. I have generally noticed in conversion that the most complete change takes place in that very point in which the man was constitutionally most weak. God's strength is made perfect in our weakness. 'Well', cries one, 'suppose I have a besetting sin; how can I help it?' I reply, if I knew that four fellows were going to beset me tonight on Clapham Common, I should take with me sufficient policemen to lock the fellows up. When a man knows that he has a besetting sin it is not for him to say, 'It is a besetting sin and I cannot help it;' he must, on the other hand, call for heavenly assistance against these besetments. If you have besetting sins and you know it, fight with them and overcome them by the blood of the Lamb. By faith in Jesus Christ besetting sins go to be led captive, and they must be led captive, for the child of God must overcome even to the end. We are to be 'more than conquerors through him that loved us'. Let the love of God, then, lead you to search yourselves and say, 'that which I see not teach thou me: if I have done iniquity, I will do no more.'

FOR MEDITATION: The Christian's attitude towards besetting sin should not be to continue in it (Romans 6:1–2), to be ruled by it (Romans 6:12–14), or to be a slave to it (Romans 6:16–17), but to lay it aside (Hebrews 12:1) and to strive against it (Hebrews 12:4).

Sins of ignorance

'And if a soul sin, and commit any of these things which are forbidden to
be done by the commandments of the LORD; though he wist it not, yet is
he guilty, and shall bear his iniquity. And he shall bring a ram without
blemish out of the flock, with thy estimation, for a trespass offering,
unto the priest: and the priest shall make an atonement for him
concerning his ignorance wherein he erred and wist it not, and it shall be
forgiven him.' Leviticus 5:17–18
SUGGESTED FURTHER READING: Numbers 15:17–31

Knowledge of the law was a duty and ignorance a crime. Can one sin be
an excuse for another? It is a sin to refuse to search into the word of
God: can it be that because a man commits this sin he is to be excused
for the faults into which his wilful ignorance leads him? It is out of the
question. If sins of ignorance are not sins, Christ's intercession was
superfluous. Our text last Sabbath morning (see 18 November) was 'he
… made intercession for the transgressors'; we illustrated it by the text
'Father, forgive them; for they know not what they do.' If there is no sin
when a man does not know what he does, why did our Lord pray for
ignorant transgressors? Why ask forgiveness if there be no wrong? The
correct way of putting it would have been, 'Father, I do not ask thee to
forgive, for there is no offence, seeing that they know not what they do';
but by his pleading for forgiveness it is clearly proved that there is guilt
in the sin of ignorance. The work of the Holy Spirit would be evil instead
of a good work in the hearts of men, if ignorance were an excuse for sin,
for he has come to convince the world of sin; but if, unconvinced of sin,
they are innocent, why convince them of it? Of what use is it to quicken a
conscience, enlighten it and make it bleed over a transgression, if it
would be no transgression, provided that conscience had never been
made cognisant of it? Who shall so blaspheme the Holy Spirit as to say
that his work is needless and even idle? Sins of ignorance, therefore, must
be sinful.

FOR MEDITATION: Ignorance is associated with foolishness (Psalm 73:22;
1 Peter 2:15), blindness (Ephesians 4:18), unbelief (1 Timothy 1:13), lusts
(1 Peter 1:14) and wilfulness (2 Peter 3:5). Far from being 'bliss',
ignorance calls for repentance (Acts 3:17–19; 17:30).

SERMON NO. 1386

Christ the conqueror of Satan

'And I will put enmity between thee and the woman, and between thy seed and her seed; it shall bruise thy head, and thou shalt bruise his heel.'
Genesis 3:15
SUGGESTED FURTHER READING: Luke 5:1–11

The text evidently encouraged Adam very much. I do not think we have attached enough importance to the conduct of Adam after the Lord had spoken to him. Notice the simple but conclusive proof which he gave of his faith. Sometimes an action may be very small and unimportant, and yet, as a straw shows which way the wind blows, it may display at once, if it be thought over, the whole state of the man's mind. Adam acted in faith upon what God said, for we read, 'And Adam called his wife's name Eve; because she was the mother of all living' (Genesis 3:20). She was not a mother at all, but as the life was to come through her by virtue of the promised seed, Adam marks his full conviction of the truth of the promise, though at the time the woman had borne no children. There stood Adam, fresh from the awful presence of God; what more could he say? He might have said with the psalmist, 'My flesh trembleth for fear of thee', but even then he turns round to his fellow-culprit as she stands there trembling too, and he calls her Eve, mother of the life that is yet to be. It was grandly spoken by father Adam: it makes him rise in our esteem. Had he been left to himself he would have murmured or at least despaired, but no, his faith in the new promise gave him hope. He uttered no word of repining against the condemnation to till with toil the unthankful ground, nor on Eve's part was there a word of repining over the appointed sorrows of motherhood; they each accepted the well-deserved sentence with the silence which denotes the perfection of their resignation; their only word is full of simple faith. There was no child on whom to set their hopes, nor would the true seed be born for many an age, still Eve is to be 'the mother of all living', and he calls her so. Exercise like faith.

FOR MEDITATION: Consider some occasions when faith in God's word overcame apparently reasonable objections such as those raised by Abraham (Genesis 15:1–6), Moses (Exodus 6:10–13), Samuel (1 Samuel 16:1–4), Peter (Luke 5:4–6) and Ananias (Acts 9:10–17).

Work for Jesus

'Son, go work to-day in my vineyard.' Matthew 21:28
SUGGESTED FURTHER READING: Titus 3:1–15

The text says, 'go work'. That is something practical, something real. It does not say, 'My son, go and think, speculate, make curious experiments, fetch out some new doctrines, and astonish all your fellow-creatures with whims and oddities of your own.' 'Son, go work.' It does not say, 'My son, go and attend conferences one after another all the year round and live in a perpetual maze of hearing different opinions and going from one public meeting and one religious engagement to another, and so feed yourself on the fat things full of marrow.' All this is to be attended to in its proper proportion, but here it is 'go work'. How many Christians there are that seem to read, 'go plan'. They always figure in a way with some wonderful plan for the conversion of all the world, but they are never found labouring to convert a baby, never having a good word to say to the tiniest child in the Sunday-school. They are always scheming and yet never effecting anything. But the text says, 'Son, go work'. Yes, but those who do not like to work themselves display the greatness of their talents in finding fault with those who do work, and a very clear perception they have of the mistakes and crotchets of the very best of workers, whose zeal and industry are alike unflagging. Howbeit the text does not say, 'My son, go and criticise'; what it distinctly says is, 'go work'. I remember that when Andrew Fuller had a very severe lecture from some Scottish Baptist brethren about the discipline of the church, he made the reply, 'You say that your discipline is so much better than ours. Very well, but discipline is meant to make good soldiers. Now, my soldiers fight better than yours, and I think therefore that you ought not to say much about my discipline.'

FOR MEDITATION: When Jesus said 'go', it was usually with some express activity in mind: go and learn (Matthew 9:13), go and preach (Matthew 10:7; Mark 16:15; Luke 9:60), go and show (Matthew 11:4; Luke 5:14; 17:14), go and tell (Matthew 18:15; 28:10; Mark 5:19; Luke 13:32), go and teach (Matthew 28:19), go and do (Luke 10:37), go and prepare (Luke 22:8), go and call (John 4:16), go and wash (John 9:7) and go and say (John 20:17). Inactivity is inconsistent with Christian life.

The spur

'Whatsoever thy hand findeth to do, do it with thy might; for there is no work, nor device, nor knowledge, nor wisdom, in the grave, whither thou goest.' Ecclesiastes 9:10
SUGGESTED FURTHER READING: 2 Corinthians 8:16–23

There are choice spirits in the world, into whose ears the Holy Spirit whispers grand designs such as he does not reveal to all men. Here and there he finds a soul that he makes congenial to himself, and then he inspires it with great wishes, deep longings and grand designs for glorifying God. Do not quench them; do not starve them by holding them back, but as death is coming, do what is in you and 'do it with thy might'. No man knows what God means to do through his agency, for often the very feeblest have conceived the greatest purposes. John Pounds and his ragged-school—who was John Pounds? A poor cobbler. Robert Raikes with his Sunday-school—who was Robert Raikes? Nobody in particular, but Sunday-schools have come to something. *You* may have a sublime conception in your soul. Do not strangle it; nurse the heaven-born thought for God, and the first opportunity you can find, carry out the idea to its practical issues, and throw your might into it. There must be some young Christian here who loves his Master, and who means to do something for him before he dies. 'That thou doest, do quickly.' Do I not address some young man of a noble spirit, who feels, 'I could be wealthy; I could gain a position in my profession; I could become famous and get honour for myself, but from this hour I will lay all down at the foot of the cross, and lay myself out for the good of souls and the glory of God'? Go and do it. Do not dream, but work. Do not listen to the sirens which would enchant you by their music and draw you from the rough sea of duty. Launch forth in God's name, yield yourself up to the winds of heaven, and they will bear you straight on in the course of devoted service. The Lord help you to do with your might what you find to do.

FOR MEDITATION: Loving the Lord our God with all our might constitutes part of the greatest commandment (Deuteronomy 6:5; Mark 12:28–30) and requires obedience. But we must never forget to rely on the Lord our God as the source of all our might (Judges 6:12–16; Ephesians 3:14–16; 6:10; Colossians 1:11).

All for Jesus

'Ye serve the Lord Christ.' Colossians 3:24
SUGGESTED FURTHER READING: Mark 14:1–9

Every now and then for Jesus there ought to be a little special wastefulness of love. The woman with her alabaster box of very precious ointment would no doubt have very gladly poured water on his feet when he came into the house weary, or she would have waited at the table when he ate. But all this would not have sufficed her ardent love; she wanted to perform an extraordinary act which should be all for him: she looked out that precious box; she must break that, for she would give him something which she could not afford to give every day, in fact, which she never did attempt to give except once in her life. Brothers and sisters, think of something special you can do for Jesus. Let it cost you something, and if it pinches you, so much the better; it will be sweet to bear a pinch for him. Think of something that you could not justify in prudence if you had to sit down and talk it over. Do it for him, not to talk about to others afterwards, nor for others to blazen abroad, but do it for him: and then if they do publish it you need not be angry, for Jesus said, 'Wheresoever this gospel shall be preached in the whole world, there shall also this, that this woman hath done, be told for a memorial of her.' Be not ostentatious, but do not be in such a great worry to hide your work for Jesus, for the knowledge of it may do other people good and lead them to imitate the deed. Still do it unto Jesus only. I cannot suggest what you shall do and it would be indelicate for me to attempt to do so. Who would think of suggesting to a wife what she should give to her husband as a special private love token? These things are too choice for others to meddle with; they are secrets between the Lord and his elect, suggestions of personal love which cannot come from outside.

FOR MEDITATION: (*Our Own Hymn Book* no.710 v.3—Cento by John Hampden Gurney, 1838–51; from John Mason, 1683)
    ''Tis Thou dost crown my hopes and plans
    With good success each day;
    This crown, together with myself,
    At Thy blest feet I lay.'

The great jail, and how to get out of it

'But the scripture hath concluded all under sin, that the promise by faith of Jesus Christ might be given to them that believe.' Galatians 3:22
SUGGESTED FURTHER READING: Ephesians 2:1–10

The plan of salvation by grace has this beauty about it, that it gives men high thoughts of God. In the other systems their idea of God is that he is very much like themselves. See the Catholic's God. He is pleased with candles and delights in incense; he is a God who likes show, garments of blue and scarlet, dolls dressed up and flowers on his altars. I know not what kind of God to call him. However, that is their notion of him. They try to save themselves, and they pull God down to their standard; and every man who is a self-saver, even if he be a Protestant, lowers God in some manner. He fancies that God will accept something short of perfection. Each man has a different standard. That miserly old gentleman's standard is that he will build a row of almshouses with his mouldy leavings, and that will content the Most High. Another says, 'I never open my shop on a Sunday.' Perhaps he cheats enough on Monday to make up for it, but Sunday's rest will do for his God. Another, who is living a wicked life in private, believes the doctrines of grace and that will satisfy his God. But the man who is saved by the grace of God says, 'My God is infinitely just; nothing will content him but a perfect righteousness; as a moral lawgiver, he would not put away sin till he had laid punishment upon one who stood in the sinner's stead. He is so loving that he gave his Son; he is so just that he slew his Son on my behalf.' All the divine attributes will splendour forth before the eyes of the man who is saved by faith, and he is led to reverence and to adore.

FOR MEDITATION: (*Our Own Hymn Book* no.554 v.1—Isaac Watts, 1709)
    'No more, my God, I boast no more
    Of all the duties I have done;
    I quit the hopes I held before,
    To trust the merits of Thy Son.'

SERMON NO. 1145

The evidence of our Lord's wounds

'Then saith he to Thomas, Reach hither thy finger, and behold my hands; and reach hither thy hand, and thrust it into my side: and be not faithless, but believing.' John 20:27
SUGGESTED FURTHER READING: John 19:17–37

If you would have your faith made vivid and strong, study much the story of your Saviour's death. 'Take it: read it', said the voice to Augustine. So say I. Take the four evangelists; take the fifty-third chapter of Isaiah; take the twenty-second psalm; take all other parts of Scripture that relate to our suffering Substitute, and read them by day and night, till you familiarize yourself with the whole story of his griefs and sin-bearing. Keep your mind intently fixed upon it, not sometimes but continually. The cross is light. You shall see it by its own light. The study of the narrative, if you ask the Holy Spirit to enlighten you, will beget faith in you, and by its means you will be very greatly helped, till at last you will say, 'I cannot doubt. The truth of the atonement is impressed upon my memory, heart and understanding. The record has convinced me.' If this suffice not, frequently contemplate the sufferings of Jesus. When you have read the story, sit down and try to picture it. Let your mind conceive it as passing before you. Put yourself into the position of the apostles who saw him die. No employment will so greatly strengthen faith, and certainly none will be more enjoyable!

> 'Sweet the moments, rich in blessing, which before the cross I spend,
> Life and health and peace possessing from the sinner's dying Friend.'

An hour would be grandly spent if occupied in turning over each little detail, item and incident in the marvellous death by which you are redeemed from death and hell. You will be surprised to find how this familiarizing of yourself with it, by the help of the Holy Spirit, will make it as vivid to you as if you saw it.

FOR MEDITATION: (*Our Own Hymn Book* no.282 v.1—Isaac Watts, 1709)
'When I survey the wondrous cross on which the Prince of Glory died,
My richest gain I count but loss, and pour contempt on all my pride.'

God's thoughts and ways far above ours

'For my thoughts are not your thoughts, neither are your ways my ways, saith the LORD. *For as the heavens are higher than the earth, so are my ways higher than your ways, and my thoughts than your thoughts.'*
Isaiah 55:8–9
SUGGESTED FURTHER READING: 2 Peter 3:1–18

God's thoughts of truth are evidently not man's, for nothing but divine grace can bring man to believe the doctrines of the gospel, or keep him faithful to them. Each generation seems to bring forth a set of men who set themselves to oppose God's truth from some fresh point. We have among us a great company of men who have attained repute through daring to assail established truth, wise men if we take their own judgment of themselves, for they are never more at home than when sounding the praises of their own culture and breadth of mind. These Philistines have intruded into the temple under the pretence of trimming our lamps, but their aim is to put them out. Evangelistic light is too clear for them, and they seek to obscure it; hence they give new readings to texts which are translated by better scholars than they will ever be, and they put new interpretations upon the doctrines which their fathers held, interpretations which their sires would indignantly repudiate. Roughly speaking, these men deny everything which faith holds dear, and yet expect to be considered Christians. They tear the vitals from every truth, yet pretend to believe it. Their advanced thought, like a vampire, sucks the blood out of the veins of truth, and he who would drive away the foul thing is called a bigot and a fool. These reverend infidels are to be tolerated as ministers, or, if we decline to reckon those to be Christian ministers who spend all their energies in undermining Christianity, we are in danger of being ridiculed. It was always so. Man thinks himself so wise and good that he does not like God's thoughts concerning himself, his fall, his guilt and his danger.

FOR MEDITATION: (*Our Own Hymn Book* no.36 song 1 v.1—Isaac Watts, 1719)
   'High in the heavens, Eternal God,
   Thy goodness in full glory shines;
   Thy truth shall break through every cloud
   That veils and darkens Thy designs.'

SERMON NO. 1387

Christ, the overcomer of the world

'Be of good cheer; I have overcome the world.' John 16:33
SUGGESTED FURTHER READING: Luke 4:1–13

When men find themselves in a world like this, they generally say, 'What is our market? What can we make out of it?' This is how they are trained from childhood. 'Boy, you have to fight your own way; mind you look to your own interests and rise in the world.' The book which is commended to the young man shows him how to make the best use of all things for himself; he must take care of 'number one' and mind the main chance. The boy is told by his wise instructors, 'You must look to yourself or nobody else will look to you: and whatever you may do for others, be doubly sure to guard your own interests.' That is the world's prudence, the essence of all her politics, the basis of her political economy; every man and every nation must take care of themselves: if you wish for any other politics or economics, you will be considered to be foolish theorists and probably a little touched in the head. Self is the man, the world's law of self-preservation is the sovereign rule, and nothing can go on rightly if you interfere with the gospel of selfishness; so the commercial and political Solomons assure us. Now, look at the Lord Jesus Christ when he was in the world and you will learn nothing of such principles, except their condemnation: the world could not overcome him by leading him into a selfish mode of action. Did it ever enter into his soul, even for a moment, what he could do for himself? There were riches, but he had not where to lay his head. The little store he had he committed to the trust of Judas, and as long as there were any poor in the land they were sure to share in what was in the bag. He set so little account by estate, stock and funds that no mention is made of such things by any of his four biographers. He had wholly and altogether risen above the world.

FOR MEDITATION: (*Our Own Hymn Book* no.739 v.5—John Newton, 1779)
'As surely as He overcame,
And triumphed once for you;
So surely you that love His name
Shall triumph in Him too.'

SERMON NO. 1327

A lesson from the life of king Asa

'Herein thou hast done foolishly: therefore from henceforth thou shalt have wars.' 2 Chronicles 16:9
SUGGESTED FURTHER READING: Proverbs 3:1–8

I may be speaking as God's mouth to some of you who are now entering upon a testing time, a trouble in the family, a trial in business, or a difficulty in reference to a contemplated marriage, and you are asking, 'What course shall I take?' You know what a man of the world would do, and it has been suggested to you that such a course is the right one for you to follow. My dear brother, remember that you are not of the world, even as Christ is not of the world; mind you act accordingly. If you are a worldly man and do as worldly men do, then I must leave you, for 'them that are without God judgeth'. But if you are a man of God and an heir of heaven, I beseech you, do not follow custom, or do a wrong thing because others would do it, or do a little evil for the sake of a great good, but in your confidence possess your soul, and abide faithful to conscience and to the eternal law of rectitude. Let others do as they please, but as for you, set the Lord always before you, and let integrity and uprightness preserve you. Ask the Lord to help you. Is it not written that he 'will with the temptation also make a way to escape'? 'Cast thy burden upon the LORD, and he shall sustain thee: he shall never suffer the righteous to be moved.' Do not put forth your hand to iniquity. You may, in order to help yourself, do in five minutes what you cannot undo in fifty years, and you may bring upon yourself a lifelong series of trials by one single unbelieving action. Beware of relying on Egypt and sending for help to Assyria, for these will distress you, but not help you. Cry, 'Lord, Increase our faith.' That is what you greatly need in the trying hour.

FOR MEDITATION: (*Our Own Hymn Book* no.668 v.1—Mary Bowly, 1847)
> 'Lord, through the desert drear and wide
> Our erring footsteps need a guide;
> Keep us, oh keep us near Thy side.
> Let us not fall. Let us not fall.'

A great bargain

'Again, the kingdom of heaven is like unto a merchant man, seeking goodly pearls: Who, when he had found one pearl of great price, went and sold all that he had, and bought it.' Matthew 13:45–46
SUGGESTED FURTHER READING: 2 Corinthians 4:1–6

A merchantman endeavours to trade so as to make a profit. Whether he deals in pearls or in grain, he does not hope to obtain riches by labour. He leaves that to those who eat their bread in the sweat of their face. He tries to get his by the sweat of his brain. He is dependent not so much upon labour as upon knowledge, skill and the advantage which superior acquaintance with the article in which he deals gives to him. Now, this merchantman is, at the very commencement, in some measure a picture of the seeker after Christ. Christ and his salvation are not to be earned; they are not to be procured as the result of labour. But Christ is to be had by knowledge. What does the Scripture say? 'By his knowledge shall my righteous servant justify many', that is, through their knowing Christ they become justified. This is, indeed, another way of putting the system of salvation which is stated thus: 'how shall they hear without a preacher?' The work begins with hearing the preacher; then it goes on to believing what they hear, and through believing they are saved. This is virtually knowledge, the knowledge communicated by God's messenger or by God's word, the knowledge heard, the knowledge believed. So men come to the knowledge of him whom to know is life eternal, for when a man knows and understands Christ, so that he gives his heart to him, then is he saved. Inasmuch, then, as the merchantman seeks his advantage by superior knowledge, he becomes a type of the man who gets saved through obtaining 'the knowledge of the glory of God in the face of Jesus Christ'. In this parable we have a fit emblem of many who lay hold on Christ and find him to be their all in all.

FOR MEDITATION: Knowledge plays a vital role in the salvation of the sinner. First must come 'the knowledge of sin' (Romans 3:20); then we are well prepared to receive 'knowledge of salvation' (Luke 1:77) and 'the knowledge of the truth' (1 Timothy 2:4). Sadly many go in for the wrong kind of learning and never reach this goal (2 Timothy 3:7). How much do you know of these things?

SERMON NO. 1424

Heart-knowledge of God

'I will give them a heart to know me, that I am the LORD.*' Jeremiah* 24:7
SUGGESTED FURTHER READING: 1 John 2:3–14

It is not enough to know that our Creator is the Jehovah of the Bible, and that he is perfect in character and glorious beyond thought; to know God we must have perceived him, we must have spoken to him, we must have been made at peace with him, we must have lifted up our heart to him and received communications from him. If you know the Lord, your secret is with him and his secret is with you; he has manifested himself unto you as he does not unto the world. He must have made himself known unto you by the mysterious influences of his Spirit, and because of this you know him. I cannot explain this knowledge, but it is delightful to remember that many of you understand what it means by experience. Is it not sweet to traverse the world discerning God on every side, your Father ever near? Is it not a blessing to be in trouble and find him helping us, to be in a dilemma and to hear his voice saying, 'This is the way, walk ye in it', to be depressed in spirit and to feel that his comforts rejoice our souls, to be exulting in joy and to feel that his presence calms and sobers us and keeps us from undue delight in created things? It is inexpressibly honourable and joyful to walk with God as Enoch did, to speak with him as Abraham did of old 'as a man speaketh unto his friend', or to be hidden in the hollow of his hand, as Moses was in Horeb. This is to know God after the manner of the text. Do you know God? Have you beheld 'the glory of God in the face of Jesus Christ'? Have you discerned the Father in the Son? Do you see all the attributes of God shining mildly through the Mediator, toned down to our capacity, lest the splendour of the Deity should blind our finite sense? Do you know God by going to Jesus as your Saviour?

FOR MEDITATION: Knowledge of the truth (1 Timothy 2:4; 2 John 1) includes head-knowledge but must not be limited to that. The Christian is one who knows not only the word of truth (2 Timothy 2:15), but also the God of truth (John 17:3), Jesus the truth (John 14:6–7) and the Spirit of truth (John 14:16–17). Can you truthfully say that you have made their acquaintance?

SERMON NO. 1206

Consolation for the despairing

'For I said in my haste, I am cut off from before thine eyes: nevertheless thou heardest the voice of my supplications when I cried unto thee.'
Psalm 31:22
SUGGESTED FURTHER READING: Psalm 107:1–32

When David feared that he was cut off from God, he was wise enough to take to crying. He calls prayer crying, and it is a very significant word. Crying is the language of pain; pain cannot cumber itself with letters, syllables and words, and so it takes its own way and adopts a piercing mode of utterance, very telling and expressive. Crying yields great relief to suffering. Every one knows the benefit of having a hearty good cry: you cannot help calling it 'a good cry', for, though one would think crying could never be especially good, yet it affords a desirable relief. Red eyes often relieve breaking hearts. Madness has been prevented by the soul's finding vent. Prayer is the surest and most blessed vent for the soul. In prayer the heart runs over as the eyelids do in crying. To pray is just as simple a matter as to cry. Do not get down that book: bishops and other prayer-makers can write good prayers for people who have no particular trouble upon them, but when you really need to pray, no ready-made prayers will suit your case. You never heard of a form of common crying. I never recollect seeing in my life a form of crying for a bereaved woman, a form for a babe to cry when it is hungry, and another form for a child to cry when it is put to bed in the dark. No, forms are out of the question when we cry. Men, women and children, when in trouble, cry without a book; and so when a man really wants the Saviour, he does not require prayer-books. Never say, 'I cannot pray!' My dear friend, can you cry? You want to be saved; tell the Lord that. If you cannot say it in words, tell it with your tears, your groans, your sighs, your sobs. Prayer, like crying, is a natural utterance, and an utterance available on all occasions.

FOR MEDITATION: The great turning-point for the children of Israel enslaved in Egypt was when they cried to God for help (Exodus 2:23–25; 3:7–10). God loves to save those who in faith cry to him for help (Psalm 34:6,17; Luke 18:7–8) and the Lord Jesus Christ demonstrated this on many occasions (Matthew 9:27–29; 14:30–31; 15:22–23,28: 20:29–34; Mark 9:23–25).

SERMON NO. 1146

Jesus Christ himself

'Jesus Christ himself.' Ephesians 2:20
SUGGESTED FURTHER READING (Spurgeon): Song of Solomon 5:8–16

It is essential to disciples that they know their Lord. His nature, his character, his mind, his spirit, his object and his power we must know—in a word, we must know Jesus himself. This is the work of the Holy Spirit. 'He shall glorify me: for he shall receive of mine, and shall shew it unto you.' The Holy Spirit reveals Christ to us and in us. Whatsoever Christ has spoken while he was here, the Holy Spirit opens to the mind and to the understanding, and thus by speaking of Christ within us he carries on the work which our Lord began when here below. The Comforter is the instructor and Jesus is the lesson. I dare say you long to know a thousand things, but the main point of knowledge to be desired is Jesus himself. This was his teaching, this is the Holy Spirit's teaching, and this is the end and object of the Bible. Moses, Isaiah and all the prophets spoke of him, and the things which are recorded in this book were 'written, that ye might believe that Jesus is the Christ, the Son of God; and that believing ye might have life through his name.' Precious is this book, but its main preciousness lies in its revealing Jesus himself; it is the field which contains the pearl of great price, the casket which encloses heaven's brightest jewel. We have missed our way in the Bible if its silken clue has not led us to the central chamber where we see Jesus himself. We have never been truly taught of the Holy Spirit, and we have missed the teaching of the life of Christ, unless we have come to abide in Jesus himself. To know him is our beginning of wisdom and our crown of wisdom. To know him is our first lesson on the stool of penitence and our last attainment as we enter heaven. Our ambition is that we 'know the love of Christ, which passeth knowledge'. Here is our life study.

FOR MEDITATION: The Holy Spirit points not to himself, but to the Lord Jesus Christ (John 16:13–15). The same will be true of the Christian who is maintaining a close walk with God (2 Corinthians 4:5). Individuals who are self-centred and congregations which are church-centred both need to learn how to become Christ-centred.

Speak for yourself. A challenge!

'He is of age; ask him: he shall speak for himself.' John 9:21
SUGGESTED FURTHER READING: Mark 5:1–20

You working men, if you were all to speak up for Christ, what an effect would be produced: what an influence you would have on others like you. Of course when they hear us preach, they say, 'Oh well, you know, he is a parson. He says it professionally. It is his business to say it.' But when you tell of what the Lord has done for you, it becomes the talk: it is repeated over and over again. I know what Tom says when he gets home. He says to his wife Mary, 'What do you think of that Jack that I have been working with? Why, he has been talking to me about his soul, and he says his sin is forgiven him, and he seems such a happy man. You know that he used to drink and swear the same as I do, but he is a wonderfully different man now; and I should say, from what I see, there must be something in it. Well, he asked me home the other night, and his place is so different from ours.' 'There, you hold your tongue,' Mary will answer up pretty sharply: 'if you brought your wages home to me regularly every week, I could lay them out for you better.' 'Ah' says he, 'and that is what I have been thinking. It is just because he is a religious man that he does bring his wages home, and I think there is something real about his conversion. He does not drink as I do. He does not get mixed up with all manners of larks and follies. I should not have thought so much of it had the parson spoken to me. But now I really do think there is something good and genuine in the grace he talks about. You and I had better go next Sunday evening to the Tabernacle, or somewhere else, and hear about it for ourselves.' There are many, many souls brought to Christ in that way. We cannot do without your testimony, Jack, because your conversation is suitable to your own class.

FOR MEDITATION: (*Our Own Hymn Book* no.670 v.1—Isaac Watts, 1709)
'I'm not ashamed to own my Lord,
Or to defend His cause;
Maintain the honour of His word,
The glory of His cross.'

Christ the maker of all things new

'Therefore if any man be in Christ, he is a new creature: old things are passed away; behold, all things are become new.' 2 Corinthians 5:17
SUGGESTED FURTHER READING: Revelation 21:1–7

'Unto us a child is born' who is the virgin's son, in whom we rejoice because he comes into the world without taint of original sin, after a new fashion, as never man was born before. Coming thus into the old world, he publishes new doctrine, called gospel or good news. It is the freshest news that an anxious heart can hear, the most novel music by which a troubled breast can be soothed. Jesus Christ's teaching is still the best news of these days, as it was centuries ago. Though the world has had nearly 1900 years of the glad tidings, the gospel has the dew of its youth upon it, and when men hear it they still ask, as the Greeks did of old, 'what this new doctrine … is?' Our Lord Jesus has come to set up, by the preaching of the gospel, a new kingdom having new laws, new customs, a new charter and new riches, a kingdom which is not of this world, a kingdom founded upon better principles and bringing infinitely better results to its subjects than any other dominion that has ever been. Into that kingdom he introduces new people, who are made new creatures in Christ Jesus, who therefore love his new commandment and serve him 'in newness of spirit, and not in the oldness of the letter'. Moreover, Christ has opened for us an entrance into the kingdom of heaven above, for now we come to God 'by a new and living way, which he hath consecrated for us, through the veil, that is to say, his flesh'. When in days to come we shall meet him again there will still be novelty, for he has said, 'I will not drink henceforth of this fruit of the vine, until that day when I drink it new with you in my Father's kingdom.' Indeed, concerning our Lord and Master everything is new.

FOR MEDITATION: God makes 'all things new' (Revelation 21:5); 'think on these things': a new covenant (1 Corinthians 11:25; Hebrews 9:15), a new communion with God (Hebrews 10:20), a new creation (2 Corinthians 5:17), a new comprehension of God (Lamentations 3:22–23), a new chorus (Psalm 40:3; 96:1–3; Revelation 5:9–10; 14:3), a new conduct (Romans 6:4; Ephesians 4:22–24), a new commandment (John 13:34–35) and a new cosmos (2 Peter 3:13; Revelation 21:1). Have you been renewed?

SERMON NO. 1328

Strengthening medicine for God's servants

'I will not fail thee, nor forsake thee.' Joshua 1:5
SUGGESTED FURTHER READING: Psalm 89:1–8

Surely this word must often have brought charming consolation to the heart of the son of Nun when he saw the people failing him. There was only the venerable Caleb left of all his comrades with whom he had shared the forty years' march through the great and terrible wilderness; Caleb and he were the last two sheaves of the great harvest, and they were both like shocks of corn fully ripe for the garner. Old men grow lonely, and small wonder it is if they do. I have heard them say that they live in a world where they are not known, now that, one by one, all their old friends are gone home, and they are left alone like the last swallow of autumn when all its fellows have sought a sunnier clime. Yet the Lord says, 'I will not forsake you: I shall not die: I am ever with you. Your Friend in heaven will live on as long as you do.' As for the generation which had sprung up around Joshua, they were very little better than their fathers; they 'turned back in the day of battle', even 'The children of Ephraim, being armed, and carrying bows'. They were very apt to go aside into the most provoking sin. Joshua had as hard a task with them as Moses had, and it was enough to break the heart of Moses to have to do with them. The Lord seems to bid him put no confidence in them, neither to be discomforted if they should be false and treacherous: 'I will not fail you: they may, but I will not. I will not forsake you. They may prove cowards and traitors, but I will not desert you.' What a blessed thing it is in a false and fickle world, where he that eats bread with us lifts up his heel against us, and where the favourite counsellor becomes an Ahithophel and turns his wisdom into crafty hate, to know that 'there is a friend that sticketh closer than a brother', one who is faithful.

FOR MEDITATION: (*Our Own Hymn Book* no.745 v.1—John Fawcett, 1782)

'Afflicted soul, to Jesus dear,
Thy Saviour's gracious promise hear;
His faithful word declares to thee
That "as thy day, thy strength shall be."'

The eternal truth of God

'His truth endureth to all generations.' Psalm 100:5
SUGGESTED FURTHER READING: John 7:14–31

The old serpent who deceived our first parents has fearfully perverted our judgment and turned aside our souls from their integrity, so that we often 'put bitter for sweet, and sweet for bitter', and frequently we believe a lie and reject the truth. But 'God is not a man, that he should lie'. His very name is 'The LORD God ... abundant in goodness and truth'. This is a part of his holiness: the angels could not cry, 'Holy, holy, holy, is the LORD of hosts', if God were not true. Admit for a single moment untruthfulness on the part of God, and you have at once destroyed the wholeness, or holiness, of his ever blessed and adorable character. What makes men untruthful? Whatever it may be, it is clear that nothing of the kind can operate with God. When a man tells a lie, it is often through fear, fear of the consequences of the truth; but the eternal Jehovah cannot dread consequences: he is omnipotent; all things are in his hands. When a man utters a lie, he frequently does so because he thinks there is no other way of accomplishing his end; but the infinite wisdom of God is never short of resources: he knows how to accomplish his will and pleasure without adopting the mean devices and paltry schemes of poor pitiful man. Man sometimes promises what he cannot perform, and then he is false to his promise; but that can never be the case with the Almighty, who has only to speak and it is done, to command and it stands fast. Falsehood is the wickedness—I dare not call it the infirmity—of little natures; but as for the Great Supreme, you cannot conceive him acting in any manner that is otherwise than straightforward, upright and truthful. A God of truth and righteousness is he essentially. He must be so.

FOR MEDITATION: (*Our Own Hymn Book* no.100 version 4 v.4—Isaac Watts, 1719)
 'The Lord is good, the Lord is kind;
 Great is His grace, His mercy sure;
 And the whole race of man shall find
 His truth from age to age endure.'

SERMON NO. 1265

A solemn impeachment of unbelievers

'He that believeth not God hath made him a liar; because he believeth not the record that God gave of his Son.' 1 John 5:10
SUGGESTED FURTHER READING: Romans 1:18–25

What does Jesus say in John 8:45? He says, 'because I tell you the truth, ye believe me not.' Strange reason for not believing a statement—because it is true! Yet there are thousands of individuals whose capacity for believing a lie is enormous, but whose ability for accepting truth appears to have gone from them. When religious impostures have arisen, the very men who have heard the gospel from their youth up and have not received it because it is true, have become dupes of imposition at once. The truth did not suit their nature, which was under the dominion of the father of lies, but no sooner was a transparent lie brought under their notice than they leaped at it at once like a fish at a fly. The monstrous credulity of unbelief amazes me! I meet with people who consider themselves to be bold thinkers and philosophers, and they express their astonishment that I can really believe the things which I preach: but no sooner do I learn from them what their positive creed is, than the astonishment comes to be on my side, and is a thousand times greater than theirs could be. The faith which accepts Christ has but a small throat indeed compared with that credulity which believes, for instance, in the development of man from a protoplasm—that creed requires the swallow of the great fish which swallowed Jonah entire. A lie you will believe, but because the gospel is true you do not believe it. 'You give us a bad character,' says one. It is your true character. Some of you are so in the habit of accepting no teaching except that which chimes in with your depraved tastes and sceptical notions, that because the gospel is true, and therefore comes across your impure tastes, you cannot endure it.

FOR MEDITATION: Rejection of God's truth does not result in 'sitting on the fence' but leads to embracing lies (John 8:44; Romans 1:25), delusions (2 Thessalonians 2:10–12), fables (2 Timothy 4:4; Titus 1:14) and error (1 John 4:6). We obey either the truth or wickedness (Romans 2:8).

SERMON NO. 1207

The gentleness of Jesus

'He shall not strive, nor cry; neither shall any man hear his voice in the streets. A bruised reed shall he not break, and smoking flax shall he not quench, till he send forth judgment unto victory. And in his name shall the Gentiles trust.' Matthew 12:19–21
SUGGESTED FURTHER READING: Matthew 11:25–30

'And in his name shall the Gentiles trust.' What does this mean? Why, power, violence, harshness and severity are never trusted. You cannot win men's hearts by such means. The Parisians wrote upon the wall of the Imperial Palace, 'Infantry, cavalry, artillery;' these were the basis of the imperial power, but an empire founded upon such things melted away like snow in summer. If there had been loyal affection between the ruler and the ruled, a thousand German invasions could not have dissolved the tie. When the old Napoleon was on the rock of St. Helena, he said gloomily to one of his attendants, 'My empire has passed away, because it rested upon force, but the empire of Jesus lasts still and will last for ever, because it is based upon love.' What has Jesus done for his subjects but loved them better than anyone else could have done, suffered for them beyond all, and conferred greater blessings upon them than all the universe besides could have bestowed? By such things has he captured their hearts. You may tempt away Christ's followers from him when you can find them a better master or a more loving friend, but not till then. You shall win us to a new leader when you can show us a better; but you cannot even imagine one who could compare with the chief among ten thousand, the altogether lovely. We who are sinners of the Gentiles trust him implicitly, because he is so divinely gentle, so omnipotently tender. Saviour, no tyrant art thou! Thou dost not trample on the poor and needy, or oppress the weak and trembling! Thou art mercy itself, love embodied, grace incarnate; therefore do the people flock to thee, and in thy name do the Gentiles trust.

FOR MEDITATION: Love covers a multitude of sins (Proverbs 10:12; 1 Peter 4:8), is strong as death and cannot be quenched (Song of Solomon 8:6–7) or separated from the Christian (Romans 8:35,39), surpasses knowledge (Ephesians 3:19) and casts out fear (1 John 4:18). Are you discovering this about God's love for you?

SERMON NO. 1147

Refined, but not with silver

'Behold, I have refined thee, but not with silver; I have chosen thee in the furnace of affliction.' Isaiah 48:10
SUGGESTED FURTHER READING (Spurgeon): Psalm 66:8–12

Let the soft whisper of the text sustain you: 'I have chosen thee in the furnace of affliction.' There are tokens of consumption about you, dear sister: I see that hectic flush, but do not dread the future, for the Lord says, 'I have chosen thee in the furnace of affliction.' You have struggled hard, my brother, to rise out of your situation; but as often as you have striven you have fallen back again with broken wing to your somewhat hard lot. Do not be despondent, but abide in your calling with contentment, since the Lord has said, 'I have chosen thee in the furnace of affliction.' Young man, you have been to college and were near taking your degree; but your health is failing you, and you will never become a renowned scholar, as you hoped. Do not distress yourself because your part will be passive rather than active, for the Lord says, 'I have chosen thee in the furnace of affliction.' Merchant, your firm is going to pieces and you will be poor; but have faith in God. It is the Lord's will that you should go struggling through the rest of your life, but he says, 'I have chosen thee in the furnace of affliction.' Mother, you have lost three or four little ones; there is another sickening, and you say, 'I cannot bear it.' Yes, you will, for the Lord says, 'I have chosen thee in the furnace of affliction.' And are you here, Hannah, woman of a sorrowful spirit? Is your adversary bitter of spirit toward you? Are there those about you who grieve you and make you fret? Weep no more, for the Lord loves you when no one else does, and he says, 'I have chosen thee in the furnace of affliction.'

FOR MEDITATION: (*Our Own Hymn Book* no.748 v.2—John Kent, 1803)
"'Tis, if need be, He reproves us,
Lest we settle on our lees;
Yet, He in the furnace loves us,
'Tis expressed in words like these:
"I am with thee,
Israel, passing through the fire.'"

Amazing grace

'I have seen his ways, and will heal him: I will lead him also, and restore comforts unto him and to his mourners.' Isaiah 57:18
SUGGESTED FURTHER READING: 1 Corinthians 6:9–11

Isaiah 57:9 says, 'thou ... didst debase thyself even unto hell.' A man does that when he defies his maker and blasphemes his Saviour, when after every other word he uses an oath, and garnishes his conversation with profane expressions, as some do. What good can there be in such wanton wickedness? What is to be gained by it? I suppose the devil himself is not such a blasphemer as some people are, whom we have the misery to hear even in our streets as we walk along, for I suppose he has some method in his profanity, but they use it for mere lack of other words. Men sink to the level of the devil when they are unkind to their aged parents, or are unnatural to their own offspring. What shall I say of the abominable cruelty of some men to their wives? I believe that if the devil had a wife he would not treat her as many working men treat their wives. Creatures called men are frequently brought up before our police-courts, and the charges proved against them make us altogether disgusted with human nature. Would the fierce lion, the savage tiger or the wild boar treat his mate so ill? O how many are thus debased unto hell! Yet, should this reach the ear of anyone who has thus debased himself, let him listen to this: 'I have seen his ways. I have seen him debase himself even unto hell; yet will I heal him, lead him, and restore comforts unto him.' 'Why,' says one, 'that seems too good to be true.' It does; and were you dealing with men it would be too good to be true, but you are dealing with one of whom it is written, 'Who is a God like unto thee, that pardoneth iniquity, and passeth by the transgression of the remnant of his heritage?' 'All manner of sin and blasphemy shall be forgiven unto men'; 'the blood of Jesus Christ his Son cleanseth us from all sin.'

FOR MEDITATION: (*Our Own Hymn Book* no.248 v.1—Julia Anne Elliott, 1835)
> 'We love Thee, Lord, because when we
> Had erred and gone astray,
> Thou didst recall our wandering souls
> Into the heavenward way.'

SERMON NO. 1279

Christ the destroyer of death

'The last enemy that shall be destroyed is death.' 1 Corinthians 15:26
SUGGESTED FURTHER READING: 1 Thessalonians 4:13–18

At the coming of Christ those who are alive and remain shall not see death. They shall be changed; there must be a change even to the living before they can inherit eternal life, but they shall not actually die. Do not envy them, for they will have no preference beyond those that sleep; rather do I think theirs to be the inferior lot of the two in some respects. But they will not know death: the multitude of the Lord's own who will be alive at his coming will pass into the glory without needing to die. Thus death, as far as they are concerned, will be destroyed. But for the sleeping ones, the myriads who have left their flesh and bones to moulder back to earth, death shall be destroyed also, for when the trumpet sounds they shall rise from the tomb. The resurrection is the destruction of death. We never taught, nor believed, nor thought that every particle of every body that was put into the grave would come to its fellow, and that the absolutely identical material would rise: but we do say that the identical body will be raised, and that as surely as there comes out of the ground the seed that was put into it, though in very different guise, for it comes forth not as a seed but as a flower, so surely shall the same body rise again. The same material is not necessary, but there shall come out of the grave, or out of the earth, if it never saw a grave, or out of the sea, if devoured by monsters, that selfsame body for true identity which was inhabited by the soul while here below. Was it not so with our Lord? Even so shall it be with his own people, and 'then shall be brought to pass the saying that is written, Death is swallowed up in victory. O death, where is thy sting? O grave, where is thy victory?'

FOR MEDITATION: (*Our Own Hymn Book* no.843 v.3—Samuel Crossman, 1664)

> 'My Saviour's angels shall their golden trumpets sound,
> At whose most welcome call my grave shall be unbound.
> Sweet truth to me! I shall arise,
> And with these eyes my Saviour see.'

SERMON NO. 1329

The meat and drink of the new nature

'For my flesh is meat indeed, and my blood is drink indeed.' John 6:55
SUGGESTED FURTHER READING: Philippians 4:10–23

Do we know our own strength? I do not mean our natural strength, for that is weakness, but the strength which lies in the new nature when it has fed on Christ. Brethren, we are strong to do, strong to be, strong to suffer. And to take an easy illustration of this, look at how the saints have suffered. Take down *Foxe's Book of Martyrs*: read of Marcus Arethusa, stung to death by wasps without a sigh. Think of Blandina, tossed on the horns of bulls, exposed in a red-hot iron chair, and yet never flinching. Give up Christ? They never dreamed of such a thing. Think of Lawrence on the gridiron, and other heroes innumerable, who were made strong because Christ was in them. Turn to humble men and women over yonder there in Smithfield, who could clap their hands while every finger burned like a candle, and who could shout, 'None but Christ.' Why, they fed on the flesh and blood of Christ, and that made them mighty. They were tortured on the rack like Anne Askew, and yet they scorned to yield. Brave woman! The priests and the friars could not vanquish her. Neither could all the Bishop Bonners in the world burn Christ out of poor Tomkins. When Bonner held the poor man's fingers over the candle and said, 'How will you like that in every single limb of your body?' Tomkins smiled on the bishop and said that he forgave him the cruelty that he was doing him. Christ in a man makes him a partaker of divine strength. Do you not think that as you are not called to suffer, you ought to lay out your strength in the line of doing, giving, self-denial and serving Christ by holy living? Certainly you should try to do so, and your strength will be found equal to it. You do not know how strong you are, but Paul shall tell you—'I can do all things through Christ which strengtheneth me.' Well may you do all things if you have fed on him who 'is all, and in all'.

FOR MEDITATION: (*Our Own Hymn Book* no.761 v.4—John Kent, 1827)
'This sacred tie forbids their fears,
For all He is or has is theirs;
With Him, their Head, they stand or fall,
Their life, their surety, and their all.'

SERMON NO. 1460

A welcome discovery

'God opened her eyes, and she saw a well of water; and she went and filled the bottle with water, and gave the lad drink.' Genesis 21:19
SUGGESTED FURTHER READING: Psalm 77:1–20

Sometimes holy scripture has its well near to the troubled heart, not so much in the form of doctrine, as in the form of promise. There was never a trouble yet in human experience among God's people, without there being a promise to meet it. You have only to look long enough and you shall find the counterfoil; you shall discover that God has in his book that which exactly meets your case. 'Oh,' said Christian in Bunyan's *Pilgrim's Progress*, 'what a thousand fools have I been to lie rotting in this stinking dungeon all these weeks, when I have a key in my bosom which, I am persuaded, would fit the locks of all the doors in Doubting Castle. Come, good brother, let us try it.' And so Christian plucked up courage, and he found his key of promise, though it grated a little; and Bunyan says that one of the doors went, as he puts it in his old edition, 'damnably hard'. He did not know how to put it strong enough until he used that word. Yet the key did open every single door, and even the iron gate itself, the external gate of the castle, opened by the help of that key. Some of you have laid, fretting and worrying yourselves about things which God has dealt with already in his own word. You have said, 'Would God he would do that!' and he has done it. You have asked him to give you something, and you have got it. I have used sometimes the simile of a man in the dark dying of hunger, and yet he is shut up in the pantry. There is the food all round him, if he could only put out his hand and take it. Did he know it to be there and would he grasp it, there is just what he wants. I am persuaded, if you search the scriptures well, there is not one child of God that need despair of finding that the Master has opened a well of promise for him.

FOR MEDITATION: In our unbelief we easily invent complications which fail to take into account the nearness and accessibility of God's commandments and his way of salvation (Deuteronomy 30:11–14; Romans 10:6–9). The Psalmist was able to cope with all sorts of circumstances simply by not forgetting God's word (Psalm 119:61,83,109,141,153,176).

Infallibility—where to find it and how to use it

'It is written.' Matthew 4:4
SUGGESTED FURTHER READING: Psalm 119:1–16

Our Lord Jesus Christ, as soon as he was assailed, had his answer prepared—'It is written'. A ready reckoner is an admirable person in a house of business; and a ready textuary is a most useful person in the house of God. Have the Scriptures at your fingers' end; better still, have them in the centre of your heart. It is a good thing to store the memory with many passages of the Word, the very words themselves. A Christian ought no more to make a mistake in quoting a text of Scripture, than a classicist does when he quotes from Virgil or Homer. The scholar likes to give the very words and so should we, for every word is precious to us. Our Saviour knew so much of Holy Scripture that out of one single book, the book of Deuteronomy, he obtained all the texts with which he fought the wilderness battle. He had a wider range, for the Old Testament was before him, but he kept to one book, as if to let Satan know that he was not short of ammunition. If the devil chose to continue the temptation, the Lord had abundant defence in reserve. 'It is written' is an armoury in which hang a thousand bucklers, all shields of mighty men. It is not merely one, but a thousand, no, ten thousand weapons of war. It has texts of every kind, suitable for our aid in every emergency and effectual for repelling every attack. Brethren, study much the Word of God and have it ready to hand. It is of no use treating the Bible as the fool did his anchor, which he had left at home when he came to be in a storm: have the infallible witness at your side when the father of lies approaches.

FOR MEDITATION: The devil was not the only opponent resisted by the Lord Jesus Christ with the words 'It is written'. Consider some other occasions when the Saviour said this spontaneously (Matthew 21:13) or in reply to others (Mark 7:6; John 6:45; 8:17; 10:34). Can you think of similar situations when you could do likewise?

The parent's and pastor's joy

'I have no greater joy than to hear that my children walk in truth.' 3 John 4
SUGGESTED FURTHER READING: Job 1:1–5

Many could not truthfully repeat my text; they look for other joy in their children, and care little whether they 'walk in truth' or not. They joy in them if they are healthy in body, but are not saddened though the leprosy of sin remains upon them. They joy in their comely looks, but do not inquire whether they have found favour in the sight of the Lord. Put the girl's feet in silver slippers, and many heads of families would never raise the question as to whether she walked the broad or narrow road. It is very grievous to see how some professedly Christian parents are satisfied so long as their children display cleverness in learning or sharpness in business, although they show no signs of a renewed nature. If they pass their examinations with credit and promise to be well fitted for the world's battle, their parents forget that there is a superior conflict involving a higher crown, for which the child will need to be fitted by divine grace and armed with the whole armour of God. Alas, if our children lose the crown of life, it will be a small consolation that they have won the laurels of literature or art. Many who ought to know better think themselves superlatively blessed in their children if they become rich, marry well, strike out into profitable enterprises in trade, or attain eminence in the profession which they have espoused. Their parents will go to their beds rejoicing and awake perfectly satisfied, though their boys are hastening down to hell, if they are also making money by the bushel. They have no greater joy than that their children are having their portion in this life and laying up treasure where rust corrupts it. Though their sons and daughters show no signs of the new birth, give no evidence of being rich towards God, and manifest no traces of electing love, redeeming grace, or the regenerating power of the Holy Spirit, yet there are parents who are content with their condition.

FOR MEDITATION: As a boy 'Jesus increased in wisdom and stature, and in favour with God and man' (Luke 2:52). If you are a parent, is this the kind of desire you have for your children? Will the Christmas you have planned for them be consistent with a godly upbringing (Ephesians 6:4)?

SERMON NO. 1148

The immovability of the believer

'They that trust in the LORD *shall be as mount Zion, which cannot be removed, but abideth for ever.' Psalm 125:1*
SUGGESTED FURTHER READING: John 6:35–40

A great nobleman with a big house in a wide country is not content to be all alone, but needs servants and tenants; if he is of a generous spirit he seeks the poor. He wants poor neighbours to help and says, 'This Christmas-time I must give something away; is there nobody wanting a round of beef? Is there nobody wanting their chimney set alight with a joint? Is there nobody needing a blanket in this cold season?' Thus God must have dependants; he must have those about him who need him. He loves dependants, and I do not see why he should cast them away. Why should he? If this is what he desires, if he 'seeketh such to worship him', and if 'he is a rewarder of them that diligently seek him', why should he reject their petition? It is not the nature of God to cast away any who rely upon him; on the contrary, he is very careful that faith should never have less than she has expected. He respects the courage of faith: he never confounds it. If you open your back door and a robin comes bravely in out of the cold, do you drive him out? No, you are pleased with his assurance and give him a hearty welcome. Even so does God deal with poor trembling souls when they come to him. We read of Charles V, the German Emperor, that when a pair of birds had built their nest among the poles and lines of his pavilion, he would not allow it to be removed though the time was come for the camp to be on the march. The birds had trusted to him, and they should not be disappointed. The like zealous care does the Lord exhibit towards the trembling hopes and feeble confidences of poor souls that trust in him. There is, therefore, no reason why they should be removed, since it is not like the Lord to cast them away.

FOR MEDITATION: (*Our Own Hymn Book* no.742 v.1—Isaac Watts, 1709)
    'Firm as the earth Thy gospel stands,
    My Lord, my hope, my trust;
    If I am found in Jesus' hands,
    My soul can ne'er be lost.'

SERMON NO. 1450

Shiloh

'Until Shiloh come; and unto him shall the gathering of the people be.'
Genesis 49:10
SUGGESTED FURTHER READING: Luke 2:1–14

The interpretation which has the most support and which I think has the fairest claim to be accorded correct, is that which derives the word 'Shiloh' from the same root as the word 'Salem'. This makes it signify 'peace'. 'Until the peace, or the peace-bearer, or the peace-giver,' or, if you like it better, 'the rest, or the rest-maker shall come'. Select the word you prefer; it will sufficiently represent the sense. 'Until the peace-bringer come; until the rest-maker come.' His advent bounds the patriarch's expectation and desire. What a vein of soul-charming reflection this opens! Do you know what rest means, such 'peace, peace'? 'Thou wilt keep him in perfect peace, whose mind is stayed on thee: because he trusteth in thee', as the prophet Isaiah puts it. Have you ever said to yourself, 'There is nothing I desire or wish for; I am satisfied, perfectly content; I am without a fear, without a dread'? 'No', you say, 'I never reached that elysium.' You may be worth millions without ever coming to that pass; all the gold in the world will never fill a man's heart. You may have broad acres across which a swift horse could hardly rush in a day, but you will not have enough; all the land in the world cannot fill a heart. You may have all the beauty, rank, honour and fame that can ever come to a human being, and yet say, 'I am wretched still.' But full many who have found Jesus have been able to say, 'It is enough: I need no more.' Believing in Jesus, and learning to yield up everything to his will, living to his glory, and loving him supremely, we enjoy 'peace with God', a peace 'which passeth all understanding', which keeps our 'hearts and minds through Christ Jesus'.

FOR MEDITATION: The baby born at Bethlehem was the promised 'Prince of Peace' (Isaiah 9:6), who would bring peace on earth (Luke 2:14). The objection that this has not been fulfilled is based on a total misunderstanding. Jesus did not come to bring peace on earth between people (Matthew 10:34–36), but a different kind of peace (John 14:27). The peace he came to preach (Ephesians 2:17) is a peace between repentant sinners and God (Romans 5:1). Are you enjoying it yourself?

SERMON NO. 1157

The great birthday

'The angel said unto them, Fear not: for, behold I bring you good tidings of great joy, which shall be to all people.' Luke 2:10
SUGGESTED FURTHER READING: Hebrews 1:1–9

The angel tells us that this Saviour 'is Christ the Lord'; there is much gladness in that fact. 'Christ' signified anointed. Our Lord is anointed in a threefold sense, as prophet, priest and king. It has been well observed that this anointing, in its threefold power, never rested upon any other man. There have been kingly prophets, like David; there was one kingly priest, Melchisedec; there have also been priestly prophets, such as Samuel. Thus two of the offices have been united in one man, but all three—prophet, priest and king—never met in one thrice-anointed being until Jesus came. We have the fullest anointing conceivable in Christ, who is anointed 'with the oil of gladness above' his fellows, and who, as the Messiah, the sent One of God, is completely prepared and qualified for all the work of our salvation. Let our hearts be glad. We have not a nominal Saviour, but a Saviour fully equipped, one who in all points is like ourselves, for he is man, but who in all points is fit to help the feebleness which he espoused, for he is the anointed man. See what an intimate mingling of the divine and human is found in the angels' song. They sing of him as 'Saviour', and a Saviour must be divine, in order to save from death and hell, yet the title is drawn from his dealings with humanity. Then they sing of him as 'Christ', and that must be human, for only man can be anointed, yet that unction comes from the Godhead. Sound forth the trumpets for this marvellously Anointed One, and rejoice in him who is your priest to cleanse you, your prophet to instruct you, and your king to deliver you.

FOR MEDITATION: In his one person the Lord Jesus Christ surpasses all who took part in the Christmas story. Angels announced his birth (Luke 2:9–13), but he is superior to angelic spirits (Hebrews 1:4,14). Rulers had an interest in the place of his birth (Matthew 2:3–6; Luke 2:1–6), but he is King of sovereigns (1 Timothy 6:15; Revelation 17:14; 19:16). Wise men came to worship him (Matthew 2:1–2), but he is wiser than the wisest of sages (Matthew 12:42; Colossians 2:2–3). Shepherds hurried to see him (Luke 2:15–20), but he is the chief of shepherds (1 Peter 5:4).

SERMON NO. 1330

Coming—always coming

'To whom coming.' 1 Peter 2:4
SUGGESTED FURTHER READING: Luke 1:46–55

Some time ago, when there was a dinner given to poor people, they were told to come and they should have all they could eat. Do you know what they did, some of them? There was not to be any dinner till six o'clock. Well, that they might have a noble appetite, they did not eat any breakfast. They meant to get all they could now they had an opportunity, and so they came as hungry as possible. Many years ago, I am told, it used to be the custom of the lord of the manor, in certain villages, to give the poor people a basin of food on Christmas Day, and the rule was that whatever basin was brought his lordship always filled it. It was perfectly marvellous how the basins grew, till at last, when some of the women came with their basins, the lord of the manor looked at the huge bowls and wondered how they could dare to bring such capacious vessels. But if he was a man of a generous heart, all he would say to his steward would be, 'These people believe in my generosity. Go and fill their bowls. Fill, and fill on till you have filled them all. As long as they bring their bowls none shall say that I denied them.' And now, when you go to Christ, take a capacious vessel of large prayer and great expectation. Enlarge your desire and make up your mind to this—'I am not going in to be a miserable Christian, with barely enough grace to keep me from open profanity, to whitewash me with a respectable profession, and ensure me against the peril of everlasting perdition. I mean to take a higher aim and to seek a better portion. Gladly would I vie with saints and angels and be the most happy, the most useful, the most joyous, the most holy believer that ever lived, if God will help me so to be.'

FOR MEDITATION: On this Christmas Day we remember the time when the Lord Jesus Christ came to dwell among us, 'full of grace and truth' (John 1:14). Have you in your emptiness come to him in return to receive 'of his fulness' (John 1:16)? The only ones who will be filled are sinners who are hungry for his righteousness and goodness (Matthew 5:6; Luke 1:53).

SERMON NO. 1334

'God with us'

'They shall call his name Emmanuel, which being interpreted is, God with us.' Matthew 1:23
SUGGESTED FURTHER READING: Luke 1:26–38

Our text speaks of a name of our Lord Jesus. It is said, 'they shall call his name Emmanuel'. In these days we call children by names which have no particular meaning. They are the names, perhaps, of father or mother or some respected relative, but as a general rule there is no special meaning in our children's names. It was not so in the olden times. Then names meant something. Scriptural names, as a general rule, contain teaching, and especially is this the case in every name ascribed to the Lord Jesus. With him names indicate things; 'his name shall be called Wonderful, Counsellor, The mighty God, The everlasting Father, The Prince of Peace', because he really is all these. His name is called Jesus, but not without a reason. By any other name Jesus would not be so sweet, because no other name could fairly describe his great work of saving 'his people from their sins'. When he is said to be called this or that, it means that he really is so. I am not aware that anywhere in the New Testament our Lord is afterwards called Emmanuel. I do not find his apostles, or any of his disciples, calling him by that name literally; but we find them all doing so in effect, for they speak of him as 'God ... manifest in the flesh', and they say, 'the Word was made flesh, and dwelt among us, (and we beheld his glory, the glory as of the only begotten of the Father,) full of grace and truth.' They do not use the actual word, but they again interpret and give us free and instructive renderings, while they proclaim the sense of the august title and inform us in divers ways what is meant by God being with us in the person of the Lord Jesus Christ. It is a glorious fact of the highest importance that, since Christ was born into the world, God is with us.

FOR MEDITATION: (*Our Own Hymn Book* no.256 v.3—Charles Wesley, 1739)
  'Veiled in flesh the Godhead see;
  Hail the incarnate Deity!
  Pleased as man with men to appear,
  Jesus our Immanuel here.'

SERMON NO. 1270

A grateful summary of twenty volumes

'Unto me, who am less than the least of all saints, is this grace given, that I should preach among the Gentiles the unsearchable riches of Christ.'
Ephesians 3:8
SUGGESTED FURTHER READING: Ephesians 1:1—10

My Master's riches of grace are so unsearchable, that he delights to forgive and forget enormous sin; the bigger the sin the more glory to his grace. If you are over head and ears in debt, he is rich enough to discharge your liabilities. If you are at the very gates of hell, he is able to pluck you from the jaws of destruction. So mighty is his mercy that no case ever did or ever will exceed his power to save. I will challenge you to a contest with regard to my dear Lord and Master, that if you will sit down and think the best and largest thoughts you can of him, you will not think him to be so good and loving as he really is: if you will try and wish for the largest blessings you can conceive, you shall not be able to wish for such blessings as he is prepared to bestow; and if you will open your mouth wide and make request for the greatest favour that ever human being asked of God or man, you shall not ask for a tenth of what he is prepared to give. Come and try him! Let it be a wrestling match between your needs and Christ's abundance, and see which will win the day. I tell you that, as Aaron's rod swallowed up the rods of the magicians, so my Master's all-sufficiency will swallow up all the demands of your dreadful necessities. Only come and try him now! All that you need between the gates of hell and the gates of heaven you shall find in Christ, and you shall have it all for nothing, all for the asking for. Open your hand and take it; it is all he asks of you, that you believingly receive what he freely bestows; trust in him as dead, risen, ascended and reigning; rely upon him, and by so doing you shall find that there are unsearchable riches of grace in him.

FOR MEDITATION: Not only are Christ's riches unsearchable, but so are God's deeds (Job 5:9), greatness (Psalm 145:3) and judgments (Romans 11:33). No wonder he 'is able to do exceeding abundantly above all that we ask or think' (Ephesians 3:20)!

N.B. This sermon's title commemorated twenty years' weekly publication of Spurgeon's sermons.

SERMON NO. 1209

My restorer

'He restoreth my soul.' Psalm 23:3
SUGGESTED FURTHER READING: Psalm 51:1–19

I felt the other day heavy at heart, dull, dead: I thought of myself as though I was a branch of a tree cut off, and so I meditated thus with myself. 'If I am a branch of the vine and have been removed from my stem, my only hope is to get back into the place whence I came, be grafted in again, and begin to suck the sap again and feel the life flowing through me.' Then was it sweet to remember that there is no possible state into which a believer could fall, even if it were the most desperate that could be conceived, from which Christ cannot restore him perfectly and at once. Then for my own comfort and renewal I began with my Lord thus: I looked at him upon the cross; I stood before him as a sinner, wondered that he should die for sinners, trusted him and said to him, 'Lord, thou knowest I trust thee: I have no hope but in thee, and I cling to thee as a limpet clings to the rock; with all my heart and soul I cling.' I began to feel the sap flow from the stem into my branch at once: directly I had got into contact with my Lord by a simple faith, I felt that virtue went out from him to heal my soul. Once having established the flow of the sap, it flowed more and more; for as I thought about my salvation through him, being myself guilty and he my righteousness, I began to love him; my soul began to glow with a passion towards him, and I wanted to be telling others what a dear, good Saviour he was; and in a few moments after I had bemoaned myself as dead to him and a castaway, I felt as much warmth of love to him as I had ever done in all my life, and could say in the language of the spouse, 'Or ever I was aware, my soul made me like the chariots of Amminadib.' Now, I believe that this is the natural process to go through for the restoring of your soul.

FOR MEDITATION: The plea for restoration which came out of David's broken and contrite heart (Psalm 51:1–17) gives us an example to follow. God's promise of restoration to those of a contrite and humble spirit (Isaiah 57:15–19) gives us great encouragement to follow that example and flee to him likewise.

SERMON NO. 1149

Rightly dividing the word of truth

'Rightly dividing the word of truth.' 2 Timothy 2:15
SUGGESTED FURTHER READING: 2 Corinthians 5:11–6:2

I take a religious newspaper from America; the last copy bore these words at the end: 'If you do not want to have this paper, discontinue it NOW. If you wish to have it for the year 1875, send your subscription NOW. If you have any complaint against it, send your complaint NOW. If you have moved, send a notice of your change of residence NOW.' There was a big 'NOW' at the end of every sentence. I would say to you at the end of this year, if you wish to forsake your sins, forsake them NOW. If you would have mercy from God through Jesus Christ, believe on him NOW. What fitter time than before the dying year is gone—NOW? In that paper I read concerning Messrs Moody and Sankey. While they were preaching in Edinburgh, a man was deeply interested. There was a pause in the service and the man went out with his friend; when he reached the door he stopped and his friend said, 'Come away, Jamie.' 'No', he said, 'I came here to get good to my soul, and I have not taken it all in yet; I must go back again.' He went back and listened again. The Lord blessed him. He found Christ and so found salvation. Being a miner, he went down the pit the next day, and a mass of rock fell on him. He was taken out but could not recover. He said to the man helping him out, 'Oh, Andrew, I am so glad it was all settled last night.' I hope those killed in the railway accident on Christmas Eve could say, 'It was all settled the night before.' What a blessed thing it will be, if you should meet with an accident tomorrow, to say, 'Blessed be God, it was all settled last night. I gave my heart to Jesus, I yielded to his divine love and mercy, and I am saved.'

FOR MEDITATION: (*Our Own Hymn Book* no.1041 vv.1&2—John Newton, 1779)
'While with ceaseless course the sun rolls along the passing year,
Many souls their race have run, never more to meet us here.
Fixed in an eternal state, they have done with all below;
We a little longer wait, but how little—none can know.'

N.B. A train fell into the Oxford Canal at Shipton on 24 December 1874; 34 passengers died.

SERMON NO. 1217

A golden prayer

'Father, glorify thy name.' John 12:28
SUGGESTED FURTHER READING: Habakkuk 3:1–19

Concerning this next year upon which we are entering, I hope it will be a year of happiness to you—I very emphatically wish you all a Happy New Year—but nobody can be confident that it will be a year free from trouble. On the contrary, you may be pretty confident that it will not be so, for 'man is born unto trouble, as the sparks fly upward'. We each have some dear faces in which we rejoice; may they long smile upon us: but each one of these may be an occasion of sorrow during the next year, for we have neither an immortal child, nor an immortal husband, nor an immortal wife, nor an immortal friend, and therefore some of these may die within the year. Moreover the comforts with which we are surrounded may take to themselves wings before another year shall fulfil its months. Earthly joys are as if they were all made of snow; they melt even as the frost and are gone before we conclude our thanksgiving for their coming. It may be you will have a year of drought and shortness of bread; years lean and ill favoured may be your portion. And perhaps during the year which has almost dawned you may have to gather up your feet in the bed and die, to meet your father's God. Well now, concerning this approaching year and its mournful possibilities, shall we grow gloomy and desponding? Shall we wish we had never been born or ask that we may die? By no means. Shall we on the other hand grow frivolous and laugh at all things? No, that is ill-becoming in heirs of God. What shall we do? We will breathe this prayer, 'Father, glorify thy name.' That is to say, if I must lose my property, 'glorify thy name' by my poverty; if I must be bereaved, 'glorify thy name' in my sorrows; if I must die, 'glorify thy name' in my departure. When you pray in that fashion, your conflict is over; no outward fright nor inward fear remains.

FOR MEDITATION: (*Our Own Hymn Book* no.699 v.2—Charlotte Elliot, 1834)
    'If Thou shouldst call me to resign
    What most I prize—it ne'er was mine;
    I only yield Thee what was Thine:
    "Thy will be done!"'

SERMON NO. 1391

The two 'comes'

'And the Spirit and the bride say, Come. And let him that heareth say, Come. And let him that is athirst come. And whosoever will, let him take the water of life freely.' Revelation 22:17
SUGGESTED FURTHER READING: Luke 14:15–24

My dear friends, I do trust that this last day of the year may be to you a day of mercy. The Jews had a feast of ingatherings at the end of the year, and I earnestly pray that we may have an ingathering of precious souls to Christ before this year quite runs out: that would be a grand finish to this year of grace, and a sweet encouragement for the future. But suppose you do not come. Well, you have been invited. If a Christmas feast is provided for the poor, and a number of beggars are standing shivering outside in the sleet and snow, and will not come in though earnestly bidden, we say, 'Well, you have been invited: what more do you want?' Remember, also, that you have been invited very earnestly; 'the Spirit and the bride' and 'him that heareth' and Jesus himself have all said to you 'Come.' I am as the man 'that heareth' and I have said 'Come.' I do not know how to say it more earnestly than I have said it. How would my soul delight if every one here did come to Christ at this moment! I would ask no greater joy out of heaven to crown this year with. You are invited, and you are earnestly invited; what more do you want? If you never come, you will have this thought to haunt you for ever—'I was invited and pressed again and again, but I would not come.' I want you to remember, too, that you are called to come now, at once. You may not be bidden to come tomorrow for several reasons: you may not be alive, or there may be no earnest person near you to invite you. Can there be a better day than today?

FOR MEDITATION: (*Our Own Hymn Book* no.509 v.3—Albert Midlane, 1865)
    'Come, and welcome: do not linger,
    Make thy happy choice to-day;
    True thou art a wretched sinner,
    But He'll wash thy sins away:
    Come, and welcome,
    Time admits of no delay.'

SERMON NO. 1331

Summary of Subject Index

Subject Index

Subject Index

Section 5   **The Christian life**
Blessings from God

Subject Index

Index of original texts
and suggested further
readings
  (Spurgeon's
complete texts are
identified below by an
asterisk *).

Scripture Index

Scripture Index

1. Location of numbers (in order of appearance)

The Metropolitan Tabernacle, Newington (363)

1111–1357, 1359–1471, 1506, 1520, 2061

Christ Church, Westminster Bridge Road (1)

1358 (Wednesday 9/5/1877)

Trinity Road Chapel, Upper Tooting (1)

1697 (Thursday 27/9/1877—see 2/10)

2. Time of numbers

The time of most sermons is given on the title page; that of the undated sermons is in most cases indicated by internal references. Most of the sermons were preached on the **Lord's Day in the morning**; the exceptions are as follows:—

Sunday evening (22)—1117, 1163, 1174, 1217, 1225, 1239, 1245, 1259, 1265, 1308, 1315, 1322, 1346, 1355, 1389, 1393, 1396–7, 1414, 1506, 1520, 2061

Thursday evening (14)—1164, 1193, 1212, 1214, 1292, 1297, 1302, 1310, 1324, 1340, 1383, 1400, 1433, 1462

Thursday afternoon (1)—1697

Undated evenings, probably Sunday or Thursday (57)—1113, 1118–9, 1131, 1138, 1153, 1156–7, 1178, 1184, 1198, 1213, 1216, 1218, 1220, 1230, 1234, 1246, 1262, 1267–9, 1274, 1279–80, 1290–1, 1295, 1334–6, 1338, 1342, 1344, 1350, 1366, 1380, 1398–9, 1407, 1423–5, 1430, 1440, 1444–7, 1449, 1452b, 1454b, 1456, 1463b, 1465–6, 1470

Undated & untimed (probably Sunday or Thursday evenings) (40)—1123, 1140, 1142, 1152, 1154–5, 1158, 1180, 1196, 1210–1, 1219, 1221–4, 1263, 1285, 1289, 1339, 1341, 1364–5, 1395, 1401–2. 1405, 1421, 1443, 1448, 1451b, 1453, 1455, 1457b, 1458, 1459b, 1460, 1461b, 1464b, 1467b

Wednesday morning (1)—1358

3. Sermons preached on behalf of societies

Religious Tract Society—1233 (9/5/1875)

London Missionary Society—1358 (Wednesday 9/5/1877—see 8/5)

Hospitals of London—1360 (17/6/1877)

Sunday-School Union—1383 (Thursday 8/11/1877)

Baptist Missionary Society—1471 (27/4/1879)

4. Dating of undated sermons (see notes to chronological index)

N.B. One sermon is incorrectly dated—1168 must have been on Sunday 12, not 13, April 1874.

5. Details of omitted short written sermons

1451a (From the sick chamber)—'This year also'—Luke 13:8

1452a (From the sick room 12 January 1879)—'The sick man left behind'—2 Timothy 4:20

1454a (Written when away from his people)—'The empty seat'—1 Samuel 20:27

1457a (Written at Mentone)—'The numbered people'—Numbers 4:49

1459a (Written at Mentone)—'Satan's punctuality, power and purpose'—Luke 8:12

1461a (Written at Mentone)—'The seven sneezes'—2 Kings 4:34

1463a (Written at Mentone)—'The roes and the hinds'—Song of Solomon 2:7

1464a (Written at Mentone)—'A refreshing promise'—Isaiah 27:3

1467a (Written at Mentone)—'The oil and the vessels'—2 Kings 4:6

6. Contents of volumes used in this compilation

Vol. 19   nos. 1111–1149

Vol. 20   nos. 1150–1209

Vol. 21   nos. 1210–1270

Vol. 22   nos. 1271–1330

Vol. 23   nos. 1331–1390

Vol. 24   nos. 1391–1450

Vol. 25   nos. 1451–1471 (omitting parts listed above), 1506 (to 27 April 1879)

Vol. 26   no. 1520 (20 October 1878)

Vol. 28   no. 1697 (27 September 1877)

Vol. 34   no. 2061 (2 December 1877)

An asterisk (*) after a sermon number indicates explanatory material at the end of the chronological index

1853

	Sunday a.m.	p.m.	Weekday
18 Dec:	2 in autobiography		

1854

	Sunday a.m.	p.m.	Weekday
COMMENCED PASTORATE	28 Apr		
20 Aug:	2896*		
03 Sep:	3108		
17 Sep:	3120*		
05 Nov:	2908		
24 Dec:	2392	2915	

1855

	Sunday a.m.	p.m.	Weekday
07 Jan:	1	2	
14 Jan:	3		
21 Jan:	4	5	
28 Jan:	10		
04 Feb:	6		
11 Feb:	7–8		
18 Feb:	9		
25 Feb:	11		
04 Mar:	12		
11 Mar:	13		
18 Mar:	14	15	
25 Mar:	16		
01 Apr:	17		03 Apr: 3139
08 Apr:	18		
15 Apr:	19		
22 Apr:	20		
29 Apr:	21		

13 May:	22	23	
20 May:	24	25	
27 May:	26	27	
03 Jun:	28		
10 Jun:	29		
17 Jun:	30		18 Jun: 3126
24 Jun:	31		
01 Jul:	32		
08 Jul:	33		
TOUR OF NORTH & SCOTLAND			
05 Aug:	34		
12 Aug:	35		
19 Aug:	36		
26 Aug:	37		29 Aug: 3133
02 Sep:	41–2		04 Sep: 39–40
09 Sep:	43		
16 Sep:	38		
23 Sep:	44		
07 Oct:	45		
14 Oct:	46		
21 Oct:	47		
28 Oct:	48		
04 Nov:		49	
11 Nov:	53		
18 Nov:	50	2554	
25 Nov:	51	2563	
02 Dec:	52	54	
09 Dec:	55		
16 Dec:	56		
23 Dec:	57		
30 Dec:	58	2602	31 Dec: 59
Late weekday	2703*		

1856

	Sunday a.m.	p.m.	Weekday
06 Jan:	60	2567	
HONEYMOON IN PARIS			
20 Jan:	61–2		
27 Jan:	63		
03 Feb:	64		
10 Feb:	65		
17 Feb:	66–7	3042	
24 Feb:	68		
02 Mar:	69		
16 Mar:	70		
23 Mar:	71		
30 Mar:	72*		
06 Apr:	73 (*—dated 30 Mar a.m.)		
13 Apr:	74		
20 Apr:	75		
27 Apr:	76		
04 May:	77		
11 May:	79		
18 May:	80		22 May: 78
25 May:	81–2		
01 Jun:	83		
08 Jun:		84	
15 Jun:	86	85	
22 Jun:	87	88	
29 Jun:	89	90	
06 Jul:	91	92	
03 Aug:	93		
10 Aug:	95	96	
17 Aug:	97	98	
24 Aug:	100	102	25 Aug: 94
31 Aug:	103	108	
07 Sep:	117		
14 Sep:	3093	219	

21 Sep:		221	25 Sep: 99
28 Sep:		367	
19 Oct:	3036		

IN SHOCK AFTER MUSIC HALL DISASTER

02 Nov:	101	2562	
09 Nov:	284		11 Nov: 2598
16 Nov:	220		
23 Nov:	104		
30 Nov:	105		
07 Dec:	106		
14 Dec:	107		
21 Dec:	109		
28 Dec:	110		

Undated a.m.	2589, 3048*
Undated p.m.	2594
Undated weekday	2581
Early untimed	2572
Early weekday	2576
Autumn p.m.	2585

1857

	Sunday a.m.	p.m.	Weekday
04 Jan:	111		
11 Jan:	112		
18 Jan:	113		
25 Jan:	114		
01 Feb:	115		
08 Feb:	116		
15 Feb:	VOICE FAILED		
22 Feb:	118		
01 Mar:	119		
08 Mar:	120	121	
15 Mar:	122		
22 Mar:	123	125	

29 Mar:	124		
05 Apr:	126		
12 Apr:	127		
19 Apr:	128		
26 Apr:	129		29 Apr: 2625
03 May:	130		
10 May:	131		
17 May:	132		
24 May:	133		
31 May:	134	147	
07 Jun:	135		
14 Jun:	136		
21 Jun:	137		
28 Jun:	138		
05 Jul:	139		
12 Jul:	140		
19 Jul:	141–2		
26 Jul:	143		
02 Aug:	144	2634	
09 Aug:	145		
16 Aug:	146		
23 Aug:	148		
30 Aug:	149		03 Sep: AT ROSS-ON-WYE
06 Sep:	150		
13 Sep:	151		
20 Sep:	152		
27 Sep:	153		
04 Oct:	156	157	07 Oct: 154–5
11 Oct:	158		
18 Oct:	159		
25 Oct:	160		
01 Nov:	161		05 Nov: 178
08 Nov:	162	174	
15 Nov:	163		
22 Nov:	164		24 Nov: 2836*

29 Nov:	165
06 Dec:	166
13 Dec:	167
20 Dec:	168
27 Dec:	169

Undated p.m.	2639
Early untimed	2607/15
Early weekday	2611
Early p.m.	2616/21
Summer p.m.	2629
Autumn p.m.	2642/47/51
Winter p.m.	2656

1858

	Sunday a.m.	p.m.	Weekday
03 Jan:	170	2660	
10 Jan:	171		
17 Jan:	172		
24 Jan:	173		
31 Jan:	175		
07 Feb:	176		
14 Feb:	177		
21 Feb:	179	180	
28 Feb:	181		
07 Mar:	182		
14 Mar:	183		
21 Mar:	184		
28 Mar:	185		
04 Apr:	186		
11 Apr:	187		
18 Apr:	188		
25 Apr:	189		28 Apr: 190
02 May:	191		04 May: 192
09 May:	193		

16 May:	194	
23 May:	195	
30 May:	196	
06 Jun:	197	11 Jun: 198+199
13 Jun:	200	
20 Jun:	201	
27 Jun:	202	
04 Jul:	203	
11 Jul:	204	
18 Jul:	205	
25 Jul:	206	
01 Aug:	207	
08 Aug:	208	
15 Aug:	209	
22 Aug:	210	
29 Aug:	211	
05 Sep:	212	
12 Sep:	213	
19 Sep:	214	
26 Sep:	215	217
03 Oct:	216	
10 Oct:	218	
SICKNESS		
07 Nov:	222	
14 Nov:	223	
21 Nov:	224	
28 Nov:	225	226
05 Dec:	227	
12 Dec:	228	
19 Dec:	229	
26 Dec:	230	

Early p.m.	2664*/73
Early weekday	2668/77
Summer weekday	2681/86/90,2759

Autumn p.m.	2695,2700
Winter weekday	2707

Winter 1858–1859

Weekday	2711

1859

	Sunday a.m.	p.m.	Weekday
02 Jan:	231	232	
09 Jan:	233	244	
16 Jan:	234	239	
23 Jan:	235	282	
30 Jan:	236	254	
06 Feb:	237	262	
13 Feb:	238		
TOUR OF SCOTLAND			
27 Feb:	240		
06 Mar:	241		
13 Mar:	242		
20 Mar:	243		
27 Mar:	245		
03 Apr:	246		
10 Apr:	247		
17 Apr:	248		
24 Apr:	249		
01 May:	250		
08 May:	251		
15 May:	252		
22 May:	253		
29 May:	255		
05 Jun:	256		
12 Jun:	257		
19 Jun:	258		
26 Jun:	259		
03 Jul:	260		

10 Jul:	261	Afternoon: CLAPHAM COMMON
17 Jul:	263	
24 Jul:	264	
31 Jul:	265	
07 Aug:	266	
14 Aug:	267	16 Aug: 268–70
21 Aug:	271	
28 Aug:	272	
04 Sep:	273	
11 Sep:	274	
18 Sep:	275	
25 Sep:	276	
02 Oct:	277	
09 Oct:	278	
16 Oct:	279	
23 Oct:	280	
30 Oct:	281	
06 Nov:	288	
13 Nov:	283	
20 Nov:	285	
27 Nov:	286	
04 Dec:	287	
11 Dec:	289	
18 Dec:	290	
25 Dec:	291	

Early weekday	2715/20/24/28
Summer p.m.	2733
Summer weekday	2737/41
Autumn p.m.	2754
Autumn weekday	2746/50
Winter weekday	2763/66

Winter 1859–1860

p.m.	2772

1860

	Sunday a.m.	p.m.	Weekday
01 Jan:	292		
08 Jan:	293		
15 Jan:	294	319	
22 Jan:	295		
29 Jan:	296		
05 Feb:	297–8		09 Feb: IN PARIS
12 Feb:	299		
19 Feb:	300		
26 Feb:	301		
04 Mar:	302		
11 Mar:	303		
18 Mar:	304		
25 Mar:	305	320	
01 Apr:	306		
08 Apr:	307	321	
15 Apr:	308	310	
22 Apr:	309	322	
		324?	
29 Apr:	311		03 May: 312
06 May:	313		09 May: 314
13 May:	315		
20 May:	316		
27 May:	317	323	
03 Jun:	318	325	
HOLIDAY ON CONTINENT			
29 Jul:	326	337	
05 Aug:	327		
12 Aug:	328		
19 Aug:	329		21 Aug: 331–2
26 Aug:	330		
02 Sep:	333		06 Sep: AT HOLYHEAD
09 Sep:	334		
16 Sep:	335		

23 Sep:	336
30 Sep:	338
07 Oct:	339
14 Oct:	340
21 Oct:	341
28 Oct:	343
04 Nov:	344
11 Nov:	345
18 Nov:	346
25 Nov:	347
02 Dec:	348
09 Dec:	349
16 Dec:	350
23 Dec:	352
30 Dec:	353

Spring p.m.	2776/80
Summer p.m.	2789
Summer weekday	2785
Winter p.m.	2794/98

Winter 1860–1861

p.m.	2802/7

1861

	Sunday a.m.	p.m.	Weekday
06 Jan:	354		
13 Jan:	355		
20 Jan:	356		
27 Jan:	357		
03 Feb:	358		
10 Feb:	359		
17 Feb:	361	362	21 Feb: 3434*
24 Feb:	363	364	

TOUR OF NORTH & SCOTLAND

17 Nov:	419	
24 Nov:	420	
01 Dec:	421	
08 Dec:	422	423
15 Dec:	424	425
22 Dec:	430	426

Apr–Dec Undated p.m.	3068
Early p.m.	2819
Summer p.m.	2828/33
Summer weekday	2823/41
Autumn p.m.	2872

Winter 1861–1862

p.m.	2880/85/89/94/98
Weekday	2868

1862

	Sunday a.m.	p.m.	Weekday
05 Jan:	427		
12 Jan:	428		
19 Jan:	429		
26 Jan:	431	440	30 Jan: 432
02 Feb:	433		
09 Feb:	434		
16 Feb:	435		
23 Feb:	436		
02 Mar:	437		
09 Mar:	438		
16 Mar:	439		
23 Mar:	441		
30 Mar:	442	446	
06 Apr:	443		
13 Apr:	444		
20 Apr:	445		

27 Apr:	447	452	
04 May:	448		
11 May:	449		
18 May:	450		
25 May:	451	456	
01 Jun:	453		
15 Jun:	454		18 Jun: 455
22 Jun:	457		
29 Jun:	458	2924*	
06 Jul:	459		
13 Jul:	460	2929*	
20 Jul:	461		
27 Jul:	462		
03 Aug:	463		
10 Aug:	464		
17 Aug:	465		
24 Aug:	466		
31 Aug:	467		
07 Sep:	468	470	
14 Sep:	469		
21 Sep:	471		
28 Sep:	472		
05 Oct:	473		
12 Oct:	474	476	
19 Oct:	475	3202	
26 Oct:	477	491	
02 Nov:	478	3204	
09 Nov:	479		
16 Nov:	480		
23 Nov:	481	488	
30 Nov:	482	3206	
07 Dec:	483	616*	
14 Dec:	484		
21 Dec:	485	3221	
28 Dec:	486	496	

Untimed	2920/34/38/88		
Undated p.m.	2902		
Early p.m.	2911		

1863

	Sunday a.m.	p.m.	Weekday
			01 Jan: 3283*
04 Jan:	487		
18 Jan:	489		
25 Jan:	490		
01 Feb:	492		
08 Feb:	493		
15 Feb:	494	2835	
22 Feb:	495		
01 Mar:	495	2393	
08 Mar:	498	2993	
15 Mar:	500		
22 Mar:	501		
29 Mar:	502		
05 Apr:	503		
12 Apr:	504	505	
19 Apr:	506		
TOUR OF HOLLAND			
03 May:	507		
10 May:	508	2996	
17 May:	509		
24 May:	511		
31 May:	512		
07 Jun:	513		
14 Jun:	514		
21 Jun:	515	2972	
28 Jun:	517		
05 Jul:	518	2391	
12 Jul:	519	3210	
19 Jul:	520	3212	

26 Jul:	521	523	30 Jul: 3214
02 Aug:	522		
TOUR OF SCOTLAND			
16 Aug:	524	3216	
23 Aug:	525	3218	
30 Aug:	527		
06 Sep:	528	3220	
13 Sep:	529	3232	
20 Sep:	531	3236	
27 Sep:	532		
04 Oct:	533	3238	
11 Oct:	534	535	
18 Oct:	537	548	
25 Oct:	536		
01 Nov:	538		05 Nov: 3234
08 Nov:	539	550	12 Nov: 3240
15 Nov:	540		17 Nov: 3242*
22 Nov:	541		
29 Nov:	542		
06 Dec:	543		
13 Dec:	544		
20 Dec:	545		
27 Dec:	546		

Untimed	2943/47/52/55/60/63/67/74/79/84
Wrong year (see 1865)	3050*

1864

	Sunday a.m.	p.m.	Weekday
03 Jan:	547	3282	
10 Jan:	549		
24 Jan:	551	3250	
31 Jan:	552		
07 Feb:	553	3252	
14 Feb:	554		

21 Feb:	555	3256	
28 Feb:	557		
06 Mar:	558	3258	17 Mar: 3260
20 Mar:	560		22 Mar: 569
27 Mar:	562	3262	
03 Apr:	563		07 Apr: 3264
10 Apr:	564		
17 Apr:	565		
24 Apr:	566		28 Apr: 3266
01 May:	567		
08 May:	568		
15 May:	570		
22 May:	571		
29 May:	572		
05 Jun:	573		
12 Jun:	574		16 Jun: 582
19 Jun:	575		
26 Jun:	577		
03 Jul:	578		
10 Jul:	579		
17 Jul:	580		
24 Jul:	581		
31 Jul:	583	584	
07 Aug:	585		
28 Aug:	587		
04 Sep:	588		
11 Sep:	589		
18 Sep:	590		
25 Sep:	591		
02 Oct:	592		
09 Oct:	593	3268	
16 Oct:	595		
23 Oct:	596		
30 Oct:	597		
06 Nov:	598		

13 Nov:	599	3270	17 Nov: 3003
20 Nov:	601	602	
VISIT TO GLASGOW			
04 Dec:	603		
11 Dec:	604		
18 Dec:	605		
25 Dec:	606	3072	

Undated p.m.	3026	
Untimed	2992/97,3001/05/09/13/18/23/30	
Wrongly dated	2497 (27 Dec p.m.)	

1865

	Sunday a.m.	p.m.	Weekday
01 Jan:	607	3073	
08 Jan:	608	3056	
15 Jan:	609		
22 Jan:	611		
29 Jan:	612	3079	
05 Feb:	613		
12 Feb:	614		
19 Feb:	615		
26 Feb:	617		
05 Mar:	618		
12 Mar:	619		
19 Mar:	620		22 Mar: 624
26 Mar:	621		
02 Apr:	622		
09 Apr:	623		
16 Apr:	625		
23 Apr:	626	3062	
30 Apr:	627		
07 May:	628		
HOLIDAY ON CONTINENT			
02 Jul:	637		

09 Jul:	638		
16 Jul:	639		
23 Jul:	641		
30 Jul:	642		
06 Aug:	643		
13 Aug:	644		
20 Aug:	645	3274	
27 Aug:	647		
03 Sep:	648		
10 Sep:	649		
17 Sep:	650	3272	
24 Sep:	651		
01 Oct:	652	3276	
08 Oct:	653	3116	12 Oct: AT BRADFORD
15 Oct:	654		
22 Oct:	655		
29 Oct:	657		
05 Nov:	658		
12 Nov:	660		
26 Nov:	662		
03 Dec:	663		
10 Dec:	664		
17 Dec:	665	669	
24 Dec:	666		
31 Dec:	667		

Undated:	3050,* 3137*
Undated weekday	3044
Early undated	3038
Harvest undated	3058

1866

	Sunday a.m.	p.m.	Weekday
07 Jan:	668		11 Jan: 3278
14 Jan:	670	672	18 Jan: 3280

21 Jan:	671		25 Jan: 3286
28 Jan:	673		
04 Feb:	674	3284	
11 Feb:	675	3288	15 Feb: 3290
18 Feb:	676	3292	22 Feb: 3294*
25 Feb:	678	3296(?)	
		3457*	
04 Mar:	679	3298	
11 Mar:	680		
18 Mar:	681		20 Mar: 3122
25 Mar:	682		
01 Apr:	683		05 Apr: 3300*
08 Apr:	684	3167*	12 Apr: 3302
15 Apr:	685	3304	19 Apr: 3306
22 Apr:	687		
29 Apr:	688	3308	
06 May:	689		
13 May:	690	691	17 May: 3310
20 May:	692	3312	
VISIT TO SCOTLAND			
10 Jun:	694	2469	14 Jun: 3314
17 Jun:	695	3316	21 Jun: 3318
24 Jun:	697	3320	
01 Jul:	698		
08 Jul:	699		
15 Jul:	700		19 Jul: 3322
22 Jul:	701	3324	
29 Jul:	703	3327(?)/706	02 Aug: 3333
05 Aug:	704	3004	09 Aug: 3329
12 Aug:	705	710	16 Aug: 3353
19 Aug:	707		
02 Sep:	708		06 Sep: 3454
09 Sep:	709		13 Sep: 3339
16 Sep:	711	3337	20 Sep: 3344
23 Sep:	712	3425	27 Sep: 3471

30 Sep:	713	3331	04 Oct: 3369*
07 Oct:	714	716	
14 Oct:	715		16 Oct: 3006
21 Oct:	717		
28 Oct:	718		
04 Nov:	719	3378	
11 Nov:	720	3172	
18 Nov:	721		
25 Nov:	722	3513	29 Nov: 3366
02 Dec:	723	3382	
09 Dec:	724		13 Dec: 750
16 Dec:	725		
23 Dec:	727		
VISIT TO PARIS			
Undated p.m.	3151		
Untimed	3163		

1867

	Sunday a.m.	p.m.	Weekday
06 Jan:	728		
13 Jan:	729	3008	17 Jan: 862
20 Jan:	730		
27 Jan:	732		31 Jan: 3375
03 Feb:	733		
10 Feb:	734		14 Feb: 3380
17 Feb:	735		
24 Feb:	737		
03 Mar:	738		07 Mar: 3364
10 Mar:	739		12 Mar: 3197
17 Mar:	740		21 Mar: 756
24 Mar:	742	none	
31 Mar:	743	none	
07 Apr:	744	none	
14 Apr:	745	none	

21 Apr:	746	none	
28 Apr:	747	3392	
05 May:	748		09 May: 3335
12 May:	749	3373	16 May: 3355
19 May:	751		23 May: 3356
26 May:	752		
02 Jun:	753		
09 Jun:	754	3397*	
16 Jun:	755	3010	
23 Jun:	757		
30 Jun:	758		04 Jul: 3011
07 Jul:	759		11 Jul: 3012
14 Jul:	760	3015	
21 Jul:	761	3027	
28 Jul:	763	766*	01 Aug: 3017
04 Aug:	764		
HOLIDAY ON CONTINENT			
08 Sep:	769		19 Sep: 773
SICKNESS			
06 Oct:	774		10 Oct: 776
13 Oct:	775	778	
SICKNESS			
03 Nov:	779		
10 Nov:	780		
17 Nov:	781		21 Nov: 3170*
24 Nov:	782		
01 Dec:	783	3401	
08 Dec:	784	3351	12 Dec: 3384
15 Dec:	785	3362	
22 Dec:	786		26 Dec: 3371
29 Dec:	787	790	
Mar/Apr weekday	767,* 768*		

1868

	Sunday a.m.	p.m.	Weekday
05 Jan:	788	3275	
12 Jan:	789	802	
19 Jan:	791	3386	
26 Jan:	792		
02 Feb:	793		06 Feb: 3358
09 Feb:	794	3458	
16 Feb:	795	3390	
23 Feb:	797		
01 Mar:	798		05 Mar: 823
08 Mar:	799		
15 Mar:	800		19 Mar: 3246
22 Mar:	801	826	
29 Mar:	803	3465	
05 Apr:	804		
12 Apr:	805		16 Apr: 806
19 Apr:	807	808	
SICKNESS			
03 May:	–	809	
10 May:	810		13 May: 811
17 May:	812		
31 May:	813	816	04 Jun: 3346
07 Jun:	814		
14 Jun:	815		18 Jun: 3460
21 Jun:	817		
28 Jun:	818		02 Jul: 3376
05 Jul:	819	3451	
12 Jul:	820		
19 Jul:	821		
26 Jul:	822		
09 Aug:	824		
16 Aug:	825		
23 Aug:	827	3357	27 Aug: 835
30 Aug:	828	3421	03 Sep: 3387

06 Sep:	829		
13 Sep:	830		
20 Sep:	831	3348	
27 Sep:	833	3398(?)	
04 Oct:	834		
11 Oct:	836	3463	15 Oct: AT BRISTOL
18 Oct:	837		22 Oct: 3022
25 Oct:	838		
01 Nov:	839		
08 Nov:	840		
15 Nov:	841		19 Nov: 3429
22 Nov:	842		26 Nov: 3439
29 Nov:	843		
06 Dec:	844		
13 Dec:	845		
20 Dec:	846		
27 Dec:	847	857	31 Dec: 3323* (or 03 Jan)

Wrongly dated	3405 (21 Mar p.m.)
	3415 & 3509 (27 Jun p.m.)

1869

	Sunday a.m.	p.m.	Weekday
03 Jan:	848		
10 Jan:	849		
17 Jan:	851		
24 Jan:	852		
31 Jan:	853		04 Feb: 3436
07 Feb:	854		11 Feb: 3025
14 Feb:	855	3024	
21 Feb:	856		25 Feb: 3019
28 Feb:	858		02 Mar: 3271
07 Mar:	859		
14 Mar:	860		
21 Mar:	861		

28 Mar:	863		
04 Apr:	864		08 Apr: 3409
11 Apr:	865	882	15 Apr: 876
18 Apr:	866		
25 Apr:	867		
02 May:	868	869	
09 May:	870	3400	
16 May:	871		
23 May:	872	3029	27 May: 3396
30 May:	873		
06 Jun:	874		10 Jun: 3407
13 Jun:	875		
20 Jun:	877		
27 Jun:	878		
04 Jul:	879		08 Jul: 886(?)
11 Jul:	880		
18 Jul:	881	3031	
01 Aug:	884	3535	12 Aug: 3032
15 Aug:	885		19 Aug: 3394
22 Aug:	887		
29 Aug:	888		
05 Sep:	889		09 Sep: 3443*
12 Sep:	890		
SICKNESS			
26 Sep:	893		30 Sep: 3419
03 Oct:	894		
10 Oct:	895		
17 Oct:	896	3389*	
24 Oct:	897	3411	
31 Oct:	898		
07 Nov:	899		
SICKNESS			
26 Dec:	907	2445	
Undated p.m.	3014		

Wrongly dated	3431 (18 Jun p.m.)		

1870

	Sunday a.m.	p.m.	Weekday
02 Jan:	908		
09 Jan:	909	3035	13 Jan: 3037
16 Jan:	911	962	
		3039(?)	
23 Jan:	912		
30 Jan:	913	3041	
06 Feb:	914		10 Feb: 3413
13 Feb:	915		
20 Feb:	917	3222	24 Feb: 3417
27 Feb:	918		
06 Mar:	919	922	
13 Mar:	920		
20 Mar:	921		
27 Mar:	923	3444	
03 Apr:	924		
10 Apr:	925	930	14 Apr: 929
17 Apr:	926	3224	21 Apr: 977
24 Apr:	927		
01 May:	928	933	
08 May:	931	932	
TOUR OF SCOTLAND			
05 Jun:	934		
12 Jun:	935	936	16 Jun: 3466
19 Jun:	937	946	
26 Jun:	938	3449	
03 Jul:	939		
10 Jul:	940		14 Jul: 3423
17 Jul:	941		21 Jul: 3427
24 Jul:	942	3475	
31 Jul:	943	3557	
07 Aug:	944		11 Aug: 3486

14 Aug:	945		
21 Aug:	947	3225	25 Aug: 3442
28 Aug:	948	2858	01 Sep: 3464
04 Sep:	949		
11 Sep:	950	3437	15 Sep: 3452
18 Sep:	951	952	
25 Sep:	953	3484	29 Sep: 3244
02 Oct:	957		
09 Oct:	954	3488	13 Oct: 3473
16 Oct:	955		
23 Oct:	956		
30 Oct:	958		
06 Nov:	959		10 Nov: 3468
13 Nov:	960		
20 Nov:	961	972	
27 Nov:	963	3492	
04 Dec:	964		
11 Dec:	965		
18 Dec:	966	3506	
25 Dec:	967	2288*	

Wrongly dated	3483 (28 Sep p.m.)

1871

	Sunday a.m.	p.m.	Weekday
01 Jan:	968	2342	
08 Jan:	969		
15 Jan:	970		
22 Jan:	971		
29 Jan:	973	3558	
05 Feb:	974		
12 Feb:	975		
19 Feb:	976		
26 Feb:	978	3490(?)	
		3497(?)	

05 Mar:	979	3476	
12 Mar:	980		
19 Mar:	981	(Afternoon—WIMBLEDON)	
26 Mar:	982		
SICKNESS			
23 Apr:	987		27 Apr: 991
SICKNESS			
02 Jul:	998	none	
09 Jul:	999	none	13 Jul: 3478
16 Jul:	1000	none	
23 Jul:	1001	none	
30 Jul:	1003	3503	
06 Aug:	1004	3501	
13 Aug:	1005	3499	
20 Aug:	1006		
27 Aug:	1008	3489	
03 Sep:	1009	3496	
10 Sep:	1010	3498	
17 Sep:	1011	3512	21 Sep: 3493
24 Sep:	1012	3539	
01 Oct:	1013	3481	
08 Oct:	1014	3043	12 Oct: 3045
15 Oct:	1015	3047	
22 Oct:	1017	1037*	
29 Oct:	1018		
05 Nov:	1019		09 Nov: 3049
12 Nov:	1020		
19 Nov:	1024		
SICKNESS & ON CONTINENT			
24 Dec:	1026		
31 Dec:	1027		
Mar/Apr undated	993*		
Summer undated	3064		
Oct/Nov undated	1022*		

Wrongly dated   3525 (22 Feb p.m.)

1872

	Sunday a.m.	p.m.	Weekday
			04 Jan: 3545
07 Jan:	1028	3517	11 Jan: 3548
14 Jan:	1029	1032	18 Jan: 3521
21 Jan:	1031	3515	
28 Jan:	1033	3554	01 Feb: 3229
04 Feb:	1034		
11 Feb:	1035	3518	
18 Feb:	1036	3531(?)	22 Feb: 3361
25 Feb:	1040		29 Feb: 1042
03 Mar:	1038		07 Mar: 1056
10 Mar:	1039	2860	14 Mar: 1062
17 Mar:	1041		
24 Mar:	1043	3051	28 Mar: 2862
31 Mar:	1044	3544	
07 Apr:	1045	3507	
14 Apr:	1046	3527	
21 Apr:	1047	3540	25 Apr: 1054
28 Apr:	1048	3551	02 May: 3227
05 May:	1049	ATTU4*	
12 May:	1050		
19 May:	1051		
26 May:	1052		
02 Jun:	1053	2459	06 Jun: 2466
09 Jun:	1055	1070	
23 Jun:	1057	3223	
30 Jun:	1058		
07 Jul:	1059	3228	
14 Jul:	1060		
21 Jul:	1061		
28 Jul:	1063		
04 Aug:	1064		

11 Aug:	1065	
18 Aug:	1066	
25 Aug:	1067	1076
01 Sep:	1068	
08 Sep:	1069	
15 Sep:	1071	
22 Sep:	1072	26 Sep: 1077
29 Sep:	1073	
06 Oct:	1074	10 Oct: AT MANCHESTER
13 Oct:	1075	
20 Oct:	1078	
SICKNESS & ON CONTINENT		
08 Dec:	1084	
SICKNESS		19 Dec: 1086
22 Dec:	1087	
29 Dec:	1088	

Early undated   3129
* 05 May 'Able to the Uttermost' no.4

1873

	Sunday a.m.	p.m.	Weekday
05 Jan:	1089	3130	
12 Jan:	1090		
19 Jan:	1091	3053	23 Jan: 3134
26 Jan:	1093		30 Jan: 3136
02 Feb:	1094	3146	
09 Feb:	1095		13 Feb: 3140
16 Feb:	1096		20 Feb: 3142
23 Feb:	1098	3144	27 Feb: 3148
02 Mar:	1099		
09 Mar:	1100		
16 Mar:	1101	3150	
23 Mar:	1103	3152	
30 Mar:	1104	3055	

06 Apr:	1105		
13 Apr:	1106		
20 Apr:	1107	3154	
27 Apr:	1109	3159	01 May: 3160
04 May:	1110		08 May: 3164
11 May:	1111	3057	
18 May:	1112	1117*	
25 May:	1114	3162	29 May: 3166
01 Jun:	1115	3138	
08 Jun:	1116	3059	
TOUR OF SOUTHERN ENGLAND			
06 Jul:	1120	3169	
13 Jul:	1121		
20 Jul:	1122		
27 Jul:	1124		31 Jul: 3171
03 Aug:	1125	3173	07 Aug: 3178
10 Aug:	1126		
17 Aug:	1127	3061	
24 Aug:	1128		28 Aug: 3063
31 Aug:	1129		
07 Sep:	1130	3180	
14 Sep:	1132	3182	
21 Sep:	1133		25 Sep: 3184
28 Sep:	1134		02 Oct: 3186
05 Oct:	1135	3192	
12 Oct:	1136	3194	
19 Oct:	1137	3196	23 Oct: 3198
02 Nov:	1139		
09 Nov:	1141	3200	
16 Nov:	1143		
23 Nov:	1144		
30 Nov:	1145		
07 Dec:	1146		11 Dec: 3065
14 Dec:	1147	3157	
21 Dec:	1148	3158	

28 Dec:	1149	3230

Early undated	3112
November?	3155,* 3156*

1874

	Sunday a.m.	p.m.	Weekday
			01 Jan: 3231*
04 Jan:	1150	3127	08 Jan: 3074
11 Jan:	1151		
SICKNESS & ON CONTINENT			
22 Feb:	1159		
01 Mar:	1160	3067	
08 Mar:	1161	1163	12 Mar: 3076
15 Mar:	1162	3078	19 Mar: 1164
22 Mar:	1165		
29 Mar:	1166	3080	
05 Apr:	1167		
12 Apr:	1168		
19 Apr:	1169	3082	
26 Apr:	1170	3084	
03 May:	1171	1174*	07 May: 3086
10 May:	1172	3090	
17 May:	1173	3092	
24 May:	1175	3096	
31 May:	1176	3069	
07 Jun:	1177		11 Jun: 3098
14 Jun:	1179		
05 Jul:	1181	3099	
12 Jul:	1182		16 Jul: 3102
19 Jul:	1183	3104	
26 Jul:	1185		
02 Aug:	1186	3106	06 Aug: 1193
09 Aug:	1187	3132	
16 Aug:	1188	3109	

23 Aug:	1189		
30 Aug:	1190		
06 Sep:	1191	3071	
13 Sep:	1192	3111	17 Sep: 1212*
20 Sep:	1194	1213 (? or 24 Sep?)*	
27 Sep:	1195		
11 Oct:	1197		
18 Oct:	1199		
25 Oct:	1200		29 Oct: 3113
01 Nov:	1201	3115	05 Nov: 3117
08 Nov:	1201		12 Nov: 3094
15 Nov:	1203		
22 Nov:	1204		26 Nov: 3119
29 Nov:	1205	3121	03 Dec: 3088
06 Dec:	1206	3123	
13 Dec:	1207	1265*	17 Dec: 3125
20 Dec:	1208		
27 Dec:	1209	1217	

1875

	Sunday a.m.	p.m.	Weekday
03 Jan:	1215	2935	
SICKNESS—AT SOUTH COAST & FRANCE			
28 Mar:	1226		
04 Apr:	1227	2936	08 Apr: 2937
11 Apr:	1228	2939	
18 Apr:	1229	2940	22 Apr: 2941
25 Apr:	1231	2944	29 Apr: 2945
02 May:	1232	2946	
09 May:	1233		13 May: 2948
16 May:	1235	1239*	20 May: 2949
23 May:	1236	2950	
30 May:	1237	2951	03 Jun: 2953
06 Jun:	1238	2954	
13 Jun:	1240	2956	

20 Jun:	1241	24 Jun: 2957
27 Jun:	1242	2958
11 Jul:	1243	2959
18 Jul:	1244	22 Jul: 2961
25 Jul:	1247	2998
01 Aug:	1248	2962	05 Aug: 2964
08 Aug:	1249	2965	12 Aug: 2966
15 Aug:	1250	2968	19 Aug: 3000
22 Aug:	1251	2969
29 Aug:	1252	02 Sep: 2971
05 Sep:	1253	2973	09 Sep: 2975
12 Sep:	1254	2977	16 Sep: 2978
19 Sep:	1255	2980	23 Sep: 2981
26 Sep:	1256	1259*
03 Oct:	1257	2983	07 Oct: AT PLYMOUTH
10 Oct:	1258	2985	14 Oct: 2986
17 Oct:	1260	2987
24 Oct:	1261	2989	28 Oct: 2991
31 Oct:	1264	3002
07 Nov:	1266	2994
AT MENTONE		
26 Dec:	1270	
Undated p.m.	3161	
Untimed	3165	

1876

	Sunday a.m.	p.m.	Weekday
02 Jan:	1221	2865	06 Jan: 2866
09 Jan:	1272	2867	
16 Jan:	1273	2869	20 Jan: 1292
23 Jan:	1275	2870	27 Jan: 2871
30 Jan:	1276		03 Feb: 2873
06 Feb:	1277		
13 Feb:	1278	2874	

27 Feb:	1281	
05 Mar:	1282	2876	09 Mar: 1310
12 Mar:	1283	2877	16 Mar: 2878
19 Mar:	1284	2881	
26 Mar:	1286	2882	30 Mar: 1297
02 Apr:	1287	2883	07 Apr: 2879
09 Apr:	1288	2884	
SICKNESS			
14 May:	1293		
21 May:	1294	2886	
28 May:	1296	2887	
04 Jun:	1298	2888	08 Jun: 2890
11 Jun:	1299	2891	15 Jun: 1302
18 Jun:	1300	2892	22 Jun: 2893
25 Jun:	1301	1308	
02 Jul:	1303	2895	06 Jul: 2897
09 Jul:	1304	2899	13 Jul: 2900
16 Jul:	1305	1315	
23 Jul:	1306	2901	27 Jul: 2903
30 Jul:	1307		
06 Aug:	1309	2933	
VISIT TO SCOTLAND			
27 Aug:	1311	2904	
03 Sep:	1312	2905	07 Sep: 2906
10 Sep:	1313	2909	
17 Sep:	1314	2910	21 Sep: 2912
24 Sep:	1316	2917	28 Sep: 2918
01 Oct:	1319	2919	05 Oct: AT BIRMINGHAM
08 Oct:	1317	2486	12 Oct: 2864
15 Oct:	1318	2932	
22 Oct:	1320	1322	26 Oct: 1336*
29 Oct:	1321	2921	02 Nov: 1324
SICKNESS			
12 Nov:	1323	2922	
19 Nov:	1325		23 Nov: 2923

26 Nov:	1326	2925	30 Nov: 2926
03 Dec:	1327	2927	
10 Dec:	1328	2928	14 Dec: 2930
17 Dec:	1329	2931	
24 Dec:	1330	3309(?)*	
31 Dec:	1331	2863	

1877

	Sunday a.m.	p.m.	Weekday
07 Jan:	1332	2803	
14 Jan:	1333	2804	
21 Jan:	1337		
SICKNESS—IN PARIS & MENTONE			
18 Mar:	1343		22 Mar: 2805
25 Mar:	1345	1346	
01 Apr:	1347	2806	
08 Apr:	1348		13 Apr: 3211
15 Apr:	1349		
22 Apr:	1351	2808	
29 Apr:	1352		
06 May:	1353		08 May: 3085
			09 May: 1358
			10 May: 2809
13 May:	1354	1355	
27 May:	1356		
03 Jun:	1357	2810	07 Jun: 2812
10 Jun:	1359	2813	14 Jun: 2814
17 Jun:	1360	2816	21 Jun: 2817
24 Jun:	1361	2818	28 Jun: 2821
01 Jul:	1362	2827	05 Jul: 2834
08 Jul:	1363	2837	
15 Jul:	1367	2838	
TOUR OF SCOTLAND			
05 Aug:	1368	2839	
12 Aug:	1369	2840	

19 Aug:	1370	1389	
26 Aug:	1371		
02 Sep:	1372	2942	
09 Sep:	1373	1390	
16 Sep:	1374	2847	
23 Sep:	1375	2848	27 Sep: 1697*
30 Sep:	1376		04 Oct: 2849
07 Oct:	1377	2485	
14 Oct:	1378	2851	18 Oct: 2852
21 Oct:	1379	2853	
28 Oct:	1381		01 Nov: 1400
04 Nov:	1382	2855	08 Nov: 1383
11 Nov:	1384	2856	
18 Nov:	1385	2857	
25 Nov:	1386		
02 Dec:	1387	2061	
09 Dec:	1388	1393*	
SICKNESS			
30 Dec:	1391	SICK	
Undated p.m.	2914		
Untimed	3237b		

1878

	Sunday a.m.	p.m.	Weekday
06 Jan:	1392	1397	
13 Jan:	1394	1396	
SICKNESS—AT MENTONE			
17 Mar:	1403		
24 Mar:	1404	2773	28 Mar: 2777
31 Mar:	1406	2778	
07 Apr:	1408	2779	
14 Apr:	1409	2781	
21 Apr:	1410		
28 Apr:	1411	2782	

05 May:	1412	2783	09 May: 3243
12 May:	1413	1414	16 May: 2784
19 May:	1415		
26 May:	1416	1506*	
02 Jun:	1417		
09 Jun:	1418		13 Jun: 2786
16 Jun:	1419	2787	20 Jun: 2788
23 Jun:	1420	2790	27 Jun: 2791
30 Jun:	1422		
14 Jul:	1426		
VISIT TO SCOTLAND			
04 Aug:	1427		
11 Aug:	1428		
18 Aug:	1429		
01 Sep:	1431		05 Sep: 1433
08 Sep:	1432	2792	
15 Sep:	1434	2793	
22 Sep:	1435	2795	26 Sep: 2796
29 Sep:	1436		
06 Oct:	1437		10 Oct: AT LEEDS
13 Oct:	1438	2797	
20 Oct:	1439	1520*	
27 Oct:	1441	2799	
03 Nov:	1442	2800	07 Nov: 2801
SICKNESS			
22 Dec:	1450		
SICKNESS			

Wrongly dated	3456 (02 Oct p.m.)

1879

	Sunday a.m. p.m.	Weekday
SICKNESS		
12 Jan:	1452a (from sickroom)	
SICKNESS & AT MENTONE		

13 Apr:	1468	2742	17 Apr: 3176
20 Apr:	1469	2743	24 Apr: 2744
27 Apr:	1471	2745	01 May: 2747
04 May:	1472	2748	
11 May:	1473	2749	
18 May:	1474	1475	22 May: 1485
25 May:	1476	2751	29 May: 3208
01 Jun:	1477	3190	
08 Jun:	1478	2066	
15 Jun:	1479	2752	
22 Jun:	1480		26 Jun: 3248
29 Jun:	1481	1508	
06 Jul:	1482		
13 Jul:	1483	3188	
20 Jul:	1484	2753	
27 Jul:	1486	2755	
03 Aug:	1487		
10 Aug:	1488	1489	
17 Aug:	1490	2756	
24 Aug:	1491	2757	
31 Aug:	1492		04 Sep: 1496
07 Sep:	1493	2758	11 Sep: 3226
14 Sep:	1494	2760	
21 Sep:	1495	2761	
28 Sep:	1497	1511*	
05 Oct:	1498	2762	
12 Oct:	1499	2764	
19 Oct:	1500		
26 Oct:	1501	2765	
02 Nov:	1502		
09 Nov:	1505		

SICKNESS & AT MENTONE

Late p.m.	1577*

1880

	Sunday a.m.	p.m.	Weekday
SICKNESS & AT MENTONE			
15 Feb:	1523		
22 Feb:	1524		
29 Feb:	1525	2663	
07 Mar:	1526	2709	09 Mar: 1533
14 Mar:	1528		
21 Mar:	1529	2710	
28 Mar:	1530	2712	
04 Apr:	1531	2713	
11 Apr:	1532	2714	
18 Apr:	1534	2716	
25 Apr:	1535	2717	
02 May:	1536		06 May: 3291*
09 May:	1537	2000*	13 May: 2718
16 May:	1538		20 May: 2719
23 May:	1539		
30 May:	1540		
06 Jun:	1541	2721	10 Jun: 2722
13 Jun:	1542		17 Jun: 1629
20 Jun:	1544		
27 Jun:	1545	2723	01 Jul: 2725
04 Jul:	1549	2726	
VISIT TO SCOTLAND?			
25 Jul:	1550	2727	
01 Aug:	1551	2729	05 Aug: 2479
08 Aug:	1552	2480	12 Aug: 1595
15 Aug:	1553	2730	
22 Aug:	1554	2731	
29 Aug:	1555		
12 Sep:	1557		
10 Oct:	1561		
13 Oct:	1562	2732	21 Oct: 2734
24 Oct:	1564	2735	28 Oct: 1566

14 Nov:	1567		
21 Nov:	1568	2736	
28 Nov:	1570	2738	
05 Dec:	1571	2708	09 Dec: 2739
12 Dec:	1572	2740	
SICKNESS			

January undated	3255 (MENTONE)
Early undated	3267 (MENTONE)
Late Oct/Nov undated	1574*

1881

	Sunday a.m.	p.m.	Weekday
SICKNESS			
30 Jan:	1581	2676	03 Feb: 1630
06 Feb:	1582	1600	
20 Feb:	1584		
27 Feb:	1586		03 Mar: 1588
06 Mar:	1587	2767	
SICKNESS			
27 Mar:	1590		
03 Apr:	1591	2774	07 Apr: 2678
10 Apr:	1592	2679	14 Apr: 1693*
17 Apr:	1593		21 Apr: 2680
24 Apr:	1594		27 Apr: 1596
			28 Apr: 1633
01 May:	1597	2682	12 May: 2683
15 May:	1598		19 May: 2472
22 May:	1599		
29 May:	1601	2684	02 Jun: 1605
05 Jun:	1602	2769	09 Jun: 1632
12 Jun:	1603	1691	
19 Jun:	1604		
26 Jun:	1606	1635	
03 Jul:	1607		07 Jul: 1872

10 Jul:	1608	2685	
17 Jul:	1609	2687	21 Jul: 2688
24 Jul:	1610	2689	
31 Jul:	1611	2691	04 Aug: 1634
07 Aug:	1612		11 Aug: 1615
14 Aug:	1613		18 Aug: 2692
21 Aug:	1614		25 Aug: 1626
28 Aug:	1616	2693	01 Sep: 2694
04 Sep:	1617	1871	08 Sep: 2696
11 Sep:	1618	1620	
18 Sep:	1619		
25 Sep:	1621	2697	29 Sep: 2775
02 Oct:	1622	2699	06 Oct: 1686
09 Oct:	1623	2698	
16 Oct:	1624	2701	20 Oct: 2702
23 Oct:	1625	2704	27 Oct: AT SOUTHAMPTON
30 Oct:	1627	2705	
06 Nov:	1631	2706	
HOLIDAY AT MENTONE			
25 Dec:	1636	2340	

Summer undated	3273

1882

	Sunday a.m.	p.m.	Weekday
01 Jan:	1637	2617	
08 Jan:	1638	1640	
15 Jan:	1639	2618	19 Jan: 2619
22 Jan:	1641	2620	26 Jan: 2622
29 Jan:	1642	2659	02 Feb: 2623
05 Feb:	1643	1646	
12 Feb:	1644	2624	16 Feb: 1649
19 Feb:	1645	2626	23 Feb: 2627
26 Feb:	1647	1657	02 Mar: 1650
05 Mar:	1648	2628	

SICKNESS

09 Apr:	1653		
16 Apr:	1654	2630	
23 Apr:	1655	2631	
07 May:	1658		
14 May:	1659	2632	18 May: 2633
21 May:	1660	2635	
28 May:	1662	2636	01 Jun: 2637
04 Jun:	1663	2638	08 Jun: 1670
11 Jun:	1664		15 Jun: 2640
18 Jun:	1665	2641	22 Jun: 2643
25 Jun:	1666	2644	29 Jun: 2645
02 Jul:	1667	2646	
09 Jul:	1668	2648	13 Jul: 2649
16 Jul:	1669	2650	20 Jul: 2475
23 Jul:	1672	2652	
06 Aug:	1673	2653	10 Aug: 1680
13 Aug:	1674	2654	
20 Aug:	1675	2655	
27 Aug:	1676	1688	31 Aug: 2657
03 Sep:	1677	2658	07 Sep: 2661
10 Sep:	1678	2662	
17 Sep:	1679	1712	
24 Sep:	1681		28 Sep: 1690
01 Oct:	1682	2665	
08 Oct:	1683	2666	12 Oct: 2667
15 Oct:	1684	2669	19 Oct: 2670
22 Oct:	1685	2771	26 Oct: 2820
29 Oct:	1687	2671	02 Nov: 2822
05 Nov:	1689	2672	

AT MENTONE

24 Dec:	1698	2674	
31 Dec:	1699	2675	

Early undated	1656*

December 03, 10 or 17   3295 (MENTONE)

1883

	Sunday a.m.	p.m.	Weekday
07 Jan:	1700		11 Jan: 2555
14 Jan:	1701		18 Jan: 2556
21 Jan:	1702	2557	25 Jan: 2559
28 Jan:	1703		01 Feb: 2560
04 Feb:	1704	2561	08 Feb: 2564
11 Feb:	1705	2565	15 Feb: 2566
18 Feb:	1707	2568	22 Feb: 2569
25 Feb:	1708	2570	01 Mar: 2571
04 Mar:	1709	2573	08 Mar: 2574
11 Mar:	1710	2575	15 Mar: 2577
18 Mar:	1711	2578	22 Mar: 2579
25 Mar:	1713	2065	29 Mar: 2580
01 Apr:	1714	2582	05 Apr: 2583
08 Apr:	1715	2584	
15 Apr:	1716	2586	
SICKNESS			
06 May:	1719		10 May: 1722
13 May:	1720	2587	17 May: 1732
20 May:	1721	2588	24 May: 2590
27 May:	1723	2591	
03 Jun:	1724	2824	07 Jun: 2592
10 Jun:	1725	1746	14 Jun: 1729
17 Jun:	1726	2593	
24 Jun:	1727	2596	
01 Jul:	1728	2595	05 Jul: 1730
15 Jul:	1731		
12 Aug:	1734	1754	
19 Aug:	1735		23 Aug: 2597
26 Aug:	1736		30 Aug: 2599
02 Sep:	1737	1740	06 Sep: 2600
09 Sep:	1738	3313	13 Sep: 2768

16 Sep:	1739	2601	
23 Sep:	1741	2770	27 Sep: 2603
30 Sep:	1742		04 Oct: 1761
07 Oct:	1743	2825	11 Oct: 2604
14 Oct:	1744	2605	
21 Oct:	1745	2606	25 Oct: 1755
28 Oct:	1747	2608	01 Nov: 2609
04 Nov:	1748	2510	08 Nov: 2612
11 Nov:	1749	1750	15 Nov: 2613
18 Nov:	1751	2614	
25 Nov:	1752	1760	
TO FRANCE			
16 Dec:	1757 (Afternoon—MENTONE)		
AT MENTONE			
19 or 26 Aug p.m.:	1762*		

1884

	Sunday a.m.	p.m.	Weekday
HOLIDAY AT MENTONE			
03 Feb:	1764	1768	07 Feb: 1829
10 Feb:	1765	2525	14 Feb: 1769
17 Feb:	1766	1770	
SICKNESS			
16 Mar:	1771		20 Mar: 2526
23 Mar:	1772	1826	27 Mar: 2527
30 Mar:	1773	2528	03 Apr: 2529
06 Apr:	1774	2530	10 Apr: 2531
13 Apr:	1775	2532	17 Apr: 2533
20 Apr:	1776	2534	
27 Apr:	1777	2535	30 Apr: 1778
			01 May: 2071
04 May:	1779	2826	07 May: 1785
			08 May: 1825
11 May:	1780	1792	15 May: 2536

18 May:	1781		
25 May:	1782	2537	
01 Jun:	1783	1831	
08 Jun:	1784		
15 Jun:	1786	2541	
22 Jun:	1787		
29 Jun:	1788	1851	03 Jul: 1823
06 Jul:	1789	2542	
13 Jul:	1790		17 Jul: 1824
20 Jul:	1791	2543	31 Jul: 1797
03 Aug:	1793	2544	
10 Aug:	1794	2545	14 Aug: 1798
17 Aug:	1795	2546	
SICKNESS			
14 Sep:	1799		18 Sep: 1805
21 Sep:	1800	2547	25 Sep: 1810
28 Sep:	1801	2548	02 Oct: 2550
05 Oct:	1802		09 Oct: 1828
12 Oct:	1803	1811	16 Oct: 1833
19 Oct:	1804	2551	23 Oct: 2552
26 Oct:	1806	2553	30 Oct: 1822
02 Nov:	1807	1834	06 Nov: 1809
09 Nov:	1808	1832	
SICKNESS			
07 Dec:	1812		
14 Dec:	1813	1821	18 Dec: 1819
21 Dec:	1815	1827	
28 Dec:	1817	2549	

June (?) p.m.	undated series 2538–9, 2237, 2540
Summer weekday	1796
Wrongly dated	1837 (02 Jun p.m.)

1885

	Sunday a.m.	p.m.	Weekday

01 Jan: 1816

04 Jan: 1818

SICKNESS & HOLIDAY AT MENTONE

Date			Date
12 Apr:	1835	2493	16 Apr: 2494
19 Apr:	1836	2495	23 Apr: 2496
26 Apr:	1838	2498	30 Apr: 2499
03 May:	1839	2501	
10 May:	1840		14 May: 3303
17 May:	1841	2502	21 May: 2500
24 May:	1842	2503	28 May: 2524
31 May:	1843		
07 Jun:	1844	1850	11 Jun: 2504
14 Jun:	1845		
21 Jun:	1846	2505	25 Jun: 1861
28 Jun:	1847	2506	02 Jul: 2507
05 Jul:	1848	2508	
12 Jul:	1849	2509	16 Jul: 2510
19 Jul:	1852	1934	

VISIT TO SCOTLAND

Date			Date
02 Aug:	1853	1874	06 Aug: 2511
09 Aug:	1854	2512	
16 Aug:	1855	1878	20 Aug: 2513
23 Aug:	1856	1881	
30 Aug:	1857	1876	
06 Sep:	1858	2514	10 Sep: 1933
13 Sep:	1859	1870	
20 Sep:	1860	2068	
27 Sep:	1862	2515	28 Sep: 1864
04 Oct:	1863	2516	
11 Oct:	1865	2517	
18 Oct:	1866	2518	22 Oct: 2519
25 Oct:	1867	2520	29 Oct: 2521
01 Nov:	1868	2522	
08 Nov:	1869	2523	12 Nov: 1880
22 Nov:	1873		26 Nov: 1877

29 Nov:	1875

SICKNESS & AT MENTONE

1886

SICKNESS & AT MENTONE	Sunday a.m.	p.m.	Weekday
07 Feb:	1885	2451	
14 Feb:	1886	2452	18 Feb: 2453
21 Feb:	1887		25 Feb: 2454
28 Feb:	1888	1889	04 Mar: 2455
07 Mar:	1890	2456	11 Mar: 2457
14 Mar:	1891	2458	
21 Mar:	1892		25 Mar: 2916
28 Mar:	1893	2460	
04 Apr:	1894	2461	08 Apr: 2462
11 Apr:	1895	2463	
18 Apr:	1896		22 Apr: 2464
25 Apr:	1898		29 Apr: 2465
SICKNESS			
23 May:	1901	1938	
30 May:	1902	2081	
06 Jun:	1903		10 Jun: 2467
13 Jun:	1904	2468	17 Jun: 2345
20 Jun:	1905	2470	24 Jun: 2471
27 Jun:	1907		
SICKNESS			
11 Jul:	1909	2473	
18 Jul:	1910	2474	22 Jul: 2476
25 Jul:	1911	2481	
01 Aug:	1912	2477	05 Aug: 1916
08 Aug:	1913	2482	12 Aug: 2829
15 Aug:	1914	2483	19 Aug: 2830
22 Aug:	1915	2484	26 Aug: 2831
29 Aug:	1917	2487	02 Sep: 2832
05 Sep:	1918	2488	09 Sep: 1944

12 Sep:	1919	1930	
19 Sep:	1920	1936	
26 Sep:	1922	1939	30 Sep: 1932
03 Oct:	1923	2489	07 Oct: 1935
10 Oct:	1924	2490	
17 Oct:	1925		
24 Oct:	1926	1997*	28 Oct: 1940
31 Oct:	1927	2491	
07 Nov:	1928	2492	
14 Nov:	1931		
HOLIDAY AT MENTONE			

| Undated weekday | 2050 |
| Wrong year (see 1866) | 3294,* 3300,* 3369* |

1887

	Sunday a.m.	p.m.	Weekday
02 Jan:	1941 (Afternoon—MENTONE)		
09 Jan:	1943 (Afternoon—MENTONE)		
SICK AT MENTONE			
30 Jan:	1945	2394	03 Feb: 2395
06 Feb:	1946	2396	10 Feb: 2064
13 Feb:	1947	2397	17 Feb: 2398
20 Feb:	1949	2399	24 Feb: 2401
27 Feb:	1950	2400	03 Mar: 2402
06 Mar:	1951	2403	
13 Mar:	1952	2404	
20 Mar:	1954	2405	24 Mar: 1979
27 Mar:	1955	2406	31 Mar: 1994
03 Apr:	1956	2407	07 Apr: 1998
10 Apr:	1958	2408	14 Apr: 2440
17 Apr:	1959	2409	18 Apr: 3350*
24 Apr:	1960		
01 May:	1961	2410	
08 May:	1962	2411	12 May: 2412

	Sunday a.m.	p.m.	Weekday
15 May:	1963	2413	19 May: 2414
22 May:	1964	2415	26 May: 2416
29 May:	1965	1991	02 Jun: 2417
05 Jun:	1966	2418	
12 Jun:	1967	2419	16 Jun: 2420
19 Jun:	1968	2421	23 Jun: 2422
26 Jun:	1970		30 Jun: 2441
03 Jul:	1971		
10 Jul:	1972	2423	14 Jul: 2058
17 Jul:	1973	2424	
31 Jul:	1975		
07 Aug:	1976		11 Aug: 2425
14 Aug:	1977	2426	18 Aug: 2427
21 Aug:	1978	2428	25 Aug: 2054
28 Aug:	1980		
04 Sep:	1981	2429	
11 Sep:	1982	2442	15 Sep: 2430
18 Sep:	1983	2431	22 Sep: 2432
25 Sep:	1985	2433	
02 Oct:	1986	2434	06 Oct: 2435
16 Oct:	1987		
23 Oct:	1988	2436	27 Oct: 2437
30 Oct:	1990	2438	03 Nov: 1993
06 Nov:	1992	2439	

HOLIDAY AT MENTONE

Wrongly dated	2010 (17 May weekday)

1888

	Sunday a.m.	p.m.	Weekday
HOLIDAY AT MENTONE			
08 Jan:	2002	2350	12 Jan: 2351
15 Jan:	2003		
22 Jan:	2004	2352	26 Jan: 2353
29 Jan:	2006	2354	02 Feb: 2067

05 Feb:	2007	2355	
12 Feb:	2008		16 Feb: 2356
19 Feb:	2009	2357	23 Feb: 2358
26 Feb:	2011	2359	
04 Mar:	2012	2360	08 Mar: 2361
11 Mar:	2013	2362	15 Mar: 2363
18 Mar:	2014		22 Mar: 2364
25 Mar:	2015	2365	29 Mar: 2062
01 Apr:	2016	2059	05 Apr: 2366
08 Apr:	2018	2367	
15 Apr:	2019	2368	
22 Apr:	2020		
06 May:	2022	2369	10 May: 2370
13 May:	2023	2371	17 May: 2372
20 May:	2024	2373	24 May: 2374
SICKNESS			
17 Jun:	2029		
24 Jun:	2030	2375	
01 Jul:	2031	2376	05 Jul: 2377
08 Jul:	2032	2378	12 Jul: 2049
15 Jul:	2033	2379	19 Jul: 2380
22 Jul:	2034	2381	26 Jul: 2382
29 Jul:	2036	2383	02 Aug: 2057
05 Aug:	2037	2060	
12 Aug:	2039	2384	
19 Aug:	2040	2385	23 Aug: 2053
26 Aug:	2041	2386	
02 Sep:	2042	2051	06 Sep: 2842
09 Sep:	2043	2387	13 Sep: 2843
16 Sep:	2044	2844	20 Sep: 2845
23 Sep:	2045	2846	27 Sep: 2056
30 Sep:	2046	2388	04 Oct: 2389
07 Oct:	2047	2390	11 Oct: 2082
14 Oct:	2048		
SICKNESS & IN SOUTH OF FRANCE			

April undated   2021*

1889

	Sunday a.m.	p.m.	Weekday
SICKNESS & IN SOUTH OF FRANCE			
24 Feb:	2072		28 Feb: 2300
03 Mar:	2073		07 Mar: 2121
10 Mar:	2074		
17 Mar:	2075	2447	
24 Mar:	2076		
31 Mar:	2077	2304	04 Apr: 2301
07 Apr:	2078	2302	11 Apr: 2305
14 Apr:	2079	2306	18 Apr: 2085
21 Apr:	2080	2308	25 Apr: 2303
28 Apr:	2083	2310	
05 May:	2084	2307	
12 May:	2086	2309	
19 May:	2087	2122	23 May: 2313
26 May:	2093	2111	30 May: 2315
02 Jun:	2088	2312	
09 Jun:	2090	2311	13 Jun: 2317
16 Jun:	2090	2314	
23 Jun:	2091	2319	27 Jun: 2449
30 Jun:	2092	2316	
07 Jul:	2094	2320	
14 Jul:	2095	2321	18 Jul: 2164
21 Jul:	2096	2322	
28 Jul:	2097	2318	01 Aug: 2323
04 Aug:	2098	2324	08 Aug: 2106
11 Aug:	2099	2325	15 Aug: 2326
18 Aug:	2100	2327	22 Aug: 2328
25 Aug:	2101	2329	29 Aug: 2330
01 Sep:	2102	2331	05 Sep: 2120
08 Sep:	2103		12 Sep: 2332
15 Sep:	2104	2333	19 Sep: 2334

	Sunday a.m.	p.m.	Weekday
22 Sep:	2105	2335	
29 Sep:	2107	2336	03 Oct: 2337
06 Oct:	2108	2338	
13 Oct:	2109	2339	17 Oct: 2343
20 Oct:	2110	2341	24 Oct: 2119
27 Oct:	2112		31 Oct: 2118
03 Nov:	2113	2344	07 Nov: 2346
10 Nov:	2115	2347	14 Nov: 2348
17 Nov:	2117	2349	21 Nov: 2177*
HOLIDAY AT MENTONE			

Wrongly dated		3504 (22 Aug p.m.)

1890

	Sunday a.m.	p.m.	Weekday
HOLIDAY AT MENTONE			
02 Feb:	2128		06 Feb: 2181
09 Feb:	2129	2275	
16 Feb:	2130	2269	20 Feb: 2287
23 Feb:	2132	2180	
02 Mar:	2133	2271	05 Mar: 2259
09 Mar:	2134	2260	13 Mar: 2267
16 Mar:	2135	2270	20 Mar: 2446
23 Mar:	2136	2138	27 Mar: 2273
30 Mar:	2137	2178	03 Apr: 2251
06 Apr:	2139		10 Apr: 2276
13 Apr:	2140	2277	
20 Apr:	2141		25 Apr: 2185
27 Apr:	2142	2262	
04 May:	2143	2286	08 May: 2278
11 May:	2144		15 May: 2246
18 May:	2145	2282	22 May: 2285
25 May:	2146	2279	
01 Jun:	2147	2268	05 Jun: 2281
08 Jun:	2148		

15 Jun:	2149		
22 Jun:	2150	2152	
29 Jun:	2151	2283	03 Jul: 2264
06 Jul:	2153	2265	
13 Jul:	2154	2257	
20 Jul:	2155	2284	24 Jul: 2254
27 Jul:	2156	2247	31 Jul: 2241
03 Aug:	2157	2256	07 Aug: 2280
10 Aug:	2158	2171	14 Aug: 2261
17 Aug:	2159		21 Aug: 2195
24 Aug:	2160	2240	28 Aug: 2172
31 Aug:	2161	2255	04 Sep: 2258
07 Sep:	2162	2248	11 Sep: 2174
14 Sep:	2163	2272	18 Sep: 2250
21 Sep:	2165	2188	25 Sep: 2252
28 Sep:	2166		
05 Oct:	2167	2263	09 Oct: 2184
12 Oct:	2168	2175	16 Oct: 2242
19 Oct:	2169	2243	22 Oct: 2245
			23 Oct: 2244
26 Oct:	2170	2266	30 Oct: 2253
02 Nov:	2173	2294	
SICKNESS AT MENTONE			
Untimed	3370		

1891

	Sunday a.m.	p.m.	Weekday
SICKNESS AT MENTONE			
08 Feb:	2189	2249	12 Feb: 2223
15 Feb:	2190	2229	19 Feb: 2274
22 Feb:	2191	2230	26 Feb: 2218
01 Mar:	2192	2228	
08 Mar:	2193	2220	12 Mar: 2221
15 Mar:	2194		19 Mar: 2226

22 Mar:	2196	2227	26 Mar: 2212
29 Mar:	2197	2236	02 Apr: 2225
05 Apr:	2198	2234	09 Apr: 2239
12 Apr:	2200	2907	
19 Apr:	2201	2235	24 Apr: 2213
26 Apr:	2202	SICK	
03 May:	2203	2238	07 May: 2206
10 May:	2204	2231	14 May: 2233
17 May:	2205	SICK	
SICKNESS			
07 Jun:	2208		
FINAL SICKNESS			
26 Oct:	TO CALAIS THEN TO MENTONE		

1892

| 31 Jan: | DEATH AT MENTONE |

Completely undated sermons showing year of publication

New Park Street Period (1854–March 1861)
1860: 342
1861: 351, 360

Published posthumously
Sun a.m.: 3081, 3087
Others: 2443, 2558, 2875, 3054, 3060, 3066, 3077, 3100, 3105, 3114, 3254?
(published 'more than half a century' before 15 Jun 1911)

Metropolitan Tabernacle Period (March 1861–1891)
1863: 499, 510, 516, 526, 530
1864: 556, 559, 561, 576, 586, 594, 600
1865: 610, 629–636, 640, 646, 656, 659, 661
1866: 677, 686, 693, 696, 702, 726
1867: 731, 736, 741, 762, 765, 770–772, 777
1868: 796, 832
1869: 850, 891, 892, 900–906
1870: 910, 916
1871: 983–986, 988–990, 992, 994–997, 1002, 1007, 1016, 1021, 1023, 1025
1872: 1030, 1079–1083, 1085
1873: 1092, 1097, 1102, 1108, 1113, 1118, 1119, 1123, 1131, 1138, 1140, 1142
1874: 1152–1158, 1178, 1180, 1184, 1196, 1198
1875: 1210, 1211, 1214, 1216, 1218–1225, 1230, 1234, 1245, 1246, 1262, 1263, 1267–1269
1876: 1274, 1279, 1280, 1285, 1289–1291, 1295
1877: 1334, 1338–1342, 1344, 1350, 1364–1366, 1380
1878: 1395, 1398, 1399, 1401, 1402, 1405, 1407, 1421, 1423–1425, 1430, 1440, 1443–1449
1879: 1451, 1452b, 1453–1467, 1470, 1503, 1504, 1507, 1509–1510
1880: 1512–1519, 1521, 1522, 1527, 1543, 1546–1548, 1556, 1558–1560, 1563, 1565, 1569, 1573
1881: 1575, 1576, 1578–1580, 1583, 1585, 1589, 1628, 1634b

1882: 1651, 1652, 1661, 1671, 1692, 1694–1696
1883: 1706, 1717, 1718, 1733, 1756
1884: 1758, 1759, 1763, 1767, 1814
1885: 1820
1886: 1879, 1882–1884, 1897, 1899, 1900, 1906, 1908, 1921, 1929, 1937
1887: 1942, 1948, 1953, 1957, 1969, 1974, 1984, 1989, 1995, 1996, 1999
1888: 2001, 2005, 2017, 2025–2028, 2035, 2038, 2052, 2055
1889: 2063, 2069, 2070, 2114, 2116
1890: 2123–2127, 2131, 2176, 2179
1891: 2182, 2183, 2186, 2187, 2199, 2207, 2209–2211, 2214–2217, 2219, 2222, 2224, 2232

Republished posthumously (sometimes with new or modified titles):
(a) Previously in *The Sword and the Trowel*
1866: 2970
1867: 2982
1869: 2976, 2999, 3028
1870: 2990, 2995, 3007, 3021, 3034
1871: 3040, 3046, 3052, 3070
1872: 3075, 3083, 3089, 3101
1873: 3107, 3118, 3124, 3135
1874: 3143, 3149
1875: 3168
1876: 3174, 3181, 3187, 3193, 3199
1877: 3205, 3217, 3237a
1879: 3249
1880: 3261
1881: 3153
1882: 3279
1883: 3289, 3301, 3307
1884: 3330, 3340
1885: 3345
1887: 3479

(b) Previously in books of Sunday and Thursday evening sermons:

In *Types and emblems*
1873: 2913, 3131, 3141, 3215, 3251, 3269, 3281, 3287, 3297, 3343

In *Trumpet calls to Christian energy*
1875: 2850, 2854, 3085, 3147, 3191, 3332, 3399, 3414, 3422

In *The present truth*
1883: 3305, 3455, 3495, 3500, 3502, 3530, 3532, 3536, 3538, 3543, 3550,
3553, 3561

In *Storm signals*
1885: 2859, 3233, 3299, 3334, 3360, 3374, 3440, 3450, 3453, 3462, 3472,
3482, 3511, 3560

Published posthumously:
2289–2293, 2295–2299, 2444, 2448, 2450, 2861, 3016, 3020, 3033, 3091, 3097,
3103, 3110, 3128, 3145, 3175, 3177, 3179, 3183, 3185, 3189, 3195, 3201,
3203, 3207, 3209, 3213, 3219, 3235, 3239, 3241, 3245, 3247, 3253, 3257,
3259, 3263, 3265, 3277, 3285, 3293, 3311, 3315, 3317, 3319, 3321, 3325,
3326, 3328, 3336, 3338, 3341, 3342, 3347, 3349, 3352, 3354, 3359, 3363,
3365, 3367, 3368, 3372, 3377, 3379, 3381, 3383, 3385, 3388, 3391, 3393,
3395, 3402–3404, 3406, 3408, 3410, 3412,* 3416, 3418, 3420, 3424, 3426,
3428, 3430, 3432, 3433, 3435, 3438, 3441, 3445–3448, 3459, 3461, 3467,
3469, 3470, 3474, 3477, 3480, 3484, 3487, 3491, 3494, 3505, 3508, 3510,
3514, 3516, 3519, 3520, 3522–3524, 3526, 3528, 3529, 3533, 3534, 3537,
3541, 3542, 3546, 3547, 3549, 3552, 3555, 3556, 3559.
Able to the Uttermost 1–3, 5–20

Dating of undated sermons etc.
72–73: Both of these sermons are dated Sunday morning 30 March 1856 and
contain internal references to being preached in the morning. G.H. Pike, *The life
and work of Charles Haddon Spurgeon,* vol. 2, pp. 223–6 preserves an eye-witness
account which confirms that **72** is correctly dated; the evening sermon on that day

was not **73**. Possibly this was preached on the next Sunday morning 6 April 1856 which is unusually unrepresented.

616: This evening sermon indicates that the sermon preached in the morning considered God's calling to receive Christ and to walk in him, which was the theme of **483,** the sermon on Colossians 2:6 preached on the morning of 7 December 1862.

766: A footnote to **3017,** preached on Thursday 1 August 1867, identifies **766** as the sermon preached on the previous Sunday evening, thus dating it to 28 July 1867.

767–768: G.H. Pike, *The life and work of Charles Haddon Spurgeon,* vol. 4 pp. 200–1 records that, during the renovations carried out at the Metropolitan Tabernacle in March and April 1867 when the Agricultural Hall was used instead on Sunday mornings, an offer of Surrey Chapel for the weekday meetings was gladly accepted. **756,** preached at Surrey Chapel on 21 March 1867, would have been the first of the Thursday sermons and the undated evening sermons **767–8,** also preached there, must have been on subsequent Thursday evenings.

993: A footnote identifies **980,** preached on 12 March 1871, as the other sermon about Jeremiah mentioned as having been preached recently. Spurgeon's absence through sickness for most of April and the whole of May and June means that **993** must have been preached in late March or early April 1871.

1022: In this undated sermon published in 1871 Spurgeon indicates that he had spoken on the words 'Ye shall die in your sins' (John 8:21,24) 'the other Sunday night'. This clearly relates to the striking last section of **3043,** the Sunday evening sermon of 8 October 1871. **1022** must have been preached between mid October and late November 1871 when Spurgeon left for the continent.

1037: In this undated sermon published in 1872 Spurgeon indicates that on the previous Sunday evening he had spoken on the fact that Christians are saved with great difficulty. This appears to relate to **3047,** the sermon on 1 Peter 4:18 preached on the evening of 15 October 1871. **1037** seems to be the evening sermon of 22 October 1871.

1117: This evening sermon includes a reference to a hymn quoted earlier that day in the morning sermon; the same hymn is quoted in **1112,** preached on the morning of 18 May 1873.

1174: This evening sermon is said by Spurgeon to be exactly 24 years since his baptism which was on 3 May 1850, thus dating it to 3 May 1874.

1212–1213: A footnote to **1213** indicates that **1212** was preached on the previous

Thursday evening, thus dating **1213** to either the following Sunday evening or Thursday evening. **1212** also contains a reference to the likeness of a child to its father being in some points a caricature, a point mentioned in **1194** (Sunday morning 20 September 1874) as also having been made on the previous Thursday. Thus **1212** was preached on Thursday 17 September 1874 and **1213** on the evening of either Sunday 20 or Thursday 24 September 1874, no other sermons of Spurgeon being allocated to either of these.

1239: G.H. Pike, *The life and work of Charles Haddon Spurgeon,* vol. 5 p. 154 dates this sermon to the evening of Sunday 16 May 1875.

1259: This evening sermon includes a reference to a point made in the morning sermon of the same day to the effect that 'the more grace a man has the lower he lies before God'. The same point is found in **1256** (Sunday morning 26 September 1875) where Spurgeon likens good men to ships—'the fuller these are the lower they sink'.

1265: A footnote to this evening sermon links it to **1207,** the sermon preached that morning (Sunday 13 December 1874).

1336: A reference to a sermon preached on Matthew 11:28 'the other night' appears to point back to **1322** preached Sunday evening 22 October 1876. **1336** was probably preached on Thursday 26 October 1876, no other sermon being attributed to that evening.

1393: A footnote to this evening sermon links it to **1388,** the sermon preached that morning (Sunday 9 December 1877).

1506: A footnote to this evening sermon links it to **1416,** the sermon preached that morning (Sunday 26 May 1878).

1511: This short evening sermon published at the very beginning of 1880 was followed by a farewell address by Spurgeon's son Thomas. Such a valedictory address appears in *The Sword and the Trowel,* January 1896 and was delivered on 28 September 1879 just before Thomas Spurgeon's second voyage to Australia.

1520: Footnotes to this evening sermon link it to **1439,** the sermon preached that morning (Sunday 20 October 1878).

1574: In this sermon published at the end of 1880 Spurgeon says 'almost the last time I stood here' he 'spoke of Peter from the words—"When he thought thereon, he wept"'. This refers to Mark 14:72, the text of **2735,** preached on the evening of Sunday 24 October 1880. **1574** would appear to have been preached at the end of October or early in November 1880.

1577: Spurgeon had 'lately' spoken on the words 'Who forgiveth all thine iniquities', the theme of **1492,** preached on 31 August 1879.

1656: This undated sermon, published at about the end of April 1882, contains a reference to the gospel still being true 'in the year "eighteen hundred and eighty-two"', thus dating it to early 1882.

1693: In this undated Thursday evening sermon published in 1882 Spurgeon refers to the difficulties householders had been experiencing while completing their census forms; he also describes his reading of Colossians 3 on the previous Sunday morning. However, his description of his reading of Colossians 3:15 aptly reflects the exposition of that chapter attached to **2679,** preached on Sunday evening 10 April 1881, which was a week after the taking of the 1881 census. Allowing for a slight editorial lapse some twenty months after the event, **1693** would seem to be the missing sermon preached on Thursday 14 April 1881.

1697: This sermon was preached at the opening of the original Trinity Road Chapel on the afternoon of Thursday 27 September 1877.

1762: This undated evening sermon was preached at Exeter Hall. From 12 August to 2 September 1883 Sunday services were held at Exeter Hall during repairs to the Metropolitan Tabernacle. The four morning sermons (**1734–7**) are all dated, as are two of the evening ones—**1754** (12 August 1883) and **1740** (2 September 1883). **1762** appears to be the evening sermon of either 19 or 26 August 1883. The Thursday meetings seem to have been held at Christ Church, Westminster where **2597** and **2599** were preached on Thursdays 23 and 30 August respectively. **2600** (Thursday 6 September 1883) marked the reopening of the Metropolitan Tabernacle.

1997: A footnote to **2492,** preached on 7 November 1886, indicates that **1997** (dated Autumn 1886) was the sermon mentioned as having been preached in the evening two weeks previously, thus dating it to Sunday evening 24 October 1886.

2000: The 'two thousandth published sermon' is dated 9 May 1880 in C.H. Spurgeon, *Messages to the multitude,* and was the evening sermon on that day.

2021: This undated evening sermon is identified in a footnote to the exposition attached to **2375,** preached on 24 June 1888, as another sermon on Nathanael preached 'a short time ago'. It was published about the end of April 1888 and probably relates to one of the unrepresented dates in that month.

2177: This undated sermon, published after the death of William Olney in October 1890, is said to have been preached on a Thursday evening before Spurgeon left for his winter's rest. Internal references indicate that William Olney was present and that Spurgeon had known the congregation for 36 years. He first preached at New Park Street Chapel in December 1853 and the various factors would seem to date **2177** to Thursday 21 November 1889 just before his winter holiday at Mentone. A letter attached to **2117** and dated Mentone, Nov. 28 1889 announced his safe arrival. However, G.H. Pike, *The life and work of Charles Haddon Spurgeon,* vol. 6 p. 312 states 'On November 17 he preached for the last time before going to his winter retreat'.

2288: This sermon was preached 'On a Christmas Day Evening' and is described internally as being 'on this last Sabbath night of another year'. All but one of the relevant years in which Christmas Day fell on a Sunday can be ruled out: 1859 by a reminiscence of the New Park Street days, 1864 and 1881 by already being accounted for, 1887 by Spurgeon's absence abroad. By process of elimination **2288** seems to have been preached on the evening of Christmas Day 1870.

2664: See 'elusive dates' below.

2703: A footnote to this Thursday evening sermon (dated 1855) identifies **47,** preached 21 October 1855, as the sermon preached on the same text on a former occasion, thus placing **2703** towards the end of the year.

2815: In this sermon, preached at New Park Street Chapel on a Sunday evening early in 1861, Spurgeon remarks that he had lately been in Glasgow, which he had visited during a tour of the North and Scotland in March 1861. The only Sunday evening unaccounted for between this tour and the move to the Metropolitan Tabernacle at the end of March is 17 March 1861. **2811,** preached on Sunday evening 24 March 1861, was the final sermon at New Park Street Chapel (but see **3242** below); **368,** preached on Sunday morning 31 March 1861, was at Exeter Hall.

2836: This sermon is said to have been preached at the 100th anniversary of Amersham Baptist Chapel in November 1857. I am grateful to Sarah Charlton, Archivist at the Centre for Buckinghamshire Studies, for providing more specific details from *The Buckinghamshire Advertiser,* 28 November 1857. The history of the Baptist churches in Amersham is quite complex and 1857 does not seem to have been a centenary for any of them, but it is recorded that 'the Anniversary Sermons of "The Old Baptist Chapel" were to be preached by the Rev. C.H. Spurgeon, at two and six o'clock, on Tuesday, the 24th of November.' **2836** was the sermon preached in the evening; the description of the afternoon sermon on

1 Thessalonians 5:6 seems to indicate that it was a repetition of **163,** preached on 15 November 1857 at the Music Hall, Royal Surrey Gardens.

2896: This sermon (dated August 1854) was originally the first of Spurgeon's sermons to be printed. G.H. Pike, *The life and work of Charles Haddon Spurgeon,* vol. 1, pp. 135–143, dates it to Sunday morning 20 August 1854 and describes the occasion at length.

2924: This sermon is dated 1862 and was preached on a Sunday evening. Spurgeon indicates that he had preached in the morning to the chief of sinners and notes that some of his congregation may have been in London to visit the Great Exhibition, which opened on 1 May 1862, or to attend the Handel Festival, which took place on 23, 25 and 27 June 1862 (see Michael Musgrave, *The musical life of the Crystal Palace* (C.U.P. 1995) pp. 215–6). **2924** would appear to be the evening sermon of 29 June 1862, the morning sermon on that day being **458,** entitled 'The friend of sinners'. I am grateful to the Gerald Coke Handel Collection (housed at the Foundling Museum, London) and to the curator of the Crystal Palace Museum for providing the dates of the 1862 Handel Festival.

2929: This sermon is dated 1862 and was preached on a Sunday evening. Spurgeon indicates that he had preached in the morning on 'Repent ye, and believe in the gospel', the text of **460,** preached on Sunday morning 13 July 1862.

3048: This sermon was preached on a Sunday morning in 1856 and entitled 'The Holy Spirit in the Covenant'. Spurgeon looks back to two earlier sermons, 'God in the Covenant' (**93**) and 'Christ in the Covenant' (**103**) preached on 3 and 31 August 1856 respectively. Only the evening sermons of Sundays 21 and 28 September are accounted for; **3048** may have been on the morning of either of these. No sermons are recorded for Sundays 5 and 12 October.

3050: This sermon is dated 1863, but Spurgeon's comment that he commenced his pastorate eleven years earlier would place it in 1865. The publishers inserted a footnote referring to those eleven years as 1854–1865. **3050** also appears in the 1865 volume of the *Baptist Messenger,* the periodical which seems to have been the source for many of the partly-dated posthumously-published sermons from Spurgeon's early years.

3120: This undated morning sermon was preached at New Park Street Chapel and entitled 'A view of God's glory'. G.H. Pike, *The life and work of Charles Haddon Spurgeon,* vol. 1 pp. 125–6 refers to it as one of the earliest published sermons and includes an excerpt derived from *The Penny Pulpit,* 1854. The sermon appears in the first volume of a representative collection of sermons from *The Penny Pulpit* published in 1886 and is there dated 17 September 1854.

3137: Spurgeon's call for a day of prayer and fasting in respect of 'this cattle disease' may relate to the cattle plague of 1865 which prompted J.C. Ryle to write his famous tract *The finger of God*.

3155–3156: These were the first two sermons in an unfinished series on the Beatitudes in 1873. The third sermon (second Beatitude) is not represented in the published sermons, but the fourth to sixth (**3065, 3157, 3158** on the third to fifth Beatitudes) were preached on the evenings of Thursday 11, Sunday 14 and Sunday 21 December 1873 respectively. It is likely that **3155–6** were preached around the end of November 1873.

3167: This sermon is dated 1866 and was preached on a Sunday evening. Spurgeon indicates that in the morning he had spoken about 'the hope that salvation was possible', which seems to relate to **684,** entitled 'Hope, yet no hope. No hope, yet hope', preached on Sunday morning 8 April 1866.

3170: During this sermon Spurgeon relates that on the previous day, after months of prayer, he was talking with a friend when a letter arrived giving notification of an anonymous gift of £1,000 for the Stockwell Orphanage. The event is recorded in *C.H. Spurgeon's Autobiography,* vol. 3 p. 175 as having taken place on 20 November 1867, thus dating **3170** to Thursday 21 November 1867.

3231/3283: Internal references indicate that both these Metropolitan Tabernacle sermons were preached on a New Year's Day. The only relevant Sunday and Thursday services not accounted for by dated sermons are Thursdays 1 January 1863 and 1874. **3231** also refers back to the building of the Orphanage, which was founded in 1867. Thus it would appear that **3231** was on Thursday 1 January 1874 (the previously published sermon was **3230,** preached on Sunday evening 28 December 1873); **3283** would have been on Thursday 1 January 1863.

3242: New Park Street Chapel is given as the location of this sermon, preached on Tuesday 17 November 1863, well over two years after the move to the Metropolitan Tabernacle. This is not a mistake! New Park Street Chapel continued to be used until the end of the summer of 1866, when the now small congregation 'finally took leave of the building' (see G.H. Pike, *The life and work of Charles Haddon Spurgeon,* vol. 3 pp. 179–80).

3283: See **3231** above.

3291: Extracts from this evening sermon on Psalm 95:5, preached at the

Metropolitan Tabernacle on behalf of the British and Foreign Sailors' Society, are reproduced in *Sunday at Home,* 1880 pp. 738–41 and the date is given as 6 May 1880. A brief footnote at the end of **1539** reveals that this special sermon was also published separately at the time in May 1880. Other sermons preached on behalf of the society are **2206** and **3321**.

3294/3300: These Thursday evening sermons are wrongly dated 1886, but fit naturally into a chronological sequence of sermons from 1866 posthumously published in volume 58 of the Metropolitan Tabernacle Pulpit (see also **3369**).

3309: This is said to be the seventh sermon in a series on Christ's glorious achievements. In Spurgeon's book of the same title the fifth sermon is an addition to the original series, being **273** from the New Park Street Pulpit and listed in a footnote to **3309,** while the sixth sermon was originally presented by Spurgeon as the fifth in the series (**1325–1329**), preached on consecutive Sunday mornings from 19 November to 17 December 1876. **3309** would appear to have been originally the sixth and last sermon in the series, but to have been renumbered seventh posthumously to allow for the addition of **273**; the text of **3309** (Luke 19:10) would have been appropriate for the evening of Christmas Eve 1876, the morning sermon having been on a Christmas theme instead of the then current series.

3323: In this evening sermon Spurgeon refers back to the previous Sunday evening when his text had been Romans 13:11. This could be a reference to **857**, preached on Sunday evening 27 December 1868. Internal remarks such as 'during the past year' and 'Here is a blessed thing to think of all the year round' suggest that **3323** was preached at the turn of the year, either on Thursday 31 December 1868 or Sunday 3 January 1869.

3350: This was the inaugural address at the Annual Conference of the Pastors' College Association at Devonshire Square Chapel, Stoke Newington and dated 1887. G.H. Pike, *The life and work of Charles Haddon Spurgeon* vol.6 p. 285 indicates that the conference began on 18 April 1887.

3369: This sermon is confirmed as being on Thursday 4 October 1866, not 1886 as printed, by a reference to the forthcoming day of prayer and fasting on Monday 5 November 1866 (see G.H. Pike, *The life and work of Charles Haddon Spurgeon,* vol. 3 p. 187).

3389: In this evening sermon on John 5:25 Spurgeon indicates that he had preached on the same chapter in the morning—'we saw in the chapter a three-fold gradation of life-giving in the person of Christ'. The three points involved the raising of the physically dead, the giving of life to the spiritually dead and the universal resurrection. This three-fold description can be found in **896,** preached on John 5:28–29 on Sunday morning 17 October 1869.

3397: This sermon was preached in June. The morning sermon had been on the subject of the Holy Spirit and could have been either **574** (Sunday 12 June 1864) or **754** (Whit Sunday 9 June 1867). The latter appears more likely as the publishers incorporated several sermons from 1867 at this time (e.g. **3373, 3384, 3392, 3401**), but none from 1864.

3412: See 'elusive dates' below.

3434: This sermon is said to have been preached at the Metropolitan Tabernacle on Sunday evening 21 February 1861. However, 21 February was a Thursday and services did not commence at the Metropolitan Tabernacle until the end of March 1861! (**886** is also described as being on a Sunday but carries a correct date for a Thursday, while **3398** and **3531** are described as being on Thursdays but carry correct dates for Sundays.)

3443: This Thursday evening sermon is dated 9 September 1896, an obvious misprint for 9 September 1869!

3457: A footnote to this Sunday evening sermon indicates that the morning sermon on the day was **678,** preached on Sunday morning 25 February 1866. **3457** certainly refers back to **678,** but **3296** is also dated Sunday evening 25 February 1866! (Duplication of dates also occurs on 30 March 1856 (see **72–3** above), 22 April 1860, 29 Jul 1866, 16 Jan 1870 and 26 Feb 1871. **3415** and **3509** are double-booked for Sunday 27 Jun 1868, a totally incorrect date!)

ATTU4: This is the only dateable sermon among the twenty undated evening sermons comprising Spurgeon's *Able to the Uttermost*, published in 1922 as a follow-up after publication of the Metropolitan Tabernacle Pulpit had ceased in 1917. Spurgeon says that the previous Friday was exactly 22 years after his baptism, which was on 3 May 1850, thus dating this communion sermon to Sunday evening 5 May 1872.

ELUSIVE DATES

2664: In this evening sermon preached early in 1858 Spurgeon reports that on the next Sunday a place with disreputable connections would be opened for a Sabbath concert in connection with the preaching of the gospel and that 'The Messiah will be performed as the great inducement for attracting them'. A footnote identifies the venue as the 'Alhambra Palace' and adds that the experiment was abandoned after one attempt as being likely to do more harm than good. The Alhambra Palace had once been used for exhibitions but first opened as a theatre on 18 March 1858. Beyond that it has proved impossible to track down the date of the concert. I am grateful to Jane Pritchard of the Theatre Museum for providing a reference from *The Globe,* 6 April 1858, which reports that 'A week or two there was preaching, but the Nonconformist minister who undertook to conduct the special services, did not like his name being mixed up with applications for spirit licenses, dancing, and such secular affairs, and he withdrew his countenance and his oratory.'

3412: This sermon has up to now defied dating despite containing various clues. It was preached on a wintry and snowy night. Two years previously Spurgeon had stood 'on the little wooden bridge in the village of Handeck, on the Swiss side of the Grimsel Pass' which could have been during his continental tours of 1865 or 1867; mention of this event also appears in *The Sword and the Trowel,* February 1868. On the previous Sunday night he had mentioned that a young person had attended the chapel for two years without anybody ever speaking to her and he had said that he was ashamed of some of his congregation.